THE STATE
OF THE
PRESIDENCY

William D. Young
1980

THE STATE
OF THE
PRESIDENCY

Second Edition

THOMAS E. CRONIN

Colorado College
and
University of Delaware

Little, Brown and Company
Boston   Toronto

Acknowledgments

The author gratefully acknowledges permission to use excerpts from the following works:

Thomas E. Cronin, "An Imperiled Presidency," in *Society* (November–December, 1978). Published by permission of Transaction, Inc. from *Society*, Vol. 16, No. 1. Copyright © 1978 by Transaction, Inc.

Thomas E. Cronin, "Small Program, Big Troubles: Policy Making." This chapter appeared originally as a chapter contributed to a volume of essays prepared in honor of Jeffrey L. Pressman—*American Politics and Public Policy*, Walter Dean Burnham and Martha Wagner Weinberg, eds. Copyright © 1978 by The Massachusetts Institute of Technology. Reprinted by permission of The MIT Press.

Lloyd N. Cutler, "A Proposal for a Continuing Public Prosecutor," excerpts from a speech delivered at the University of California (November 18, 1974). Reprinted in *Watergate Reorganization & Reform Act of 1975*, Hearings Before the Committee on Government Operations, U.S. Senate (July 1975), pp. 208–210. Reprinted by permission of Lloyd N. Cutler.

Richard E. Neustadt, *Presidential Power*, pp. 119, 121, 122, 123. Copyright © 1960 by John Wiley & Sons, Inc. Reprinted by permission of John Wiley & Sons, Inc.

Richard E. Neustadt, *Presidential Power*, pp. 125, 126, 127, 128. Copyright © 1976 by John Wiley & Sons, Inc. Reprinted by permission of John Wiley & Sons, Inc.

Bradley H. Patterson, Jr., "The President's Cabinet: Issues and Questions," pp. 17–18. Reprinted from *Public Administration Review*, © 1976 by The American Society for Public Administration, 1225 Connecticut Avenue, N.W., Washington, D.C. All rights reserved.

David R. Schaefer, excerpts from a letter sent to Thomas E. Cronin (January 17, 1979). Reprinted by permission.

PREFACE

This book is about the political values and political pressures that shape presidential performance. It is also an analysis and interpretation of the promise of the presidency and the constraints on presidential leadership.

To understand the American presidency one must first understand the conflicting values in our democratic republic. One must understand that in many ways the presidency was not designed to perform the countless leadership functions that we have come to demand of it. In this book, I place the presidency in the context of the passionate cycles, paradoxical yearnings, and changing perspectives of the American people. Throughout I have tried, as well, to debunk many of the myths about the presidency. This book is written with deep respect for the office of the president. But the limits of the presidency, as well as the need for multiple sources and diverse centers of leadership, must be understood if America is to achieve its potential as a nation. Doubtless, a president can powerfully affect the future of the nation, but depending too much on a single office is a gamble, weakens our civic fabric, and inevitably will centralize responsibility far more than is wise.

The analysis also seeks to clarify and assess the presidential election system, presidential-congressional relations, presidential-bureaucratic relations, role of the cabinet and the White House staff, and, finally, how presidents become involved in the policy-making process. Special attention is paid to how we recruit presidents and develop expectations of them, our definition and their definition of the job, and how we hold them accountable. I also evaluate various reforms that are repeatedly proposed to make the presidency more effective and more accountable. Often, not surprisingly, reforms that would make the presidency more effective would make it less accountable, and vice versa. That is part of the challenge (and fascination) of studying the institution.

Many questions treated here first caught my attention when I served on the White House staff as a White House Fellow back in the mid-1960s. During the 1970s I interviewed over 100 senior White House aides and several dozen cabinet officials and Executive Office advisers representing the top aides and advisers to Presidents Kennedy, Johnson, Nixon, Ford, and Carter. Quotes without references in these chapters almost always come from my extensive interviews with these officials.

Much of this book and many of my interpretations, however, have been arrived at more by talking with average citizens around the nation than with Washington officials. I have gone to considerable lengths to discuss the politics and problems of the presidency with persons in all sections of the nation. I have also made extensive use of the oral histories now available at the various presidential libraries.

I have attempted to outline the patterns of performance and the larger features of the landscape of national political life. The presidency necessarily changes with the incumbent, the crisis, and the season, but the constants are greater than is usually appreciated. Presidential frustration is far more the rule than presidential triumph. The job of the president in a democratic society is obviously an exacting one and often, as I shall try to persuade you, thankless and almost no-win. As a nation we need to be more sensitive to this, for our assessment of presidential leadership as a failure often lies in our values and our illusions about the nature of the political enterprise in America. I welcome the reader to the exploration, and I hope my examination of this vital institution will encourage development of personal views, even if they are contrary to the interpretation presented here. Please write to me of your differences and your suggestions.

THOMAS E. CRONIN

Colorado College

CONTENTS

THE STATE
OF THE
PRESIDENCY

CHAPTER 1

THE PRESIDENTIAL PUZZLE

The presidency is not merely an administrative office. That is the least of it. It is more than an engineering job, efficient or inefficient. It is pre-eminently a place of moral leadership. All our great Presidents were leaders of thought at times when certain historic ideas in the life of the nation had to be clarified.

> — Franklin Roosevelt,
> *New York Times,* 13 November 1932.

To become President, Lincoln had had to talk more radically on occasion than he actually felt; to be an effective President he was compelled to act more conservatively than he wanted.

> — Richard Hofstadter, *The American Political Tradition* (Vintage, 1948), p. 164.

We give the President more work than a man can do, more responsibility than a man should take, more pressure than a man can bear. We abuse him often and rarely praise him. We wear him out, use him up, eat him up. And with all this, Americans have a love for the President that goes beyond loyalty or party nationality [sic]; he is ours, and we exercise the right to destroy him.

> — John Steinbeck, *America and Americans* (Bonanza Books, 1966), p. 46.

We need an effective presidency, capable of swift and informed action in case of emergency. We need a competent president who can express the national purpose and can renew the public understanding of and commitment to it. We need a president who has the political skills and character to enlist the energies and allegiance of Congress, career public employees, his party, and the nation not only to see that the laws are faithfully executed but also to encourage the tremendous forces for good at large in the country.

But we also need to know what presidents cannot do. Too many of us have for too long been beguiled into believing that our contemporary presidents just do not measure up to the flawlessly heroic nine-foot-tall storybook leaders of our past who are etched in the marble statuary of Washington, D.C. A senior reporter with the *New York Times* once called me and asked a series of questions about President Carter. His intent was to try to capture what Jimmy Carter stood for and what, if anything, Carter had achieved. He was frustrated, even exasperated. He was convinced Carter was merely bending with the wind, following public opinion rather than leading it, being shaped by events rather than shaping them. He was convinced, too, that many of our previous presidents had been very different. I tried to argue the other way, at least to put things in perspective. He appreciated my points, but, like most of us, he still wanted to believe that history belongs to heroes.

To understand the presidency, we need to appreciate the limits of the presidency, the constraints on presidents, and the exaggerated expectations we visit on both. We overestimate the powers of the office and underestimate the economic, social, and cultural factors that so often shape presidential performance and so greatly shape the people we place in the presidency. Few if any of our presidents have been the giants American mythology makes them out to be. There is virtue in placing both presidents and the presidency under the microscope. A healthy skepticism about the promises presidents make and about our own expectations for national leadership is needed. This is not easily achieved, however, for if we have learned anything in recent years, it is that the American people demand more, not less, of their presidents.

The aim of this book is to reassess the purposes, powers, and performance of the American presidency. What was the presidency intended to do? What do we now expect of it? What is the contemporary job of the president? What does the job do to its occupant? Exactly how is the presidency organized and staffed? What are the environmental and institutional constraints? Three additional questions guided the research and writing of this book: How can the presidency become a more effective executive and political leadership institution? How can the presidency be made more accountable, more responsive? Why do we tolerate the vicious cycle of overpromising, underdelivering, and deception and the resulting public disaffection or self-destructive attitude that, in turn, weakens the legitimacy that alone can permit individuals in a democracy to provide leadership?

The institution of the American presidency has been the center of great controversy and debate for several years. It may have served us well for most of our nearly two hundred years, but there is growing disillusionment. Confidence in the credibility of presidents has diminished. Public approval of how they handle the job has diminished. Americans are no longer surprised when presidential promises go unfulfilled; we almost have come to expect this as the natural way of national politics.

We run the risk of a confused and cynical public that is turned off with politics in general, seizing on the arrogance or inadequacies of recent presidencies and condemning not only the abuses but also much that is essential in the presidency. Surely we need to understand how and why the presidency works as it does rather than to punish the institution for the acts of a few individuals who temporarily misused or abused its powers.

It is said of the presidency that it is the most powerful political office in the world. It is said too that we have a concentration of power in the presidency that threatens our liberties and has rendered obsolete the division of powers contemplated by the Republic's founders. But presidential power is often illusive. Presidential capacity to make the country a significantly better place, from whatever point of view, is more constrained than is generally appreciated. John Steinbeck said it well when he wrote, "What is not said or even generally understood is that the power of the chief executive is hard to achieve, balky to manage, and incredibly difficult to exercise. It is not raw, corrosive power, nor can it be used willfully. Many new Presidents, attempting to exert executive power, have felt it slip from their fingers and have faced a rebellious Congress and an adamant civil service, a respectful half-obedient military, a suspicious Supreme Court, a derisive press, and a sullen electorate."[1]

THE PRESIDENCY AND ITS PARADOXES

Why is the presidency such a bewildering office? Why do presidents so often look powerless? Why is the general public so disapproving of recent presidential performances, so predictably less supportive the longer a president stays in office?

The search for explanations leads in several directions. Each individual president molds the office, as does the changing political environment. The Vietnam and the Watergate scandals must also be considered. The personalities of Lyndon B. Johnson and Richard M. Nixon doubtless were factors that soured some people on the office. Observers also claim that the institution is structurally defective—that it encourages isolation, palace guards, groupthink, and arrogance.

Yet something else seems at work. Our expectations of, and demands on, the office are frequently so paradoxical as to invite two-faced behavior by our presidents. We seem to want so much so fast that a president, whose powers are often simply not as great as many of us believe, gets condemned as ineffectual. Or a president often will overreach or resort to unfair play while trying to live up to our demands. Either way, presidents seem to become locked into a rather high number of no-win situations.

The Constitution is of little help in explaining any of this. The founding politicians were purposely vague and left the presidency imprecisely defined. They knew well the presidency would have to provide the capability for swift and competent executive action; yet they went to considerable lengths to avoid enumerating specific powers and duties, so as to calm the then widespread popular fear of monarchy.

The informal and symbolic powers of the presidency today account for as much as the formal ones. Further, presidential powers expand and contract in response to varying situational and technological changes. Thus, the powers of the presidency are interpreted in ways so markedly different as to seem to describe different offices. In some ways the modern presidency has virtually unlimited authority for nearly anything its occupant chooses to do with it. In other ways, our beliefs and hopes about the presidency very much shape the character and quality of the presidential performances we get.

The modern (post–Franklin Roosevelt) presidency is bounded and constrained by various expectations that are decidedly paradoxical. Presidents and presidential candidates must constantly balance themselves between conflicting demands. It has been suggested by more than one observer that it is a characteristic of the American mind to hold contradictory ideas simultaneously without bothering to resolve the potential conflicts between them. Perhaps some paradoxes are best left unresolved, especially as ours is an imperfect world and our political system is a yet to be perfected system held together by many compromises. But we should, at least, better appreciate what it is we expect of our presidents and would-be presidents. For it could well be that our paradoxical expectations and the imperatives of the job make for schizophrenic presidential performances.

We may not be able to resolve the inherent contradictions and dilemmas of these paradoxes. Still, a more rigorous understanding of these conflicts should make possible a more refined sensitivity to the limits of what a president can achieve. Exaggerated or hopelessly contradictory public expectations tend to encourage presidents to attempt more than they can accomplish and to overpromise and overextend themselves.

A more realistic appreciation of presidential paradoxes might help presidents concentrate on the practicable among their priorities. A more sophisticated and tolerant consideration of the modern presidency and its paradoxes might relieve some of the burden so a president can better lead and administer in those critical realms in which the nation has little choice but to turn to him. Whether we like it or not, the vitality of our democracy still depends in large measure on the sensitive interaction of presidential leadership with an understanding public willing to listen and willing to provide support when a president can persuade. Carefully planned innovation is nearly impossible without the kind of leadership a competent and fair-minded president can provide.

Each of the following twelve paradoxes is based on apparent logical contradictions. Each has important implications for both presidential performance and public evaluation of presidential behavior. A better understanding may lead to the removal, reconciliation, or more enlightened toleration of the contradictions to which they give rise.

Paradox: The Decent and Just but Decisive and Guileful Leader

Opinion polls indicate that people want a just, decent "man of good faith" in the White House. Honesty and trustworthiness repeatedly top the list of qualities that the public values most highly in a president. Almost as strongly, the public also demands the qualities of toughness, forcefulness, and even a touch of ruthlessness.

Franklin Roosevelt's biographers agree that he was vain, devious, manipulative, and had a passion for secrecy. These are often the standard weaknesses of great leaders, they note. Most of the significant advances in the world have been made by people with drive, ambition, and a certain amount of irrational confidence in themselves.

We admire modesty, humility, and a sense of proportion. Yet most of our great leaders have been vain. The faults are perhaps part of being a success in politics; you don't get to be a political leader by being a wallflower.

Adlai Stevenson, George McGovern, and Gerald Ford were all criticized for being "too nice," "too decent." Being a "Mr. Nice Guy" is easily equated with being too soft. The public dislikes the idea of a weak, spineless, or sentimental person in the White House. Even Gerald Ford's own aides said he was "too nice for his own good." He seldom cracked the whip or exercised discipline over his staff and cabinet.

Would-be presidents simultaneously have to win our trust by displays of integrity, and yet to become president ordinarily requires calculation, single-mindedness, and the practical knowledge of gutter fighting.

This paradox may partially explain the extraordinary public fondness for President Dwight D. Eisenhower — blessed with a benign smile and a reserved, calming disposition, he was also the disciplined, strong, nononsense five-star general with all the medals and victories to go along with it. His ultimate resource as president was this reconciliation of decency and proven toughness, likability alongside demonstrated valor.

A second aspect of this paradox is that while people want a president who is somewhat religious, they are deeply wary of one who is too much so. Presidents often go out of their way to be photographed going to church or in the presence of noted religious leaders. Nixon, who was not by any definition religious in the usual sense, held highly publicized Sunday services in the White House itself.

John Kennedy, however, encountered considerable difficulties because of his Catholic affiliation. Jimmy Carter faced similar problems from certain Catholics and Jews as well as some Protestants as a result of his deep and open "born again" convictions. One answer to this paradox is found in the history of America, which was founded by refugees fleeing from religious persecutions; Americans want moral leadership on occasion, but they do not want a president who will inhibit religious freedom and diversity. Nor do they want preachiness or public policies guided solely by moral principles as opposed to considerations of power and national interests.

One of the ironies of the American presidency is that those characteristics we condemn in one president, we look for in another. Thus a supporter of Carter's told this writer in 1978 that Carter wasn't "rotten enough," "a wheeler-dealer," "an s.o.b." — precisely the virtues (if they can be called that) Lyndon Johnson was most criticized for ten years earlier.

Sociologist Andrew Greeley offers this explanation or apology for the deceptiveness of presidents:

> The political leader . . . is forced by the nature of the circumstances in which he finds himself to evade and avoid, to sugarcoat and to mislead more than the rest of us. He does so not because he is dishonest (though he may be), not because he likes to manipulate people (though it is very possible that he does), but because his role is essentially one of "conflict management." [2]

Plainly, we demand a double-edged personality. We, in effect, demand the *sinister* as well as the *sincere*, President *Mean* and President *Nice* — tough and hard enough to stand up to Khrushchev or Brezhnev or to press the nuclear button and compassionate enough to care for the ill fed, ill clad, ill housed. The public in this case really seems to want a kindhearted son of a bitch or a clean wheeler-dealer, hard roles to cast and an even harder role to perform over eight years.

Paradox: The Programmatic but Pragmatic Leader

We want both a *programmatic* (committed on the issues and with a detailed program) and *pragmatic* (flexible and open, adjustable) person in the White House.

There is a saying that if politicians really indulged in principle, they would never have a chance for the White House. We may admire consistency in the abstract, but in politics consistency has its costs. The late Everett Dirksen, a popular Republican senator from Illinois, used to say that "I'm a man of fixed and unbending principle, but my first fixed and unbending principle is to be flexible at all times."

Lyndon Johnson, when he was in the U.S. Senate, was called a superb politician in part because of his flexible pragmatism. Political writer Garry Wills illustrates with this story: "In 1953 he told a journalist friend that Vice President Nixon was 'just chicken shit.' The next week Nixon returned from South America a mistreated national hero, and the first to hug him at the airport was Senator Johnson. The journalist asked him about his earlier opinion of Nixon. 'Son,' Johnson replied, 'in politics you've got to learn that overnight chicken shit can turn to chicken salad.' " Wills concluded, "The politician's views insofar as they are distinguishable, must be endlessly reversible." [3]

Franklin D. Roosevelt proclaimed that the presidency is preeminently a place for moral leadership; Governor Jerry Brown aptly notes that "a little vagueness goes a long way in this business."

A president who becomes too committed risks being called rigid; a president who becomes too pragmatic risks being called wishy-washy. The secret, of course, is to stay the course by stressing character, competence, rectitude, and experience and by avoiding strong stands that offend important segments of the population.

Jimmy Carter was especially criticized by the press and others for avoiding commitments and stressing his "flexibility" on the issues. This prompted a major discussion of what came to be called the "fuzziness issue." Jokes spread the complaint. One went as follows: "When you eat peanut butter all your life, your tongue sticks to the roof of your mouth, and you have to talk out of both sides." Still, the toothful southerner's "maybe I will and maybe I won't" strategy proved effective in overcoming critics and opponents who early on claimed he didn't have a chance. Carter talked quietly about the issues and carried a big smile. In fact, of course, he took stands on most of the issues, but being those of a centrist or a pragmatic moderate, his stands were either not liked or dismissed as nonstands by most liberals and conservatives — especially the purists.

What strikes one person as fuzziness or even duplicity appeals to another person as remarkable political skill, the very capacity for compromise and negotiation that is required if a president is to maneuver through the political minefields that come with the job.

Most candidates view a campaign as a fight to win office, not an occasion for adult education. Barry Goldwater in 1964 may have run with the slogan "We offer a *choice* not an echo," referring to his unusually thematic strategy, but Republican party regulars who, more pragmatically, aspired to win the election preferred "a *chance,* not a *choice.*" Once in office, presidents ofen operate the same way; the electoral connection looms large as an issue-avoiding, controversy-ducking political incentive. Most presidents strive to *maximize their options,* and hence leave matters up in the air or delay choices. JFK mastered this strategy, whereas on Vietnam, LBJ permitted himself to be trapped in a corner that seemed to allow no escape, because his options had so swiftly dissolved. Indeed, this yearning to maximize their options may well be the core element of the pragmatism we so often see when we prefer moral leadership.

Paradox: The Innovative and Inventive Yet Majoritarian and Responsive Leader

One of the most compelling paradoxes at the very heart of our democratic system arises from the fact we expect our presidents to provide bold, innovative leadership and at the same time respond faithfully to public-opinion majorities.

Columnist Walter Lippmann once warned against letting public opinion become the chief guide for leadership in America, but he just as forcefully warned leaders: Don't be right too soon, for public opinion will lacerate you! Hence, most presidents fear being in advance of their times. They must *lead us,* but also *listen to us.*

Put simply, we want our presidents to offer leadership, to be architects of the future and providers of visions, plans, and goals, and at the same time we want them to stay in close touch with the sentiments of the people. To *talk* about high ideals, New Deals, big deals, and the like is one thing. But the public resists being *led* too far in any one direction.

Most of our presidents have been conservatives or at best "pragmatic liberals." They have seldom ventured much beyond the crowd. They have followed public opinion rather than shaped it. John F. Kennedy, the author of the much-acclaimed *Profiles in Courage,* was often criticized for presenting more profile than courage; if political risks could be avoided, he shrewdly avoided them. Kennedy was fond of pointing out that he had barely won election in 1960 and that great innovations should not be forced upon the public by a leader with such a slender mandate. Kennedy is often credited with encouraging widespread public participation in politics, but he repeatedly reminded Americans that caution is needed, that the important issues are complicated, technical, and best left to the administrative and political experts. As political scientist Bruce Miroff writes in *Pragmatic Illusions,* Kennedy seldom attempted to change the political context in which he operated:

> More significantly, he resisted the new form of politics emerging with the civil rights movement: mass action, argument on social fundamentals, appeals to considerations of justice and morality. Moving the American political system in such a direction would necessarily have been long range, requiring arduous educational work and promising substantial political risk. The pragmatic Kennedy wanted no part of such an unpragmatic undertaking.[4]

Presidents can get caught whether they are coming or going. The public wants them to be both *leaders* of the country and *representatives* of the people. We want them to be decisive and rely mainly on their own judgment; yet we want them to be very responsive to public opinion, especially to the "common sense" of our own opinions. It was perhaps with this in mind that an English essayist once defined the ideal democratic leader as an "uncommon man of common opinions."

Paradox: The Inspirational but Don't Promise More than You Can Deliver Leader

We ask our presidents to raise hopes, to educate, to inspire. But too much inspiration will invariably lead to dashed hopes, disillusionment, and cynicism. The best of leaders often suffer from one of their chief virtues — an instinctive tendency to raise aspirations, to summon us to transcend personal needs and subordinate ourselves to dreaming dreams of a bolder, more majestic America.

We enjoy the upbeat rhetoric and promises of a brighter tomorrow. We genuinely want to hear about New Nationalism, New Deals, New Frontiers, Great Societies, and New American Revolutions; we want our fears to be assuaged during a "fireside chat" or a "conversation with the President"; we want to be told that "the torch has been passed to a new generation of Americans . . . and the glow from that fire can truly light the world."

We want our fearless leaders to tell us that "peace is at hand," that the "only fear we have to fear is fear itself," that "we are Number One," that a recession has "bottomed out," and that "we are a great people." So much do we want the "lift of a driving dream," to use Nixon's awkward phrase, that to understate the state of the nation is to seem unpresidential to the American people.

Do presidents overpromise because they are congenital optimists or because they are pushed into it by the demanding public? Surely the answer is a mixture of both. But whatever the source, few presidents in recent times have been able to keep their promises and fulfill their intentions. Poverty was not ended; a Great Society was not realized. Vietnam dragged on and on. Watergate outraged a public that had been promised an open presidency. Energy independence remains an illusion just as crime in the streets continues.

A president who does not raise hopes is criticized for letting events shape his presidency rather than making things happen. A president who eschewed inspiration of any kind would be rejected as un-American. For people everywhere, cherishing the dream of individual liberty and self-fulfillment, America has been the land of promises, of possibilities, of dreams. No president can stand in the way of this truth, regardless of the current dissatisfaction about the size of big government in Washington and its incapacity to deliver the services it promises.

William Allen White, the Kansas publisher, went to the heart of this paradox when he wrote that Herbert Hoover is a great executive, a splendid desk man, "but he cannot dramatize his leadership. A democracy cannot follow a leader unless he is dramatized."

Paradox: The Open and Sharing but Courageous and Independent Leader

We unquestionably cherish our three branches of government with their checks and balances and theories of dispersed and separated powers. We want our presidents not only to be sincere but to share their powers with their cabinets, Congress, and other "responsible" national leaders. In theory, we oppose the concentration of power, we dislike secrecy, and we resent depending on any one person to provide all of our leadership. In the early 1970s repeated calls for a more open, accountable, and deroyalized presidency were heard.

Just the same, however, Americans long for dynamic, aggressive presidents even if they do cut some corners. We still celebrate the gutsy presidents who made a practice of kicking Congress around. It is still the Jeffersons, Jacksons, Lincolns, and Roosevelts who get top billing. The great presidents were those who stretched their legal authority and dominated the other branches of government. This point of view argues, Watergate notwithstanding, that the country in fact yearns for a hero in the White House, that the human heart ceaselessly reinvents royalty.

Some scholars even suggest that the less popular presidents were often our greatest leaders. We honor our mediocre presidents during their incumbency. Lincoln wasn't popular by Gallup- and Harris-poll standards, they point out. Nor was Harry Truman, one of the most disapproved presidents during his last few years in office.

Although some people would like to see a demythologized presidency, others claim we need myth, we need symbol. As a friend of mine put it, "I don't think we could live without the myth of a glorified presidency, even if we wanted to. We just aren't that rational. Happily, we're too human for that. We will either live by the myth that has served us fairly well for almost two hundred years or we will probably find a much worse one."

In theory we want presidents to consult widely and use the advice of such colleagues as cabinet members and other top advisers. We like the idea of collegial leadership. But would we want a president to sacrifice his own ideas and priorities for the benefit of conforming to the advice of his cabinet officers? No. We elect the president, not his advisers. One of the most fondly remembered Lincoln stories underscores this point. President Lincoln is supposed to have taken a vote at a cabinet meeting that went entirely against him, but he announced it this way: "Seven nays and one aye, the ayes have it." The late Harold Laski also made this point well when he wrote:

> A President who is believed not to make up his own mind rapidly loses the power to maintain the hold. The need to dramatize his position by insistence upon his undoubted supremacy is inherent in the office as history has shaped it. A masterful man in the White House will, under all circumstances, be more to the liking of the multitude than one who is thought to be swayed by his colleagues.[5]

We want our president to be not only both a lion and a fox but more than a lion, more than a fox. We want simultaneously a secular leader and a civil religious mentor; we praise our three-branched system, but we place capacious hopes upon and thus elevate the presidential branch. Only the president can give us heroic leadership, or so most people feel. Only a president can dramatize and symbolize our highest expectations of ourselves as almost a chosen people with a unique mission. Note too that only presidents are regularly honored with a musical anthem of their own: "Hail to the Chief."

Paradox: Taking the
Presidency Out of Politics

The public yearns for a statesman in the White House, for a George Washington or a second "era of good feelings" — anything that might prevent partisanship or politics as usual in the White House. In fact, however, the job of a president demands that he be a gifted political broker, ever attentive to changing political moods and coalitions.

Franklin Roosevelt illustrates this paradox well. Appearing so remarkably nonpartisan while addressing the nation, he was in practice one of the craftiest manipulators and political-coalition builders to occupy the White House. He mastered the art of politics — the art of making the difficult and desirable possible.

A president is expected to be above politics in some respects and highly political in others. A president is never supposed to act with his eye on the next election; he's not supposed to favor any particular group or party. Nor is he supposed to wheel and deal or to twist too many arms. That's politics and that's bad! No, a president is supposed to be "President of all the people," or so most people are inclined to believe. Yet he is also asked to lead his party, to help fellow party members get elected or reelected, to deal firmly with party barons and congressional political brokers. Too, he must build political coalitions around what he feels needs to be done.

To take the president out of politics is to assume, incorrectly, that a president will be so generally right and the general public so generally wrong that a president must be protected from the push and shove of political pressures. But what president has always been right? Over the years, public opinion has usually been as sober a guide as anyone else on the political waterfront. And, lest we forget, having a president constrained and informed by public opinion is what a democracy is all about.

In his reelection campaign of 1972 Richard Nixon sought, in vain, to display himself as too busy to be a politician: he wanted the American people to believe he was too preoccupied with the Vietnam War to have any personal concern about his election.

If past is prologue, presidents in the future will go to considerable lengths to portray themselves as unconcerned with their own political future. They will do so in large part because the public applauds the divorce between the presidency and politics. People naively think that we can somehow turn the job of president into that of a managerial or strictly executive post. (The six-year, single-term proposal reflects this paradox.) Not so. The presidency is a highly political office, and it cannot be otherwise. Moreover, its political character is for the most part desirable. A president separated from, or somehow above, politics might easily become a president who doesn't listen to the people, doesn't respond to majority sentiment or pay attention to views that may be diverse, intense, and at variance with his own. A president immunized to politics would be a president who would too easily become isolated from the processes of government and removed from the thoughts and aspirations of his people.

In all probability, this paradox will endure. A standard diagnosis of what's gone wrong in an administration will be that the presidency has become too politicized. But it will be futile to try to take the president out of politics. A more helpful approach is to realize that certain presidents try too hard to hold themselves above politics — or at least to give that appearance — rather than engage in it deeply, openly, and creatively. A president in a democracy has to act politically in regard to controversial issues if any semblance of government by the consent of the governed is to be achieved.

Paradox: The Common Man Who
Gives an Uncommon Performance

We like to think that America is the land where the common sense of the common person reigns. We prize the common touch, the up-from-the-log-cabin "man of the people." Yet few of us settle for anything but an uncommon performance from our presidents.

This paradox is splendidly summed up by a survey conducted by the Field Research Corporation, a California public-opinion organization. Field asked a cross section of Californians in 1975 to describe in their own words the qualities a presidential candidate should have. Honesty and trustworthiness topped the list. But one of the more intriguing findings was that "while most (72%) prefer someone with plain and simple tastes, there is also a strong preference (66%) for someone who can give exciting speeches and inspire the public." [6]

It has been said that the American people crave to be governed by a president who is greater than anyone else but not better than anyone else. We are inconsistent; we want our president to be one of the folks but also something special. If a president gets too special, however, he gets clobbered. If he tries to be too folksy, people get bored. The Lincoln and Kennedy presidencies are illustrative. We cherish the myth that anyone can grow up to be president — that there are no barriers, no elite qualifications — but we don't want a person who is too ordinary. Would-be presidents have to prove their special qualifications — their excellence, their stamina, their capacity for uncommon leadership.

The Harry Truman reputation, at least as it flourished in the 1970s, demonstrates the apparent reconciliation of this paradox. Fellow commoner Truman rose to the demands of the job and became an apparently gifted decision maker, or so his admirers would have us believe.

Candidate Carter in 1976 nicely fitted this paradox as well. Local, down-home farm-boy-next-door makes good! The image of the peanut farmer turned gifted governor contributed greatly to Carter's success as a national candidate, and he used it with consummate skill. Early on in his presidential bid, Carter enjoyed introducing himself as a peanut farmer *and* a nuclear physicist — yet another way of suggesting he was down to earth but cerebral as well.

A president or would-be president must be bright but not too bright, warm and accessible but not too folksy, down to earth but not pedestrian. Adlai Stevenson was witty and clever, talents that seldom pay in politics. Voters apparently prefer plainness and solemn platitudes, but these too can be overdone; witness Ford's talks, no matter what the occasion, which dulled our senses with the banal. When Jimmy Carter once gave a fireside chat even the fire fell asleep. The "catch 22" here, of course, is that an uncommon performance puts distance between a president and the truly common man. We persist, however, in wanting an uncommon common man as president.

Paradox: The National Unifier — National Divider

One of the paradoxes most difficult to alleviate arises from our longing for a president who will pull us together again and yet be a forceful priority setter, budget manager, and executive leader. The two tasks are near opposites.

Our nation remains one of the few in the world that calls upon its chief executive to serve also as its symbolic, ceremonial head of state. Elsewhere, these tasks are spread around. In some nations there is a monarch *and* a prime minister; in other nations there are three visible national leaders — the head of state, a premier, and a powerful party chief.

In the absence of an alternative, we demand that our presidents and our presidency act as a unifying force in our lives. Perhaps it all began with George Washington, who so artfully performed this function. At least for a while, he truly was above politics, a unique symbol of our new nation. He was a healer, a unifier, and an extraordinary man for all seasons. Today we ask no less of our presidents than that they should do as Washington did.

We have designed a presidential job description, however, that impels our contemporary presidents to act as national dividers. Presidents must necessarily divide when they act as the leaders of their political parties, when they set priorities that advantage certain goals and groups at the expense of others, when they forge and lead political coalitions, when they move out ahead of public opinion and assume the role of national educators, when they choose one set of advisers over another. A president, as a creative executive leader, cannot help but offend certain interests. When Franklin Roosevelt was running for a second term, some garment workers unfolded a great sign that said, "We love him for the enemies he has made." Such is the fate of a president on an everyday basis; if he chooses to use power he will usually lose the goodwill of those who preferred inaction over action. The opposite is, of course, true if he chooses not to act.

Look at it from another angle. The nation is torn between the view that a president should primarily preside over the nation and merely serve as a referee among the various powerful interests that actually control who gets what, when, and how and a second position, which holds that a president should gain control of government processes and powers so as to use them for the purpose of furthering public, as opposed to private, interests. Obviously, the position that you take on this question is relevant to your value of the presidency and the kind of person you'd like to see in the job.

Harry S. Truman said it very simply. He noted that 14 million or 15 million Americans had the resources to have representatives in Washington to protect their interests, and that the interests of the great mass of other people were the responsibility of the president of the United States.

The president is sometimes seen as the great defender of the people, the ombudsman or advocate general of "public interests." Yet this should be viewed as merely a claim, for enough presidents have acted otherwise, even antagonistically, to mass or popular preferences.

This debate notwithstanding, Americans prize the presidency as a grand American invention. As a nation we do not want to change it. Proposals to weaken or devitalize it are dismissed. Proposals to reform or restructure it are paid little respect. If we sour on a president, the conventional solution has been to find and elect someone we hope will be better.

Paradox: The Longer He Is There, the Less We Like Him

Every four years we pick a president, and for the next four years we pick on him and at him, and sometimes pick him apart entirely. Because there is no adequate prepresidential job experience, much of the first term is an on-the-job learning experience. But we resent this. It is too important a job for on-the-job learning, or at least that's how most of us feel.

Too, we expect presidents to grow in office and to become better acclimated to their powers and responsibilities. But the longer they are in office, the more they find themselves involved in crises with less and less public support. An apocryphal presidential lament, "Every time I seem to grow into the job, it gets bigger," is not unfounded.

Simply stated, the more we know of a president, or the more we observe his presidency, the less we approve of him. Familiarity breeds discontent. Research on public support of presidents indicates that approval peaks soon after a president takes office and then slides downward until it bottoms out in the latter half of the four-year term. Thereafter, briefly, it rises a bit but never attains its original levels. This pattern of declining presidential support is a subject of debate among social scientists. Unrealistic early expectations are, of course, a major factor, guaranteed to ensure a period of disenchantment.

Peace and prosperity can help stem the unpleasant tide of ingratitude, and Eisenhower's popularity remained reasonably high in large part because of his (or the nation's) achievements in these respects. For other presidents, however, their eventual downslide in popularity was due nearly as much to the public's inflated expectations as to the presidents' actions. It was often as if the downslide in popularity would occur no matter what the president did. If this seems unfair, even cruel, it is, nonetheless, what happens to those skilled and lucky enough to win election to the "highest office in the land."

All this occurs despite our conventional wisdom that the *office makes the man* — "that the presidency with its built-in educational processes, its spacious view of the world, its command of talent, and above all its self-conscious historic role, does work its way on the man in the Oval Office," as James MacGregor Burns puts it.[7] If we concede that the office in part does make the man, we must admit also that time in office often unmakes the man.

Paradox: The Reassuring the Public While Accentuating a Sense of Crisis Leader

Although a president is expected to exude hope, reassurance, and an I'm OK we're OK sense of confidence, the public nevertheless likes to see presidents visibly wrestling with crises. Presidents Ford and Carter learned, sometimes painfully, about this paradox when they found that more political support was available when the United States was at odds with the Soviet Union than when the two countries were in agreement. It is almost easier, they found, to go to the brink of war with the Soviets than to defend advances in détente or new SALT agreements. President Kennedy found that "the politics of confrontation" with Cuba as well as that with Khrushchev were politically helpful.

Presidents are simultaneously asked to build a lasting peace and at the same time maintain United States superiority as the number one superpower. Promote peace, yes. But don't yield anything to the Soviet Union! Moreover, presidents who wish to appear presidential must accentuate the nation's sense of being in a severe predicament. They perceive that a sense of heightened crisis must be created. FDR did it, as did Kennedy, especially in the summer of 1961 when he launched a fallout-shelter program.

This paradox, in a sense, is the inevitable outgrowth of our belief system that is based on both laissez-faireism (fear of big government and the desire to be left alone) and interventionism (reliance on the strength and authority of the United States government to solve national and international problems). Whether it be the Soviet or the Cuban threat or an energy crunch, the public expects presidents to solve the problem, to protect the country. There is, however, a genuine reluctance on the part of citizens to pay the price for such strength.

We expect our president, as the most visible representative of big government, to solve the entire scope of our problems by mustering all the powers and strengths to which that office entitles him — and then some — but we are unwilling to allow him to infringe upon our rights in any significant way. We don't especially like calls for sacrifice. Energy conservation is illustrative. We applauded Carter's efforts to put forth solutions to the "energy problem" but then criticized him for trying to force sacrifices in the form of higher gas prices and other individual hardships.

Stated another way, we want strong, effective presidential leadership, yet at the same time we are profoundly cautious about concentrating power in one person's hands.

Paradox: The Active in Some Areas and at Some Times but Passive in Other Areas or at Other Times Leader

There are times when we want our president to be engaged actively in doing certain things, and there are other occasions when we would like to see him sit back and let things run their course. But different people will disagree on whether the times demand presidential passivity or activity.

If you are not directly concerned about a matter one way or another, it is easy to say the president should not take action. When the president and the executive branch are doing something you consider important, however, that's just an instance of society organizing itself to perform an urgent task. Thus a subject you are especially interested in deserves all the presidential attention it can get.

In the abstract, everyone is against the "imperial presidency," but one person's waste is another's means of survival. People want a strong presidency, but at the same time they don't want it interfering in their lives or initiating any more new taxes. There is a fair amount of disagreement on precisely how much and what kind of presidential leadership we want; this has always been the case and will continue to be so.

Some have wanted to curtail the functions and authority of the presidency because they think it has too much power. Others no longer trust the presidency on a variety of specific issues such as war making or tax reform. Still others want to tie a president's hands for personal reasons or for the benefit of special interests.

Historically, conservatives have been more opposed to a strong presidency than liberals. This has changed. The conservatives may fear a very powerful planning presidency at home but they want a powerful presidency for national-security leadership. Liberals, of course, have generally applauded a strong presidency when it has been in the hands of a Roosevelt, a Truman, or a Kennedy. Overall, it does appear that in much of the debate over the proper range of presidential power, our attitudes are considerably shaped by the party and the kind of leader at the moment in control of the White House. Put another way, conservatives and liberals have favored or opposed a powerful presidency according as it suited their immediate purposes.

Writing about shifts of the public mood in America, historian Arthur M. Schlesinger, Sr., once claimed that "a period of concern for the rights of the few has been followed by one of concern for the wrongs of the many. . . . An era of quietude has been succeeded by one of rapid movement." [8] A period of affirmative government is followed by backlash and a period of lull. Schlesinger plotted these shifts of mood from 1765 to 1947, noting the liberationist or progressive eras with an asterisk. I have taken the liberty of updating the Schlesinger "tides" through 1980.

* 1765–1787	1787–1801
* 1801–1816	1816–1829
* 1829–1841	1841–1861
* 1861–1869	1869–1901
* 1901–1919	1919–1931
* 1931–1947	1947–1960
* 1960–1973	1973–

This examination of shifting public moods is of interest here because it is clear that a president is constrained by the dominant national mood or climate of expectations. Sometimes the coming of a new, colorful president can help to recast or shift the national mood. More often, however, the national mood responds to major events, to challenges, to times of testing. Admittedly, full accounting for these shifts remains somewhat elusive. Still, President Carter's difficulties arose in no small measure because he sought to lead a nation that had turned inward, introspective, and perhaps neonarcissistic. The nation had become self-centered rather than nation-centered. One of Carter's problems came about because he is a man of strongly activist inclination who came along at a time when programmatic passivity (at least in social and regulatory programs) was what many Americans seemed to want. The people acted as if what they really wanted was a second Ford administration, whereas Carter, or so it seemed, sometimes wanted to act as if it were 1933 or 1963. Political analysts may quarrel with whether there really was a surge to conservatism in the 1970s. They may be right in this contention. Still, it is a fact in national politics that the illusion of a shift usually gets interpreted as an actual shift.

Paradox: What It Takes to Become President May Not Be What Is Needed to Govern the Nation

To win a presidential election takes ambition, ambiguity, luck, and masterful public-relations strategies. To govern the nation plainly requires all of these. However, it may well be that too much ambition, too much ambiguity, and too heavy a reliance on phony public-relations tricks actually undermine the integrity and legitimacy of the presidency.

Columnist David Broder offered an apt example: "People who win primaries may become good Presidents — but 'it ain't necessarily so.' Organizing well is important in governing just as it is in winning primaries. But the Nixon years should teach us that good advance men do not necessarily make trustworthy White House aides. Establishing a government is a little more complicated than having the motorcade run on time." [9]

Likewise, ambition (in very heavy doses) is essential for a presidential candidate, but too much hunger for the office or for success at any price is a danger to be avoided. He must be bold and energetic, but in excess these characteristics can produce a cold, frenetic candidate. To win the presidency obviously requires a single-mindedness, yet our presidents must also have a sense of proportion, be well rounded, have a sense of humor, be able to take a joke, and have hobbies and interests outside the realm of politics.

To win the presidency many of our presidents (Lincoln, Kennedy, and Carter come to mind) had to talk as more progressive or even populist than they actually felt; to be effective in the job they felt compelled to act as more conservative than they wanted to.

Another aspect of this paradox is the ambiguous or misleading positions candidates take on issues in order to increase their appeal to the large bulk of centrist and independent voters; such positions may alienate people later, after the candidate has won, when they learn that his views and policies differ. Such prepresidential pledges as LBJ's "We will not send American boys to fight the war that Asian boys should be fighting," Richard Nixon's "open presidency," and Jimmy Carter's "I will balance the budget by 1981" backfired when they were later violated.

One of the most difficult to perform campaign sleight of hands is how to win without proving that you are unworthy of the job you are seeking. Thus it is a common temptation for all candidates, including some incumbents, to run a "bureaucrats-are-bums" anti-Washington kind of campaign. Many of our successful presidential candidates adopt this strategy. The public is against government waste and cronyism. There is always too much red tape and "fat" in government.

Just the same, we expect a president to be able to work closely and effectively with Congress and civil servants. A candidate who is forever poor-mouthing Washington officials will breed resentment, and if he gets to the White House, he will have a difficult time winning sustained co-operation from these same officials when he needs their help to get things done. Then, too, as Carter found out in the Bert Lance affair, a candidate who gets too pious about how standards have to be raised in Washington will be called a hypocrite if he and his top aides are caught in compromised conflict-of-interest positions.

Moreover, as Henry Fairlie points out, "There is something more than a little deceitful, and certainly a lot that is absurd, in a presidential candidate who is trying to get to Washington by saying that he is running 'against Washington,' and one hoping to be elected to the most powerful office in the world by proclaiming that he is against big government." [10] This is especially true for a Democratic candidate.

We often also want both a "fresh face," an outsider, as a presidential candidate and a seasoned, mature, experienced veteran who knows the corridors of power and the back alleyways of Washington. The frustration with past presidential performances leads us to turn to a "fresh new face" uncorrupted by Washington's politics and its "buddy system." We also feel more secure in passing on the presidency to the more experienced politician who is adept at political bargaining with old Washington cronies and old enough in outlook not to attempt anything rash or naive. This explains both why the Carter candidacy was so appealing to many in 1976 and why the Carter presidency may well encourage a search for insiders or at least perceived veterans rather than outside fresh faces next time. This also explains why Carter aide Hamilton Jordan had to "eat" his words several months after he made this statement: "If, after the inauguration [1977], you find a Cy Vance as Secretary of State and Zbigniew Brzezinski as head of national security, then I would say we failed. And I'd quit. But that's not going to happen. You're going to see new faces, new ideas." The outsiders from Georgia apparently needed the old hands to steady their administration. Aides like Jordan time and again found that running the government is altogether different from running for the

White House. They also learned that taking charge is not the same as taking hold of the executive branch.

Political scientist Samuel Huntington calls attention to yet another way this paradox works. To be a winning candidate, he notes, the would-be president must put together an *electoral coalition* involving a majority of voters advantageously distributed across the country. To do this, he must appeal to all regions and interest groups and cultivate the appearance of honesty, sincerity, and experience. But once elected, the electoral coalition has served its purpose and a *governing coalition* is the order of the day:

> The day after his election the size of his majority is almost — if not entirely — irrelevant to his ability to govern the country. What counts then is his ability to mobilize support from the leaders of the key institutions in society and government. He has to constitute a broad governing coalition of strategically located supporters who can furnish him with the information, talent, expertise, manpower, publicity, arguments, and political support which he needs to develop a program, to embody it in legislation, and to see it effectively implemented. This coalition must include key people in Congress, the executive branch, and the private-sector "Establishment." The governing coalition need have little relation to the electoral coalition. The fact that the President as a candidate put together a successful electoral coalition does not insure that he will have a viable governing coalition.[11]

Candidates plainly depend upon television to transform candidacy into incumbency. Research findings point out that candidates spend well over half their funds on radio and television broadcasting. Moreover, this is how most people "learn" about the candidates. Approximately two-thirds of the American public reports that television is the best way for them to follow candidates, and about half of the public acknowledges that their best understanding of the candidates and issues is derived from television coverage.

Thus, television is obviously vital. But the candidate has to travel to every state and hundreds of cities for at least a four-year period to capture the exposure and the local headlines that earn for him the visibility and stature of a "serious candidate." For the most part, it becomes a grueling ordeal, as well as a major learning experience. In quest of the Democratic nomination for president, Walter F. Mondale of Minnesota spent most of 1974 traveling some 200,000 miles, delivering hundreds of speeches, appearing on countless radio and television talk shows, and sleeping in Holiday Inn after Holiday Inn all across the country. He admitted that he enjoyed some of it, but said, too, that he seldom had time to read or to reflect, not to mention time for a sane family life. Eventually he withdrew on the grounds that he simply had neither the overwhelming desire nor the time, as an activist United States senator, to do what was necessary in order to win the nomination.

What it takes to *become* president may differ from what it takes to *be* president. To become president takes a near megalomaniac who is also glib, dynamic, charming on television, and hazy on the issues. Yet we want our presidents to be well rounded, careful in their reasoning, clear and specific in their communications, and not excessively ambitious. It may well be that our existing primary-convention system adds up to an effective obstacle course for testing would-be presidents. Certainly they have to travel to all sections of the country, meet the people, deal with interest-group elites, and learn about the challenging issues of the day. But with the Johnson and Nixon experiences in our not-too-distant past, we have reason for asking whether our system of producing presidents is adequately reconciled with what is required to produce a president who is competent, fair-minded, and emotionally healthy.

CONCLUSIONS

Perhaps the ultimate paradox of the modern presidency is that it is always too powerful and yet it is always inadequate. Always too powerful because it is contrary to our ideals of a "government by the people" and always too powerful, as well, because it now possesses the capacity to wage nuclear war (a capacity that unfortunately doesn't permit much in the way of checks and balances and deliberative, participatory government). Yet always inadequate because it seldom achieves our highest hopes for it, not to mention its own stated intentions.

The presidency is always too strong when we dislike the incumbent. Its limitations are bemoaned, however, when we believe the incumbent is striving valiantly to serve the public interest as we define it. For many people, the Johnson presidency captured this paradox vividly: many who felt that he was too strong in Vietnam also felt that he was too weak to wage his War on Poverty (for some it was vice versa).

Like everyone else, presidents have their good days and their bad days, their creative leadership periods and their periods of isolation, their times of imperiousness and ineptitude. On good days, we want the presidency to be stronger. On bad days, we want all the checks and balances that can be mustered. It also turns out that on good days, the presidency is never strong enough. And on bad days, it is too strong already — as when Nixon asserted the impoundment, executive privilege, and war powers to their hilt in the early 1970s. The dilemma of the presidency nowadays is that you can't have it both ways. "Take away power on his bad days, and it's not available when there are good things to be done," notes James L. Sundquist of the Brookings Institution.[12] In the nearly two centuries since President Washington took office we have vastly multiplied the requirements for presidential leadership and made it increasingly difficult to lead. Serious students of the presidency all conclude that more power, not less, will be needed if presidents are to get the job done. There are just too many constraints on governmental action — when the president is at his best. Certainly this is no time for mindless retribution against the already fragile institution of the presidency.

But if the presidency is to be given more power, should it not also be subject to more controls? Perhaps so. But how do you institute controls that will curb the powers of a president who abuses the public trust and at the same time not undermine the capacity of a fair-minded president to serve the public interest? The riddle here arises because we sometimes disagree over which days are good and which are bad. Thus Ford's extensive use of the veto power was applauded by some but condemned by others. Ford's pardon of Nixon was thought by many to be a terrible misuse of the pardon power, but it was cheered by almost as many others.

Finally, although we sometimes do not approve of the way a president acts, we nevertheless approve of the end results. Thus Lincoln is often criticized for acting outside the limits of the Constitution, but he is at the same time forgiven because of the obvious necessity for him to violate certain Constitutional principles in order to preserve the Union. FDR was often flagrantly deceptive and manipulative not only of his political opponents but also of his staff and allies. FDR even relished pushing people around and toying with them. But leadership effectiveness in the end comes down to whether a person acts in terms of the highest interests of the nation. "And one has to conclude — certainly most historians will conclude — that Roosevelt was profoundly right in the use of the federal government to help the poor people in need. And he was also profoundly right in helping to lend the weight of this nation to counter Hitler." [13]

Neither presidents nor the the general public should be relieved of their respective responsibilities of trying to fashion a more effective and fair-minded leadership system simply because these paradoxes are pointed out and even widely agreed upon. It is also not enough to throw up our hands and say, "Well, no one makes a person run for that crazy job in the first place."

The situation analyzed here doubtless also characterizes the positions of governors, city managers, university presidents, and even many corporate executives. Is it a new phenomenon, or are we just increasingly aware of it? Is it a permanent or a transitory condition? My own view is that it is neither new nor transitory.

We shall have to select as our presidents people who understand these paradoxes and have a gift for the improvisation necessitated by their contrary demands. Too often in the past we have selected those who have simply learned to manipulate these paradoxes for electoral purposes.

Although the presidency will surely remain one of our nation's best vehicles for creative policy change, it will also continue to be a hard-pressed office, laden with the cumulative weight of these paradoxes. We need to probe the origins and to assess the consequences of these paradoxes and to learn how presidents and the public can better coexist with them, for it is apparent that these paradoxes often serve to confuse the public in their evaluation of presidents, not to mention the job ambiguity they cause for presidents.[14]

Collectively these paradoxes and contradictory expectations are the toughest challenge to presidential leadership. They constitute a tough unwritten code of conduct for our presidents, perhaps a code so difficult to follow that our presidents will almost certainly be the scapegoats when anything goes wrong. But do we not blame the victim? The public's expectations are often too contradictory and too high to be fulfilled by one man alone. When Americans realize that the presidency is incapable of dealing with everything well, and that politics in general is not suited to provide answers to every social and economic malaise, then there may be less savaging of the president.

The paradoxes of the presidency do not lie in the White House but in the emotings, feelings, and expectations of us all. There exists some element in the American mind, and perhaps in the minds of people everywhere, that it is possible to find a savior-hero who will deliver us to an era of greener grass and a land of milk and honey. When this pseudomessiah fails we inflict upon him the wrath of our vengeance. It is almost a ritual destruction; we venerate the presidency, but we destroy our presidents. Perhaps this is only logical when we elect a person expecting superhuman strength, character, and restraint, and invariably get a rather fragile, overworked, fallible, and mortal human.

The paradoxes of the presidency present the nation with a special problem, for often the high and conflicting expectations and the pressures to meet them force a president to abandon attainable goals in favor of unattainable hopes. This, of course, fills people with false hope and later frequently leads to disillusionment. The textbook, or storybook, presidency that these paradoxes help create should, of course, be exposed and lessened where possible. Progress will be slow. For even if the presidency cannot realistically be all things to all people, it will always mean many things to many people. As long as people continue to hope and to dream, as long as there remains an American Dream (or Dreams), so also these paradoxes will shape how presidents go about their work.

NOTES

1. John Steinbeck, *America and Americans* (Bonanza Books, 1966), p. 46.

2. Andrew Greeley, *Building Coalitions: American Politics in the 1970's* (New Viewpoints, 1974), pp. 229–30.

3. Garry Wills, "Hurrah for Politicians," *Harper's*, September 1975, p. 49.

4. Bruce Miroff, *Pragmatic Illusions: The Presidential Politics of John F. Kennedy* (David McKay, 1976), p. 31. For a somewhat similar treatment of several earlier presidents, see Richard Hofstadter, *The American Political Tradition* (Vintage, 1948).

5. Harold J. Laski, *The American Presidency* (Harper & Bros., 1940), p. 93.

6. See Mervin Field, "Public Opinion and Presidential Response," in John Hoy and Melvin Bernstein, eds., *The Effective President* (Palisades Press, 1976), pp. 59–77.

7. James MacGregor Burns, *Presidential Government* (Houghton Mifflin, 1974), p. 296.

8. Arthur M. Schlesinger, Sr., *Paths to the Present* (Houghton Mifflin, 1964), p. 93.

9. *Boston Globe*, 7 January 1976, p. 19.

10. Henry Fairlie, *The Parties* (St. Martin's Press, 1978), p. 213.

11. Samuel Huntington, "The Democratic Distemper," in N. Glazer and I. Kristol, eds., *The American Commonwealth 1976* (Basic Books, 1970), p. 27.

12. James L. Sundquist, written remarks prepared for a seminar, American University, Washington, D.C., 22 April 1976, p. 2. I am indebted to Sundquist for his suggestions.

13. James MacGregor Burns, remarks at annual meeting, International Society of Political Psychology, New York City, 3 September 1978. See also his *Leadership* (Harper & Row, 1978).

14. I am aware that this discussion deals with at least two different kinds of conflicting expectations. The first deals with different desires held by the public. The gentle but decent yet guileful and decisive paradox is an example of this. Our second kind of conflict deals with the different kind of behavior required to cope with different aspects of the presidency. Here, as in the conflict between the candidate and the president as the national executive, I am obviously pointing to the different roles a president has to provide whether he wants to or not. The latter are somewhat less tractable, for there we are speaking about some of the central problems of the institution.

CHAPTER 2

THE PRESIDENTIAL SELECTION PROCESS

He shall hold his Office during the Term of four Years. . . .
No person except a natural born Citizen, or a Citizen of the
United States at the time of the Adoption of this Constitution,
shall be eligible to the Office of President; neither shall any
person be eligible to that Office who shall not have attained
to the Age of thirty-five years, and been fourteen Years a
Resident within the United States.

— U.S. Constitution, Article II.

I am convinced . . . that the [presidential selection] system
itself is becoming increasingly irrational, self-defeating and
destructive of the ultimate goal of electing the most important
political leader in a free society in the world.

— Walter F. Mondale, *The Accountability
of Power* (McKay, 1975), p. 30.

The way things now stand, in [the 1980] election a decision of
major national importance will again be entrusted to the
outdated, flawed mechanism of the electoral college. Most
importantly, the Nation will again run the serious risk that
due to the workings of this system the candidate obtaining
the most popular votes might not be selected as President.

— Hon. Jonathan B. Bingham (D–N.Y.)
Congressional Record 26 February 1979, p. H 882.

Can anyone remember when a kind word was said about the way we elect our presidents? Perhaps not for a generation have a large majority of Americans felt they had a choice between first-rate candidates. Although Americans may prize the institution of the presidency, they are far less confident about the procedures and machinations of the presidential selection process.

The selection process itself is so full of paradoxes and ironies and unintended consequences that a current saying is that "elections are rarely our finest hour." It is the purpose of this chapter to explore and explain how we elect our presidents. The following questions will be discussed: Who becomes president? What do we look for in prospective presidents? What must a person do to get taken seriously as a presidential candidate? How important are the primaries? Are the national conventions still needed? What about the so-called advantages of incumbency? What has been the effect of the Twenty-second Amendment? Why do people vote or not vote for president? Finally, what about the controversial electoral college and its role in presidential elections?

WHO BECOMES PRESIDENT?

It has been observed that our presidents are usually middle-aged white male Protestant lawyers from the larger states. There have been exceptions, but the observation holds reasonably well. In the twentieth century only two have come from medium-sized states. About half have been lawyers, served in Congress and held city or county public positions.

Presidential candidates are almost invariably selected from a small pool of professional politicians who have served as governor, member of Congress, or vice president. In a sense, there is an "on-deck circle" of about fifty individuals in any given presidential election year: governors of the larger states, prominent male U.S. Senators under the age of sixty-five, and a few recent governors or vice presidents who have successfully maintained themselves in the news media.

Americans often gripe about the small number of able people who vie for the presidency. Is this the best we can do? With our large and highly educated population, why can't we produce Washingtons, Jeffersons, Madisons, Franklins, and the like? Or, as James Reston put it a few years ago, "The more you look at the men who are now running for President, the more you have to wonder about the men who are not running." [1] Where did the men come from who became our twentieth century presidents?

Doubtless, there is many a talented business entrepreneur, university president, or other outstanding individual who might make as capable a president as the score or so of activist politicians who inevitably become

Twentieth Century Presidents — Where They Came From
(N = 15)

Lawyers	7
Members of Congress	7
City or county elective or public positions	7
Governors	6
Vice presidents	6
State legislators	4
Businessmen	3
Cabinet officers	2
University presidents	2
Generals	1

Last Job Before Becoming President
(N = 15)

Vice president	5*
Governor	4
U.S. Senate	2
Cabinet officer	2
Law practice	1
University president	1

Total 15

the serious candidates. Seldom, however, are these nonprofessional politicians willing to enter the political thicket at age fifty-one or fifty-six or sixty-one. Some, perhaps many, do not want to disclose their finances and subject their families and themselves to the brutal public scrutiny involved in a presidential race. The demanding presidential campaign, especially with the thirty or more primary elections, is unappealing even to the career politician.

Are great men never selected? This is a perennial topic. Some say that many men of substance and character have indeed been elected. Some say that events make the men, not the other way around. Still others contend that merit is always difficult to assess. Was Charles Evans Hughes better than Woodrow Wilson in 1916? Was Eisenhower better than Stevenson in 1952? And so on. Supporters of winners do not complain as much, but supporters of losers almost always see flaws in our way of nominating and electing presidents. Greatness is, of course, in the eyes of the beholder. Greatness is also something that is not necessarily the same as popularity. Some of our most respected presidents just barely won election.

* Note that all five of these twentieth-century presidents were elevated to office when presidents died or (in Nixon's case) resigned from office. The last vice president to win the presidency by running as an incumbent vice president was Martin Van Buren in 1836.

Those we now respect were sometimes not applauded when they were in office.

In practice, then, only a few dozen individuals (all white male politicians) are considered as "serious" potential presidents. The evidence is strong that usually by about January of election year one or two front-runners have emerged from this pack to go on to the semifinal, the nominating convention. The country probably deserves a large array of possibilities, but this is unlikely to be the case in the near future. Both parties and the public will usually be presented with a virtual fait accompli. In practice, name familiarity, access to large financial resources, and the substantial spare time necessary to prepare for the primaries give certain candidates advantages over others.

WHAT WE LOOK FOR IN
OUR PRESIDENTS

A presidential candidate must be at least thirty-five years old, must have lived within the United States for fourteen years, and must be a "natural born citizen." Whether a person born abroad of American parents is qualified to serve as president has never been decided. Many scholars believe that such a person would be considered "natural born" even if not native-born.

What are the qualities Americans desire in their presidential candidates? Honesty and integrity head the list of desired characteristics. The "Honest Abe" and "I will never tell a lie" sentiment lives. We are keenly aware, the more so because of Watergate, of the need for a president to set a tone, and to serve as an example, of credibility. Dishonesty and the trait of saying one thing and doing another are the qualities we dislike the most.

Intelligence, a capacity to clarify, communicate, and mobilize, as well as flexibility, compassion, and open-mindedness are also leading characteristics sought in presidential candidates.

Most voters look for a moderate candidate. They generally vote against extremists of any kind and for the middle-of-the-road, don't-rock-the-boat candidates. This has led to the aphorism that "the only extreme in American politics that wins is the extreme middle."

The three overriding factors that influence how persons vote in presidential elections are their *party orientation*, their *public-policy preferences*, and *the way they perceive the integrity, character, and judgment of the candidates*.

Parties may be decaying as organized, vital institutions in America, but they are still important factors when the votes are counted. Not as partisan a people as we were earlier in this century, we are now better educated with multiple sources of political information, no longer dependent upon party leaders for welfare, patronage, or certain other intermediary services. Still, more than two-thirds of Americans identify themselves as Democrats or Republicans. People still vote party for president. Most of the time, most Republicans vote Republican, most Democrats vote Democrat. Republicans are a more cohesive party in the general election. More than 80 percent of Republicans voted for Barry Goldwater in 1964, 95 percent voted for Nixon in 1972, 89 percent for Ford in 1976. Democrats, twice as numerous, are less unified, less predictable. Carter got more than 80 percent of the Democratic vote in 1976, but George McGovern in 1972 got only 67 percent of the Democratic vote. A third of the people calling themselves Democrats voted for Richard Nixon that year.

Party membership is based on inheritance, memories, and emotional factors as well as rational calculations. Always important, issues or public-policy preferences play an even more complicated role in how people cast their presidential vote. In certain years — 1800, 1860, 1896, 1936, and 1964 — issues played a larger, more clear-cut role than in other years — 1956, 1960, and 1976. Sometimes both major candidates take the same position on a major issue, as in 1968 when both Nixon and Hubert Humphrey said they favored ending the war, honorably, in Vietnam.

Issues seem to be less important in many elections because of the tendency for both parties to offer candidates who take policy stands near the midpoint of public opinion. Thus both candidates often echo the public mood rather closely. Moreover, candidates' policy preferences are often deliberately highly ambiguous. Clear-cut policy stands are often infrequent and inconspicuous as candidates devote much more attention to their concerns about general goals, problems, and past performance. One student of election strategy sums up the experience:

> If perceptions of parties' and candidates' stands are often confused or absent altogether, the reason is not necessarily apathy or lack of cognitive skill on the part of the citizenry. To be sure, voters do not receive or retain every scrap of available information about politics: it would be costly and irrational to do so. But often the information is simply not available. The extreme ambiguity of candidates' policy stands — the low emphasis with which they are taken, and the lack of specificity in even the least ambiguous statements — add greatly to the costs of obtaining such information and sometimes make it altogether unobtainable.[2]

There was a steep increase in ideological consistency in public attitudes in the 1960s and early 1970s. Attitudes about issues came to be an increasingly significant factor in whether and how people voted. The number of persons who could distinguish between the parties on ideological grounds increased. So also the number of people who paid attention to political issues went up. This led some scholars to suggest that political parties were needed when imperfect information existed, but that in an era of higher education and ample campaign television coverage parties are less relied upon as a guide to voting. Yet in the 1976 election, the party again played a more dominant role than the issues. Normally (1964 and 1972 were perhaps aberrations), then, most issues most of the time get fuzzed over as candidates boast, from coast to coast, how wonderful their administration will be. Only the candidates' names appear on the national ballot; no issues are listed.

Personality and character also count. In local elections people often just rely on party labels. But with governors, U.S. Senators, and especially with presidents and the availability of extensive television coverage, people plainly intrude their own personal judgment on the decision of who is most fit to win office.

Many people deplore the fact that a candidate's personality and style are evaluated as equal to or more important than issues and substance. But a candidate's personality is a perfectly legitimate and, indeed, a proper subject for voters to weigh. There is little doubt that a candidate's sense of self-confidence and his personal style of conduct can and usually do affect how he would behave in office. "Presidents do far more than respond to the issue preferences of the voters. They have enormous discretionary power, and their personalities can importantly affect the way they handle issues and decide public policy." [3]

The basic insecurities of certain presidents have also led to failure in the White House. We have reason to be alert to whether a candidate can accept criticism and whether he demands absolute loyalty from subordinates. "The great danger is that a President who feels threatened by events or harassed by 'enemies' will precipitate a crisis in order to shore up his own inner doubts and confound his opposition." [4]

The experience of the 1960s and 1970s suggests that although Americans still yearn for strong, decisive leaders, they also want persons who can restore trust in government. They want individuals who keep their word, who tell the truth. They want persons who are not rigid, defensive, compulsive, self-striving, and torn by self-doubt and self-pity, or who are wont to blame their problems on "enemies" and proceed to punish those on their "enemies list."

Political scientist James David Barber, a pioneer in studying presidential character, urges us even to look first at a candidate's character. The issues of an election year will change, but the character of the president will last. Politics, he says, is politicians. There is no way to understand it without understanding them. We need to look very closely at the rhetoric, skill, and world view of presidential candidates. Barber finds that Wilson, Hoover, Johnson, and Nixon were persons who displayed tendencies toward compulsiveness and rigidity and were not as desirable as FDR, HST, and JFK. These latter candidates combined a high volume and fast tempo of activity with marked enjoyment of politics and people. They, these "activist-positives" as Barber calls them, manifested strong self-esteem and distinct success in relating to their environment.[5] Barber's analysis has had an influence on opinion makers, members of the press who cover national elections, and even on some presidential candidates. His book has also raised almost as many questions as it has answered. Yet he has correctly identified the importance of evaluating character and personality in presidential elections.

Rexford Tugwell, a onetime brain truster to FDR, tried his hand at defining the qualities that contribute to successful political careers. He was writing about specific political success stories of his own acquaintance, but his generalizations are instructive. All were, Tugwell writes, hearty, full-blooded types, vital, overflowing with energy, restless, driven by ambitions long before their compulsions had any focus.

> They were unintellectual in the scientific sense.
> They were strongly virile and attractive.
> All were extroverts, enjoying sensual pleasures.
> All were superb conversationalists; all knew the uses of parables.
> All were insensitive to others' feelings except as concerned themselves.
> All seemed to have thick skins because they were abused, but this was only seeming; all were hurt and all were unforgiving; and all were anxious for approval.
> All were ruthless in the sense of not reciprocating loyalty; they punished friends and rewarded enemies.
> All had thick armor against probings. Not even those nearest to them knew their minds.
> All were driven by an ambition to attain power in the political hierarchy, and all allowed it to dominate their lives.[6]

However much we seek the well-rounded leader for all seasons, we invariably get ambitious, vain, and calculating candidates who rarely know what is to be done (though they are willing to try). The men who run and win view presidential campaigns less as dialogues or programs for adult education as a fight to win office, a fight to get there. Once they get there, they will experiment and try and see what works. The voters may like a person who knows all the answers — but few candidates will make commitments that are not reversible once in office. One of the first laws of presidential politics seems to be to promise a fresh approach but avoid specificity, to give the appearance of executive ability but not spell out what one intends to execute — at least not in any risky detail.[7]

THE INVISIBLE PRIMARY

Some political analysts contend that "nothing that happens before the New Hampshire presidential primary (usually held in February of election year) has any meaning." In times past it was a confession of weakness for a presidential candidate to get too organized before the New Hampshire primary. Now, however, candidates work for two, three, and even four years before that primary to prepare for their race. Thus Jimmy Carter announced his candidacy for the White House on December 12, 1974, almost two full years before the 1976 election, and he admits he made his decision in 1972, four years before the election. Hence, "the invisible primary," the determining events of an election that actually occur a year or more before the New Hampshire primary.[8] Since 1936 the active candidate who ranked as most popular within his own party in the Gallup poll taken one month before New Hampshire's primary has won his party's nomination 85 percent of the time. Pre-primary activity is indeed significant. Actually, most primaries appear "more as a ritual encounter, a symbolic show whose results reinforce a victory already decided." [9]

What can be called the invisible primary consists of what a candidate does during the two years prior to election year to assure that his candidacy will be taken seriously. A candidate needs to be convincing on at least several "tracks" before he gets mentioned as a serious contender. All of the following are needed:

to become as well known as possible
to raise substantial sums of money
to attract and organize a staff
to identify issues and build a supportive constituency
to devise a "winning" strategy
to devise an effective relationship with the media
to develop a psychological preparedness and a self-confidence that radiates hope

These do not necessarily occur in this order. Nor does this short list exhaust the self and organizational testing of this period. Surely, however, these are the essentials without which a candidate has little chance of being taken seriously.

The first need of a would-be president is to become known. No other effort commands as much time as the battle to gain name recognition. Candidates like Roosevelt, Eisenhower, Kennedy, and Reagan had a leg up on most others because they had become celebrities or had inherited a well-known name even before they ran for the presidency. Candidates like Carter, George Bush, and Walter Mondale have to go out and become known the hard way — by crisscrossing the nation, visiting city after city, and giving unremitting, bone-numbing speeches and interviews.

The second major need for a presidential candidate is money. Large sums are needed to pay for staff, travel, and later in the campaign for crucial television and radio advertising. Money is convertible into many other resources. It is exceedingly difficult to raise money for a presidential race unless you look like a "sure winner" or unless you take especially strong positions on controversial issues. A conservative such as Goldwater or George Wallace can much more easily raise money than a moderate such as Hubert Humphrey or Birch Bayh. Making matters worse, the national media generally follow the "star system" of giving primary coverage to those who are already well known or to the controversial candidates who command intense followings.[10]

The process of raising money in large sums is a compromising and often a corrupting system. The burden of raising millions for a presidential race is often at the heart of why many able persons do not consider making the race. It is also at the heart of why some people are turned off by our political process. When does a political contribution become a bribe? When does systematic campaign soliciting become equivalent to a conspiracy to extort funds? The Watergate and Tongsun Park disclosures highlighted some of these problems.

A 1974 national campaign law set a ceiling of $10 million for each presidential candidate for preconvention campaigning. Because of inflation the limit stood at $12 million or more in 1980. The ceiling applies only if a candidate accepts federal funds to help finance his or her preconvention efforts. If a candidate raises at least $5,000 in each of twenty states in contributions of no more than $250, he or she can qualify for federal funds to pay for up to half his or her preconvention expenses. In essence, contributions of up to $250 are matched dollar for dollar by the U.S. Treasury.

Attracting loyal staff, identifying key issues, and devising a sensible strategy are all vital to the successful launching of a candidacy. Often underestimated is the capacity to evolve a good working relationship with reporters and television interviewers. Some candidates, great speakers who are superb at raising funds, perform poorly when interviewed by the press. Sometimes, too, the great stump speaker looks foolish and too "hot" on television. Friends of Hubert Humphrey generally admitted that Humphrey and television were not made for each other. He was an outstanding orator of the old school at political rallies, but he talked too fast and too much for the television viewer.

What might be called the psychological test — how a candidate reacts to the strain, the temptations, and the intense public scrutiny of the campaign — is one of the most important. Arthur Hadley asks:

> How much does the candidate want the presidency? How much of his private self and belief will be compromised to the public man? To what extent will he abandon family, friends and other normal joys of life, and how does he handle this isolation?[11]

Some candidates develop self-doubts. Some develop a tendency to tell audiences what they want to hear, and over the course of a few weeks they become so inconsistent as to look ridiculous. Others, such as Edmund Muskie, become plagued by a need for more sleep. Muskie also found his presidential bid in 1972 exacerbated his inability to control his temper. The exacting invisible primary period is always an exhausting ordeal and a formidable test, as well, of whether an individual can hold up physically and can control himself emotionally.

THE PRESIDENTIAL PRIMARIES

Presidential primaries began as an outgrowth of the Progressive movement's efforts in the early twentieth century to eliminate "boss rule" and to encourage popular participation in government. Presidential primaries began to take shape after 1905 when the La Follette Republicans in Wisconsin provided a system for the direct election of members of the state's delegation to the national nominating convention, and now about thirty-six, including most of the big, vital states, are using some type of presidential primary.

The concept of popular participation in the nomination of the presidential party nominees evolved slowly during our country's history. First we relied upon the congressional caucus system, which did not allow for direct popular participation at all. Until 1828 members of Congress from each party met and selected the person they wanted as their nominee. With the growth of democratic sentiment and the coming of the Age of Jackson, the national nominating convention system began to emerge as the replacement. In 1828 state legislatures and state party conventions were relied upon to nominate party nominees. After that national conventions took hold, although it was not until 1840 that national party conventions were accorded full recognition.

It was not until about 1912 that primaries began to be used (about twelve states used them that year) in enough places to begin to have a serious impact on the presidential nominations. Many party leaders, however, have never been enthusiastic about primaries, in large part because they believe they undermine the two-party structure by strengthening the hand of candidate loyalists and issue-oriented zealots at the expense of the party regulars. Primaries allow people to vote who may have little or no loyalty to the party and no interest or stake in the party's future. The pre-primary method plainly permitted party regulars and long-time party professionals to control who would be on the party's ticket.

The importance of primaries has waxed and waned during this century, but they have become increasingly important since the 1950s.

Candidates in the past twenty-five years or so have viewed the primaries as an essential test to demonstrate their vote-getting appeal.

Not all states have adopted the primary system. About fifteen states select a certain number of delegates to the national convention through local or district conventions or allow a state committee or convention of party officials to choose the remaining delegates.

The rules for primaries vary from state to state and from party to party. Usually, however, voters elect delegates directly or by showing a preference for a presidential candidate. Some of the early primaries, such as those in New Hampshire, Florida, and Wisconsin, can be important in giving a psychological lift to a front-runner or a new challenger. Later primaries, such as those in California, Ohio, and New Jersey, can be important in giving the final edge to one candidate over others as he heads into the national convention.

In recent years the system of presidential primaries has become one of the most passionately debated aspects of the presidential selection process. Critics say it is a case of "democracy gone mad." Adlai Stevenson, a three-time presidential candidate, observed that the primary system is a "very, very questionable method of selecting presidential candidates, and actually it never does. All it does is destroy some candidates." David Broder goes so far as to say the main thing primaries do is eliminate people, not nominate them:

> The elimination of candidates occurs, not because of the actual votes they receive, but because they get discouraged; volunteers and contributors desert them and the press sours on them when the returns are disappointing. What happens, and what is written and broadcast, the day after the primary is more important than what happens at the polls.[12]

Others contend that the primary system has persuaded some competent and well-balanced persons not to compete; whereas those who possess near-psychopathic ambition and drive enter primaries and lust in their hearts for victory.

Nearly always, the criticism of the primaries ends up focusing upon these alleged flaws: the system takes too long, costs too much, highlights entreprenurial personalities at the expense of issues, makes pseudoenemies out of true political allies, invites factionalism, often favors colorful ideological candidates over moderates, and frequently does not even affect the outcome of the nomination process. Critics especially point to the Goldwater and McGovern nominations as examples of flaws in the primary system.

Primary voters are older, have higher incomes, are more educated, and are more politically active than are primary nonvoters. Turnout is relatively low. (In 1976 about 29 million voters participated in the primaries, about 20 percent of the voting-age population. Their votes determined the selection of nearly three-quarters of the delegates to both the Republican and Democratic conventions.) This low turnout leads some analysts to conclude that as a democratic institution designed to stimulate popular participation, the presidential primary has limited effectiveness.

Not surprisingly, the frequent and sustained criticism of primaries leads people to suggest that the primaries be abolished or reformed. A national primary — a one-shot winner-take-all event in August or September of election year — is supported by a majority of adults answering two Gallup poll surveys. Others favor regional (multistate) primaries or a return to state conventions as a better means by which to select competent presidential nominees.

The primary system surely has its blemishes, but it has also served us well, better in my judgment than the proposed alternatives would serve us. Although "the people" do not fully control the nominating process, it is clear that primaries have increased the public's power in influencing who will be convention delegates.

Primaries have decreased the party leaders' firm control over the nomination process. Students of our party system are worried about this. They would prefer a system that sends responsible party regulars of the state and local parties to the national convention, not bound by rigid instructions from a primary verdict, but as representatives, free to seek out the national interest according to their best judgment. They contend that these party regulars would be delegates concerned with the majority of the party's rank and file and also with the acceptability and electability of a candidate. This view perceives party regulars as those who are most informed and best qualified to select the nominee.[13]

It is true that primaries do allow, on occasion, for a Goldwater or a McGovern to be nominated. But the primaries also allow for fresh faces and younger new blood to emerge, as happened in 1960 and 1976. The 1976 campaign showed that the Democrats, for example, could emerge from the primaries as a fairly unified party. It also demonstrated that even a little-known candidate with modest resources could mount a successful challenge. By giving candidates several opportunities to present themselves to the public, our present procedures make it possible for a candidate to win substantial support during a relatively short period. Abolishing this aspect of the presidential selection process could prevent the infusion of new blood into the presidential race. Further, the alternative, to return to the choosing of the nominee by a small establishment group is unacceptable to most Americans today. People are demanding more involvement, not less.

Modest participation in the primaries suggests the need for improvements. Placing the names of all the major candidates on the ballot increases participation. Universal voter registration would also increase participation. Newspapers and television could do a better job of getting to the heart of candidates' views, exploring inconsistencies, and piecing together the candidates' positions on various policies.

One of the virtues of the primary system is that candidates are required to present themselves to the people. Candidates have got to organize their thoughts, to clarify and define key issues. They are required to communicate with all kinds of people and to react under pressure. Most of the time it is an excellent learning experience — for candidates and the public. The extended primary allows room for the people to sharpen and alter their initial views of candidates.

The chances of destroying or eliminating a truly outstanding front-runner in the primaries are slim. Critics of the primaries are hard-pressed to cite examples of this. Moreover, the fact that relative newcomers or dark-horse candidates have emerged as front runners only two or three times since 1936 in no way decreases the importance of primaries. On the contrary, it generally means that the front-runner has succeeded in surviving a challenge to what has been termed his greatest asset, the presumption of victory.

The primaries were designed to give the people the right to be involved in the choice of their party's nominee and should not be abandoned because qualified persons choose not to run. The convention can still draft a "dark horse" if there is no popular favorite. Primaries may be imperfect, but so are democratic societies. They are an inexact and overlong way of coming up with nominees, but the system is not as flawed as critics contend.[14]

Return to state conventions or the ancient congressional caucus procedure would only serve to increase the influence of political bosses and special interests, who find it easier to bring pressure to bear on a few individuals in those old "smoke-filled rooms" than on entire electorates. Moving to a national or even a regional primary would lessen contact between candidate and voter, virtually prevent the less well-known candidate from running, and increase reliance on television advertising.

Perhaps it is naive to believe that candidates who have more direct contact with the electorate and are dependent on their votes for nomination as well as election will focus more on the voters' needs than on the needs of special interests. Yet this would be the case if we continue improving our use of state presidential primaries. Constant attention and further improvements are needed in order to obtain the high standards that have been set.

Despite flaws, primaries are the most effective of the existing means of involving the populace in the nominating process. If, as the critics have remarked, primaries are democracy gone mad, the response can only be to paraphrase Shakespeare: Ah, but there is some method in this madness.

NATIONAL PARTY CONVENTIONS

For most of the past 130 years the national conventions have performed (or tried to perform) the following functions. They have nominated presidential candidates acceptable to most factions within the party. By winning plurality victories in the primaries a candidate can secure the nomination without being acceptable to virtually all elements within a party. It is only the acquiescence of these other interests at the convention that signal to the party's rank and file that the nominee is the legitimate party standard-bearer. Carter and Ford won that legitimization at the 1976 conventions. But Goldwater and McGovern failed at their conventions in 1964 and 1972 respectively.

It has always been the purpose of a convention to select or ratify nominees who possess a strong likelihood of winning voter support in November. The goal is to produce a winning ticket. Thus a second function of a convention is to shape the vice-presidential choice in such a way as to both strengthen the ticket and reconcile factional cleavages within the party.

A more general function of conventions is the task of trying to unify a party that is not inherently unified. This is a time not to examine differences but to seek unity in the face of disagreements and diversity. It is naturally in the party's and the ticket's interest to whip up enthusiasm and rally the party faithful to work for the national ticket.

Conventions also hammer out party platforms. Platforms are generally less meaningful than the campaign statements of the presidential candidates, but they are a useful guide to the major concerns of a party. They are often inclusive "something-for-everyone" reports. A platform is invariably a compromise of sectional views, diverse caucuses (women, blacks, etc.), and the policy preferences of dominant party elites. The winning candidate is often willing to concede a plank in the platform to one of the runner-ups in the primaries. This can be a quid pro quo offer to a faction or a candidate-based organization within the convention that must be won over to unite the party. Thus Gerald Ford's people virtually had to agree to a more hawkish foreign and defense policy plank as a means to placate the Ronald Reagan forces at the 1976 Republican convention.

If the party has an incumbent president, the platform is often drafted in the White House or approved by the president and his top policy advisers. Seldom is a platform critical of its incumbent president adopted by a party.

Criticism of the national party nominating conventions has been loud and frequent. President Eisenhower called them a national disgrace. Critics contend conventions are too big, unwieldy, unrepresentative, and irresponsible. Others say they function with too much concern for selecting a winner and not enough attention to selecting the best-qualified person.

Similarly, it is felt that vice-presidential choices are often made too hastily with too much regard for balancing the ticket and too little regard for selecting a person who may also become president. People mention the selections of Agnew (1968), Eagleton (1972), and Dole (1976) as illustrative of this problem.

Another concern about our national conventions is that

> The nominating machinery is susceptible to capture by a well-organized, disciplined extremist faction of the party, working behind the scenes in the party convention states. This militant minority may select a party nominee who is the darling of the activists, but who enjoys only limited national voter appeal. The takeover of the GOP nominating machinery in 1964 by the conservative Goldwater faction is cited as a classic example. In defying the usual custom of selecting a nominee of moderate views, the right-wing Goldwater faction brought down upon the GOP one of the most crushing general election defeats that the party has ever suffered.[15]

The most recent complaint about national conventions has come about in the wake of the Democratic party's McGovern-Fraser commission reforms of the early 1970s. This commission was established to try to improve the delegate selection processes and to "open up" the Democratic party. Some political analysts contend that the basic thrust of the McGovern-Fraser reforms was to end the traditional dominance of regular party leaders and to make the Democratic convention of the 1970s less representative of the party rank and file. Jeane Kirkpatrick's book, *The New Presidential Elite*, offers strong criticism of these reforms and suggests that so long as they are in effect the party conventions will not be able to perform their traditional functions as well as they once did. A sample of her critique:

> The Democratic experience of 1972 . . . illustrates the errors of concluding that "open" processes and thousands of meetings will produce a convention in which "the people" are represented. Herein lies the reason that conventions based on "open" participatory politics may turn out (as in 1972) to be less representative of party rank and file (and other voters) than conventions peopled by labor leaders, political "bosses," and public officials. The middle income symbol specialist elected by those who turned out for a party conference or ward meeting is likely to feel his job is to represent those who chose him — that is, to represent other politically active middle-class symbol specialists. But the "boss" and the labor leaders, even if also middle income professionals, know that they represent different and broader constituencies. A characteristic of the "new breed" may be its remoteness from the party rank and file, and a major consequence of the new rules may have been to open the way for selection of delegates unrepresentative of and unaccountable to either the party rank and file or any ongoing organization whose welfare depends on responsiveness to that rank and file.[16]

The larger criticism here is that according to the new rules many and perhaps even a majority of the delegates to the Democratic convention are not acting as responsible members of a party, with all the memories, past participation in, and future commitment to it, so much as they are acting as members of a candidate-centered organization whose loyalties are almost exclusively to a specific candidate and his or her issues.

This last criticism is a serious charge and it deserves to be examined. Initial research suggests, however, that much of this lament does not stand up to critical analysis. "Greater participation . . . does not mean that party leaders must automatically lose. All it means is that party leaders must compete with nonleaders for influence." [17] Nor are issue activists inclined to be party wreckers. Issue activists supported JFK in 1960, LBJ in 1964, and Carter in 1976 — even though all were moderates. "The groups advantaged by the [new participatory] process are not homogeneous, they are not necessarily more or less representative than the party organization people they have replaced . . . , and their participation does not necessarily guarantee continued internal divisions in the Democratic party." [18] The Carter experience in 1976 overcame many of the difficulties of 1972. Carter's supporters liked him more as a person than for his issues. Vietnam as an issue had ended and in the process healed some of the divisions in the Democratic party. Thus, in many ways, the 1976 Democratic convention was a textbook convention. Unity, reconciliation, and legitimation of the Carter-Mondale ticket all took place amid spirited fraternal activities.

On balance, the national conventions have served us quite well. New rules changes, the far greater role of television, and the reality that nominees are more and more "selected" and "nominated" in the state primaries require us to reexamine the traditional functions of the convention. Although substantial change has taken place, the conventions still serve many intended goals. Despite their deficiencies, they have nominated some capable leaders, Lincoln, the Roosevelts, Wilson, FDR, Eisenhower, and JFK among them. Conventions have had many triumphs and only a few outright failures.

Many of the criticisms of the convention process are really criticisms of elections in general. Elections may not be the ideal way to select leaders, but they remain the least bad of the known available devices.

The most popular alternative to the conventions — the national primary — is unacceptable. H. L. Mencken once said that "for every complex problem in our society there is a solution that is simple, plausible, and wrong." This applies to the national primary idea, which would, I believe, carry democratic participation to excess. A national primary would favor wealthy candidates by enlarging the role of money spent to gain name recognition. Big money buys television, which buys elections. A national primary would also attract the already well known. With a large number of likely aspirants, a national primary would typically require a runoff, with the result that voters would have to take part in three national elections in a row. Political scientist William Crotty points to these added flaws in the proposed national primary idea:

> While well intentioned, the national primary concept represents a radical alternative that could destroy what is left of the party system. The elections would resemble nonpartisan contests and southern primaries with all their attendant ills: low turnout, a confused voting public, little policy coherence, a tendency toward emphasizing demagogic and personal excesses, a lack of accountability by office-holders to organized party electorates, an undue emphasis on media influence, high personal expenses, and disorganized public relations-type campaigns. Party supporters would probably have less direct say in deciding their parties' nominee in a national primary system designed to award them such power than they do at present.[19]

Conventions may not be a perfect process, but they are an acceptable alternative and they still perform several much needed functions.

THE INCUMBENCY "ADVANTAGE"

The advantages of incumbency for a president seeking reelection are traditionally revered as a political article of faith. For a sitting president, the benefits of incumbency are easily distinguishable: instant recognition, full access to government research resources, the ability to dominate events, constant media exposure, and a ready-made party organizational structure at his disposal.

Regardless of his real record of accomplishment, an incumbent president is supposed to benefit from a public-relations machine that shows the president as a man of action, a commander in chief, a traveling statesman, and a strategic crisis manager. Not the least of his assets is a loyal White House staff that, in the unavoidable blurring of presidential and political functions, performs a myriad of services for him and hence his candidacy.[20] A president and his party can also raise money far more easily, and the resources of his office provide millions of dollars' worth of publicity.

A rival for the presidency is generally a political candidate and little more. He is a seeker whose motives are unclear, a pursuer with a feverish gleam in his eye. He covets what his rival already possesses. The most he can give is promises.

Another important asset of an incumbent is the distorted perception and aura of the presidency as a form of elective kingship, as the symbolic apex of the country with all the power and mystique that suggests (a subject treated in more detail in chapter 3). In that vein, Woodrow Wilson declared as part of the Blumenthal Lectures at Columbia University in 1907: "His is the only national voice in affairs. Let him once win the admiration and confidence of the country, and no other single force can withstand him, no combination of forces will easily overpower him. His position takes the imagination of the country. He is the representative of no constituency, but of the whole people." [21]

That, as Wilson himself sadly learned several years later, may have been an exaggerated portrayal; nevertheless, it accurately reflects the broad horizons of presidential appeal.

Perhaps the most important asset for the incumbent is the selective or manipulative use of government contracts, patronage, release of previously impounded funds, and other political controls over the economy. President Nixon's manipulation of milk prices is alleged to have aided his campaign treasury in the 1972 election. In what was called "the incumbency-responsiveness program," Nixon aides sought to maximize their control over the federal government's enormous resources to their best advantage. Federal grants were evaluated according to political benefits. Political appointments and ambassadorships were sometimes promised in exchange for large campaign contributions. And corporations were "encouraged" to contribute to the upcoming Nixon campaign in a near-extortionist manner.

Political scientist Edward Tufte, who studied the relationship of the economy's performance and election outcomes, concluded that short-run economic performance has a good deal to do with ensuring an incumbent's reelection. The Nixon manipulations of 1972 are not alone. Tufte finds positive support going back to 1948 for the not surprising hypothesis "that an incumbent administration, while operating within political and economic constraints and limited by the usual uncertainties in successfully implementing economic policy, may manipulate the short-run course of the national economy in order to improve its party's standing in upcoming elections and to repay past political debts." Tufte adds, "In particular, incumbents may seek to determine the *location* and the *timing* of economic benefits in promoting the fortunes of their party and friends." [22] In short, every administration that seeks reelection has some leeway to influence economic performance in the short run by advancing expenditures and postponing taxes. And a friend at the head of the Federal Reserve Board helps too.

A discussion of the advantages of incumbency certainly suggests that the odds of unseating an incumbent president are formidable. Yet the record is far from clear-cut; indeed, incumbency is sometimes as much a burden as a benefit. Since the Jacksonian era, which inspired the rise of mass political parties and the party convention system, five presidents have been denied party renomination: Tyler, Fillmore, Pierce, Andrew Johnson, and Arthur. Another seven, John Adams, Van Buren, Cleveland, B. Harrison, Taft, Hoover, and Ford, were defeated for a second term after winning their party's nomination. Against these twelve failures, incumbent presidents have been successful in winning both the nomination and the election only fourteen times — including three reelection triumphs by Franklin Roosevelt.

Incumbency, then, is a double-edged sword. It can help a president who presides over a period of prosperity and peace and projects an image of being in charge of events. But it can just as readily act against a president associated with troubled, perplexing times, who does not seem to be in full possession of his office. Put another way, prosperity favors the ins; depression favors the outs. Distrust of politicians and low morale in the nation favors the outs; strong confidence in the national government favors the ins.

An incumbent is necessarily on the defensive; his record is under detailed scrutiny, its every flaw and unfulfilled promise exposed to microscopic examination. The American people can conveniently, if often unfairly, blame a whole range of problems on a president, whereas the astute challenger presents a smaller target. He can talk about secret plans and make a rash of promises without detailing what they would cost and who would wind up paying for them. A challenger is also in a far better position to present illusory problems as real ones and to play upon public fear about such things as missile gaps, inflation, and crime in the streets in ways that may distort reality while conveniently winning headlines. The challenger can take the offensive and try to convince the voters that he would do better.

The incumbent is often judged against the idealized model of the perfect president, and not unnaturally, he is found wanting. He may at times be the symbol of the nation's pride, but he can just as readily be the nation's most convenient scapegoat. Few incumbents can match the legendary images of the storybook presidency: "Our imagination has been seized by the larger-than-life, charismatic leader who towers above his contemporaries, enjoys extraordinary personal renown, and leads in the grand style." [23]

If the incumbent gains from his image as an experienced "statesman," he often loses from his image as a "politician." A political motive is easily ascribed to almost everything the incumbent does. Presidents who seem to be preoccupied with putting their reelection needs ahead of the public interest suffer accordingly.

Moreover, as one White House aide to President Ford put it, "People forget what you have done for them and remember only what you did to them." Thus, if taxes and inflation go down, people will ascribe it to American ingenuity and the success of the free enterprise system. But if taxes and inflation go up, it gets blamed on a failure of presidential leadership. In the past generation the presidency has gradually acquired more responsibility for peace, prosperity, and improvement in the quality of life than it has the authority to implement. It is a case of demanding more of the presidency, even as we deny it the capacity to act. The "what have you done for us lately" refrain is even more recurrent in an age of heightened single-issue, narrow special-interest-group politics.

So the disadvantages of incumbency are not so minor. They never have been. The seeming political invincibility of FDR and Eisenhower may have encouraged political analysts to forget about these disadvantages. Perhaps, too, considerable talk of the "two-term tradition" confuses more than it clarifies. In fact, the "American presidential tenure experience comes closer to being a one-term tradition." [24] Twenty-one American presidents (counting Cleveland twice for his two discontinuous terms) were elected to only a single term. Eleven were elected to two four-year terms; one (FDR) to four four-year terms. Five, like Gerald Ford, were never elected. So the presumed rhythm of eight years in the White House is exaggerated and misleading.

On balance, it appears that although the advantage usually lies with the incumbent, particularly in modern times, these advantages are not nearly so overwhelming as the received wisdom would have it. The extent to which incumbency can be translated to both renomination and reelection depends on several factors that clearly must be examined in context — the state of the economy, party strength, the political character of the incumbent as well as challenger, and the extent to which the president has a successful record.

THE TWENTY-SECOND AMENDMENT

Proposed by Congress in 1947 and ratified by the states in 1951, the Twenty-second Amendment to our Constitution provides that no person shall be elected president more than twice. Also, any person serving more than two years of another president's term is eligible for only one elected term. In practical terms, this amendment provides that the minimum time a president can serve and not be eligible for reelection is six years and one day, with the maximum time being nine years, 364 days.

The four-year term with silence as to reeligibility became a provision of the original Constitution as a compromise to effect a reconciliation of extreme views. Several of the framers wanted the president to serve during "good behavior," meaning so long as he honored the Constitution, acted within the laws, and conducted himself according to acceptable moral norms. Others favored a seven-year term. Still others thought a second term should be prohibited absolutely. Both Thomas Jefferson and James Monroe, although neither had been at the Constitutional Convention, argued in favor of a periodic rotation in office. It was their belief that reeligibility made it possible for an able, ambitious person to hold presidential office for life. Both the Virginia and New York delegations proposed an eight-year, or two-term, limit be imposed. Their resolutions failed in the new Congress. But between 1789 and 1947 no less than 270 resolutions to limit eligibility for reelection were introduced in Congress.

Alexander Hamilton, writing in *The Federalist,* No. 72, said that the framers felt restrictions on the tenure of the president were illogical. It was ill-founded, he continued, to place a man in office for a certain length of time and then tell him he no longer had the opportunity to serve. In order for a person to even attain such a high office, he must have considerable skills and ability. If, in fulfilling the requirements of his office, the public approves of the president's action, they should have the opportunity and option of reelecting him ". . . in order to prolong the utility of his talents and virtues, . . ." [25] Modern advocates of unlimited reeligibility echo Hamilton and contend in addition that we may on occasion find ourselves trapped in a severe national emergency and be anxious to keep the incumbent in office.

How and why was the Twenty-second Amendment adopted? Most people agree the movement to enact the Twenty-second Amendment was "born" in 1940 on the day Franklin Roosevelt was nominated for his third term. The main reason for the proposal of the amendment was an attempt by Republicans to "get even" with Roosevelt. Republicans controlled both houses at the time, the Senate by six votes and the House by almost sixty votes. Republicans in both houses voted unanimously in favor of the proposed amendment. They were joined by some Democrats, mainly from the South, who had soured on the New Deal and FDR. Republican-dominated statehouses readily ratified the proposal.

Those who proposed the amendment feared the public was sometimes incapable of deciding whether or not a man who has served two terms as president actually has the best interests of the people at heart. They had this fear in part because they believed that a clever president, like FDR, could manipulate news and symbols in such a way as to distort reality. Further, the presidency is an office with such extreme access to power that a person occupying the office for too long could easily become corrupt or even dictatorial. Proponents argued too that there is no indispensable man in a democracy. Prolonged incumbency also might encourage rigidity, and thus the "Twenty-second Amendment protects us from periodic hardening of the governmental arteries!" [26]

Most political scientists and historians who have studied the Twenty-second Amendment conclude it places unnecessary restrictions on both presidents and people. Historian Henry Steele Commager sums up the prevailing attitude this way:

What right, after all, does one generation have to impose on succeeding generations their choice of a President? An electorate which believes strongly in limiting a President to one or two terms can express the belief very easily at the ballot box — just what the American people did when they rejected Hoover after one term in 1932; just what they refused to do when they rejected the two-term tradition in 1940 and 1944. Imposing a restriction on the freedom to repeatedly reelect a President is to violate the essential principle of democracy — that a people have a right to exercise a free and untrammeled ballot, even if they exercise it badly.[27]

There is also a widespread but arguable view that the inability to run again for a third term weakens a president's power. President Harry Truman, for example, testified that any officeholder who is ineligible for reelection loses a lot of influence. What was accomplished by means of the Twenty-second Amendment, said Truman, was to take a man and put him "in the hardest job in the world, and send him out to fight our battles in a life-and-death struggle — and you have sent him out to fight with one hand tied behind his back, because everyone knows he cannot run for reelection." Truman added, "If he is not a good President, and you do not want to keep him, you do not have to reelect him. There is a way to get rid of him and it does not require a constitutional amendment to do it." [28]

Many presidents have complained of their "lame duck" periods — those periods when it is known that they will be leaving. During such periods, presidents get even less deference and cooperation than they otherwise do. Members of Congress, bureaucrats, cabinet officers, and foreign leaders have all taken advantage of presidents during this period. To be sure, the two-term tradition has also had this effect. But history suggests that many presidents in their second term (Wilson, Coolidge, Truman, to name a few) seriously considered running again, and that possibility just may have made them both more responsible and stronger in leadership situations. "If a President knows definitely that he is finished politically and, also if he feels his power beginning to weaken, he may be led to take actions which he would not take if the possibility existed of his again facing the electorate." [29]

What is the likely future of the Twenty-second Amendment? It remains one of the most controversial parts of the Constitution. Most people support the custom of a two-term tradition but view it as unnecessary and probably unwise to have it hardened into a constitutional prohibition. Most people would gladly leave it up to the people to decide whether or not a president should stay in office yet one more term. Doubtless, the real meaning of its enactment was not fully appreciated in 1951.

Ironically, although the amendment was pushed and passed primarily by Republicans, only Republican Eisenhower has been constrained by it. Because of his age and heart trouble, Eisenhower would have sought retirement anyway. Soon after Richard Nixon's easy reelection in 1972 a committee of Friends of Richard Nixon formed to press for reconsideration of the Twenty-second Amendment. Needless to say, their efforts were overtaken by other events.

So the amendment lives on. Few citizens understand its meaning. Circumstances that would lead to its repeal are hard to imagine. An emergency at the end of a president's second term might lead to a major repeal effort, but there might not be enough time to repeal it in such a crisis situation if partisan feelings were mobilized. Some experts say that we could move swiftly to repeal the measure in a truly serious crisis. Perhaps so. Meanwhile, the prohibition stands. Presidents will have to live with it and make the best of it. Most of our recent presidents, not surprisingly, have favored its repeal but have not mobilized supporters to this end.

THE GENERAL ELECTION

Presidential candidates are not free agents who can choose among strategies at will. Their strategy is seldom based on choice. It is usually forced on them by circumstance. For example, about every eight or twelve years there is a strong underlying desire to throw out the party in office. (In 1920, 1932, 1952, 1960, 1968, and 1976 voters seemed in part to be punishing those in office who were unable to improve things.) Slogans such as "It's time for a change" or "Throw the rascals out" are a familiar refrain as voters turn incumbents out of office with an almost predictable alternation.

Between 65 and 75 percent of the voters usually have made up their minds as to how they will vote by the end of the national conventions (late August of election year, a good eight or ten weeks before election day). The basic organizational effort of a candidate must be aimed at stirring up the support of voters at the grass roots. The strategy that makes the most sense is to get out all possible supporters and potential supporters and to target only secondary resources at converting the opposition. Supporters need general reassurance on both substantive as well as stylistic matters, but opponents want to know specific policy plans and program ideas.

A lot depends on how the candidate conducts himself. Our election process usually, although not always, excludes broad policy questions. Of necessity, then, in addition to observing the candidates' party, the people assess the contenders not so much on what they believe but on how good a job they might do.[30] This is why we carefully watch how they answer tricky questions and whether or not they keep their cool with hecklers. Many of us, during the Ford-Carter television debates, were more attentive to whether or not they looked nervous than to what they were saying.

Why did people vote for Jimmy Carter in 1976? A *CBS News* survey provided people with a list of ten reasons and invited them to check as many as three. Here is how they responded.[31]

	Percent
He's my party candidate	29
He seems more capable	28
He cares about people like me	21
He's the lesser of two evils	19
He's not part of the crowd running things now	18
He has strong qualities of leadership	16
I like his vice president	16
I trust him	14
He impressed me during the debates	13
I feel more comfortable with him	11

Public financing of the general election lessens the contender's dependence on wealthy special interests. However, candidates still need to build a coalition of well-organized interest groups to get out the vote. Nor can they afford to offend most of the so-called single-issue groups. More than anything else, presidential electoral politics is coalitional politics. Interest groups help to get others involved in a campaign. They can help mobilize voters on election day. Groups are seldom neutral. They lean to one party or one kind of candidate over others. Groups want access to the political system and they want someone favorable to their interests in the White House.

Candidates find the general election fraught with dynamic tensions. Issue-oriented enthusiasts urge them to "speak out on the vital issues." Party regulars urge them to work closely with the party bosses. Television consultants urge them to devote most of their time to brief television spots and talk-show appearances. Public-relations aides urge them to invoke patriotic symbols and quote from prestigious heroic sources. Campaign managers generally urge that debating all the issues and trying to educate the public is the worst possible way to run a campaign.

Political scientist John Kessel points to some of these tensions:

> The course of action that is acceptable to one group in his coalition is opposed by another. The detailed discussion of policy nuances appreciated by the activist will bore the nonactivist, and the simplistic appeal that attracts the apathetic voter may seem unworthy to the attentive elite.

The ringing call for partisan support will not produce independent votes, and the less passionate analysis directed at independents may lose the faithful worker who began ringing doorbells in February. The interplay of all these tensions lends dynamism to the campaign, and presents a different challenge to the candidate. He must make his way carefully lest he forfeit vital support, yet at the same time convey those qualities of confidence that win the trust of the people.[32]

Do elections matter? The answer is yes, but usually in a very general kind of way. That is, elections rarely give a president or a country a specific mandate. A national election in the United States is not a plebiscite or referendum on a number of specific issues. Candidates tend to mute and fuzz over differences of view as often or more often than they clarify their policy stands. Hence, we often vote without a clear idea of what the candidates will do if elected.

Candidates who win by a large margin usually claim they have won a mandate from the people. Such a claim is often unjustified, however, especially in elections such as those in 1964 and 1972 where the "landslide" was more a factor of the negative perceptions toward the defeated than positive perceptions toward the victors.

The debate over whom to vote for usually centers, as it did in 1976, around which candidate is best equipped to handle the job and the problems at hand rather than around the detailed specifics of how to solve the big issues of the day. In this sense our elections represent mandates to get the job done, but we leave the means up to the judgment of the president. Elections sometimes set limits on what can be done, but they seldom determine the precise content of public policy.

Presidential elections are important in terms of who is to handle the issues and with what broad leeway. But elections seldom are direct policymaking events. The general mood in the nation on issues and the partisan and ideological balance in the recently elected Congress are probably as important if not much more so in shaping how a president will act. The cautions of the late V. O. Key, Jr., are worth citing: "Retrospective judgments by the electorate seem far more explicit than do its instructions for future action. . . . The vocabulary of the voice of the people consists mainly of the words 'yes' and 'no'; and at times one cannot be certain which word is being uttered." [33]

NONVOTING IN PRESIDENTIAL ELECTIONS

Nearly half of voting-age Americans do not vote in presidential elections. (About 47 percent did not vote in 1976.) The proportion of voting Americans to those not voting has decreased steadily in recent years. Voting participation apparently peaked in this century in the 1950s and in the 1960 election (with an average of 61.4 percent). Surveys suggest also that since the mid-1960s, fully 15 million individuals who were once regular voters have dropped out of the political process. A growing percentage of young people are failing to enter as political participants. Some part of the decline in voting is rightly attributed to a marked increase in the proportion of the electorate under 35 years of age, a traditionally low-turnout group. This rise of nonvoting or "refraining" from voting has taken place in the same period that significant steps have been made in reducing the mechanical and legal constraints to registration. The poll tax has been outlawed. The 1965 Voting Rights Act ended most of our ballot-box discrimination practices. Residency requirements for national elections have been reduced. About half of the states have introduced innovative voter registration methods. A handful of the states now permit election-day registration.

Analysts believe that America has lower voting rates than just about all other democracies in the world because we still make it difficult for people to register to vote. Irregular registration hours, inconvenient locations of registrars, lack of absentee registration in many states, early cutoff dates, and a periodic purging of recent nonvoters from the registration lists all contribute to lower voting rates. Yet even if all the states made registration much easier, turnouts in presidential elections would probably grow by only about 8 to 10 percent. Streamlined registration laws would mean an increase of from 10 million to 15 million above the actual number of votes in 1980 or 1984. Still, the vast number of unregistered voting-age persons would remain unregistered. Further, large numbers of even the registered would refrain from voting.

Why? The primary explanations for nonvoting are attitudinal — disinterest, powerlessness, and distrust. Nonvoters ought not to be described as a cohesive group. There is just about as much diversity among nonvoters as among voters. Moreover, the old view that nonvoters are almost entirely poor, uneducated minorities is misleading. At least a third of those who choose not to vote in presidential elections do so not because of misery or dissatisfaction, but because of contentment or indifference to politics.[34]

Dissatisfaction with the caliber of the candidates, the limited number, and the difficulty in distinguishing differences among their stands on issues lead many to think that voting is not the effective act it may once have been. All candidates seem pretty much the same to the American voters, and it is true that they are offered less choice than in comparable Western democracies. Voters complain that too many politicians "talk in circles" and "say one thing, then do another."

Just as ticket splitting and being an Independent rather than a

Democrat or a Republican are becoming fashionable, so also refraining from voting may be becoming an accepted norm. Abstinence occurs in part because some people feel that voting for the lesser of two evils demeans the right. Refraining is a way for them to show they don't approve of either candidate and, in effect, it is a kind of peaceful protest. As a friend of mine put it: "A vote constitutes an endorsement of the candidate and unless given with conviction, or at least hope, is a form of self-deception. I think I'm being more honest with myself and more in keeping with the sense of freedom than the voter who casts his ballot just because it is expected of him."

A significant amount of nonvoting is caused by a feeling of power-lessness or political impotence. This feeling, in turn, is generally caused by distrust, disillusionment, and disenchantment with government. The "Don't vote, it only encourages them" bitterness toward politicians is illustrative. "Watergate proved that elected officials are only out for themselves" is the way some folks see it. Others indicating this power-lessness frequently respond:

It doesn't make any difference who is elected because things never seem
   to work right.
The government seems to act too secretly.
One person's vote really won't make any difference.
Most elections are already decided in advance.
The choice of candidates is just limited to Democrats and Republicans.[35]

Several political analysts think that nonvoting has increased as presi-dential elections have become predominantly television spectacles. TV elec-tions, they say, promote the rise of candidates whose primary attribute is charisma. Exposure to presidential politics through television may confuse many viewers and discourage them from voting. Perhaps the inconsistencies and inadequacies of the candidate become magnified by television. Perhaps, too, a public conditioned to continuous entertainment from its television sets is unlikely to respond positively to continuously smiling candidates uttering platitudes. Nor are they likely to be turned on by the typical presidential debate, which refers to countless initials such as IMF, GNP, SALT, HUD, and so forth and undoubtedly leaves many a viewer with the feeling of being confused and left out. Televised debates, despite their flaws, do increase voter interest and cause voters to pay more at-tention to the campaign than do the primaries and conventions. But studies suggest that it is still unclear whether this interest leads to higher voter turnout.

Just as many analysts contend that the erosion of our two-party system is the underlying factor in increased nonvoting. Analyst Curtis Gans puts it this way:

For 40 years [1920–1960] the public had every confidence that in voting Democratic or Republican it was making a meaningful choice which would be reflected in public policies candidates would implement once in office.

But in the 1960's, that certitude broke down. The '60's left the nation with a Republican Party controlled at its bottom by ideological zealots and at its top, to a lesser extent, by corporate giants. That decade also saw the arena of national debate on central issues of public policy — Vietnam, detente, jobs, the environment — shift to the Democratic Party, rather than remain an interparty dialogue. The fact that the debates were never resolved left the Democratic Party fraught with conflict, without a clear sense of direction or the ability to deliver a political program.

Faced with one party that was fast becoming ideologically irrelevant, and the other incapable of contributing to the public good, it is little wonder that the average citizen saw no choice and no reason to vote.[36]

If citizens voluntarily avoid the voting booth because they see little concrete impact of their vote, the mystery is not why so many refrain from voting but why so many continue to vote. In comparative terms, an impressive number of votes are cast every four years in national, state, and local elections, as well as party primaries, not to mention school board elections and referendums. Americans vote in more kinds of elections and for longer ballots than do other Western nations.

David Broder of the *Washington Post* says the real question "is how long anyone can govern without the legitimacy that comes from a genuine and representative mandate from the electorate." [37] Broder is right in posing the question. But available evidence suggests that the American government and our form of democracy will go on much as it always has. The rise in nonvoting has not especially bothered recent presidents or most members in Congress. Indeed, they almost seem complacent with the relatively restricted electorate they have. There is little evidence that a slim mandate or a small voter turnout affects very much how a president leads. Lincoln, Kennedy, and Nixon barely won, while Harding and Eisenhower won easily.

Election-day registration and voting should be easily accessible to all citizens. It is the right to vote — or to refrain from voting — that counts.

Our parties and candidates so often trade in ambiguities that it is little wonder so many voters stay home. Moreover, our politics is so often the politics of moderation that it is little wonder citizens see slight relationship between voting and the important issues in their lives. Most Americans, most of the time, are nonpolitical. Politics is not a central interest, not a central concern. If people believed their lives depended more directly on what presidents and governments do or, conversely, if the legitimacy of the American system depended on high voter turnout, it would doubtless be obtained.

THE DEBATE OVER THE ELECTORAL COLLEGE

Every four years, political observers grumble about our electoral college system — largely because it does not assure victory to the presidential candidate who wins a majority of the popular votes. But nothing seems to get done. The complexity of the electoral college system discourages the average voter from understanding its dangers. The road to electoral college reform is littered with the wrecks of hundreds of previous efforts. Moreover, if the disease is clear, the remedy is not.

Experts and political strategists differ in their estimates of the consequences of electoral reform. Politicians and commentators are divided and deadlocked over whether to retain the electoral college or to amend the Constitution to provide for direct popular election of the president.

Many observers believe that it may take the election of another popular vote loser to prompt the sustained action needed to amend the U.S. Constitution. Others feel that merely one more close election, such as that in 1960, 1968, or 1976, may be enough. Whatever change does occur will have important consequences for the health of the political system, for the quality and balance of our political parties, and for the kind of democracy we have. These considerations are not merely housekeeping matters. They speak directly to the integrity of our political system.

Public support for abolishing the electoral college system is growing. Repeated Gallup and Harris polls since 1966 show a steady rise in support for a constitutional amendment to change the way we select presidents. About 75 percent of those surveyed say they approve of direct popular election of the president. A constitutional amendment overwhelmingly passed in the House of Representatives in 1969 but foundered because of a filibuster the next year in the U.S. Senate. In 1977 President Carter became the first Democratic president to support abolishing the electoral college system.

The Senate has been the chief obstacle in the way of electoral college reform. Birch Bayh, the U.S. Senate's leading advocate of direct popular election, conducted nine days of hearings on his direct vote proposal during 1977. He barely succeeded in getting his measure, Senate Joint Resolution 1, out of committee. Opposition came from most of the committee's Republicans, from Committee Chairman James Eastland and Senators John McClellan and James B. Allen. The Senate did not act on Bayh's amendment.

But Senators Eastland and William Scott of Virginia have retired, Senators McClellan and Allen are dead, and Senator Edward Kennedy became chairman of the Judiciary Committee in 1979. Senator Bayh had approximately forty-five co-sponsors for his measure in 1978, including active support from the majority and minority leaders as well as strong backing from President Carter. Senators Robert Dole, Howard Baker, and

Robert Byrd are supporters, as are several of the younger, moderate members in both parties. Bayh also felt that he would have had the votes to overcome a filibuster in 1977. (Until 1975, it took two-thirds of the senators to close off debate. Under the new 1975 cloture rules, if sixteen senators sign a petition, two days later the question of curtailing debate is put to a vote. If three-fifths — sixty — of the total number of senators vote for cloture, no senator may speak for more than one hour.) Hearings on this measure were held again by Senator Bayh in the spring of 1979. On July 10, 1979, the Senate rejected the Bayh direct vote plan once again, giving it only a 51 to 48 margin instead of the two-thirds vote needed. It needed 66 votes for two-thirds of the 99 members present on that occasion.

WHAT IS THE ELECTORAL COLLEGE?

The Founding Fathers might well be amazed to find the electoral college system still in operation. Thomas Jefferson thought it was defective. John Roche, a contemporary historian, aptly describes it as a jerry-rigged improvisation that has subsequently been endowed with a high theoretical content.

For a long time the convention in Philadelphia accepted the idea that the president should be elected by Congress, but it was feared that either Congress would dominate the president or vice versa. Election by the state legislatures was rejected because of distrust of those bodies. Only after extensive deliberations was the electoral college system decided upon. It was at the time an ingenious and original compromise. Everyone got something: large states got electoral votes based on their population; small states got an assurance of at least three electoral votes and a contingency procedure based on the one-state–one-vote principle; those who feared the "tyranny of the majority" got an indirect method of electing presidents; and those who feared the national legislature got a method in which the states could play a major role. Evidence suggests, however, that no one was exactly sure how well it would work.

Alexander Hamilton said the compromise was an excellent answer to the problem. It was good, he noted, that the people in the states in one way or another would help choose the electors. But he seemed more impressed that the immediate election would be made by a small, capable, and judicious elite who would be most likely to possess the information and discernment requisite to so complicated an investigation.

Others believed that once Washington had finished his term or terms, the electors would fail to produce majorities and the president, consequently, would be chosen by contingency means in the House of Representatives. George Mason thought selection would be made in the House nineteen out of twenty times.

Plainly, as compromises go, it was a gamble.

The framers expected electors to be designated by state legislatures. The electors would be distinguished citizens who would, in fact as well as in form, nominate and then elect the president and the vice president. The rise of national political parties changed all this. By the election of 1800, electors by custom had become party agents, usually pledged in advance to vote for designated party candidates.

How does the system work today? In making their presidential choice in November, voters technically do not vote for a candidate but choose between slates of presidential electors selected by state political parties. The slate that wins a plurality of popular votes in the state casts all the electoral votes for that state. A state has one electoral vote for each senator and each representative. The District of Columbia has three votes, granted it by the Twenty-third Amendment. There are 538 votes in the electoral college today. A candidate must get 270 or more to win the presidency.

Technically, a president is not elected on election day. Victorious slates of electors travel to their state capitols on the first Monday after the second Wednesday in December, where they cast ballots for their party's candidates, perhaps listen to some speeches, and go home. Ballots are then sent from the state capitols to Congress, where early in January they are formally counted by House and Senate leaders and the next president is finally announced.

If no candidate secures a majority of electoral votes the decision then goes to the House. This has happened twice, once in 1800 and again in 1824. People feared it might happen again in 1968 if George Wallace received enough electoral votes to keep Richard Nixon or Hubert Humphrey from obtaining a majority. In the House, each state delegation casts a single vote. If a delegation is evenly divided, the state forfeits its votes. Further, the influence of a third-party "spoiler" candidate may be significant, because the House chooses a president from among the top *three* candidates. Consecutive ballots are taken until a candidate wins a majority (twenty-six) of the state delegations.

THE CASE FOR THE DIRECT
ELECTION OF PRESIDENTS

Advocates of the direct popular system argue that *everyone's vote should count equally, that people should vote directly for the candidate, and that the candidate who gets the most votes should win.*

Perhaps the most disliked feature of our present electoral arrangements is that the electoral college method can elect a president who has fewer popular votes than his opponent. This can happen because all of a state's electoral votes are awarded to the winner of the state popular vote regardless of whether the winning candidate's margin is 1 vote or 3 million votes. Ironically, the major defect here — the unit-rule provision — is not a part of the Constitution. This winner-take-all formula (unit rule) is merely a state practice, first adopted in the early nineteenth century for partisan purposes, and gradually accepted by the rest of the states to ensure maximum electoral weight for their state in the national election.

Plainly, the electoral college benefits the large "swing" states at the expense of the middle-size states. The smaller states are also advantaged by the "constant two" electoral votes. Thus, in 1976, Alaska got 1 electoral vote for every 40,000 popular votes, whereas Minnesota got 1 for every 194,956 popular votes.[38]

But the fact that California casts 45 electoral votes and New York casts 41 to Alaska's 3 and Minnesota's 10 overshadows all other inequalities. The eleven largest states control 272 electoral votes, more than a majority of the electoral college. The "voting power" of each individual in these large, competitive states far exceeds that of most voters elsewhere in the nation. Political scientist Lawrence Longley says, "A citizen voting in California in the present electoral college as apportioned in the 1970's is found to have 2.5 times the potential for determining the outcome of the Presidential election as a citizen voting in the most disadvantaged area — the District of Columbia."[39]

In contrast to the complexities and dangers of the electoral college system, the direct vote method is appealing in its simplicity. It is based on a one-person–one-vote principle. It more clearly makes a president the agent of the people and not of the states. (Particularly is this the case compared with the contingency provisions of our present system.) Governors and senators are elected by statewide direct popular voting, and they are supposed to be agents of the states. The president should be president of the people, not president of the states.

The direct-vote plan would also do away with the present electors who occasionally have voted for persons who did not win the plurality vote in their states. This is the often-discussed "faithless elector" problem. Since our first election, fewer than a dozen electors have been faithless among almost eighteen thousand. These few miscast votes have never made a difference. Still, the process seems anachronistic and potentially dangerous. For this reason there are few defenders of this aspect of the electoral college.

In sum, proponents of the direct vote say it is the most forthright alternative and far preferable to the present system. They contend that voters, when they are choosing a president, think of themselves as national citizens, not as residents of a particular state. In the words of the American Bar Association, the present system is "archaic, undemocratic, complex, ambiguous, indirect and dangerous." [40] The direct popular vote system is simple, democratic, and clear cut.

DEFENSE FOR RETAINING
THE ELECTORAL COLLEGE

Defenders of the electoral college are outnumbered in Congress, in the general public, and in the ranks of major interest groups. Yet those who defend the electoral college system do so with intensity and strong conviction.

First, it is said that we should not lightly dismiss a system that has served us so well for so long. The late Alexander Bickel of Yale Law School wrote:

> We are well served by an attachment to institutions that are often the products more of accident than of design, or that no longer answer to their original purposes and plans, but that offer us the comfort of continuity, and challenge our resilience and inventiveness in bending old arrangements to present purposes with no outward change. The English know this secret, and so does the Common Law that we inherited from them. We have, of course, many institutions and arrangements that, as they function, no longer conform to the original scheme, and we have bent most of them quite effectively to the purposes of our present society, which in all respects differs enormously from the society of nearly two hundred years ago. The Supreme Court is one such institution, and the Presidency itself is another. The fact that we have used them without modifying their structures has lent stability to our society and has built strength and confidence in our people.[41]

Defenders of the electoral college system stress that, despite some imperfections, it works. They point out that we have not had a popular-vote loser elected by the college in ninety years. They feel that the chance of this happening is not as dangerous as the likely consequences of a move to a direct vote. They quote John F. Kennedy who defended the electoral college by arguing that the question does not merely involve certain technical details of the election process but a whole solar system of subtle, interrelated institutions, principles, and customs. Defenders also quote Lord Falkland's epigram that "when it is not necessary to change, it is necessary not to change" or Livy's pronouncement that "the evil best known is the most tolerable."

Political scientist Austin Ranney, in testimony before the Senate Judiciary Committee, put it this way:

> It seems to me that the evil the amendment [Bayh's S.J.R. 1] seeks to prevent is unlikely to happen. What you are dealing with here, therefore, is not a very pressing problem. . . .

There seems to me to be a real possibility — I cannot say certainly any more than the proponents of the amendment can say certainly that we are going to have a minority President — there seems to me a certainty that several things would happen to our political parties, to our mode of campaigning, to the kinds of candidates that might enter in the whole process.

So I wind up remaining to be convinced that the imminence and the size of the evil that this amendment addresses itself to are such that we ought to go ahead and risk the evils that might ensue, whatever those probabilities might be.[42]

It was with these fears in mind that Senators James Eastland, James Allen, Strom Thurmond, William Scott, Paul Laxalt, Orrin Hatch, and Malcolm Wallop opposed the direct vote of the president. Specifically, these senators, in a minority report to the U.S. Senate, argued that direct election would:

cripple the party system and encourage splinter parties
undermine the federal system
lead to interminable recounts and challenges and encourage electoral fraud
necessitate national control of every aspect of the electoral process
give undue weight to numbers, thereby reducing the influence of the small states
encourage candidates for president, who represent narrow geographical, ideological, and ethnic bases of support
encourage simplistic media-oriented campaigns and bring about drastic changes in the strategy and tactics used in campaigns for the presidency

Others point out that the elections in 1824 and 1876, in which the popular-vote losers were elected president, had little to do with the electoral college: The present system did not exist in 1824; there were no parties, no popular vote in six states, and no unit electoral vote in six others. Moreover, it was the House of Representatives, not the electoral college, that put in Adams. In 1876, Tilden had a majority in the electoral college, and a rigged electoral commission put in Hayes. Hence, there was only one occasion in nearly two hundred years when the electoral college system denied the popular-vote winner the presidency. Is that reason enough to justify taking a gamble on the direct-vote method?

An additional factor has motivated groups such as the NAACP and ADA and writers such as Alexander Bickel and Wallace Sayre to oppose the direct vote and defend the electoral college. In 1977 the Americans for Democratic Action said:

Perhaps the only way that significant American minorities can have an impact on the political process is as the deciding factor as to which major candidate can win a given state and a given set of electoral votes. In this way urban interests and rural, blacks, Latinos and other minorities, the handicapped and the elderly, the young, the poor, the rich and the middle-aged can all compete for some attention and some share of public policy. If direct election were instituted, the need for taking into account the needs and desires of minorities would no longer exist. Candidates would campaign for the American middle as their particular pollster describes that middle and would be beholden to no group, no cause and no interest. Those who constitute America's minorities, whether they be farmers or urban dwellers, would all suffer.[43]

Consequently, with the direct vote the weight given to small blocks of voters would be far less than it is today. Minorities such as blacks and Jews might especially be disadvantaged. "Jewish voters, less than 3 percent of the electorate, must be given some attention now because they can tip the scales in New York or Illinois or California." [44]

Would Direct Vote Cripple the Party System?

Proponents of the electoral college system say that it minimizes the impact of minor parties and, because of the unit-rule provision (used by all states except Maine), encourages a politics of moderation. They point out, too, that under the present system losers at party nominating conventions generally abide by their party's choice. But with a direct vote these same losers would be tempted to go after the presidency anyway, hoping to force a runoff election. John Sears, campaign manager for Ronald Reagan in 1976, says that if the direct-vote method had been in operation he would have counseled Reagan to bypass the Republican convention altogether.

An American Enterprise Institute document puts this point of view as follows:

> The critics [of direct vote] suggest that the major parties are, on the national level, only loosely assembled aggregates of state party organiza- tions and factional interests; such internal discipline as they possess comes primarily from their ability to make their nominations stick. They are able to do this, it is argued, primarily because winner-take-all discourages disgruntled losers and their partisans from launching a campaign on their own. Once winner-take-all is removed, say the opponents of direct elec- tion, the major parties will lose their most potent weapon for enforcing their nominating decisions.[45]

Arthur Schlesinger also fears that tiny parties or single-cause candi- dates would be able to magnify their strength through the direct-vote scheme. "Anti-abortion parties, Black Power parties, anti-busing parties, anti-gun control parties, pro-homosexual-rights parties — for that matter, Communist or Fascist parties — have a dim future in the Electoral College. In direct elections they could drain away enough votes, cumulative from state to state, to prevent the formation of a national majority — and to give themselves strong bargaining positions in case of a run-off." [46]

Under the present system, the votes for these marginal parties or single-issue candidates never really get counted, although they sometimes can help one of the major parties and hurt the other. For example, in 1976, Eugene McCarthy may have cost Jimmy Carter as many as four states. But under the direct-vote system, each vote cast for a minority party would count. Carried over from state to state, this vote might add up to 5 percent, 15 percent, or more. This would, it is argued, increase the incentives for these kinds of parties to send a message, register their strength, flex their muscles — and, it is claimed, cause the proliferation of splinter or third parties.

Proponents of the direct vote just as strongly argue that their plan will not undermine the two-party system. They point out that we have a direct vote in the states and that the two-party system is safely intact in most of our states.

Supporters of the Bayh amendment say that the two-party system is shaped and sustained not by the electoral college and the winner-take-all provision but by the election of almost all public officials in the United States by single-member districts. Citing the writings of Maurice Duverger, they note that almost every government in the world that elects its officials from single-member districts and by plurality vote has only two major parties, whereas countries that use multimember districts and pro-portional representation have a multitude of parties.

They point to George Wallace's effectiveness under the present sys-tem. Wallace was encouraged by the electoral college arrangements to try to carry enough states in a three-way race to enable him to force the two major candidates into a deadlock and bargain with them in the House vote. In effect, the electoral college rewards regional third parties (like Wallace's American Independent Party) and punishes third parties with a national constituency.

The Bayh direct-vote plan stipulates that a candidate must obtain at least 40 percent of the popular vote to win. To prevent that and cause a runoff, a third party would have to win more than 20 percent of the vote and the two major parties would have to split the rest almost evenly. Says Tom Wicker of the New York Times, "That's no more in-centive, and probably less, to a minor party than its chance, under the present system, to prevent an electoral majority and throw a presidential election into the House." [47]

Finally, under the direct-vote system organizers and supporters of third parties would doubtless have to make the same calculations as to whether their efforts would take votes from the major-party candidate closest to them in policy convictions. Do they really want to be a spoiler party and thereby ensure the victory of the least preferred party and have it in office for the next four years?

Despite these assurances from the direct-vote advocates, there is at least the possibility that our party system will be drastically altered. We really have a party-and-a-half system in the United States at this time. The House of Representatives is now, and is likely to remain, decidedly in Democratic hands. The senate is somewhat that way, but much less so than the House. Only the presidency is a competitive institution at the national level.

Political scientist Aaron Wildavsky contends that with the direct vote we would eliminate the requirement that pluralities be created state-by-state. This could easily undermine the remaining basis of party competition. "What is likely," he adds, "is that more and more voters will move into the primary of the majority party. Fewer and fewer voters will move into the party of the minority. The minority party, of course, will become more extreme . . . until eventually it disappears." [48]

Would Direct Vote Undermine Federalism?

Defenders of the electoral college say that the current system is part of the subtle structure of federalism, which over the years has thwarted factionalism and helped maintain liberty, that is, to tamper with the electoral college is to tamper with federalism. The electoral college imposes a state-oriented strategy upon presidential candidates. Each candidate must forge a coalition of supporters within each state, especially the big states. To move to a direct vote would lessen the bargaining power of state officials. Countering this argument, others as diverse in their views as Robert Dole and former Senator Mike Mansfield feel that the federalism issue is phony because the electoral college encourages candidates to ignore the noncompetitive states.

"If states are abolished as voting units," writes Theodore H. White, "TV becomes absolutely dominant. Campaign strategy becomes a media effort to capture the largest share of the national 'vote market.' " [49] Of course, television is absolutely essential in the existing arrangement. But White and others think it will be relied upon even more in the future, with candidates concentrating on hundreds of thousands of easily accessible votes in New York, Los Angeles, and Chicago. Who needs Idaho? Direct-vote advocates admit major metropolitan areas are advantaged by the electoral college but point out that suburbs are advantaged even more. Staff aides to Senator Bayh claim black voters would have more impact in a direct vote. The NAACP thinks otherwise.

The federal principle refers not only to the division of responsibilities between nation and states but also to how we elect our national officers.

The Senate, for example, is entirely a creature of the federal principle. Political scientist Judith Best suggests that "if federalism is an anachronism, if cross-sectional, concurrent majorities are no longer necessary to maintain liberty, then perhaps we should abandon federalism for the national legislature as well as for the executive." She adds:

> To do one without the other, particularly to make the President the recipient of the only all-national mandate, could change our governmental solar system, could change the balance in executive-legislative relationships to the advantage of the President. The authenticity of the voice of the Congress, speaking for a concurrent majority, could be seriously undermined by a truly plebiscitary President claiming to speak most directly and clearly for the general will. The sobering experience of the Watergate era should make us reluctant to further aggrandize the Presidency.[50]

Direct popular election would bring about demands for a uniform ballot in all states, for uniform voter qualifications. Centralization would also be needed for uniform rules governing challenges and recounts. State laws vary considerably on these matters. For example, may a defeated candidate from a national party convention obtain a ballot listing as a new party or as an independent candidate? In 1976 Eugene McCarthy faced challenges to his access to the ballot in several states, notably New York. As it was, thirteen different candidates qualified for a place on the ballot in six or more states, but no state ballot contained all thirteen names.

For all practical purposes, the states would have to yield a certain amount of their constitutionally granted control over the electoral process to some form of federal elections commission. Elections expert Richard Smolka raises this additional point: "The question of candidates' access to the ballot, a technical question in many respects, nevertheless requires a specific definition of political party, a definition on which state laws, court decisions, and political scientists do not agree." [51] Once members of Congress attack details of this nature, they are also likely to regulate further the presidential primary process, the methods of voting, and hence, at least indirectly, to influence the national conventions. One likely side effect of these new regulations will be that even more states will hold state elections in nonpresidential election years. There is already a trend in this direction. If so, the eventual effect of these changes could be a lower turnout of voters in state elections *and* in presidential elections.

Advocates of the direct vote say one of its virtues is simplicity. But questions of runoff elections and recounts in closely contested elections bother advocates of the present system. Political analysts warn a recount can be a bloody, lengthy, and delayed process, as was the Wyman-Durkin 1974 recount and the new election in New Hampshire. Yet election specialists say a national recount could be accomplished in a reasonably short time, perhaps two weeks or less, and that the recount issue is not paramount.

Defenders of the direct vote contend that it would not undermine federalism in any way. "The vitality of federalism," columnist Neal Peirce writes, "rests chiefly on the constitutionally mandated system of congressional representation and the will and capacity of state and local governments to address compelling problems, not on the hocus-pocus of an eighteenth-century vote count system." [52]

Would Direct Vote Affect the Legitimacy of the Winner?

The direct-vote method could easily produce a series of 41 percent presidents. Lincoln was the only president with a vote that small (and he wasn't on the ballot in several states). Then, too, in a runoff election, the direct-vote method might increase the possibility that the presidency would be won by the person who finishes second.

In an era when confidence and trust in the national government have eroded, the direct vote would almost ensure that we would have minority presidents all the time. We have had fifteen minority presidents (that is, persons who won with less than 50 percent of the vote), but the present electoral college system is a two-stage process in which the popular votes are converted into electoral votes. In every election this has the effect of magnifying the vote margin of the winner, so much so that only once in the past hundred years has a president received less than 55 percent of the electoral college vote (Wilson received 52 percent).

Steven Brams and Peter Fishburn recently discussed a system called *approval voting* that might remedy part of this problem. They proposed that voters would vote for as many candidates as they thought worthy of the office. Under this system, which could operate together with the direct vote, several candidates might receive a majority and the one with the most votes would win office. Brams and Fishburn believe the "legitimacy of election outcomes in the eyes of voters would certainly be enhanced if the winning candidate received the support of a majority of the electorate. This would be true even if he was the first choice of fewer voters than some other candidate, because this fact would not show up in the approval-voting returns."

Brams and Fishburn are not sure of all the side effects of this alternative voting scheme, but they do believe fringe candidates would probably drain little support from centrist candidates because, for strategic reasons, fringe-candidate supporters would probably also tend to vote for a centrist:

> Barring unforeseen changes, it seems likely that at the same time approval voting would give some additional support to strong minority

candidates like George Wallace, it would also help centrist candidates —
including perhaps nominees of new parties — both in winning their
party's nomination in the primaries and conventions and prevailing
against more extreme candidates in the general election. Coupled with the
greater opportunity it affords voters to express their preferences, and the
greater likelihood it provides the winning candidate of obtaining majority
support, approval voting would seem to be an overlooked reform that
now deserves to be taken seriously.[53]

A case might be made for using approval voting in party primaries, but
its consequences for the two-party system in the general election pose
problems. Additional centrist candidates might easily draw support away
from major-party candidates and bring chaos and confusion. To be sure,
as Brams and Fishburn themselves point out, these new centrists might
not bring about drastic policy changes because they would not win high
approval unless they were middle-of-the-road candidates. Yet they could
displace the major-party candidates, and if this happened with any
frequency, it would probably hammer the last nail into the coffin of our
two-party system.

No electoral system is neutral. Trade-offs are very much in evidence
in this debate. Electoral college supporters clearly want to discourage third
parties and protect a party system that pits one moderate-centrist party
against another moderate-centrist party. Moreover, electoral college sym-
pathizers strongly prefer the idea of cross-sectional concurrent majorities
over simple majorities. Direct popular vote advocates clearly want all
votes to count equally and the candidate with the largest number of
popular votes to win. Both schools are concerned with the legitimacy, or
public acceptance, of the election process and outcome. As political
scientist William Keech notes: "A decision about which system of electing
the president to prefer depends on values, on priorities among those
values, and on estimates of the likely consequence of change." [54]

There are liabilities or likely adverse effects with either the direct-
vote or the electoral college system. Opponents of the direct vote may have
overstated their case. The dire consequences they foresee seem exaggerated.
Still, they pose enough uncertainty about the possible ill effects of direct
vote that even skeptics should consider seriously a sensible compromise.

It was with this goal in mind that the Twentieth Century Fund, a
New York-based nonprofit research foundation, appointed a task force
in late 1977 — a task force on which I had the pleasure of serving. Its
members were divided along the predictable lines, with defenders of the
present system taking the view that the probable foreseeable and unfore-
seeable consequences of shifting to a direct vote might amount to a cure
that was worse than the disease. Others, including myself, argued the
merits of the direct-vote plan. We did agree, however, on the weaknesses
of the two contending election schemes. We did agree, also, that a fair and

democratic election system should maximize the likelihood that the candidate with the most popular votes would win, encourage healthy competition through a vigorous two-party system (without unduly restricting new third parties), promote voter participation, ensure public acceptance of the election outcome, and sustain the vitality of the federal system. With these core values in common, we set about designing a compromise election system. What follows is adapted from the discussions of what we — the twelve-person Task Force on Reform of the Presidential Election Process of the Twentieth Century Fund — devised.[55]

THE NATIONAL BONUS PLAN COMPROMISE

The compromise plan retains the existing 538 state-based electoral votes but adds a national pool of 102 electoral votes that would be awarded on a winner-take-all basis to the candidate who wins at least 40 percent of the popular votes nationwide. There would thus be a combined total of 640 state and national electoral votes, and the candidate with a majority would be the winner. As a consequence, the existing federal bonus (of two electoral votes for each state plus the District of Columbia) would be balanced by this *national bonus* given to the nationwide popular winner.

The National Bonus Plan, a reform alternative to the existing system, would virtually eliminate the major flaw in the electoral college arrangements. The new system, for example, would make it unlikely for the popular-vote winner to lose the election, as happened in 1888 and could have happened in 1960 and 1976.[56]

Because a constitutional amendment is required to establish the National Bonus Plan, a few other changes for simplicity could also be incorporated. Under the National Bonus Plan, there is no need for the office of elector or for the electoral college. Instead, the practice of having designated "electors" would be eliminated and all electoral votes — those now assigned and those proposed under the National Bonus Plan — would be allocated automatically on a winner-take-all basis to the popular-vote winner in each state and in the nation as a whole. Thus the "faithless elector" problem would be eliminated.

In the unlikely event that no candidate receives a majority of the total electoral vote under the National Bonus Plan, it is recommended that a runoff be held between the two candidates receiving the most popular votes. This runoff would be held within thirty days of the first national election, and the candidate who wins a majority of electoral votes would be elected president. A reasonable alternative would provide for a direct-popular-vote runoff.

We also recommended a mandatory re-tally to assure the accuracy of official totals. In addition, we proposed that a second, independent authority or agency recheck the tallies of the vote-recording devices within a short, specified time after the first tally and that the second total be registered even if the election is neither close nor disputed. It was felt that the use of automatic vote-registering and -counting procedures minimizes fraud and error, and that these procedures should be extended to every precinct in the nation. An accurate national count is absolutely essential if direct election is enacted.

The National Bonus Plan and these additional correctives introduce novel features to the existing system, but they are constitutional innovations that are similar to the original balancing efforts of 1787.

These innovations should bring about an improvement in the fairness, and an enhanced public acceptance, of the electoral process without being a drastic or sweeping restructuring of the system. The plan retains some of the familiar features such as the federal principle, but it eliminates or minimizes most of the problems that plague the presidential election process.

In addition to improving and simplifying the present election process, this set of reforms would encourage broader voter participation, enhance voter equality, and encourage party competition in the states. As against the existing system, it would:

go a long way toward assuring the election of the candidate with the largest number of popular votes

reduce the possibility of a deadlock and make the contingency-election procedure more representative

eliminate the so-called faithless elector

enhance voter equality

encourage greater voter turnout

As against direct election, it would:

avoid a proliferation of candidates and help maintain the two-party system

preserve the federal or cross-sectional character of the presidential election process

lessen the likelihood of minority presidents

lessen the likelihood of runoff or second elections

lessen the likelihood of regional or sectional candidates emerging as major candidates

At one and the same time, then, this new proposal would remedy most of the problems of the electoral college system and avoid the numerous potential problems and risks that might be encouraged with direct election.

Potential Drawbacks of the
National Bonus Plan

Initial reaction to the National Bonus Plan has been favorable. It has been praised as an "ingenious plan," "a notable accomplishment," a "practicable, worthy and needed reform." Edwin M. Yoder, Jr., an editor of the *Washington Star*, says, "After many years of superficial discussion, the electoral college has at last had the thoughtful public study it deserves but rarely gets." [57] A staff member at the White House writes (in a personal communication to me), "It is an intriguing plan. It seems to satisfy the objections of the opponents of direct election and yet it still would appear to accomplish the goals of that proposal. We're very interested in it. . . ." Meanwhile, Senator Birch Bayh feels strongly that his direct-vote plan is the best reform, although there is reason to believe he would find the National Bonus Plan a convenient fall-back position. Congressman Jonathan Bingham, a New York Democrat, introduced the National Bonus Plan as a constitutional amendment in the 96th Congress. [58]

There have been some objections to the National Bonus Plan. First, it is noted that smaller states such as Idaho and South Carolina might lose almost as much under this plan — both in a diluted electoral vote and in lessened control over state election law — as under direct popular vote.

Southern states in general have a lower voter turnout and consequently in a nationwide race would lose some voting power to such states as Minnesota and Massachusetts, which have high turnout rates. On the other hand, voter turnout in the South has improved in recent years, and when and if voter registration reform wins passage even higher turnouts may be expected in the South. Further, the National Bonus Plan would, in effect, persuade all states to encourage rather than discourage voter participation.

Political scientist Allan P. Sindler, a thoughtful student of the presidential election process, fears that the National Bonus Plan might be deficient in that it could allow a plurality leader with a highly sectional base of voting support to win the 102 bonus votes and thereby win the presidential election. It is his view that having a geographic spread is important in sustaining the federal principle and "is also a very important desideratum in itself in affirming a requirement of a 'qualitative' majority and not simply a quantitative one." [59] He points out that a major difference between the vote patterns of a major party and third party is that the former have the stronger showing across the larger geographic spread. Third-party candidates tend to concentrate their strength in one section of the country or to spread their support thinly across the nation. Sindler frankly admits wanting to protect two-partyism and to discourage multi-partyism. To achieve this, he would devise some additional safe-guard, such as requiring the plurality leader to carry a majority of House districts, or states, by plurality vote, or meet some other similar geographic criteria. His suggestion deserves consideration by those who would shift us away from the electoral college. It would, however, not help to simplify matters, and it would make the system harder for the average citizen to comprehend. Still, it might enhance the public acceptance of the outcome of presidential elections.

Some skeptics call the National Bonus Plan a Rube Goldberg con-traption — a gimmick that actually is a direct vote in disguise. To be sure, it would achieve most of what a direct vote would achieve, but it does so in a more acceptable way. But the direct-vote plan has not passed, and it consistently runs into a buzz saw of opposition: "Small state conservatives who think they might lose some advantage; blacks who believe the swing vote of big, metropolitan states would be reduced; and federal system 'traditionists,'" as Neal Peirce sums up the opponents' direct vote.[60] Too many people still fear the unknown and the possible repercussions of the direct popular election of the presidents.

The National Bonus Plan brings to a common position those who advocate direct election of the president and those who support the electoral college. Direct-vote advocates, who believe reform should go all the way to a one-person–one-vote system, may be harder to win over than defenders of the electoral college. Yet Neal Peirce, a leading direct-vote advocate who was a member of the Twentieth Century Fund task force, calls the National Bonus Plan an innovative proposal that might well break the long-standing logjam on electoral college reform. He adds that ideally he favors a simple direct-election amendment; "however, as be-tween the existing system, with all its perils, and the National Bonus Plan, I find the National Bonus Plan infinitely preferable." [61]

Some critics say we overestimate the public's insistence on a one-man–one-vote system. But sooner or later there is going to be another presidential election in which one candidate wins the popular vote but loses the presidency. At that time the furor and heated emotion of the moment may cause a rush to change the system in a radical or overly simplistic way. The National Bonus Plan may be a reasoned alternative for such an occasion.

Our presidential selection process, obviously, is neither tidy nor easy to understand. It has evolved in varying and often unpredictable ways since the framers met in Philadelphia. It seeks to achieve a variety of often contending purposes. Yet it is one of the grand compromises so often found in the structure of the American political system that seek to paper over regional, political, and even ideological differences. The old tensions of how strong a central government we really want and of how strong and powerful a central leader we are willing to tolerate are never far behind the scenes. Then, too, the questions of just how much democracy we really want and how much we actually trust the judgment of the common man are often involved in our attitudes about the presidential election system. Finally, the whole selection process, along with its design and redesign, from time to time, is also a manifestation of the American quest to preserve a politics of coalitions, moderation, and pragmatism.

NOTES

1. James Reston, "The Men Who Are Not Running for President," *New York Times,* 9 November 1975, p. E15.

2. Benjamin I. Page, *Choices and Echoes in Presidential Elections* (University of Chicago Press, 1978), p. 281.

3. William R. Keech, "Selecting and Electing Presidents," in Thomas E. Cronin and Rexford G. Tugwell, eds., *The Presidency Reappraised* (Praeger, 1977), p. 98.

4. Erwin Hargrove, "What Manner of Man?" in James David Barber, ed., *Choosing the President* (Prentice-Hall, 1974), p. 19.

5. James David Barber, *The Presidential Character,* rev. ed. (Prentice-Hall, 1977).

6. Rexford G. Tugwell, *The Art of Politics* (Doubleday, 1958), pp. 242–43.

7. On this point see Rexford G. Tugwell, *The Brains Trust* (Viking, 1968), pp. 410, 423–24. Also see Page, *op. cit.,* chap. 6.

8. This discussion summarizes and borrows from Arthur T. Hadley, *The Invisible Primary* (Prentice-Hall, 1976).

9. *Ibid.,* p. 2.

10. See Walter F. Mondale's personal reflections on his efforts to gain name recognition and media attention in his bid for presidential nomination in the mid-1970s, *The Accountability of Power* (McKay, 1975), pp. 33–40.

11. Hadley, *op. cit.,* pp. 14–15.

12. David Broder, "What the Primaries Really Mean," *Boston Globe,* 7 January 1976, p. 19.

13. See, for example, David S. Broder, "One Vote Against the Primaries," *New York Times Magazine,* 31 January 1960, p. 9ff., and Jeane J. Kirkpatrick et al., *The New Presidential Elite* (Russell Sage Foundation and Twentieth Century Fund, 1976). See also, James W. Ceasar, *Presidential Selection: Theory and Development* (Princeton University Press, 1979).

14. One of the most useful and most balanced studies of the presidential primaries is found in William R. Keech and Donald R. Matthews, *The Party's Choice* (Brookings Institution, 1976). See also William J. Crotty, *Political Reform and the American Experiment* (Crowell, 1977), chap. 7.

15. James W. Davis, *National Conventions* (Barron's Educational Series, 1973), pp. 69–70. See also Judith H. Parris, *The Convention Problem* (Brookings Institution, 1972).

16. Kirkpatrick, *op cit.,* p. 330.

17. Robert T. Nakamura and Denis G. Sullivan, "Party Democracy and Democratic Control," in Walter Dean Burnham and Martha W. Weinberg, eds., *American Politics and Public Policy* (M.I.T. Press, 1978), p. 33.

18. *Ibid.,* p. 38. See also Denis G. Sullivan's review of the Kirkpatrick volume, *American Political Science Review,* September 1978, pp. 1068–69.

19. Crotty, *op. cit.,* p. 229.

20. I draw upon two articles I co-authored: See, Thomas E. Cronin and Dom Bonafede, "Incumbency, Two-Edged Sword," *Los Angeles Times,* 7 March 1976, and Stephen

Hess and Thomas E. Cronin, "The Incumbent as Candidate," *Washington Post*, 20 August 1972.

21. Woodrow Wilson, *Constitutional Government in the United States* (Columbia University Press, 1908), pp. 67–73 *passim*.

22. Edward R. Tufte, *Political Control of the Economy* (Princeton University Press, 1978), pp. 2–3.

23. John W. Gardner, personal communication to the author, 17 October 1978.

24. Harry A. Bailey, Jr., "Presidential Tenure and the Two-Term Tradition," *Publius*, Fall 1972, p. 106.

25. Alexander Hamilton, *The Federalist* (Stratford Press, 1945), pp. 485–86.

26. Reo M. Christenson, "Maybe Two Terms *Are* Enough," in his *Heresies, Right and Left* (Harper & Row, 1973), p. 149. Christenson presents a provocative and helpful debate on the pros and cons of the two-term tradition.

27. Henry Steele Commager, "How Long Should a President Serve?" *Parade*, 16 September 1973, p. 11. See also the strong sentiment opposed to the Twenty-second Amendment, *Senate Judiciary Hearings*, 86th Cong., 1st sess., 4 May 1959, p. 6.

28. Harry S. Truman, *Senate Judiciary Hearings*, 86th Cong., 1st sess., 4 May 1959, p. 7.

29. Political scientist Sam Huntington, *Congressional Record*, 17 April 1957, p. A3075.

30. This is a point also made by Nicholas von Hoffman, *Make Believe Presidents* (Pantheon, 1978), p. 219.

31. *National Journal*, 6 November 1976, p. 1588.

32. John H. Kessel, "Strategy for November," in James David Barber, ed., *Choosing the President* (Prentice-Hall, 1974), p. 119. Also see Steven J. Brams, *The Presidential Election Game* (Yale University Press, 1978), chap. 4.

33. V. O. Key, Jr., *Politics, Parties and Pressure Groups*, 5th ed. (Crowell, 1964), pp. 543–44.

34. Arthur Hadley, *The Empty Polling Booth* (Prentice-Hall, 1978), p. 40. See also the useful article by Richard Rose, "Citizen Participation in the Presidential Process," *Society*, November/December 1978, pp. 43–48.

35. See the results of the Peter Hart poll, released by the Committee for the Study of the American Electorate, 5 September 1976, mimeo. Partial results were printed in *Newsweek*, 13 September 1976, p. 16.

36. Curtis B. Gans, "Elections by Default of the Nonvoters," *Los Angeles Times*, 8 October 1978, p. VI-5. See also his "The Empty Ballot Box," *Public Opinion*, September/October 1978, pp. 54–57, and his "The Empty Voting Booths," *Washington Monthly*, October 1978, pp. 27–30. For some similar views, with more blame placed on party "reformers," see Everett Carll Ladd, Jr., *Where Have All the Voters Gone?—The Fracturing of America's Political Parties* (Norton, 1978).

37. David S. Broder, "Non-Voting: A Threat to Government Legitimacy," *Washington Post*, 2 July 1978, p. B7.

38. Neal R. Peirce, *The People's President* (Simon & Schuster, 1968), pp. 141–42.

39. Lawrence D. Longley, "The Case Against the Electoral College" (Paper prepared for the 1977 Annual Meeting of the American Political Science Association, Washington, D.C., September 1974), p. 15. See also the useful volume by Lawrence D. Longley and Alan G. Braun, *The Politics of Electoral College Reform*, 2nd ed. (Yale University Press, 1975). On the other side of the debate see Wallace Sayre and Judith Parris, *Voting for President* (Brookings Institution, 1970).

40. *Electing the President: A Report of the Commission on the Electoral College Reform*, American Bar Association, January 1967, p. 3.

41. Alexander Bickel, "Is Electoral Reform the Answer?" *Commentary Reports* (1968), p. 3. See also his *The New Age of Political Reform* (Harper & Row, 1968).

42. Austin Ranney, *The Electoral College and Direct Election,* Hearings before the Committee on the Judiciary, U.S. Senate, 95th Cong., 1st sess. (1977), p. 269.

43. *Ibid.,* p. 398.

44. Jack H. Germond and Jules Witcover, "What Direct Elections Would Do to U.S.," *Boston Globe,* 23 March 1977, p. 19.

45. *Direct Election of the President* (Washington, D.C.: American Enterprise Institute), June 1977, p. 19.

46. Arthur Schlesinger, Jr., "The Electoral College Conundrum," *Wall Street Journal,* 4 April 1977.

47. Tom Wicker, *New York Times,* 27 March 1977, p. E17.

48. Aaron Wildavsky, *Hearings* (1977), *op. cit.,* p. 225. See also his "The Plebiscitary Presidency: Direct Election as Class Legislation," *Commonsense,* Winter 1979, pp. 1–10.

49. Quoted in *Direct Election of the President, op. cit.,* p. 21.

50. Judith A. Best, "The Case for the Electoral College" (Paper prepared for the 1977 Annual Meeting of the American Political Science Association, Washington, D.C., September 1977), pp. 24–25.

51. Richard G. Smolka, "Possible Consequences of Direct Election of the President," *State Government,* Summer 1977, p. 140.

52. Neal R. Peirce, a partial dissent, in *Winner Take All:* Report of the Twentieth Century Fund Task Force on Reform of the Presidential Election Process (Holmes and Meier, 1978), p. 15.

53. Steven Brams and Peter Fishburn, "Approval Voting," *American Political Science Review,* September 1978, and Brams, *The Presidential Election Game* (Yale University Press, 1978), chap. 6.

54. *Winner Take All, op. cit.,* p. 67.

55. The entire report and a perceptive and helpful background paper by Professor William Keech are found in *Winner Take All, op. cit.*

56. Analysis indicates that under our present electoral college arrangement in a race as close as the Carter-Ford contest, the likelihood of a divided verdict is about 23 percent. A "divided verdict" is the possibility that one candidate wins in the electoral college while another wins the popular vote. Under the national bonus plan a similar analysis indicates that the likelihood of a divided verdict in races as close as the Carter-Ford election would be about 3 percent. See Samuel Merrill, "Empirical Estimates for the Likelihood of a Divided Verdict in a Presidential Election," *Public Choice,* Vol. 33, #2, 1978, pp. 127–133. And personal communication, Samuel Merrill to Thomas E. Cronin, May 22, 1979, pp. 1–2.

57. Edwin M. Yoder, Jr., "The Electoral College: An Antique That Works," *Washington Star,* 23 March 1978.

58. Jonathan B. Bingham, *Congressional Record,* 26 February 1979, pp. H882-H883. The amendment carries the title, H.J.Res. 223.

59. Personal communication, Allan P. Sindler to Thomas E. Cronin, December 29, 1978, p. 2. I am in debt to Sindler for his discussion of these plans with me.

60. Neal Peirce, "Electoral College Reform: A New Plan for an Old Idea," *Washington Post,* 18 March 1978, p. A19.

61. Peirce, *Winner Take All, op. cit.,* p. 15.

CHAPTER 3

THE
TEXTBOOK
AND
PRIME–TIME
PRESIDENCY

His is the only national voice in affairs. Let him once win the admiration and confidence of the country, and no other single force can withstand him, no combination of forces will easily overpower him. His position takes the imagination of the country. He is the representative of no constituency, but of the whole people.

> — Woodrow Wilson, *Constitutional Government in the United States* (Columbia University Press, 1908), pp. 67–73 *passim.*

[O]nly the President represents the national interest. And upon him alone converge all the needs and aspirations of all parts of the country, all departments of government, all nations of the world. . . . We will need in the Sixties a President who is willing and able to summon his national constituency to its finest hour — to alert the people of our dangers and our opportunities — to demand of them the sacrifices that will be necessary.

> — John F. Kennedy, speech during the presidential campaign, 14 January 1960.

The President is the only person who can speak with a clear voice to the American people and set a standard of ethics and morality, excellence and greatness. He can call on the American people to make a sacrifice and explain the purpose of the sacrifice, propose and carry out bold programs to protect, to expose and root out injustice and discrimination and division among the population. He can provide and describe a defense posture that will make our people feel secure, a foreign policy to make us proud once again.

> — Jimmy Carter, quoted in an interview, *National Journal*, 7 August 1976, p. 993.

Nothing is more evident in the twentieth century than the steady accumulation of presidential responsibilities. Less evident but equally important are the heightened public expectations of the president. One of the strongest forces shaping the American presidency during most of the past forty years has been a faith in charismatic presidential leadership, a belief that a strong power-maximizing president can conquer all, make us secure and even make us feel good. This romantic — benevolent father, Big Daddy, — vision of the presidency loomed especially large in the 1940 to 1966 period. During the next decade (1967–1977) it would recede in importance but never really be repudiated. Once Vietnam, Watergate, and Nixon were removed from the national political landscape the demand for a very powerful presidency would be with us again, this time not only for national-security purposes but for economic and domestic policy as well.

This chapter will review the existence and the origins of what may be called the textbook presidency, or the cult of the presidency. The textbook presidency describes and extols a chief executive who is generally benevolent, omnipotent, omniscient, and highly moral. How has this textbook presidency been presented in the texts? How has prime-time television contributed to magnifying the promise of the American presidency? What explains the development of the often unrealistic and sometimes absurd expectations we place upon our presidents? What are some of the consequences of these expectations?

Textbooks summarize current thinking and guide the work of contemporary researchers. For more than twenty years after the Franklin D. Roosevelt presidency, most textbook treatments of the presidency seriously inflated presidential competence and beneficence. There developed a view that America needs a strong central government and it needs strong central leadership to attain the strong government. Further, only a strong presidency and strong presidents could provide it with the needed leadership. Social scientists as well as reporters, in an undeniably patriotic stance, helped make the case for a strengthened presidency. What resulted very often was a storybook view that whatever was good for our president must be the right thing. We were told the president is the embodiment of all that is good in America: courage, honesty, integrity, and compassion. We began to hail the power-maximizing president; we said the president needs help, the president alone speaks for the public interest, the president is the most knowledgeable and competent person in the nation to make decisions for us, the president is the chief source of progressive and creative initiative. Writers occasionally criticized particular policies of national leaders who failed to live up to the newly elevated standard, but nearly everyone preferred to believe in the high promise of the presidency. Only in the late 1960s and early 1970s did disillusionment with the presidency temporarily still this textbook devotion. But after a trial period in which the public turned to Congress rather than to the presidency for leadership, the prevailing view once again took hold that only the president can get things done, only the president can lead legislatively, only the president can negotiate effectively with other nations, and only the president can make the country governable. If Ford and Carter were clear about anything in the mid-1970s it was that they wanted to offer us a scaled-down, nonimperial, unmajestic presidency. But that got them both in trouble. People rejected the idea of a minimal president. Americans no more wanted to devitalize the American presidency in the late 1970s than they had in the late 1950s.

Most social scientists and writers no doubt merely mirrored the predominant popular views of the times. As will be discussed in more detail, the extraordinary events of the period, most especially World War II, the development of atomic weapons, and cold-war episodes such as the Cuban missile crisis, made old conceptions of the presidency outmoded. Citizens looked to presidential leadership with a mixture of awe, support, and trust. Where else could they look?

But as we turned to our presidents for more and more kinds of leadership we also helped to promote false notions and myths. Too many of us misattributed the promise of America to the politician who temporarily held our country's highest office. Treated as exalted figures, presidents began to believe and act that way. Too little concern was expressed about the possibility of the abuse of presidential power. Too little concern was paid to the need for strengthening various checks and balances or at least adapting them to the new needs of a new era. In the long run, rising expectations hurt presidents, who were led to make exaggerated promises and encouraged to go to great lengths "to look presidential" as if in the textbook mold. What was needed was a better sense of proportion and a respectful skepticism about what it was that a president could achieve. The imaginary, legendary, and hoped-for presidencies needed to be counterbalanced by a discussion of the real presidency with all its complexities and paradoxes.

The promise of the American presidency may have been overstated, but denying the importance and the need for effective presidential leadership would be equally misleading. That is not the intent here. The following discussion of the textbook and prime-time presidency should be viewed primarily as a part of an attempt to reformulate the possibilities for an effective presidency that is also accountable, and realistic as well as *within* the specifications of the Constitution.

THE TEXTBOOK PRESIDENCY
OF THE FIFTIES AND SIXTIES

Franklin D. Roosevelt personally rescued the nation from the depths of the Great Depression, and the stalwart soldier of freedom, with Harry Truman, brought World War II to a proud conclusion. The courageous

Truman personally committed the nation to resist communist aggression around the globe. General Eisenhower pledged that as president he would "go to Korea" to end that war — and he did. John F. Kennedy pledged to put a man on the moon, and even though it took a while, this was achieved. Kennedy also pledged he would get tough with the Russians and Cubans and he did this, almost majestically, during the Cuban missile crisis of 1962. These are the prevailing idealized images that most American students read and remember. For convenience, if not always accurately, textbooks give eras or major events such labels as "the Wilson years," "the Roosevelt revolution," "the Eisenhower period," and "the Kennedy Camelot years."

Presidents were expected to perform as purposeful activists who knew what they wanted to accomplish and relished the challenges of the office. The student learned from textbooks that the presidency was "the great engine of democracy," "the American people's one authentic trumpet," and "the central instrument of democracy." [1] With the New Deal presidency in mind, these textbooks portrayed the president instructing the nation as a national teacher and guiding the nation as national preacher. Presidents, they said, should expand the role of the federal government to cope with the increasing nationwide demands for social justice and a prosperous economy. The performances of Harding, Coolidge, and Hoover were lumped together as largely similar and rejected as antique. The retiring reluctance of Eisenhower generally elicited a more ambiguous appraisal: after a brief tribute to him as a wonderful man and a heroic military leader, he was categorized as an amateur who lacked both a sense of direction and a progressive, positive conception of the presidential role. What was needed, most texts implied, was a person with the foresight to anticipate the future and the personal strength to unite us, to steel our moral will, to move the country forward and make it governable. The vision, and perhaps the illusion, was that if Americans could only identify and elect the right person, their loftiest aspirations would be fulfilled.

Studies of how people developed their attitudes about government and politics stressed at the time that children's views of authority and government center on an American president, a towering, "glittering mountain peak" of benevolence, power, and wisdom, someone who can win and end wars as well as cure the nation's socioeconomic ills.[2] As children grow older and are exposed to textbooks and discussions of current events, however, it was commonly assumed that the views derived from norms taught in grade school or by parents become more tempered, and that teenagers or young adults become, perhaps, even cynical about political leaders. But introductory high-school and college textbooks at the time usually reinforced rather than refined youthful expectations about presidential leadership.[3]

With minor variations college texts of the 1950s and 1960s stressed that the contemporary presidency was growing dramatically larger, gaining significantly more resources and responsibilities. This expansion was often described metaphorically as "wearing more hats." With rare exception texts not only devised and approved but openly celebrated an expansive theory of presidential power. Students read that more authority and discretion in determining policy devolves to the president during war and crises and that because the country was engaged in sustained international conflict and acute domestic problems, presidents were constantly becoming more powerful.[4] One text pointed out, "As the world grows smaller, he will grow bigger." Another exclaimed that the "President . . . bears almost the entire burden of the formulation of national policy and the definition of the national purpose." The following presidential job descriptions have been taken from five of these introductory texts:

The president is the most strategic policy maker in the government. His policy role is paramount in military and foreign affairs.[5]

He [John F. Kennedy] also became the most important and powerful chief executive in the free world. His powers are so vast that they rival those of the Soviet Premier or of any other dictator. He is the chief architect of the nation's public policy; as President, he is one who proposes, requests, supports, demands, and insists that Congress enact most of the major legislation that it does.[6]

The evolution of the Presidency is the story of a frequent and cumulative increase in the role — or, better, the roles — that the President can play and is expected to play in the American political system, and, more recently, in the world. Every "great" President has left the office somewhat altered and enlarged. The Presidency is like a family dwelling that each new generation alters and enlarges. Confronted by some new need, a President adds on a new room, a new wing; what began as a modest dwelling has become a mansion; every President may not use every room, but the rooms are available in case of need.[7]

The President of the United States of America is, without question, the most powerful elected executive in the world. He is at once the chief formulator of public policy as embodied in legislation, leader of a major political party . . . chief architect of American foreign policy. And his power and responsibility are increasing.[8]

If the President is a king, it is equally clear that he is no mere constitutional monarch. For in an era in which many monarchies all over the world have disappeared, and the power of kings has declined, the power of the President has enormously increased . . . through subtle and unusually informal changes, attributable mainly to the fact that the President is the literal embodiment of American mass democracy and . . .

the symbol of the pervasive egalitarianism which from the beginning has characterized the emergent forces of the American democratic ideal.[9]

To the teenager or young adult, textbook discussions of the extensive resources available to the president cannot help but convey the impression that a president must have just about all the inside information and good advice anyone could want, especially when they point out the vast arrays of experts, strategic support staffs, and intelligence systems. Usually, too, a lengthy listing is included of the National Security Council, the Cabinet, the Office of Management and Budget, the Council on Environmental Quality, the Council of Economic Advisers, White House domestic-policy staffs, and countless high-level study commissions. A casual reading of such chapters fosters the conclusion that a contemporary president can both set and shape the directions of public policy and can see to it that these policies *work as intended*.

The conviction that the president knows best, that his advisory and information systems are unparalleled, was readily encouraged by a passage like the following:

> Presidential government is a superb planning institution. The President has the attention of the country, the administrative goals, the command of information, and the fiscal resources that are necessary for intelligent planning, and he is gaining the institutional power that will make such planning operational. Better than any other human instrumentality, he can order the relations of his ends and means, alter existing institutions and procedures or create new ones, calculate the consequences of different policies, experiment with various methods, control the timing of action, anticipate the reactions of affected interests, and conciliate them or at least mediate among them.[10]

The same theme is outlined in Theodore White's *The Making of the President 1960*: "So many and so able are the President's advisers of the permanent services of Defense, State, Treasury, Agriculture, that when crisis happens all necessary information is instantly available, all alternate courses already plotted." [11] Elsewhere, White pays lavish tribute to America's "action-intellectuals," whom he designates as the "new priesthood" of national policymaking. These "best and brightest," recruited from prestigious universities and research centers, are credited with being a benign and "propelling influence" upon our government, "shaping our defenses, guiding our foreign policy, redesigning our cities, reorganizing our schools." [12]

Clinton Rossiter's *The American Presidency,* published in 1956 and still widely read, contains one of the most lucid venerations of the American presidency. Rossiter describes the presidency sympathetically as a priceless invention that not only has worked extremely well but also is a symbol of the continuity and destiny of the American people.

Few nations have solved so simply and yet grandly the problem of finding and maintaining an office or state that embodies their majesty and reflects their character. . . .

There is virtually no limit to what the President can do if he does it for democratic ends and by democratic means. . . .

He is, rather, a kind of magnificent lion who can roam widely and do great deeds so long as he does not try to break loose from his broad reservation. . . .

He reigns, but he also rules; he symbolizes the people, but he also runs their government.[13]

Rossiter, both fully aware of his own biases and seemingly quite convinced that the myth of presidential greatness and grandeur was to be cultivated, writes about the Lincoln legacy:

Lincoln is the supreme myth, the richest symbol in the American experience. He is, as someone has remarked neither irreverently nor sacrilegiously, the martyred Christ of democracy's passion ·play. And who, then, can measure the strength that is given to the President because he holds Lincoln's office, lives in Lincoln's house, and walks in Lincoln's way? The final greatness of the Presidency lies in the truth that it is not just an office of incredible power but a breeding ground of indestructible myth.[14]

Such lavish prose hardly discourages awe and admiration, if not exactly reverence, for the presidency.

Perhaps the most respected specialized treatment of the presidency written in the 1950s or 1960s was Richard Neustadt's *Presidential Power* (1960).[15] Neustadt's insights countered much of the conventional wisdom by stressing the highly political and bureaucratic context in which presidents must operate, the obstacles posed to presidential directives by Washington empire builders, and the scarce resources available to a president who wants to reverse policy directions. Although his analysis found the president's position limited and tenuous, one in which he must grasp for just enough power to get by the next day's problems, Neustadt argued vigorously for a more powerful president — one who would guard his options and would impose his will. His study held on to the hope that a shrewd and manipulative leader could and should be a powerful engine of change. Indeed, an aggressive, ambitious politician, determined to get his way and ever distrustful of the motives of others, was what was needed. Because the Neustadt study is so central to the conception of the presidency in the 1960s it is treated in detail in the next chapter.

Post–New Deal textbooks on government emphasize also the importance of personal attributes: "The President's values, his qualities of character and intellect, his capacity for leadership, his political skills, his definition of his own role, and the way he performs it — *these are fundamental determinants* [emphasis added] of the working of the American government and of American politics." [16] Emphasizing a president's personality or character or offering psychohistories of past presidents captures the attention of students and adults alike. In studying presidential leadership we should, of course, seek some clues and rough guidelines as to the kind of person who can handle the job and also form some idea of how the presidency affects the occupant. But despite the flurry of this type of research, major methodological pitfalls still exist. The links between personal character and presidential policymaking are important, but social scientists have been unable to predict with rigor exactly which personal characteristics will produce the most desirable leadership in public policy.

Recent research, notably the work of James David Barber, Alexander George, and Erwin Hargrove, has alerted us to the need for a democratic temperament, openness, and the capacity to listen, as well as to the value of a sense of joy in presidents. But stressing desirable personality characteristics may well have a tendency to create merely another kind of textbook presidency tradition. Can we be content with the verdict that a happy, healthy president — one who loves life and enjoys his job — is sufficient for the country? "The point is that a president can be a healthy personality and yet have a deficient view of the world" or an undesirable set of values.[17]

Not surprisingly, the personalization of the presidency is also reflected in campaign rhetoric. Presidential candidates proclaim how personally courageous and virtuous a president must be. Nelson Rockefeller recited a litany of necessary qualities in 1968:

> The modern Presidency of the United States, as distinct from the traditional concepts of our highest office, is bound up with the survival not only of freedom but of mankind. . . . The President is the unifying force in our lives. . . . The President must possess a wide range of abilities: to lead, to persuade, to inspire trust, to attract men of talent, to unite. These abilities must reflect a wide range of characteristics: courage, vision, integrity, intelligence, sense of responsibility, sense of history, sense of humor, warmth, openness, personality, tenacity, energy, determination, drive, perspicacity, idealism, thirst for information, penchant for fact, presence of conscience, comprehension of people and enjoyment of life — plus all the other, nobler virtues ascribed to George Washington under God.[18]

John Kennedy as a presidential candidate similarly emphasized the crucial personal requisites of a potential president. Certain men, he claimed, could so enjoin the nation's best inclinations that these United States could and would "move forward" — and he promised to be that type of individual. Four years later Lyndon B. Johnson went even further, asserting that the president of this country must be able to "ignite a fire in the breast of this land, a flaming spirit of adventure that soars beyond the ordinary and the contented, demanding greatness from our society and achievement in our government."[19]

The personalized presidency is as well a central feature of contemporary political journalism. No one did more to embellish this perspective than Theodore White, whose *Making of the President* volumes not only enjoy frequent university use but also serve as texts for the millions of adults who savor the explanations of an insider. White's concentration on the styles and personalities of the candidates promotes a benevolent, almost liturgical, orientation toward the presidency. His narrative histories have an uncanny knack of creating suspense about the outcome of an election well after it actually took place. The melodramatic style promotes a heightened sense of reverence for the eventual victor akin to that felt for royalty. White first describes the field of seven or eight competing hopefuls, which becomes four or five; eventually the field is narrowed down to two or three national candidates. Finally, one person remains. Clearly, it seems from White's approach, the victor in such a drawn-out and thoroughly patriotic ritual deserves the nation's deepest respect and approval. Moreover, White subtly purifies the victorious candidate. In what must be the classic metamorphosis at the root of the textbook image of the presidency, the individuals who assume the presidency seem to change physically and, it is implied, spiritually. White says about President Kennedy's first days in the White House in 1961: "It was as if there were an echo, here on another level, in the quiet Oval Office, of all the speeches he had made in all the squares and supermarkets of the country. . . . He had won this office and this power by promising such movement to the American people. Now he had to keep the promise. He seemed very little changed in movement or in gracefulness from the candidate — only his eyes had changed — very dark now, very grave, markedly more sunken and lined at the corners than those of the candidate." [20] He writes of Richard Nixon soon after his ascendancy in 1969:

> He seemed, as he waved me into the Oval Office, suddenly on first glance a more stocky man than I had known on the campaign rounds. There was a minute of adjustment as he waved me to a sofa in the barren office, poured coffee, put me at ease; then, watching him, I realized that he was not stockier, but, on the contrary, slimmer. What was different was the movement of the body, the sound of the voice, the manner of speaking — for he was calm as I had never seen him before, as if peace had settled on him. In the past Nixon's restless body had been in constant movement as he rose, walked about, hitched a leg over the arm of a chair or gestured sharply with his hands. Now he was in repose, and the repose was in his speech also — more slow, studied,

with none of the gear-slippages of name or reference which used to come when he was weary; his hands still moved as he spoke, but the fingers spread gracefully, not punchily or sharply as they used to.[21]

To summarize, four propositions can be singled out as the main elements of the textbook ideal.

Omnipotent-Competent Dimension:

1. The president is *the* strategic catalyst for progress in the American political system and the central figure in the international system as well.
2. Only the president can be the genuine architect of United States public policy, and only he, by attacking problems frontally and aggressively and by interpreting his power expansively, can slay the dragons of crisis and be the engine of change to move this nation forward.

Moralistic-Benevolent Dimension:

3. The president must be the nation's personal and moral leader; by symbolizing the past and future greatness of America and radiating inspirational confidence, a president can pull the nation together while directing its people toward fulfillment of the American Dream.
4. If, and only if, the right person is placed in the White House, all will be well; and somehow, whoever is in the White House is the best person for the job — at least for a year or so.

The significance of the textbook presidency is that the whole is greater than the sum of the parts. It presents a cumulative presidential image, a legacy of past glories and impressive performances — the exalted dignity of Lincoln, the Wilsonian eloquence, the robust vitality of the Roosevelts, the benign smile and lasting popularity of Eisenhower, the inspirational spirit of Kennedy, the legislative wizardry of Lyndon Johnson, the globe-trotting of the first-term Nixon — which endows the White House with a singular mystique and almost magical qualities. According to this image, the office of the presidency seems to clothe its occupants in strength and dignity, in might and right, and only men of the caliber of Lincoln, of the Roosevelts, or of Wilson can seize the chalice of opportunity, create the vision, and rally the American public around that vision.

THE ROOTS OF THE
TEXTBOOK-PRESIDENCY TRADITION

How are we to explain the tendencies to exaggerate the promise of the presidency? No simple explanation is satisfactory; rather, several mutually reinforcing factors no doubt contributed to a runaway inflation in the capabilities attributed to presidential leadership.

1. the rise of the president as "the leader of the free world"
2. the need for a national symbol of reassurance
3. the values of liberal pundits and textbook writers
4. the vast expansion of government coupled with the gradual relinquishment of powers to the president by Congress
5. the desire for national stability and regime loyalty
6. the constraints on research and writing about the presidency
7. the rise of prime-time television coverage of presidential campaigns and presidential performance

The President as the
Leader of the Free World

A critical aspect of the rise in the attention paid to the presidency came as a result of World War II. That war radically altered our foreign-policy outlook and our position in the world. An American sense of mission developed and we began to take an active and vital interest in the destiny of practically every nation around the world.

Textbook images have always been with us but toward the end of World War II certain events began to take place that would embellish the textbook notions for an entire generation of Americans. It was then that the image of President Roosevelt in his black cape and his head high with upturned hat was pictured in all our newspapers as he rode in an open jeep at the front. It was then also that he was seen as the wartime leader discussing world affairs with Churchill and Stalin.

Here was the real beginning of the president as leader of the free world. The United States was now providing leadership and protection for other nations. Shortly thereafter we invented the atomic bomb. For the first time in history a president of the United States became the only person in the world who had the power to destroy the human race. These were new images that would undeniably alter our conception of the presidency.

Truman would intervene in Korea, halfway around the world. Truman would supply arms and money to Turkey, Greece, and elsewhere. The United States was rebuilding Europe. In instance after instance the idea of the United States as world leader and the image of the president as a permanent commander in chief of the free world's militia heightened the promise and the role of the president.

This was the root also of the imperial presidency — of a presidency that reached out to control and shape world events. Tom Wicker puts the matter well:

> So I think in that very short span at the end of World War Two and the beginning of the Korean War, the idea of the leader of the free world, the man who can wipe out the human race, the commander-in-chief with all that intones, all the vibrations that has for us, I think this

created the modern imperial presidency, and it did it in a way that really had nothing to do with institutional processes or cycles. It was because of the on-going events of history then.

And I would suggest . . . that from that period that I am talking about, from Roosevelt in his black cape to John Kennedy at the Cuban Missile Crisis, the imperial presidency was highly successful, and that that is what sustained it. And also it was sustained and perceived as being highly successful because it was fundamentally a foreign policy phenomenon; it didn't have much to do with domestic affairs and that was very congenial to the years of the Fifties and the early Sixties, when due to the Cold War and due to America's emergence in the world as a world power and due to the new possession of nuclear weapons, the center of things was seen as being in foreign policy, rather than domestic policy.[22]

These images of a president as an international figure not only enlarged the responsibilities of a president but also, at least initially, encouraged people to believe that a president must have greater leeway in such matters — including the power to withhold information from Congress or the people. The rise of extensive secret negotiations and diplomacy by executive agreements followed, along with the view that a president could even lie to us if the best interests of the survival of the free world would thus be served. Arthur Schlesinger, Jr., even though he now admits that he, along with other historians, devised exaggerated views of presidential omniscience, points out that the whole thrust of the cold war seemed at the time to compel the growth and superordinate status of the presidency: "Above all, the uncertainty and danger of the early cold war, with the chronic threat of unanticipated emergency always held to require immediate response, with, above all, the overhanging possibility of nuclear catastrophe, seemed to argue all the more strongly for the centralization of the control over foreign policy, including the use of the armed forces, in the presidency." [23]

The Presidency as a
National Symbol of Reassurance

A basic human tendency is to believe that history belongs to heroes, to believe that someone, somewhere, can and will cope with the major crises of the present and future. In the post–New Deal, post–Franklin Roosevelt era, most Americans have grown accustomed to expecting their president to fill this role. Who, if not the president, is going to prevent the Communists from burying us, pollution from choking us, crime and conflict from destroying our cities, oil-producing nations from freezing us to death, and pornography from slipping into our neighborhood bookstores and theaters? Within the complexity of contemporary political life, the presidency serves our basic need for a visible national symbol to which we can attach our hopes. Something akin to a presidential cult has emerged in the United States, just as personality cults, hero worship, reverence for aged leaders, and other forms of authority worship have flourished in most societies. Although Americans like to think of themselves as hardheaded pragmatists, they persistently regard notable former presidents as folk heroes.

Certain presidents, those who have enlarged the office and enlarged the place of the nation on the global landscape, are placed on a pedestal rather than under a microscope. Portraits of Washington, Jefferson, Lincoln, the Roosevelts, and Kennedy occupy many a classroom wall alongside the American flag. Even mediocre presidents have sometimes become, for a while, national heroes to at least a sizable portion of the populace.

Why do we have this yearning for the unique or heroic prophet among us? Michael Novak, who has wrestled with this question, concludes that a president's actions

> . . . seep irrepressibly into our hearts. He dwells in us. We cannot keep him out. That is why we wrestle against him, rise up in hatred often, wish to retch — or, alternately, feel good, feel proud, as though his achievements were ours, his wit the unleashing of power our own.
>
> Hands are stretched toward him over wire fences at airports like hands extended toward medieval sovereigns or ancient prophets. One wonders what mystic participation our presidents convey, what witness from what other world, what form of cure or heightened life. The president arouses waves of "power," "being," "superior reality," as if where he is is history. . . . His office is, in quite modern and sophisticated form, a religion in a secular state. It evokes responses familiar in all the ancient religions of the world. It fills a perennial vacuum at the heart of human expectations.[24]

To be sure, not everyone would go so far as Novak in this liturgical interpretation of the role of the president. Novak's analysis appeared after Vietnam and Watergate and he writes as though he still believes rather strongly that — certain tragedies of the presidential promise notwithstanding — presidents, for better or worse, play a crucial psychological role in our lives, even though we like to think we are rational democrats.

Political scientists have usually not read in such meaning or at least have not infused their view of the presidency with connotations of a civil religion. As the following passage from one notable social scientist's text illustrates, the typical textbook interpretation merely generalized freely from past performances to a bright, optimistic future: "When presidents are great heroes elected by a vast and vigorous majority, or when they are forced by a catastrophe and crisis to unexpected greatness, then the Presidency is as powerful as the sun, obscuring all other stars with its own light. But when neither heroic personality nor calamitous circumstance expands its influence, then it is only one star among many almost unnoticeable in a Milky Way. Yet through all this fluctuation one can discern a long-run trend of increasing brightness." [25] Even Dwight Eisenhower and Eugene McCarthy, who spoke out against expansive and possessive presidential leadership, venerated the possibilities for moral leadership in the office and assumed that presidents should unify and uplift the American people and liberate them from their weaknesses.[26]

The incumbent president was first in the Most-Admired-Man Poll annually conducted by Gallup from 1953 to 1972, except in 1967 and 1968, when a war-weakened Lyndon Johnson lost out to former President Eisenhower. The view that "if they were not the most-admired men in the country they wouldn't have been elected president" is apparently widely held. Perhaps because of our need for reassurance that things will work out satisfactorily, we admire more readily the dramatic actions of people in high places who are willing to cope with the exigencies of crisis and perplexity. As political scientist Murray Edelman puts it: "Because it is apparently intolerable for men to admit the key role of accident, of ignorance, and of unplanned processes in their affairs, the leader serves a vital function by personifying and reifying the processes." [27]

The Values of
Liberal Pundits and Textbook Writers

Those who wrote about the presidency in the post–World War II period were predominantly liberal and internationalist in political outlook. Influenced in large part by world events, they supported a strong presidency because they believed that a strong presidency would best serve their values. There developed what might be called a Lippmann-Kennan-Niebuhr-Morgenthau view of the presidency as a national-security leader. This view held that the requisite needs of negotiation and quick response to changing world events did not lend themselves to public participation. The common man could not possibly acquire the skills or knowledge to participate in foreign-policy decision making.

According to Walter Lippmann, a president must consult not the people but the necessities of a given situation and then devise policies that he believes are in the public interest. The public could judge these policies at the next election, after the policies had had a chance to work and after the president had had a chance to explain their necessity. In a similar way, Congress would merely amend or deny, but the president would initiate.

The duty and challenge of a president, according to this school, was to articulate the national purpose and to mold public opinion. Hans Morgenthau wrote that public opinion was a dynamic thing, created and continuously being changed by the very policies for which its support is sought. Public opinion does not exist before a presidential policy is developed, except perhaps as a vague and inarticulate disposition. Too often the presidential will has been paralyzed by the unfounded fears of, and misplaced deference to, public opinion. "Hence the task of the President is both clear and decisive. He must reverse the established pattern of subservience to public opinion and become its molder." [28]

Part of this favorable disposition toward the presidency may lie in the ideological heritage of recent generations. In the 1930s and 1940s it doubtless was hard *not* to identify with American political institutions, perhaps symbolized in the presidency, because at the time they were coming under international attack.

> Across the sea, Hitler defiantly taunted the democracies as impotent. Praise for the efficacy of the Fascist dictatorship in Italy was heard in surprisingly high places in the democracies. Some doubts were being expressed as to the ability of the presidential system to supply the bold dynamic leadership required for solution of the problems of modern government. A question was raised as to whether efficiency and democracy were compatible. Was constitutional government under a President and a Congress a luxury of an earlier age that could not be afforded in modern crisis government? [29]

One reaction to this was to feel that the presidency should be more of a place for strong, activist, vigorous leadership. The personal magnetism of Franklin Roosevelt seemed to fill this need. FDR upstaged his colleagues and most world leaders as he magnified the personal role and heroic style of a confident, competent president in the context of tumultuous times. The mantle of world leadership was passing to the United States, isolationism had been defeated, and the American era had begun. Understandably, these developments, especially the dramaturgy of the New Deal presidency, affected young, liberal academics and their future interpretations of the presidency. For example, "Under Roosevelt, the White House became the focus of all government — the fountainhead of ideas, the initiator of action, the representative of the national interest." [30]

Most writers of the fifties and sixties identified with the considerable liberal faith in the possibilities of structural reforms. This liberal viewpoint advocates that better and faster reforms are more likely to be achieved through a vigorous chief executive than through alternative institutions. In the 1950s and 1960s academics frequently turned to the presidency in despair because Congress, dominated by southerners of a conservative coalition, held out such little hope for those progressive, redistributive reforms that intellectuals believed were urgently needed. Moreover, many of them believed, in part correctly, that the biases of the electoral college would usually encourage more liberalism in the White

House than on Capitol Hill. They expected White House leaders to respond better than local politicians to the public interest because the federal government enjoyed an expanding and more progressive tax base. One result of these shared values among text authors is that text discussions of the presidency move back and forth between what the presidency is to what it ought to be, and it becomes difficult to separate the factual from the normative, the real from the imaginary.

Political scientist William Andrews says the presidency theory of this 1960 consensus school rested on the partisan political bias of the members of that school. Events in later years would show their bias to be vulnerable:

> Since 1960, writers on the presidency have been learning, to their chagrin, that the presidency can thwart their purposes as well as serve them. The power that they urged upon the presidency has been used to support policies of which they disapprove. Power *per se* is neutral. Power wielders may not be. Some power wielders are "good guys," others "bad guys," depending on the viewer's perspective. That lesson has been surprisingly hard for constitutional theorists to learn. Even today, the most common response of critics of the presidency is to urge that power be shifted from it to Congress. Yet, by the time that transfer is accomplished, the "good guys" may be back in the White House and the "bad guys" back in Congress.
>
> Constitutional theory cannot depend upon this "report card" approach. It is very thin indeed if it evaluates an institution on the basis of the constitutional theorist's agreement with its incumbents or its policies of the moment and adjudges it, thereby, to be worthy of more or less power for the indefinite future. Such constitutional theory has been dissolved in the policy and partisan preferences of the theorists. If those preferences leak out of the institution, the constitutional theory goes with them.[31]

In any event, the idealized view of the Roosevelt years — a halo effect that characterizes most of the recent treatments of the presidency — seems to have emerged more distinctly in the 1950s and 1960s than during the years FDR was in office. Perhaps a delayed reaction was at work; members of the older generation may have been less inclined to idealizing a hero than a younger, more impressionable generation of writers who may have been more easily mesmerized by the Roosevelt performance. Many of the textbook writers of the 1950s and 1960s were teenagers or young adults during the depression years, and many became involved in one way or another in the executive branch in helping to fight or manage World War II. It is also plausible that myths of Roosevelt's ability reached a peak only well after he was removed from the continual congressional and journalistic barbs to which he certainly was subjected in his day.

Government Expansion and the
Transfer of Power from
Congress to the President

Government today does vastly more in domestic and economic affairs than it did in the nineteenth century, and a president is the most visible leader of that level of government, the national establishment, which nearly monopolizes the rich and expanding monetary resources made up of the personal and corporate income tax and social insurance taxes. As cities, states, and even Congress proved inadequately equipped to assist the nation in the 1930s, people turned to the White House for leadership. Proponents of the textbook presidency feel that in the absence of a strong president, our system of checks and balances simply does not produce decisions quickly enough. Most high-level fights within the executive branch come to the president. Legislation often languishes without his support. The presidential voice is amplified so that it looms larger and louder than that of any rival. Presidential leadership is an absolute necessity, or so it seems to them, if the system is to work at all. To them, the concept of the all-powerful presidency is rooted in experience as well as in fancy. This is where national goals must be set — where else? Who else could determine national priorities in such a fast-paced, complex era?

Congress played an instrumental role in this expansion of the presidency. In the early 1970s it became fashionable to blame presidents for usurping congressional powers. But very nearly the reverse actually took place; Congress willingly yielded power time and again. It began in the early twentieth century, under Theodore Roosevelt. An early high point was Wilson's diplomacy at the end of World War I. But equally important was the Budget and Accounting Act of 1921. This act, in effect, made the president the government's general manager. This was plainly a congressional initiative.

Again in 1946 Congress initiated the landmark Employment Act of 1946 that, in effect, mandated presidents to be the general manager of the economy, the chief economic stabilizer. From then on every president would have a sizable staff of White House economists helping to prepare the annual economic report to Congress. From then on it was the president, not Congress, who would be recognized as the initiator of anti-unemployment and anti-inflation policies. As James Sundquist notes, "Before 1946 there was no requirement that the President have an economic policy and most of them didn't. After 1946 the President had to have an economic policy, so the economic leadership of the government was handed to the President by the Congress quite voluntarily." [32]

Congress yielded power, or at least an enlarged mandate, to the presidency for several reasons. First, they were overwhelmed or overtaken by events. The country wanted faster action and practical solutions. Congress recognized that as a deliberative body it had severe limits for setting broad policy goals and for acting quickly in foreign- and economic-policy situations. It also recognized it could not manage or plan very well. That the presidency might not do these things exceedingly well either did not matter; the view was that there was more unity and more potential for swift, informal action in the executive than in Congress. So Congress became something akin to a loyal opposition. Having yielded considerable managerial and policy responsibilities to the president, congressional leaders organized themselves to oversee, oppose, and occasionally veto presidential government.

The Desire for
National Stability and Regime Loyalty

A president may be elected by a small margin, but after election he is supposed to speak for all the people. Textbooks suggest that one may question a presidential candidate vigorously, but not a new president; after the election, it is one's duty to unite behind the legitimized winner because united we stand, divided we might not. The mood is one of beginning anew, of reasoning together, and of joining together with renewed support for both presidency and nation, as if the president were the pilot of an aircraft and the rest of us passengers. We all, consequently, have a stake in his success. We feel we must give the man a chance; to behave otherwise is unpatriotic or smacks of unsporting partisanship. The losing party receives little sympathy during postelection periods; the time for complaints is the next election, or at least not the first year or so while the new man is trying hard to get on with the job.

Some political scientists point out that childhood romanticisms and deferential respect for the presidency may be blessings in disguise in terms of national stability. A study of children's images of the presidency has argued:

> From the point of view of the stability of the American political structure, some such attachment early in life has positive consequences. As the child grows to adulthood, he is exposed to considerable debate and conflicts over the merits of various alternative incumbents of the Presidency and of other roles in the political structure. There is constant danger that criticism of the occupant will spill over to the role itself. Were this to occur under certain circumstances respect for the Presidency could be seriously impaired or destroyed. But the data here suggest that one of the factors that prevents this from occurring is a strong parental-like tie with respect to the President's role itself, developed before the child can become familiar with the contention surrounding the incumbent of the office.[33]

Our system of adversary elections, in which ambitious and competing hopefuls strive to outdo each other in their promises and denunciations, is counterbalanced, then, by an institution of ritualistic unification. The presidential role symbolically absorbs much of the discontinuity and tension promoted during the often hectic election period.

Constraints on Writers

The textbook presidency emerges also from the modes of analysis employed by the typical textbook writer. Normally, an author relies on some combination of the public record, prior texts, cabinet, and White House staff memoirs, and perhaps some interviewing of Washington officials. Newspaper and magazine commentary serves as a supplement. Reliance on such sources will usually encourage a positive orientation toward presidents and the office. Many newsmen who have covered presidential campaigns have been converted into an admiring claque. Theodore White, for example, now admits that he gave himself over to the loyalty of JFK's friendship, adding that he frankly viewed Kennedy as a hero. Those who have worked closely with presidents are unlikely to downgrade their experiences. As Theodore Sorensen said: "The inaccuracy of most Washington diaries and autobiographies is surpassed only by the immodesty of their authors." Former members of the White House inner circles, John Dean excepted, are modest about neither their own role nor their claims for the strengths and virtues of their presidents. Literate members of the White House press corps, referred to by some presidents as their "newspaper cabinet," are similarly afflicted. To preserve their access to the president, a requisite for their economic survival, they must treat presidents graciously, or else risk becoming victims of intensified White House animosity and manipulation. Then, too, upon the inquiry of outside academic investigators, insiders may "forget" those plans or strategies that did not work and unwittingly embellish the record of presidential and personal performances. Any mention of mistakes or uncertainties, shortcuts or foul play is usually off the record.

Another methodological technique that leads to overdramatizing the presidency is the reliance on exciting presidential biographies and case histories of international crises and domestic emergencies. Writing as well as reading about presidential personalities is always more fun and usually a lot easier than writing and reading about the complexities of the institution of the presidency. Case studies of Roosevelt's first hundred days; of Truman's decisions to drop the atomic bomb, enter Korea, and create the Marshall Plan; of Eisenhower's summit conferences; of Kennedy's Cuban missile blockade and "victory" over the steel price-rise; and of Nixon's historic journey to China also come to mind. To be sure, documents, press accounts, and memoirs about these incidents are readily available. But to study presidential performance only in the context of crisis or presidential personality and summitry is to magnify the importance of the job and the man at the expense of other major determinants of policy.

Most text writers probably would agree that introductory government texts have two preeminent functions: to enlighten students and to train citizens. Text authors are certainly motivated by the goal of instructing students about the realities of the highly competitive, complex, and inchoate process of determining national policy. In addition, they and sometimes their editors are motivated by the goals of socializing students by teaching them the norms of their culture and of cultivating respect for their society's political institutions. Often, the latter goal seems to require a glossy, controlled picture of the institutions of national leadership, one that inspires loyalty but conflicts with reality. When this occurs, as one text writer remarked in conversation, the author almost invariably emphasizes citizen training, usually at the expense of instruction. On balance, most authors willingly accept the assignment of combating student cynicism by stressing the practicality of the democratic system and pointing out the benefits and opportunities of the American Dream. Large introductory American government texts expose students to the whole spectrum of political institutions and processes. Almost always, the authors treat each institution separately: there may be one chapter on the Constitution, another on elections, perhaps a chapter on political parties and interest groups, two on Congress, one on the courts, and so forth. Unfortunately, the resulting compartmentalism often gives the impression that the men and women who populate these institutions and the processes in which they engage are not only distinctly different but also largely unrelated. A chapter may stress the informational and representational roles performed by interest groups and lobbyists, but only scant mention will be made of their activities in relation to the presidency. Likewise, little attention will be paid to the way in which federal bureaucrats or mayors and governors become involved in the implementation of presidential policy. In the chapter on Congress and the president, the student learns that a major function of Congress is to question and review presidential program requests and occasionally to oppose — in short, not to be taken in by the president's overtures. A chapter on the presidency suggests the centrality of the office and its paramount role in initiating and controlling public policy and leaves the impression that national policy is almost entirely the product of a president and the "best and the brightest" at his command. This picture of government is overly hierarchical and neat: a nearly omnipotent presidency really runs the country, but because this is a democracy rather than a monarchy, such institutions as Congress and the court system serve occasionally as the nation's insurance policy between elections.

Of late, analysis of White House staffs and presidential advisory processes has improved. It has moved beyond the image of a lonely president making inspired decisions in the quiet of his Oval Office. Yet, a misplaced emphasis and oversimplification remain in the portrayal of presidential counselors and staff associates as the real policymakers. The Bay of Pigs defeat, consequently, is credited solely to overzealous and misinformed CIA leaders. Innovative peace negotiations are credited to Henry Kissinger, who is possessed, so the argument goes, of a vision so clear and a grip on reality so tenacious that the achievements of the Nixon administration in foreign policy must be labeled brilliant. The ineffectiveness of the war on poverty is explained in terms of the defective vision of a small band of social-science advisers and presidential aides. The Watergate mess is blamed on overzealous underlings. The net impression is that public policy is controlled, if not by the president, then by a handful of presidential intimates. The student remains grievously ignorant of the large number of elite, economic, and institutional forces behind policy formulation and implementation and of the complex transactions and ambiguities that more accurately characterize most national policy developments.

The Television-Magnified Presidency

During Jimmy Carter's 1977 honeymoon period his media adviser, Barry Jagoda, believed he had come up with a match for Johnny Carson and Walter Cronkite.

> We've got the biggest star in television. Jimmy Carter may be the biggest television star of all time. He is the first television President. . . . He looks normal on television, natural; most of all he's comfortable. . . . Television has become a regular part of his life. It's no big deal. That's what we set out to do: to make television neutral. . . . If a picture is worth a thousand words, a television show is worth millions.[34]

Since its invention, television has become an increasingly important part of presidential politics. Television has dramatically changed the very nature of the office, the kind of men who hold it and how the public responds to presidents. A president who is knowledgeable in its use can use it to shape public opinion, to gain support for his policies, and to boost his chances for political survival. It is estimated that 98 percent of the population has at least one television set at home and that the average set is on more than six hours a day. Television is the source from which most people now receive their news. It is also usually rated the most believable of their sources for following public events. The younger and less educated people are, the more they watch television and depend on it for interpreting political developments.

"No mighty king, no ambitious emperor, no pope, no prophet ever dreamt of such an awesome pulpit, so potent a magic wand," writes Fred, W. Friendly of television as a tool in presidential politics.[35] Television, needing figures and celebrities larger than life, seizes on presidential candidates, especially the winners, and magnifies them. Television fixes on a president and makes him the prime symbolic agent of government. If there is a balance of powers within the government, it rarely shows on television.

So much media news time is devoted to presidential elections that people might well expect an election to produce a savior rather than a president. Jimmy Carter's proud 1976 campaign boasts that he was not a lawyer, not a liar, *and not from Washington* beguiled some people into believing that here was *a man of faith* who could not only restore trust in government but be the textbook moral leader they were looking for. "For what the nation has been beguiled into believing ever since 1960 is surely the politics of evangelism: cast to be messiahs, the conviction that Presidential incantations can be substituted for concrete programs, the belief that what matters is not so much the state of the nation as the inspiration quotient of its people." [36]

Television has downgraded local news and elevated national phenomena. Presidential travels and addresses are accentuated, and events are divorced from meaningful interpretation. The major networks are invariably committed to an almost mindless superficiality in their coverage of the presidency. In the hands of shrewd presidents, symbolic actions carefully displayed via videopolitics are often as effective while they last as concrete action itself.

John F. Kennedy was especially helped by television. As an attractive, articulate, and glamorous candidate, television aided his efforts to become known and to be taken seriously. Moreover, his father's wealth could afford the high cost of a well-produced advertising campaign. Also, the 1960 presidential debates allowed Kennedy to look as competent if not more so than his better-known opponent Richard Nixon. No wonder that, once elected, Kennedy quickly tried to convert television into a large presidential megaphone. Political scientist Michael J. Robinson notes that Kennedy reveled in the use of television, more than tripling Eisenhower's rate of network appearances:

> Kennedy gave the networks their first real opportunity to televise the President in his office, at work, and during his press conferences. In return, Kennedy tacitly accepted the unstated privilege of using the networks to build a more plebiscitary Presidency than any since Franklin Roosevelt. There is some irony here, in that Kennedy's innovative use of television . . . helped expand the "imperial presidency" more quickly than most television journalists would care to admit. Under Kennedy television overwhelmingly concentrated on the Presidency for the first time. By the

time of his death, Kennedy had helped to make both network journalism and the Presidency more powerful forces in American politics.[37]

Later in this same analysis Robinson acknowledges that, whereas television has probably made the office more powerful, it may also have rendered presidential authority less legitimate. How is that? Television allows us to see, close up, most of the shortcomings of our presidents, thus deromanticizing somewhat the actual performance of presidents. If Robinson is right, this simultaneous effect — enhanced importance but lessened legitimacy — further fuels the exaggerations of the textbook presidency. Simply put, television glamorizes the coming of a president and leads us to consider a president as more crucial to effective leadership, but it also brings proximity and familiarity and with these the risks of unpopularity if not contempt. So it has been for the post-Kennedy presidents. Television has helped to make them more important but less popular.

Pollsters and countless academic studies report a high correlation between presidential addresses to the nation or well-timed press conferences and a rise in public support. President Truman was the first to use television addresses to the nation, but both he and Eisenhower used television sparingly. Kennedy, one of the most skillful practitioners of presidential television, used it nineteen times to reach out with major statements directly to the American people. Like Truman and Eisenhower, Kennedy often used television to report to and reassure the American people during periods of crisis. But he also initiated a new use of television, the "conversation." President Johnson not only used television frequently but, unlike earlier presidents, demanded the networks make television time available to him without an explanation. The networks disliked this habit but reluctantly relented. So insistent and unpredictable were Johnson's desires that the networks finally converted a small White House theater into a presidential studio. Three cameras were kept warm for immediate use.[38] Johnson would demand time and go on television whenever he wanted, often overriding the wishes of the television executives.

Johnson was aware, of course, of the potential power television might give him in molding public opinion, in rallying support, in bringing pressure on the other branches of government. Congress and the Supreme Court and the bureaucracy had severely limited or even nonexistent access to television airwaves. They cannot request time whenever they want, especially during prime time. Some members of Congress have attempted to do this, but they are refused for the most part. The Supreme Court has never tried to get access to the airwaves. The bureaucracy, of course, has no real chance to gain direct access to the airwaves.

Presidents usually like the televised press conferences because they can control most of what goes on at them. Thus a president can usually find friendly questioners if he does not like the direction in which the session is moving. A president can answer questions briefly or not at all and he can leave little opportunity for follow-up questions because other press members have their pet questions to ask and are eager to change the subject. Seldom do reporters follow up one another's questions. Through his press secretary, a president can plant questions for reporters to ask so that the president can get across certain, specific points. A president also has the advantage of calling a press conference quickly, so that the press is not particularly prepared to ask tough, pointed questions.

President Carter, one of several recent presidents who has promised an open presidency, was not above trying to manipulate televised press conferences. On July 20, 1978, during an evening "prime-time" session with the White House press corps, he declared a legitimate news story to be off limits. "I will not answer questions on the subject," he said of the controversial resignation under fire of his drug-policy adviser, Dr. Peter Bourne. Dr. Bourne, a psychiatrist and longtime Carter supporter and political adviser, prescribed a small amount of Quaalude, a tightly controlled but often abused drug that reduces anxieties, induces sleep, and is sometimes used as a "recreational" drug because of its effects. Bourne wrote the prescription, but to a fictitiously named patient, although he later acknowledged it was for one of his White House assistants. It turned out, too, that he had written prescriptions for a number of other White House aides. Rumors of marijuana and cocaine use by White House staffers spread throughout Washington. Was this a legitimate news issue? Was it proper for reporters to ask the president questions concerning it? Carter said he felt that because some legal investigations might be in progress he did not want to comment on the matter. But several reporters and others questioned Carter's right to rewrite the informal rules of presidential press conferences. "To the doctrine of executive privilege he has tried to add Presidential preference," wrote William Safire. Carter, in effect, "sought to change the open press conference format into a forum using newsmen as props for the airing of views on matters of the President's choosing." [39] John Herbers, who covered the Nixon and Ford years at the White House for the *New York Times*, concluded that the press conferences have become the president's, not the public's, device:

As a televised spectacular . . . the conference is seriously flawed. In the informal news conferences that mayors, governors, congressmen, and others hold daily, a reporter can develop not only the hard news but the insights and feel for the officials that is important to the interpretive copy he writes. The Presidential press conference is staged and plastic. Why should a President, who is performing his job on a day-to-day basis, have to be so elaborately briefed and coached for thirty minutes of questioning? Scores of people are put to work [in the White House and executive branch] long before the event anticipating questions and suggesting answers. It is an institutionalized system that grew, I believe, out of the cult of the Presidency, which holds that the President is no mere mortal who might answer, "I don't know much about that subject at this stage. I will try to provide answers later." As it is, we do not know whether the answers he gives are his or those of some unnamed assistant who told him what to say. We do not have much sense of his own grasp of the government, or his style, or substance.[40]

Television places in a president's hands enormous powers not provided for in our Constitution, powers over reality, perception, and over the whole way in which issues are presented and discussed in America. The Constitution did not intend this disparity in which a president's work and his presence dominates the attention of citizens who sit in their living rooms in silence, able only to listen. Michael Novak writes that the Constitution envisaged that a president would argue as a man among men. He adds, "If we are to reform the presidency, the heart of the matter is the president's power over reality, his symbolic power. The social reality of the United States cannot be left to definition by one man alone."[41]

Presidential television has produced a troubling problem for democratic politics. The problem is the near-monopoly enjoyed by presidents who skillfully use that medium in determining the way issues get shaped and even over the way political participation often takes place in the American political arena. A president's words and actions receive far more television coverage than the efforts of any other political figure. Moreover, a president's access to the political consciousness of the average citizen is unmatched in its immediacy and directness. To be sure, not all presidents use television to their maximum advantage. Even their television advantage is no match for a Watergate. But most presidents have used television to focus national attention on what they want to accomplish and have sought to influence and shape the televised activities of other leaders and governmental institutions in such a way as to preserve their own superior visibility and public preeminence. Political scientist Bruce Miroff makes this point:

> The President, I suggest, dominates the public space through his superior capacities of initiating action, defining reality, and enacting political drama. This domination is commonly justified by the assumption that he is a surrogate for a citizenry incapable of action on its own. Presidential dramas in the public space attract vicarious participation, providing many Americans with political meaning and sometimes with a sense of political potency — at the cost of making actual participation unappealing, diverting people from their own interests, and mystifying existing power relationships.[42]

Television, in short, serves to amplify the president's claim to be the only representative of all the people. Television promotes the image of the president as the towering figure in the national politics. Television allows a president an added extraconstitutional advantage in diminishing the role of others who would compete with him. For, as Miroff notes, "Public awareness of issues is largely governed by the problems he has defined and the battles he is engaged in fighting. His role in the public space is so prominent that it is sometimes hard for others simply to be seen on any large scale." [43] We have today a "television presidency" and a video politics that have altered our political system in ways that are constantly underestimated and in ways that we are still trying to comprehend.

CONSEQUENCES OF THE TEXTBOOK AND PRIME-TIME PRESIDENCY

The textbook presidency exaggerations may appear useful to some and amusing to others, but they are not without cost to society. Some of the consequences are reflected in the quality of civic participation, in the potential for cynicism toward government, and in the distorted perceptions within the presidential establishment. Finally, the largest cost may be the way in which presidents are led to act — often as if they are more concerned with "looking presidential" than with being responsible or accountable.

The Effect on Citizen Politics

The relationship between moral leader and layman is often viewed as a one-way street. If the president is indeed the national chaplain, how is it possible to cultivate a democratic citizenry that is active and not passive, that may, on selective occasions, responsibly dispute with this national moral eminence? The average citizen, nurtured in the belief that presidents are personally powerful enough to end war, depression, corruption, and all like manner of civic malaise, finds it difficult to disagree strongly with the president under any circumstances. Students are instructed that it is proper to state one's differences in letters to congressmen or even to the White House. But because of the deference to his textbook image, the president can usually expect a highly favorable ratio in telegram and mail responses to his television reports on major issues.

There are, of course, those who engage in protest, perhaps to discredit presidential claims or to weaken the incumbent president, hoping to obtain a more suitable leader — probably one more like the textbook version — or more suitable policies at the next election. But protestors and demonstrators are dismissed by large numbers of Americans as self-righteous and unpatriotic critics, elitist easterners, or congenital defeatists. The "love it or leave it" slogan includes a basic respect for the presidency as well as the country.

The most popular course of action is quietly to rally around the president and offer him permissive support, hoping by such action — or inaction — to strengthen his and the nation's resolve to meet the present challenge. A related pattern of behavior, that of benign indifference, is selected by citizens who feel secure in the belief that presidents know best. Thus, a president usually may assume that when major difficulties are faced, most Americans, at least for a while, will trust and follow him, often tendering him even increased support. In the process a citizen's loyalty to the nation often mindlessly blends into loyalty to the president, a confusion much to be desired by incumbent presidents and indeed often promoted by them. As a result, public support comes not only from those who feel the president is right but is also measurably inflated by those who, regardless of policy or situation, agree with their president merely because he is the only president they have.

Presidents and press alike might be well advised to de-escalate claims that the American people or the great silent majority of middle Americans are strongly behind the president on a certain policy matter. This may or may not be the case, regardless of the polls; in all likelihood, a substantial portion of the people really do not know much about the subtleties — or crudities — of the policy or do not much care. For those few who are inclined to protest the actions of their president, textbook wisdom seems to encourage a direct, personal confrontation. If the president personally is so powerful and independent, it appears logical to picket him, march on his White House, or try to break or get rid of him in order to change policy; but breaking or changing presidents does not necessarily insure any major shift in specialized policy subsystems. Cast as superhuman, presidents and even presidential candidates are supported passionately, but they also run the risk of assault and assassination.

Thus, although the vast majority of Americans support and honor their presidency, presidents are prime targets for psychotics and extremists. Regrettably, presidents become deeply loved and roundly hated, unduly worshipped and unduly feared. On both sides of the presidential popularity equation, the president's importance is inflated beyond reasonable bounds. On one side, there is a near-mindless faith that a president enjoys a monopoly of national civic virtue and wisdom and that any detractor must be an irreverent, effete snob or a nervous Nellie. On the other side, a president becomes the most crooked of all politicians, the perpetuator of poverty and racism, the tool of the establishment, and the primary source of a choleric national disposition.

An Invitation to Cynicism and Despair

The idealized textbook view portrays the president, the architect of policy, as the lobbyist for all the people, the representative of the otherwise unrepresented. Pointing out that he is often quite dependent on one or another political and policy elite both inside and outside the federal government is regarded as indecorous. Perhaps textbook writers, along with many political scientists of the 1950s and 1960s, overreacted defensively to the allegations of sociologist C. Wright Mills and others about the existence of a cabalistic power elite.

But what happens when the citizen who was reared on the sanitized textbook version of the presidency learns that the presidential establishment sees to it that the government extensively subsidizes corporate farmers, opposition political forces in Allende's Chile, Lockheed Aircraft, home-building companies, and the like; or that the presidency is sensitively deferential to monopolistic organizations such as ITT and the Teamsters' Union because of their political and financial clout? What happens when the student learns too about deliberate government suppression of information about massacres of Vietnamese citizens, irregularities in defense contracting, illegal campaign practices, political fixes, Watergate conspiracies, and advertisements and telegram campaigns rigged to give the appearance of public support for devious presidential policies? Cynicism, a crisis of confidence, and a diminution of the feeling of legitimacy in the institution of the presidency seem inevitable, and indeed these have occurred. The paradox is that when misunderstood and misused, those very characteristics that nourish the potential for responsible leadership in the presidency — its pronounced visibility, its mystique, and its exalted legacy — can also undermine it.

Distortions of Presidential Perceptions

If the mythical textbook image of the presidency has costly implications for the quality of the relationship between citizens and the presidency, it affects fully as much the ways in which presidents and their associates conceive of themselves and of their jobs. The reverence and loyalty rendered a new president are a rich resource, but an overindulgent citizenry can distort the president's psychological perspective and sense of balance. Though some of his observations are overstated, former presidential press secretary George Reedy's criticisms of the monarchical trappings of the contemporary White House deserve attention:

> The atmosphere of the White House is calculated to instill in any man a sense of destiny. He literally walks in the footsteps of hallowed figures — of Jefferson, of Jackson, of Lincoln. The almost sanctified relics of a distant, semi-mythical past surround him as ordinary household objects to be used by his family. From the moment he enters the halls he is made aware that he has become enshrined in a pantheon of semi-divine mortals who have shaken the world, and that he has taken from their hands the heritage of American dreams and aspirations. Unfortunately

for him divinity is a better basis for inspiration than it is for government.[44]

The Gaullist plebiscitary image of the American presidency that was allowed to grow up in the Nixon White House — so obvious from the deference shown him by oversolicitous and overzealous aides — is an illustration of this type of distortion. The quality of advice necessary to balanced presidential decision making can be adversely affected by too respectful an attitude toward the chief executive. So acute did this problem become in the Nixon presidency that John Ehrlichman's Watergate testimony conjured up the image that the president is too busy to be bothered, that bad news should be kept away, and that the dignity of the office somehow was demeaned or compromised if heated debate and advocacy were allowed to occur in the presidential presence. It was only a short step to the autocratic views that "the President *is* the government," to quote Ehrlichman, and that, "every President has a right to conduct foreign policy in a way *that helps him most*" (italics added), to quote Henry Kissinger.[45] Daniel P. Moynihan put it this way at the time: "I am of those who believe that America is the hope of the world and for that time given him, the President is the hope of America." [46]

Protecting a president and his power too assiduously sometimes can lock the president into a disastrous policy.[47] Thus, former Nixon White House aide Egil Krogh led the plumbers operation because he believed sincerely that "freedom of the President to pursue his planned course was the ultimate national security objective." Only after his conviction did he recognize that sincerity and loyalty "can often be as blinding as worthy." His advice to future young people in high governmental posts sums up the classic problem: "I hope they will recognize that the banner of national security can turn perceived patriotism into actual disservice. When contemplating a course of action, I hope they will never fail to ask, 'Is this right?' " [48]

H. R. Haldeman, Nixon's chief of staff, writes in his memoir of his service in the White House that Nixon had to be protected from his own darker side. He would often, says Haldeman, issue mean-spirited and weird orders that were best ignored. Moreover, because Nixon was insecure with people whom he did not know well, he had to be carefully programmed and isolated. By 1978, with ample time to reflect on the experiences with Nixon, Haldeman realized that he and other White House aides in an effort to make the president look presidential actually helped to do him in:

> By presenting Nixon, or attempting to, as 100 percent pure and good, we were setting him up for a disastrous fall when it was demonstrated that he fell short of that absolute — as all humans must. Had he been

more accurately portrayed as he really was, complete with flaws, there is no doubt in my mind that he would have succeeded. . . .[49]

LOOKING PRESIDENTIAL

Everyone knows that public relations play a large role in presidential elections. But most people underestimate the way the concern for a president's popularity and reelection gets elevated to an end in itself and the purposes for which presidential powers were granted get shunted aside. Machiavelli's *The Prince* includes a chapter entitled "How a Prince Must Act in Order to Gain Reputation." Contemporary presidents could easily include a chapter in their memoirs that would vastly expand on Machiavelli.

The American public has become conditioned by the media not to believe in the reality of a public act until it has been transformed into a dramatic or theatrical gesture before the cameras. National personalities, including presidents, know they must try to acquire the attributes of show business. The publicity imperatives of looking presidential, of achieving star quality or what journalists might call magnetism and charisma, promote a zealous presidential press-agentry. The need to protect the image has added television advisers, pollsters, and countless "media" specialists to the White House staff. So important did one of these aides become in the Carter administration that he was referred to as the Secretary of Symbolism.

When Vice President Richard Nixon "lost" to John F. Kennedy in the television debates of 1960 he and his aides tried to review what had gone wrong. Nixon's verdict: "At the conclusion of our post mortem, I recognized the basic mistake I had made. I had concentrated too much on substance and not enough on appearance." [50] Later in his presidential career, Nixon would often go to great lengths to accentuate style and appearance over substance. For example, in 1972, as the presidential primaries were in progress, President Nixon went to China for seven days. Through careful media planning, and a well-calculated, long stopover en route, Nixon managed to arrive in China and return to Washington, D.C., precisely during prime-time television viewing. For seven days his presence in China dominated the television airwaves and helped him to fend off various presidential challengers in his own and the opposition party.

In most presidential campaigns, would-be presidents are told to talk about integrity, religious conviction, love of family, and the need for more honesty in government. They are repeatedly advised by public-relations advisers to avoid controversial issues. President Ford steered clear of most policy issues in 1976 and nearly won a major come-from-behind victory. His chief advertising executive acted on the principle that voters are far more influenced by their feelings about the candidate's personal traits than by positions on issues:

> The first commercial we made was a five-minute documentary on President Ford's family. It opened on a birthday party for Susan. She was shown hugging her father as the band played Happy Birthday. We then cut to a series of film clips in which the President's children talked warmly about their father. Michael Ford, a seminary student, talked about the family's feelings about religion in extremely moving terms. The commercial ended with the President giving Betty an affectionate kiss on the cheek.
>
> It sounds, I know, about as corny as a commercial can get. But it was an honest portrayal of a loving family, and it worked because it touched that deep yearning for traditional American values that lay deep in most voters' hearts.
>
> Our most successful commercial, one we ran heavily at the end of the campaign, featured our campaign song, "Feeling Good About America" . . . played by marching bands, sung quietly by a chorus, played softly under Ford's voice as he talked about trust.[51]

Jimmy Carter received the same kind of public-relations advice from his friends and advisers. Charles Kirbo, his senior political mentor, told him "not to run his campaign on an intellectual approach to issues, but on a restoration of confidence in government. I thought," said Kirbo, "people would buy that. They were worn out on the issues." [52] As soon as the election ended, Patrick H. Caddell, Carter's well-paid pollster, advised the new president to keep on stressing style and personality rather than programs. Caddell put it this way: "Too many good people have been defeated because they sought to substitute substance for style." [53] So, time and again, policy decision and implementation become secondary to selling the appearance of leadership, selling the personality, helping the man to become known, liked, and trusted. "Let's PR it through," was the way H. R. Haldeman sometimes put it, as if the whole enterprise was viewed as "the faking of the presidency." The imperatives of the script outlined below may seem irreverent, but they are wholly relevant to an understanding of public leadership in the United States today.

Don't Just Stand There; Do Something

More than any course of action, indecisiveness can hurt a president's popularity, or so White House people seem to believe. For many people nothing is more reassuring than a president who seems to know what to do and is willing to act, especially when others are confused. Declaring oneself is always more popular than remaining neutral, especially in the face of a threat to the status quo. The accepted PR technique is to be positive, seize the initiative, have plans — even secret plans if necessary — announce new programs, fly here and there, appoint a new commission, make new appointments. Above all, do not convey the impression that you are sitting on your hands or, worse yet, are asleep. Never, never, take a vacation. All vacations must be working vacations. This appearance of always being at work was perhaps carried to an extreme when Nixon observed in an interview: "The worst thing you can do in this job is to relax, to let up."

History too rarely rewards the president who knows when to sit tight. The textbooks praise the activists even when things go wrong. Texts should also measure a president for what he has not done, for troubles he did not get us into. John Quincy Adams and Dwight Eisenhower deserve more praise on this score than they usually get for *not* going to war with France and in Vietnam respectively. As Stephen Hess adds, "While doing something may be imperative, the pressures to act often mean the alternatives are not carefully weighed." [54]

Logically, President Kennedy should have suffered a great loss of popularity after the Bay of Pigs failure, but his popularity actually rose by seven to ten points. Nixon's popularity dropped markedly when in his first term he failed to act decisively on inflation, and it dropped again dramatically in his second term when he failed to respond with dispatch to Watergate revelations. George Gallup explains this phenomenon this way: "People tend to judge a man by his goals, by what he is trying to do, and not necessarily by what he accomplishes or by how well he succeeds. People used to tell us over and over again about all the things that [Franklin] Roosevelt did wrong and then they would say, 'I'm all for him, though, because his heart is in the right place; he is trying.' That's the most important thing in the world. . . ." [55]

Harry Truman aide Clark Clifford similarly recognized the public's hunger for novelty and image-accentuating presidential activity. Clifford counseled: "A president who is also a candidate must resort to subterfuge. . . . He cannot sit silent; he must be in the limelight. . . . He must resort to the kind of trip Roosevelt made famous in the 1940 campaign — the 'inspection tour.' No matter how much the opposition and the press pointed out the political overtones of those trips, the people paid little attention, for what they saw was the Head of State performing his duties." [56] With guidance from this Clifford script and a little help from Thomas Dewey, Truman went on to win an upset victory in the 1948 elections.

The political incentives of the 1960s seemed to deflect energies away from rigorous policy experimentation and planning. The thinking seemed to be that it was better to act immediately and to worry about planning later. The curse of activism, regardless of its cost, seemed always at work. Presidents and congressional leaders were eager for quick results; they felt they were elected not to study policies but to make them and put them into operation. As one Kennedy-Johnson counselor told me:

> People were always wanting to turn pilot projects into full-scale programs all over the place before they knew the result or before they tested whether things would work. Often we would argue this brief before the President. But again and again between the presidential message and later when it was enmeshed in congressional committees, the departmental and lobbying interests had worked on it in such a way that the program idea would get expanded and markedly changed in scope. Political advisers would always say that to line up the right number of votes you had to spread the program around. So before you had a chance to debug a program it was being launched nationwide! The Budget Bureau lost any influence it might have had on many programs because they were set up so rapidly and thrown into the political processes too quickly — everybody wanted results right away. This was also in the character of President Johnson. He was impatient about problem-resolving programs; he wanted to do things right away and as fast as he could on a large scale.

Bend Over Backward to Disprove Your Stereotypes

Most presidents seem to behave in such a way as to counteract the notable stereotypes people have of them — sometimes for the better, but often for the worse. The public feared General Eisenhower might be swayed easily by his military advisers and that another war might result. Eisenhower not only disproved such fears but made large cuts in the military budgets. His military policies won little praise from the generals in the Pentagon. Indeed, once elected, he may have been the least popular modern president in the eyes of the military establishment.

John Kennedy constantly behaved as if he were trying to counteract his image as young, inexperienced, and not tough enough to deal with world leaders. As a result, he overcompensated, as in the Bay of Pigs humiliation, in the perilous, if successful, handling of the Russian missile sites in Cuba, and in the escalating involvement in Vietnam. And to still the people's fear of a Catholic president, Kennedy became so cautious about any commitments to the Church that his policies and practices have been characterized as perhaps the most anti-Catholic since those of Millard Fillmore.

Johnson, like Nixon, seemed determined to be a different kind of person as president than he had been previously. Aaron Wildavsky notes, for example, that "Johnson delighted in showing that he was not the canny politician everyone thought they had elected, the man who would always trim his sails so as to keep close to the people, but rather the statesman who would insist on doing right in Vietnam no matter what anyone thought."[57] Many people also doubtless thought of Lyndon Johnson as a

parochial southerner who would be relatively weak on civil-rights initiatives. Johnson himself recalled that while he was in Congress he had
voted against six major civil-rights bills, feeling that such legislation was
written more to humiliate the South than to help the black people. "I
represented a conservative constituency. One heroic stand and I'd be back
home, defeated, unable to do any good for anyone, much less the blacks and
underprivileged," he wrote.[58] But as his national responsibilities (and
ambitions) grew, he sought to demonstrate that a southerner could rise
above regional attitudes. In 1964 and 1965 Johnson seemed determined
to prove once and for all that he should not be identified solely as a
southerner and a compromiser who somehow would wriggle out of the
controversy over civil rights. He later recalled in his memoirs how he
tried to outdo the Kennedy commitment:

> When I sat in the Oval Office after President Kennedy died and reflected
> on civil rights, there was no question in my mind as to what I would do.
> I knew that, as President and as a man, I would use every ounce of
> strength I possessed to gain justice for the black American. My strength
> as President was then tenuous — I had no strong mandate from the
> people. I had not been elected to that office. . . . Even the strongest
> supporters of President Kennedy's civil rights bill in 1963 expected parts
> of it to be watered down in order to avert a Senate filibuster. . . . I had
> seen this "moderating" process at work for many years. I had seen it
> happen in 1957. I had seen it happen in 1960, I did not want to see it
> happen again. . . . I made my position unmistakably clear: We were
> not prepared to compromise in any way. . . . I wanted absolutely no
> room for bargaining. And I wanted everybody to know this, from the
> lowliest bureaucrat to the members of my cabinet, from the poorest black
> in the slums to the richest white man in the suburbs, from the staunchest
> Baptist in the South to the most devout Catholic in the North.[59]

The Ford presidency suggests an example of a stereotyping that, however much the president and his aides tried to disown, persisted and later
became a factor that led to his defeat. Ford's reputation as a clumsy
bumbler, a Bozo the Clown klutz, quite rightly angered the president.
Ford was a youthful, athletic man, a graduate of Yale University Law
School and a veteran member of Congress who was widely respected in
Washington. He was also widely liked by the public. Still, an alleged
physical clumsiness was translated into suggestions of mental ineptitude.
Ford's press secretary says this unfair typecasting was his and Ford's biggest
continuing media problem. Ron Nessen, the press secretary in question,
suggests Ford's own staff sometimes were of little help in countering the
stereotype:

> Members of the White House staff were not without blame in perpetuat-
> ing the myth that Ford was a dullard. Describing to journalists their role
> in briefing Ford for major decisions or overseas trips, staff members often

made it sound like they were giving Ford a cram course, as if they were tutoring a backward schoolboy. Particularly bothersome to me were the stories suggesting that Ford was learning foreign policy at the feet of Henry Kissinger.

Whenever the president made an especially impressive appearance, the effect was frequently diluted by Ford staff members who rushed to tell reporters what a great job they had done coaching and rehearsing Ford, as if he were a brainless puppet they had to manipulate.[60]

Nessen and Ford spent a lot of their time trying to make the president look more competent, more presidential, but in the end they were basically beaten by a stream of cartoons, Johnny Carson jokes, and Chevy Chase imitations that portrayed Ford in less becoming ways.

Don't Be Soft: Appear Resolute and Dominant and Accentuate the Sense of Crisis.   Machiavelli summed it up well when he said that "above all a prince must endeavor in every action to obtain fame for being great and excellent." [61] A president can appear more presidential if he can accentuate the nation's sense of being in a desperate predicament. This enlarges on the uncertainties and isolates the leader from the people and even more from the sets of checks and balances that usually prevail. Therefore, because the important and critical problems are not necessarily those that people want to hear about, a self-enhancing technique is to place critical problems in an unreal light and pose illusory ones as if they were critical. When challenged for doing so, a president can condemn his critics as obstructionists on the one hand and as mindless romantics on the other. He can label them as radicals, Nervous Nellies, or ivory-tower intellectuals. A clever policy is to practice the politics of confrontation, to elevate external challenges to a call for a state of national emergency, and to know the value of keeping his subjects' minds uncertain and astonished, watching and waiting for his remedies.

John Kennedy sounded the clarion call on innumerable occasions; his appeal to the nation to build fallout shelters during one of his early crises is an illustration of jolting the people and making them uncertain. Both Kennedy and Nixon publicly activated and put the Strategic Air Command and other nuclear air missions on alert — quite possibly as a means to excite the nation and create an aura of precariousness.

Another means of creating a sense of importance is to proclaim every new presidential action as a constitutional duty, as the nation's number-one priority, and as the right of every citizen. Whatever the content of his program and the direction of his commitments, the president can claim to be a reform leader dedicated to innovations and responsible change. Lyndon Johnson had a fondness that verged on a weakness for making nearly every novel social-reform idea that came along his major priority — until, of course, so many things were top priority that the very term was reduced to near meaninglessness. Also, presidential opponents can be confronted with stern and irreconcilable dichotomies; they can, for example, love the country or leave it, have peace with honor or peace with dishonor, support either prudent fiscal policy or budget-wrecking activities. Such simplistic pronouncements ensure good headlines, place the opposition on the defensive, and inhibit serious dialogue.

Also, a president can avoid dwelling on his mistakes — avoid any admission of them, if possible — and deny categorically that he ever was involved in any wrongdoing or mistaken endeavors. If necessary, he can shield himself behind national security and issue "no comment" statements rather than clarifications or further elaboration. A former administrative assistant to Franklin Roosevelt recalled an admonition by FDR to this then-young aide, who had suggested that some retraction or acknowledgment of error be released to the press: "My son, I've been involved in politics a very long time and I probably have made hundreds of mistakes, but I learned long ago *never* to talk about them!" [62] The lesson was clear: there is little incentive in politics to call attention to one's mistakes; whatever press space is available should be used to call attention to one's achievements.

President Carter tried, mostly in vain, to win support for his energy programs by calling our energy crisis "the moral equivalent of war." But a self-centered nation mostly looked the other way and failed to respond. Even a much watered down energy program took nearly two years to get through the Congress.

Claim to Be a Consensus Leader When the Polls Are Favorable and a Profile-in-Courage Leader When They Are Not. Presidents can attempt to prolong the presidential honeymoon as long as possible; after all, a president must replace partisan politics with consensus politics, be the leader for the entire country, and unite all factions. When the popularity ratings drop, he can emphasize that although he is the president of all the people, he has a special responsibility to represent the underrepresented or the badly represented. This is a convenient strategy, particularly when he is faced by a majority opposition against part of his legislative program. He can say that he represents the silent majority, the next generation, the minorities, the young, or the ill fed, and thereby become portrayed as a moral leader. He can claim he is doing what is right rather than what is popular or easy.

The prerogative of claiming moral considerations in making an unpopular decision is a well-established presidential tradition. Consider President Nixon's explanation of why he sent United States troops to Cambodia in the spring of 1970:

I have noted, for example, that a Republican Senator has said that this action I have taken means that my party has lost all chances of winning the November elections, and others are saying that this move against enemy sanctuaries will make me a one-term President. . . . I would rather be a one-term President and do what I believe is right than to be a two-term President at the cost of seeing America become a second-rate power and to see this nation accept the first defeat in its proud 190-year history.[63]

In the early years of his administration, Lyndon Johnson proudly walked around with assorted favorable polls stuffed in his pocket; their results were ever mentioned in his conversations to illustrate the virtues of his consensus strategy. As time wore on, public support and consensus politics diminished measurably and so, understandably, did Johnson's high evaluation of the polls. Later in his presidency Johnson took the tack that he was doing what was right even if he was hurt significantly in the polls: "In this job a man must set a standard to which he's working. In my case, it is what my grandchildren think when I'm buried out there under the tree on the ranch. I think they will be proud of two things. What I did for the Negro and seeing it through in Vietnam for all of Asia. The Negro cost me 15 points in the polls and Vietnam cost me 20." [64]

Travel Widely, Be a Statesman. Run for a Nobel Peace Prize, and Be Your Own Secretary of State. Consensus is easier to achieve on national defense and international peace aims than on the more divisive internal problems affecting the nation. Having achieved celebrity-number-one status at home, every president since Theodore Roosevelt has been mindful that no other prize is more cherished than a Nobel Prize for Peace. Lending one's name to a doctrine, as Monroe, Truman, and Eisenhower did, is most presidential. Thus, to make history's list of great presidents a president can first claim to be making the world safe for democracy and, second, making the American dollar safe for the world. He can appear to be an architect for a lasting peace and for generations of peace; as a statesman he can appear to be bipartisan and above politics. He can concentrate on foreign affairs with trips, summits, treaties, negotiations, and plans for generations of peace and still seem like an effective, or at least an adequate, president. Ford became so caught up in the new excitement of traveling here, there, and everywhere that party elder statesman Barry Goldwater had to admonish him by saying, "I think it would be a good thing for the country if President Ford put Air Force One in the hangar for at least eight months," implying that Ford should stay at home and begin realizing the real problems we have here.[65] After all Nixon's travels, Ford's peregrinations caused people to see through this presidential ploy of staying 35,000 feet above their problems.

Carter vowed that he would not travel as much as his predecessors and he limited himself to one trip abroad his first year. But soon he too was off to Latin America, Europe, and Asia, and he openly boasted of being the first president to visit a black African nation when he visited Nigeria in mid-1978. He seemed to especially enjoy having himself photographed as he jogged in Vienna, Korea, and elsewhere.

Don't Let the Vice President or Any Other Member of the Cabinet or White House Staff Upstage or Outshine You. A president can avoid party responsibilities and fund-raising activities by delegating these to his vice president, attorney general, or party officials. Highly partisan and divisive activities may be assigned routinely to the vice president to keep him busy, to ensure that his popularity does not outstrip the president's, and to demonstrate, by contrast, that the president is above politics. Johnson's use of Humphrey and Nixon's use of Agnew in these ways are illustrative, as were Nixon's difficulties in retaining such strong-willed cabinet members as Hickel, Connally, Richardson, and Peterson.

The president can also accentuate his role as symbolic leader: he can cater to the American passion for a benevolent father image or superhero. The PR script may even require him to own dogs, preferably several, and to attend church fairly regularly even if he has not in the past. One textbook finds it significant to mention that the president "usually attends church on Sunday." [66] Ceremonial activities and close association with entertainment and sports superstars, astronauts, and winners in high-visibility professions are major priorities. Charisma, at least for a while, can be manufactured, borrowed, and staged. But attractive politicians are to be kept out of the cabinet, off your staff, and always at camera-arm's length. Unretired politicians make questionable cheerleaders.

Claim Credit When Things Go Right and Decentralize Blame. Choose Problems for Their Potential Credit Value. President Kennedy knew the value of expropriating credit when policies worked and decentralizing blame when they did not. At the conclusion of some White House discussions for handling a complex foreign-policy problem, Kennedy cheerfully told some of the participants: "I hope this plan works. If it does, it will be another White House success. If it doesn't, it will be another State Department failure." [67] Nixon's classic statement in this regard was his assertion that he had the responsibility for Watergate but would not accept the blame.

Precisely because presidents prefer to be loved, not excoriated, their counselors are always under orders to find problems they can solve or at least appear to solve. Presidents can urge their staffs to concentrate on those programs that can get passed, on what they can do well, on those matters for which credit is obtainable.

Proclaim an Open Presidency and an Open Administration but Practice Presidency-by-Secrecy, Manage the News, and Circumvent the White House Press Corps. Presidents can hold numerous news conferences during their honeymoons and later, after the idyllic time period has ended, appeal directly to the people by direct address over the heads of the Washington press, especially when unkept promises or unresolved scandals can make news conferences embarrassing. So distrustful was Nixon of the press and press conferences that he held fewer news conferences than any president in forty years. He gained extensive prime-time exposure, perhaps more than any other president, but only when he had well-crafted speeches, messages, or emergency announcements. These, of course, were the labor of many minds and skilled public-relations counselors, not of a man standing alone before the uncertainties and hostile barbs of the prepared press. The news can be what the White House says it is. Presidents can generously say that press conferences will be held when they will serve the public interest, but the appropriate time for a press conference is always decided backstage by the White House public-relations executives.

The phrase "compelling reasons of national security" can always serve as a cloak of justification. Reliance on secrecy, however, can tempt presidents and their aides to conceal grievous mistakes, deviousness, and a host of other activities to account for which would be embarrassing. Vietnam, Watergate, the Cambodian bombings, and similar events speak eloquently to the point.

Some presidents, it seems, have thought that the best policy toward the White House press corps was to make them comfortable and leave them ignorant. As one political scientist summed it up: "Like the movie star [the political star] is known primarily through pictures on screens and billboards, voices from loudspeakers, anecdotes in newspapers and magazines. These are appearances, and, as such, they are subject to certain kinds of manipulation. Like the movie star, the politician has the possibility of becoming a mythical character. In both cases, also, the myth can be a managed one." [68]

History and Historians Reward Him Who Protects and Strengthens the Powers of the Presidency. According to this axiom, presidents should expand the executive powers and the executive office and leave the presidency a larger, more capable institution. They can always rationalize that even if such actions arouse controversy in the short run, posterity almost always praises such enlargements. Then, too, presidents are criticized if they are too weak, conciliatory, or seem to lack machismo. Lincoln, they may recall, is praised because he had the courage to violate one clause of the Constitution to preserve the rest. Of course, a president can try to defeat congressional measures that lessen presidential discretion. He can decry such efforts as reactionary and contrary to the spirit of strict construction of the Constitution. When doing so, he may recall that the Supreme Court invariably is more friendly to the presidency than to Congress.

If All Else Fails, Wage War on the Press, Impugn Its Objectivity, Undermine Confidence in Its Fairness and Integrity.   According to this part of the PR script, being president means never having to say you're sorry — or wrong. Any credibility problems are supposedly due to the press, not to the presidency. In fact, the press may also be responsible for hindering some projects that have not performed well or for sabotaging national security. Television, as "the" presidential medium, dramatizes the individual and can portray an individual's sense of stability and calm during emotional events and his sense of moral certitude in times of great confusion. When a president's popularity sags and when he is hedged in by Congress and the Supreme Court, television provides an obvious platform from which to dress up old platitudes in new slogans to proclaim bold initiatives. A dramatic new video performance can often resuscitate some of his former supporters. Nixon's team especially tried to manage the press, although nearly every president has tried to lessen its influence. According to his aides, Nixon was constantly ordering his staff to get this or that opponent. "On one occasion, Nixon wanted somebody brought in 'full-time' to 'destroy' the 'press' image, as if people like Colson and Buchanan were not doing enough of that already," writes one ex-Nixon staffer.[69]

Another twist to this Hollywood script is the maneuver of exposing it and campaigning — or seeming to campaign — against it. Fully understanding the publicity imperatives that make up the script, the shrewdest of presidents would write a profiles-in-courage kind of book to denigrate both the past uses and misuses of it and to denounce Machiavellianism and all its contemporary manifestations. But this presupposes not only that presidential candidates can appreciate fully all its implications, but also that if elected they could cope with the burdens of office without resorting to it themselves.

The danger of the textbook presidency and this "how-to-look presidential" script lies in its misplacement of values: in the subordination of policy substance to presidential style, in the subordination of doing what is right but controversial to postponement, ducking, or coverup. A president, elected for reasons often unrelated to his leadership capabilities, can engineer a public reputation quite inconsistent with his substantive performance as a leader, at least for a while. The selling of the presidential administration and its image can be as devious, if not more so, as the original selling of the presidential candidate. A president is pressured, on the one hand, by exaggerated expectations of what he can accomplish and, on the other, by a large, restless, and often overzealous public-relations machine. Too often, these script imperatives not only subordinate substance to style but also affect substance directly. The wrong people are hired for important White House counseling posts. The wrong people are asked for advice. Debates and multiple advocacy are thwarted. Telling the truth becomes dangerous. Manipulation becomes an end in itself, and a mindless confusion sets in about the proper ends and means.

Conclusions have been liberally sprinkled throughout this chapter. A combination of events, textbook treatment, and television amplification have left us with unrealistic expectations about the presidency. The presidency, an already impossible job, has become sometimes the sole focus of our hopes and aspirations as a nation. Presidents have in the end been led to "act," to fake and to mislead as they try to live up to the illusory notion that the right person in one job single-handedly can solve the nation's problems. Despite Watergate and Vietnam, much of the illusion endures. Some think it is too late to reverse the tide. The plea here, however, is that a more substantive and critical approach to the presidency would not only prepare our young with a more objective understanding of politics, leadership, and civic participation, it could also contribute to a more effective and healthy presidency.

NOTES

1. Fifteen introductory college texts on American government and another twenty more specialized studies of the presidency or national policymaking were examined, with special attention to the types of images, perception, and facts given about presidential performance. The case made in this section is merely illustrative; no claim of exhaustive quantitative analysis is implied.

2. David Easton and Jack Dennis, *Children in the Political System* (McGraw-Hill, 1969) and Fred I. Greenstein, *Children and Politics* (Yale University Press, 1965). Note that Watergate would have a definite negative effect on the way children regarded the president. A general loss of affection, respect, and esteem for the president became widespread and was well documented by several studies. See, for example, Harold M. Barger, "Demythologizing the Textbook President: Teaching about the President after Watergate," *Theory and Research in Social Education*, vol. 4, Aug. 1976, pp. 51–66; and F. Christopher Arterton, "Watergate and Children's Attitudes Toward Political Authority Revisited," *Political Science Quarterly*, Fall 1975, pp. 477–96.

3. See the discussion in Byron G. Massialas, *Education and the Political System* (Addison-Wesley, 1969), chap. 3.

4. Educational films about the presidency and recent presidents usually outdo even the texts in overstating and romanticizing presidential influence and greatness.

5. Robert Carr, Marver Bernstein, and Walter Murphy, *American Democracy in Theory and Practice*, 4th ed. (Holt, Rinehart and Winston, 1965), p. 447.

6. William A. McClenaghan, *Magruder's American Government* (Allyn and Bacon, 1962), p. 262.

7. Robert A. Dahl, *Pluralist Democracy in the United States* (Rand McNally, 1967), p. 90.

8. William H. Young, *Essentials of American Government,* 9th ed. (Appleton-Century-Crofts, 1964), p. 251.

9. Rowland Egger, *The President of the United States* (McGraw-Hill, 1967), p. 4.

10. James M. Burns, *Presidential Government* (Avon Books, 1965), pp. 326–27.

11. Theodore H. White, *The Making of the President 1960* (Pocket Books, 1961), p. 441.

12. Theodore H. White, "The Action Intellectuals," *Life,* 9 June 1967, pp. 43–76; 16 June 1967, pp. 44–74; 23 June 1967, pp. 76–85. For a later study that shatters such illusions see David Halberstam's *The Best and the Brightest* (Random House, 1972).

13. Clinton Rossiter, *The American Presidency,* rev. ed. (New American Library, 1960), pp. 17, 68–69, 84, 250.

14. *Ibid.,* p. 102.

15. Richard E. Neustadt, *Presidential Power* (Wiley & Sons, 1960). This pioneering analysis of New Deal and post–New Deal presidential performance had an important influence on political science. Neustadt's thesis that a leader's power hinged upon his capacity to persuade and that his capacity to persuade rested upon his image and reputation was provocative. Neustadt's optimism about the potential for effective presidential leadership, however, is more tempered in later writings, especially *Alliance Politics* (Columbia University Press, 1970). See also the assessment of his argument by Peter W. Sperlich, "Bargaining and Overload: An Essay on Presidential Power," in Aaron Wildavsky, ed., *The Presidency* (Little, Brown, 1969), pp. 168–92.

16. Burton P. Sapin, *The Making of United States Foreign Policy* (Brookings Institution, 1966), p. 90.

17. Erwin C. Hargrove, "Presidential Personality and Revisionist Views of the Presidency," *American Journal of Political Science,* November 1973, p. 826. See also Alexander L. George, "On Analyzing Presidents," *World Politics,* January 1974; Erwin Hargrove, *The Power of the Modern Presidency* (Random House, 1974); James David Barber, *The Presidential Character* (Prentice-Hall, 1972), p. 446. Also useful are articles by James David Barber, "Strategies for Understanding Politicians," *American Journal of Political Science,* Spring 1974, pp. 443–67; and Arthur Schlesinger, Jr., "Can Psychiatry Save the Republic?" *Saturday Review/World,* 7 September 1974, pp. 10–16.

18. Nelson A. Rockefeller, *Unity, Freedom and Peace* (Vintage, 1968), pp. 152–53.

19. Lyndon B. Johnson, *My Hope for America* (Random House, 1964), p. 14.

20. White, *The Making of the President 1960, op. cit.,* pp. 450–51.

21. Theodore H. White, *The Making of the President 1968* (Atheneum, 1969), p. 428.

22. Tom Wicker, remarks at a conference on the separation of powers, University of Texas, Austin, Texas, November 1977, transcript, pp. 109–10.

23. Arthur M. Schlesinger, Jr., "Congress and the Making of American Foreign Policy," *Foreign Affairs,* Fall 1972, pp. 94–95. See also his *The Imperial Presidency* (Houghton Mifflin, 1973).

24. Michael Novak, *Choosing Our King* (Macmillan, 1974), p. 5.

25. William H. Riker, *Democracy in the United States,* 2nd ed. (Macmillan, 1967), p. 188.

26. See, for example, Eugene McCarthy, "Thoughts on the Presidency," *New York Times,* 30 March 1968, editorial page.

27. Murray Edelman, *The Symbolic Uses of Politics* (University of Illinois Press, 1967), p. 78.

28. Hans J. Morgenthau, *The Purpose of American Politics* (Vintage, 1960). See also James Nathan, "The Roots of the Imperial Presidency: Public Opinion, Domestic Institutions, and Global Interests," *Presidential Studies Quarterly,* Winter 1975, pp. 63–74.

29. Herbert Emmerich, *Essays on Federal Reorganization* (University of Alabama Press, 1959), p. 62.

30. William E. Leuchtenberg, *Franklin D. Roosevelt and the New Deal* (Harper & Row, 1963), p. 327.

31. William G. Andrews, "The Presidency, Congress and Constitutional Theory," in Aaron Wildavsky, ed., *Perspectives on the Presidency* (Little, Brown, 1975), pp. 38-39.

32. James Sundquist, remarks at a conference on the separation of powers, University of Texas, Austin, Texas, November 1977, transcript, p. 72.

33. Robert D. Hess and David Easton, "The Child's Changing Image of the President," *Public Opinion Quarterly,* 24 (Winter 1960): 644.

34. Barry Jagoda, Carter media adviser, quote in Richard Reeves, "The Prime-Time President," *New York Times Magazine,* 15 May 1977, p. 17.

35. Newton Minow, *et al., Presidential Television* (Basic Books, 1973), Foreword, p. vii.

36. Anthony Howard, "No Time for Heroes," *Harper's,* February 1969, pp. 91–92.

37. Michael J. Robinson, "Television and American Politics: 1956–1976," *Public Interest* (Summer, 1977), p. 11.

38. Minow, *op. cit.,* p. 45. See also, in general, William C. Spragens, *The Presidency and the Mass Media in the Age of Television* (University Press of America, 1978).

39. William Safire, "Carter's Pills," *New York Times,* 24 July 1978, p. A17.

40. John Herbers, *No Thank You, Mr. President* (Norton, 1976), p. 75. He dedicates his volume to his colleagues on the White House beat "that they may find a way to separate imagery from substance, the phony from the real."

41. Novak, *op. cit.,* p. 259.

42. Bruce Miroff, "Monopolizing the Public Space: The Presidency as a Barrier to Democratic Politics" (Paper delivered at 1978 Annual Meeting of the Southwestern Political Science Association, Houston, Texas, April 1978), p. i.

43. *Ibid.,* p. 13.

44. George E. Reedy, *The Twilight of the Presidency* (World, 1970), pp. 14–15.

45. John Ehrlichman, quoted in *Time,* 30 July 1973, p. 17; Henry Kissinger, statement before the Senate Foreign Relations Committee, quoted in *Los Angeles Times,* 9 September 1973.

46. Daniel P. Moynihan, White House press release, December 21, 1970, p. 11.

47. See the useful elaboration of this point in Alexander L. George, "The Case for Multiple Advocacy in Making Foreign Policy," *American Political Science Review,* September 1972, pp. 762–63.

48. Statement by Egil Krogh, Jr., released by his attorney after he was sentenced in U.S. District Court for his role in the plumbers' break-in of the office of Daniel Ellsberg's psychiatrist, *New York Times,* 25 January 1974, p. 16.

49. H. R. Haldeman, with Joseph Di Mona, *The Ends of Power* (New York Times Books, 1978), pp. 324–25.

50. Richard Nixon, *Six Crises* (Pyramid Books, 1968), p. 366.

51. Malcolm MacDougall, "The Packaging of an (Ex) President — Wrap Well with Traditional Values," *Boston Globe,* 3 April 1977, p. A3. See also Vic Gold, *PR in President* (Doubleday, 1977).

52. Charles Kirbo, quoted in Kandy Stroud, *How Jimmy Won* (Morrow, 1977), p. 202.

53. Patrick H. Caddell, quoted in James T. Wooten, "Pre-Inaugural Memo Urged Carter to Stress Style Over Substance," *New York Times,* 4 May 1977, p. 1.

54. Stephen Hess, *Baltimore Sun,* 3 July 1978, p. A11.

55. George Gallup, *Opinion Polls* (Center for the Study of Democratic Institutions, 1962), p. 35.

56. Clark M. Clifford, quoted in Joseph Goulden, *The Superlawyers* (Dell, 1973), p. 86.

57. Aaron Wildavsky, "The Presidency in the Political System," in Wildavsky, ed., *Perspectives on the Presidency*, 2nd ed. (Little, Brown, 1975).

58. Lyndon B. Johnson, *The Vantage Point* (Holt, Rinehart and Winston, 1971), p. 155.

59. *Ibid.*, p. 157.

60. Ron Nessen, *It Sure Looks Different from the Inside* (Playboy Press, 1978), p. 165. See also Ford's own discussion of some of these incidents: Gerald R. Ford, *A Time to Heal* (Harper and Row/Reader's Digest, 1979).

61. Niccolo Machiavelli, *The Prince and the Discourses* (Modern Library, 1950), pp. 81–82.

62. Personal interview with James Rowe, October 1973.

63. Richard Nixon, quoted in the *New York Times*, 1 May 1971.

64. David Wise, "The Twilight of a President," *New York Times Magazine*, 3 November 1968, p. 131.

65. Quoted in an editorial, the *New York Times*, 14 December 1974.

66. See W. H. Hartley and W. S. Vincent, *American Civics* (Harcourt, Brace and World, 1971), p. 86.

67. John F. Kennedy, quoted in Harlan Cleveland, *The Future Executive* (Harper & Row, 1972), pp. 95–96.

68. Stanley Kelley, *Presidential Public Relations and Political Power* (Johns Hopkins University Press, 1956), p. 221.

69. Douglas Hallett, "A Low-Level Memoir of the Nixon White House," *New York Times Magazine*, 20 October 1974, p. 56. This view is also expressed in H. R. Haldeman, *op. cit.* For additional public-relations techniques and how public officials use them, see the account by one of Spiro Agnew's press secretaries: Vic Gold, *I Don't Need You When I'm Right: The Confessions of a Washington PR Man* (Morrow, 1975).

CHAPTER 4

PRESIDENTIAL POWER

Taken by and large, the history of the presidency is a history of aggrandizement, but the story is a highly discontinuous one. Of the thirty-three individuals who have filled the office not more than one in three has contributed to the development of its powers; under other incumbents things have either stood still or gone backward. That is to say, what the presidency is at any particular moment depends in important measure on who is President. . . .

> — Edwin S. Corwin, *The President: Office and Powers*
> (New York University Press, 1957), pp. 29–30.

In a relative but real sense one can say of a President what Eisenhower's first Secretary of Defense once said of General Motors: "What is good for the country is good for the President, and vice versa."

> — Richard E. Neustadt, *Presidential Power*
> (Wiley & Sons, 1960), p. 185.

What the country needs today is a little serious disrespect for the office of the Presidency; a refusal to give any more weight to a President's words than the intelligence of the utterance, if spoken by anyone else, would command; an understanding of a point made so aptly by Montaigne: "Sit he on never so high a throne, a man still sits on his bottom."

> — Arthur M. Schlesinger, Jr., *The Imperial Presidency*
> (Houghton Mifflin, 1973), p. 411.

All presidents are leased similar formal constitutional powers, but the amount of power of any one administration invariably exceeds the legal limits. The Founding Fathers arranged for an office broadly defined as well as vaguely outlined. The power granted, they felt, should be a broadly discretionary residual power available when other governmental branches failed to meet their responsibilities or failed to respond to the urgencies of the day.

As Edward S. Corwin and the best of our writers on the American presidency have never ceased to point out, there is a plasticity in our fundamental conception of the presidency and its powers.[1] The exact dimensions of executive power at any given moment is largely the consequence of the incumbent's character and energy combined with the overarching needs of the day, the challenges to system survival and regeneration. Some presidents have been power maximizers. The Jacksons, Lincolns and Roosevelts are illustrative. Certain of them became shrewd party leaders. Some saw themselves as direct agents of the American people, as the people's choice with mandates to carry out in exchange for the grant of powers. Still others employed the "take care that the laws be faithfully executed" clause of the Constitution to broaden the notion of executive power well beyond the boundaries envisioned by most of the framers of the Constitution. Plainly, an office underdefined on paper became enlarged with accumulated traditions and with the cumulative legacy of some often brilliant achievements.

Tocqueville rightly observed that if executive power was weaker in the United States than in European countries (in the early 1800s), the reason for this was more in circumstances than in laws. He added that "it is generally in its relations with foreign powers that the executive power of a nation has the chance to display skill and strength."[2] If the United States had remained a small nation, isolated and removed from the other nations of the world, the role of the executive would doubtless have remained weak, certainly much weaker than the presidency we have come to know in the late twentieth century. Just the opposite has been the case, of course. Had the presidential office been incapable of expanding, the nation may well not have survived. Presidential powers and presidential leadership have been essential for both progress and stability.

One of the more persisting of presidential paradoxes from the standpoint of presidents is the realization that there is much less power there, however defined, than the candidates had thought when they ran for the office. Lyndon Johnson did his best to pyramid available power resources to the office soon after he found himself there. But he never stopped complaining that his responsibilities always exceeded his powers. Thus it is not surprising that although LBJ did not have much advice for his successor, he did have this notable caution or warning:

Before you get to be president you think you can do anything. You think you're the most powerful leader since God. But when you get in that tall chair, as you're gonna find out, Mr. President, you can't count on people. You'll find your hands tied and people cussin' you. The office is kinda like the little country boy found the hoochie-koochie show at the carnival, once he'd paid his dime and got inside the tent: "It ain't exactly as it was advertised." [3]

Richard Neustadt's celebrated *Presidential Power,* first published in 1960, has studied this same problem in detail. His work is a veritable manual of personal power: how to get it, how to keep it, and how to use it. James Reston called it the nearest thing America has to Machiavelli's *The Prince.* Presidents Kennedy and Johnson were influenced by the Neustadt work. Kennedy studied it carefully and employed Neustadt as as a consultant on staffing and varied policy questions. Johnson almost naturally seemed to conduct himself according to the Neustadt power principles, even more so than Kennedy.

In 1976 Neustadt's book was reissued, with an afterword essay on JFK, written earlier, and a lengthy introductory essay entitled "Reflections on Johnson and Nixon." [4] In the new edition and supplement Neustadt assesses how the often traumatic Johnson and Nixon experiences have influenced the presidency. He also clarifies and amends and offers some second thoughts on his well-known generalizations about the sources and strategies of effective presidential leadership.

The publication of Neustadt's new edition provides a good opportunity to review and reappraise his widely praised model of presidential effectiveness. How does it stand up in the aftermath of Vietnam, Watergate, and the Ford and Carter experiences? Have the intervening years validated or undermined his basic premises? Where do we stand now in our attitudes about presidential power?

CONCEPTIONS OF PRESIDENTIAL POWER

Presidential Power was hailed in the early 1960s as a brilliant and pioneering contribution to our understanding of the operational realities of presidential leadership. It was widely read then and it remains widely read today, especially in courses on the presidency around the country.

What accounts for its reception? It broke away from the traditional emphasis on leadership traits, the compartmentalized listings of functional tasks, and the then dominant tendency to study the presidency in legal or constitutional terms. Instead, Neustadt used organizational and administrative behavior as frames of reference for the study of what a president must do if he wants to influence events and why and how presidents so often lose the ability to influence. His stress was on the *shared* powers of the office rather than the separation of powers. He emphasized the reciprocal character of influence, the constant personal calculations and trade-offs that motivate people to cooperate or not to cooperate with presidential initiatives.

The message of the 1960 book is that the presidency is neither as powerful as many people thought nor should its strengthening be feared as many others believed. Neustadt called upon future presidents to acquire as much power as they could, for he noted that the formal institutional powers were fragile, alas, even puny, compared to the responsibilities.

The overriding theme is that presidential power is the power to persuade, and the power to persuade comes through bargaining. Bargaining, in turn, comes primarily through getting others to feel that it is in their own self-interest to cooperate. The president is depicted as being constantly challenged by threats to his power and constantly needing to enhance his reputation as a shrewd bargainer, in fact, as one operating an entrepreneurial "do-it-yourself" business. Tenacity and proper timing were also essential.

Neustadt viewed Franklin D. Roosevelt as the many splendored prototype. Roosevelt had that rare combination of self-confidence, ambition, political experience, sense of purpose, and Neustadt's elusive term "sensitivity to power" that was necessary to harness formal authority with effective personal performance and thus make the presidency work. Roosevelt had absolutely no problems, Neustadt tells us, of acting presidential and seizing for his personal use all the latent resources that could be squeezed out of the office. "Roosevelt had a love affair with power in that place. It was an early romance and it lasted all his life." [5] "[H]e saw the job of being President as being FDR." [6] "Roosevelt always knew what power was and always wanted it." [7] In short, Roosevelt had the will to power, the driving ambition and uncommon sense of knowing how to deal with people — and these combined almost always to leave him in the driver's seat.

Neustadt was especially impressed with the way Roosevelt juggled assignments, kept people guessing, put men of clashing temperaments, outlooks, and ideas in charge of his major projects. FDR loved dividing authority and keeping his organizations temporary and overlapping. To some people this might have been the art of manipulation, but to Neustadt it was the essence of leadership. Sixteen years later, Roosevelt remains the Neustadt model, particularly the robust, playful Roosevelt temperament: "Roosevelt's sense of fun combined with Roosevelt's sort of confidence remain for me what they were . . . : a target at which to aim." [8]

In his 1960 treatise, Neustadt, in effect, rates FDR as a great president. President Truman, with whom Neustadt had worked in the White House, is rated a *good* president, but by no means an equal to Roosevelt. To be sure, Truman loved to make decisions, but he lacked "bureaucratic feel," he lacked FDR's sense of timing, and he was instinctively just a judge, whereas FDR had been instinctively an aggressive intelligence operative. "Truman's sensitivity to power was no match for his predecessor's. Truman's past experiences had been less relevant and lacked Roosevelt's instinct for the uses of Executive power." [9] And "the help that Truman gave himself in calculating power status was help of an uneven sort; his power sense was equally uneven. His methods in the Presidency brought him into contact with details and with decisions more consistently than Eisenhower, but the timing of these contacts was not on a par with Roosevelt's from the standpoint of protecting personal power." [10]

President Eisenhower gets low marks in the 1960 book; *fair,* or perhaps *poor,* but not what we want in the White House. Neustadt quotes approvingly Speaker Sam Rayburn's description of Eisenhower, "good man, wrong profession." We are told that Eisenhower's self-image was that of the good man above politics. He disdained politics and felt the presidency was, or ought to be, the source of a unifying, moderating influence above the struggle, and hence, above the pulling and hauling and bureaucratic political infighting. Neustadt holds up the Eisenhower presidency as a model of how-not-to-succeed. Eisenhower's strategies were almost literally the opposite of those employed in Roosevelt's presidency, says Neustadt. "Eisenhower often was reported in the press to have transformed the White House into an Army Headquarters. That he did not do — nobody could — but he did manage to impart more superficial symmetry and order to his flow of information and of choices than was ever done before. Thereby, he became typically the last man in his office to know tangible details and the last to come to grips with acts of choice. . . . [The staff systems] workings often were disastrous for his hold on personal power." [11] In short, Eisenhower's conduct often rendered him a helpless prisoner of the office, "a sort of Roosevelt in reverse." [12]

Professor Neustadt's book is sometimes described as an impressionistic account. This is unfair. For Neustadt's closely reasoned analysis, based on his own participant observations, extensive interviews, and a close reading of available diaries and memoirs, is replete with rich empirical propositions, many of which taken as a whole approximate an exchange theory of influence relationships.

There was a widespread agreement among political scientists in the early and middle 1960s that Neustadt's analytical treatment of presidential power was a perceptive and astute description of how to strengthen the hand of a president one liked. Neustadt's propositions made sense to most people. Here is a list of several of them, slightly rephrased:

1. To be a leader, a president must have a will for power. If he lacks a consuming hunger for power and a penchant for shrewdly handling people, then he is not fit for the office.

2. The skill of a president at winning others over to his support is the necessary energizing factor to get the institutions of the national government into action. He and only he supplies the agenda for action for the Washington political community.

3. A president cannot be an introvert, or above the battle, or above politics, or simply work from within the confines of his own ideas; a sensitivity to the thoughts and feelings of others and an ability to create solutions that compromise contesting points of view are what distinguishes effective leadership from nonleadership.

4. The members of Congress act the way they think they have to in order to get reelected and to "look good." A president's job is to get congressmen and other influential members of the government community to think his requests are in their own best interests.

5. A president has to ride events and crises to gain attention. Most Americans grow attentive only as they grow directly concerned with what may happen in their lives.

6. A president should never rely on others to determine his power stakes. He should be his own intelligence officer, his own expert on crucial power relationships. Moreover, he should be concerned with details, gossip, and the intricacies of human sensitivities. A president who delegates the job of being chief politician to others is a president who will not exercise much influence.

7. The lesson from case experiences is that when it comes to power, nobody is expert but a president, and if he too acts as a layman it will be fatal.

8. Popularity and public prestige produce favorable credit for a president among the professional Washington community. But public disapproval heightens and encourages resistance from the Washington community (defined as members of Congress, bureaucrats, the press, governors, diplomats, etc.).

9. Presidential power is not easy to come by and even the most skillful of presidents will have to get by catch-as-catch-can, always sensitive to the need for multiple channels of information, always frugal in using power resources to get his way, and always employing the art of persuasion in a bargaining situation, thereby avoiding at almost all costs the direct issuing of a confrontational command.

Thus, *Presidential Power* held out hope that a shrewd and artfully manipulative leader could and would be a powerful Hamiltonian engine of change. An aggressive, ambitious politician, determined to get his way and ever distrustful of the motives of others, seemed to be the remedy for the post-Eisenhower years. The foremost problem of the presidency in the late 1950s, or so most people believed, Neustadt concluded, was how the presidency could regain control over the drifting Washington policy apparatus. Forceful leadership was needed and *only* the president could fill the leadership vacuum.

In retrospect, Neustadt's greatest contribution to the understanding of the presidency is his notion that the power of a president rests ultimately on his ability to persuade others. Because a president shares authority with other institutions, he cannot merely command. Rather he must constantly bargain and trade in an effort to gain his ends. Thus, he argued, don't study the institution of the presidency or its formal powers as ends in themselves; seek instead to understand how these are used to enhance the personal power of individual presidents, and thus their success as leaders and policymakers. This was wise advice. This alone assures Neustadt's analysis a very special place in our ever-expanding shelf of presidency studies.

PRESIDENTIAL POWER RECONSIDERED

Sixteen years later, in 1976, Professor Neustadt published a calm, mostly untroubled set of reflections on the post-Eisenhower presidency. In spite of the many abuses of presidential power in the Johnson and Nixon years, Neustadt argues that his earlier conclusions are basically still valid. Yes, there have been some changes in the arena within which a president must seek power, and he offers a few reinterpretations and amendments to his earlier views. However, in a very real sense we are informed that, at least concerning presidential power, the more things change, the more they stay the same. Early in these reflections Neustadt makes this plain:

> Since April 1960, when *Presidential Power* first came out, there have been events aplenty, not alone Vietnam and Watergate, but assassinations, riots, inflation, recession, even a nuclear confrontation, to say nothing of changes in our world relationships, political *and* economic. Still, these do not appear to have altered very much the general character of presidential power. Nor do they disclose to me a likely shift of central role from President to Congress or the courts, or elsewhere, of the sort that Wilson found emergent in a turn from Congress to the Presidency.[13]

Neustadt does discuss various changes that have at least marginally affected presidential power. Most of these tend to work toward isolating the president from people on the one hand and increasing a president's discretion on the other. Thus, the tightening of a president's appointment schedule and the growth of television as a means of one-way communication on the president's terms tend to isolate the White House occupant. Another difference, perceptively noted by Neustadt, with respect to the cabinet is not merely the infrequent meetings in the Kennedy-Nixon era or the decline in status, but rather that, in Truman's time, a cabinet member had a *right* to see the president, whereas by Ford's time, this had become a *privilege* to be granted or withdrawn according to the presidential mood at the time.

One of the few changes that Neustadt notes, which brings the American people into the policymaking arena on a broader scale, is the idea of legitimacy, the feeling that if a significant number of people question a president's behavior, they are likely to resist his bargaining and perhaps even undermine his claim to leadership.

Perhaps most noteworthy in these new reflections are his amendments to his 1960 interpretations and his explanations of Johnson and Nixon. He now feels that Eisenhower's concern with his own and his office's prestige, and hence credibility, was a more impressive contribution to the presidency than had been previously credited to him. It had been difficult for Neustadt as a young, liberal, Democratic professor to accept Eisenhower's low-profile leadership. An older Neustadt, comparing Eisenhower to Johnson and Nixon rather than to FDR, now writes that Ike's shunning of controversy and his conscious enhancing of the presidency's legitimacy were eminently sensible in that they added to Ike's potential to govern. Although he does not really develop this point, it may be that an older Neustadt now realizes, as we all do after the 1960s and 1970s, that presidents should be measured not only by what they do but also by what they do not do. Eisenhower's refusal to be drawn into Indochina is illustrative.

Elsewhere Neustadt acknowledges that his emphasis on the need for experienced politicians of "extraordinary temperament" in his 1960 study was "singularly unhelpful." He now says it is the quality not the quantity of prior political experience that counts. Beware the insecure, driven candidate. Drive is needed, but carefully distinguish *drive* from *drivenness*. The former is a necessity, the latter may be fatal. Neustadt says of Johnson and Nixon: "Each man was a driving man and driven, tending to excess, compulsive in seeking control, taking frustration hard." [14] But is this a useful distinction, prospectively? For example, neither Lyndon Johnson in 1960 nor Richard Nixon in 1960 or in 1968 appeared excessively driven. Indeed Johnson often seemed reluctant about running for president. On the other hand, many analysts said that Jimmy Carter in 1976 was the most driven presidential candidate they had ever observed. Many added, too, that these days it seems as if anyone lacking such all-consuming ambition is not likely to get there. Yet, once in the White House, Carter did not evidence this rigidity or drivenness. At times he seemed even deficient in this category.

On the matter of experienced politicians, it is obvious that both Nixon and Johnson epitomized this description. In addition, however,

Buchanan, Arthur, McKinley, Coolidge, and Gerald Ford were all veterans in the art of politics, yet none of them was able to provide effective presidential leadership. This is not to say we can begin to look elsewhere — outside the career of politics — for our future presidents. It is merely to underscore that being an experienced politician is at best a desirable characteristic for a would-be president, but hardly a sufficient one.

Neustadt admires the pioneering work of James David Barber and although he does not accept Barber's typology he clearly joins Barber and others who urge us to examine more carefully the political and managerial experiences of presidential candidates.[15] He says, for example, look carefully to see whether presidential candidates enjoyed their earlier political responsibilities and were "at ease" with them, and whether there was an "enjoyment of one's self," a capacity to laugh at themselves and avoid taking themselves too seriously. Again on Johnson and Nixon: "Perspective is precisely what those others lacked. Their solemnity about themselves was of a piece with their intensely personal reactions to frustrations."[16]

Further, Neustadt appears to criticize Johnson and Nixon for attempting to amass too much power. Maximizing power, he suggests now, cannot be a president's sole criterion for choices. There had been little in his 1960 version to anticipate this. In terms of power as a source of clues to policy, we are told that for both Johnson and Nixon, the short-run tangibles seem to have overshadowed long-run risks. Their sensitivity to their power stakes simply didn't work for them. Johnson chose to gamble that the maximum duration of the Vietnam War would be the two-and-a-half-year figure some of his aides passed along to him. Nixon, similarly, was woefully inexpert in distinguishing the crucial from the irritating. Nixon also was inexpert in distinguishing the implications over time from effects of the moment. Says Neustadt: the 1960 discussion of power stakes is still valid but "not nearly as helpful as I once had hoped."[17]

What to do now? Neustadt suggests a process of "backward mapping" whereby a president would consider his desired outcome and backtrack from there, determining how he arrived at each successive step. Specifically, the author advises us that Lyndon Johnson would have discovered, among other things, that the massive bombing of Hanoi would not achieve his desired end. Maybe so, but this notion of backward mapping comes close to the old and usually unrealistic admonition to practice rational-man decision-making calculations.

Neustadt now also admits that he underestimated the negative influence of palace-guard loyalty on a president's power stakes. He laments the fact that several recent presidents have allowed a swelling of the presidency. Thus, Nixon's White House aides put the whole elaborate center of their system in the White House, attracting vast amounts of second-string activity, and at the same time tried to spare Nixon the details. Thinking they were doing him a service, they were in practice helping to do him in. Roosevelt still provides the model, says Neustadt. "For Roosevelt, the President was not the Presidency, both ought to be staffed, the President should weigh advice from both. He sought advice as well from everybody else that he could get his hands on. . . . Roosevelt never thought that staffs had a monopoly on judgment or on information either." [18]

Ultimately, Neustadt holds firmly to most of his 1960 views. Presidents still share most of their authority with others and are no more free today to rule by sheer command. "Persuasion in a sense akin to bargaining remains for major purposes the order of his day." [19] Despite Watergate and Vietnam and the so-called reassertion of Congress, the presidency's advantages as a leadership institution have not suffered. Congress, cabinet, party leaders, the establishment, and others need him rather more than he needs them. Indeed, writes Neustadt, they are less colleagues today than customers, to whom he has to sell more than consult.

But the gap between presidential responsibility and capability is an ever-widening one. Neustadt bemoans the post-Watergate outpouring of proposed legislation that would make a bad president weak because it would enfeeble the good presidents as well. He dismisses the idea that we could succeed for long in lowering our expectations of the office. He believes in the inevitability of high expectations.

He closes his 1976 reflections with a few ideas whereby public support for presidents might be enhanced and stabilized. One suggestion calls for a president who will master the medium of television and utilize it to mobilize suburbanites and public-interest groups across the country. Kennedy was the precursor. The new master of the medium would fashion not a "party" or a "movement" but a league of followers who could help provide the support a president badly needs to govern. Both Presidents Ford and Carter found it difficult to follow this advice. Perhaps, however, a Reagan presidency could have risen to the challenge of public communication.

Neustadt's final suggestion is a strengthened party leadership in Congress as a basis for restoring and enlarging "the collegial relationship downtown." Neustadt relishes the notion of a link between the powers of the president and those of the House Speaker. "When we find a President who handles television as well as TR did the press, let us encourage him to try to put his friends in Congress, and encourage them to try to build a leadership he cannot help but hear." [20] His suggestion about presidents' involving themselves at the primary stage of the congressional nomination process will strike most political analysts as being highly questionable from a practical standpoint, no matter how desirable that idea may be in theory. Neustadt here seems to ignore the fact that incumbency in congressional elections has become so powerful that there is relatively little a president can do to affect who gets elected to Congress. Moreover, it would appear that congressional elections have increasingly little to do with national issues and presidential politics.[21]

An attempt to sketch his model of presidential leadership is provided in Figure 4.1, taking both the 1960 and 1976 variables into account. Readers will doubtless have their own variations on this sketch, which is presented here more to encourage efforts to map out the Neustadt model than to suggest this as definitive.

Unresolved Questions

What of the problems and confusion raised by *Presidential Power*? Have they been addressed well enough in these 1976 reflections? What of the book's worth today as a guide to understanding the American presidency and the politics of leadership?

Perhaps the most frequent complaint about the 1960 study was that it seemed too preoccupied with the will to power, the acquisition of power, and increasing power, divorced from any discussion of the purposes to which power should be put. Such extraordinary emphasis on means without any clear discussion of ends left the impression that the art of leadership is the art of manipulation. Neustadt was faulted too for his failure to emphasize the role that a "sense of direction" plays in presidential leadership, and how a president would call upon or consider ideological values in his power exchanges.

One critic went so far as to suggest that Neustadt "baptizes" political ambition just as Dale Carnegie and kindred self-help manuals baptize greed. Does power tend to purify, and absolute power to purify absolutely? Many of his readers would have liked a more thoughtful discussion of the ends of presidential power, of the ethical boundaries. What are the higher claims on a president and how does the creative president join together the ethic of responsibility and the ethic of ultimate ends?

Neustadt's prime objective is to examine a president's capability as a seeker and wielder of influence, influence of a president upon others involved in the governing process. His analysis implies it is wise, indeed necessary, for a president to build up a vast reserve of power. No doubt Neustadt was trying to steer away from having to make value judgments about the content and consequences of presidential power. But his concentration and emphasis on the acquisition of power left him open to the charge that certain presidential activities that might look like "effective leadership" according to Neustadt were merely actions of a blatant power grab quite unrelated to substantive policy leadership.

Put another way, Neustadt's methodology "does not allow political science to distinguish between the use and the abuse of Presidential power.[22] He made little claim beyond that, although he does suggest that a president's sensitivity to the means of power had a good deal to do

FIGURE 4.1
NEUSTADT'S MODEL OF PRESIDENTIAL LEADERSHIP
(WITH 1976 AMENDMENTS)

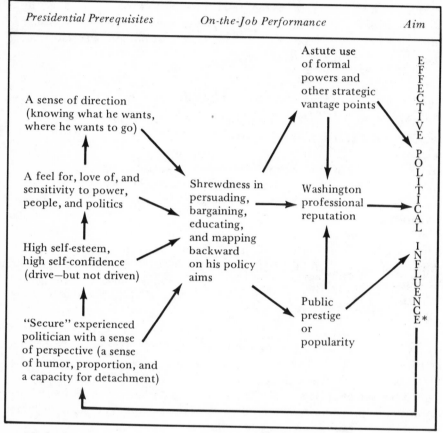

Presidential Prerequisites   *On-the-Job Performance*   *Aim*

* Defined as the capacity to get power and use it to have his views felt and to allow his views to succeed in the framing and implementation of public policy.

with "viable" public policy. To some people, this seems as if in Neustadt's terms, public purpose *is* linked directly to presidential power. In any event, he does not apologize for this focus (nor for this implicit theory of political and social change). Certainly he does not try to broaden it in his 1976 essay.

John Hart notes that the passage of the Tonkin Gulf Resolution in 1964 would show, according to Neustadt's frame of reference, President Johnson as an effective wielder of influence; that the action led to a disastrous Vietnam War policy is irrelevant. "Johnson would rate highly on Neustadt's scale insofar as this episode was concerned." [23] Examples of influence seeking and even influence wielding are Nixon's extensive policy impoundments and his efforts to centralize more administrative authority at the White House level, but they are not now viewed as acceptable presidential leadership.

Neustadt, however, chose to write primarily, perhaps even exclusively, about the means of leadership. He made little claim beyond that. He does not apologize for this focus, nor does he try to broaden it in his 1976 essay. This will not quiet certain critics. They will, and with some reason, contend the analysis and discussion of power devoid of content is a shallow, even an empty, exercise. In Neustadt's defense it can be said the ends were, and perhaps still remain, implicitly embedded in the liberal vision of the 1960s.

A second criticism of Neustadt's book was that it is too worshipful of presidential power. It seems to say: Find the right president and teach him what power is all about and progress will be realized. It portrays presidents as potential saviors. If only we had the Second Coming of Franklin Roosevelt, all would be well! It comes close to suggesting we need a "Big-Daddy" figure on whom to lean to make the system work. Further, the book speaks almost exclusively about the Washington political community and makes little or no reference to the people's role or to social movements.

Two problems arise from this emphasis on FDR and on presidents as the answer to our needs. First, Neustadt fails to take into account the degree to which presidents are almost invariably stabilizers or protectors of the status quo rather than agents of redistribution or progressive change. Neustadt gives little attention to the way the prevailing American elite values, or ideology, severely limit a president's freedom. Bruce Miroff wrestles with some alternative interpretations in his *Pragmatic Illusions: The Presidential Politics of John F. Kennedy*.[24] One gets the impression from reading Neustadt that he thinks that a president can roam at will, providing he is shrewd enough to be able to persuade others that their interests are the same as his. In fact, however, all of our presidents have had to prove their political orthodoxy and their acceptability to a wide array of established powers, especially corporate leaders, entrenched interest-group leaders, and so on. Thus, Neustadt raises countless hopes that the presidency will be an instrument for the progressive transformation of American politics. (Neustadt apparently sees no other alternative.) This complaint is a provocative one and it will doubtless be a lasting one.

The plight of the president in the special-interest state is of course one of the reasons Neustadt is on the side of the presidency as opposed to other forces in American life. President Carter, whom many people hoped would be sufficiently fresh and sufficiently unburdened by campaign debts and the traditional ways of doing business in Washington, fell prey to the tenacious pressure groups. Carter expressed his plight this way:

Almost every pressure that I feel on me as President that leads to later inflation comes from a very fine group of people — those who want to build weapons, those who want to build highways, farmers, educators, veterans, and others — all have demands upon the Federal Government that are legitimate. But when you add them all together, it creates an almost impossible financial circumstance, and the budget deficits increase because very fine people press for special attention to their problem which is very costly.[25]

The point is that a president's options are necessarily limited, if not by the accommodations he makes to get elected, then by the accommodations he makes to get reelected or to keep his party or friends in power.

Just how much and how often can we turn to the White House and hope that a benevolent and bright president will provide truly inspired leadership? Sometimes we must turn there, but a reading of history suggests that breakthroughs and leadership often come from the bottom (or at least the middle) up. Civil-rights workers, consumer organizers, women's rights activists, environmental protectionists, tax-revolt champions, and antiwar protestors are illustrative of the catalysts that more often than not bring about policy change in the United States. John W. Gardner, himself a citizen-activist, cautions that "crusading citizens' groups may not always be wise, as witness the Prohibitionists. Or they may be wise but unsuccessful in persuading their fellow citizens. For every citizens' group that changes the course of history, there are thousands . . . that never create a ripple." [26]

In Neustadt's defense it can be said that although the book is often a hymn of praise for FDR, the author really doesn't go so far as to say: defer completely to your president and trust him. He appears instead, at least most of the time, to say that without a good engineer the train just won't go.

There is, however, an undeniable elitist cast to Neustadt's formulation. There is an implicit, if not explicit, fear of the masses juxtaposed with a robust faith in the great leader. This was, of course, a prevailing and accepted view among most academics at the time Neustadt wrote. Roosevelt may have been a grand manipulator and sometimes deceptive as well, but wasn't this increasingly necessary? Leaders need a free hand. It was as if Roosevelt on occasion deceived people, including the American people, much as the physician who lies to the patient "for the patient's own good." Walter Lippmann, George Kennan, Hans Morganthau, and others had previously and often eloquently argued a similar case. What was needed was an activist helmsman to define the national interest, to subdue or avoid the passions of the electorate and the parochialisms of the special-interest groups and Congress. Look to your presidents for leadership, for in Lippmann's oft-quoted words, "The unhappy truth is that the prevailing public opinion has been destructively wrong at the critical junctures."

In a way, Neustadt's book was the culmination of revisionist thinking in the 1950s. The populist identification of the 1930s had been rejected. Intellectuals were reassessing the romantic aspects of the populist heritage. No one has captured this reversal in intellectual trends as well as C. Vann Woodward:

> Disenchantment of the intellectual with the masses was well under way in the forties. Mass support for evil causes in Germany and elsewhere helped to undermine the faith. The liberal's feelings of guilt and impotence were reflected in the interest that the writings of Sören Kierkegaard and Reinhold Niebuhr aroused, and the mood of self-flagellation was expressed in the vogue of the novels of Franz Kafka and George Orwell. The shock of the encounter with McCarthyism sustained and intensified the mood. Liberals and intellectuals bore the brunt of the McCarthyite assault on standards of decency. They were rightly alarmed and felt themselves betrayed. They were the victims of a perversion of the democracy to which they now guiltily realized they had too often turned a blind or indulgent eye. Stung by consciousness of their own naiveté, they responded with a healthy impulse to make up for lost time. . . .[27]

The writings of these intellectuals, surprisingly, are not discussed in the Neustadt book, but their theories and themes were in high fashion during the years Neustadt was preparing his treatise. He was doubtless unconsciously steeped in this new realism, this new orthodoxy about leaders and the led.

Neustadt was influenced by this tradition just as this tradition would be reinforced by him. The message is plain: the whole system revolves around an activist, persuasive president who knows how to avoid the pitfalls and the sand traps of the Washington obstacle course. Neustadt believes this still. Presidential power is as contigent, as uncertain, as tenuous as ever. The press, the attentive public, or a mindless Congress can too easily do enormous harm to a president's ambitions. Do not, Neustadt tells us, worry too much about an imperial presidency. Do not weaken the powers of the presidency. In Watergate and Vietnam we witnessed the *abuse* of power, not an *excess* of power. The absence or weakness of power can also corrupt.

In June 1978 Neustadt was asked why the disillusionment in our national leaders was so great. He began by saying Americans expect too much of their presidents. He added this was a bad time to be president. He suggested too that the times often make the leader or at least make us more respectful of a leader.

> It will continue to be a bad time until events that aren't very controllable conspire to create a background against which Carter's strong points come into sharp focus. . . . This negative mood probably will last until there is a new conjunction of personalities and events that does what FDR in the Depression did. . . .

Our perception of good leadership depends enormously on the time. One can't imagine Lincoln doing well in the 1870s, say, or the 1840s. What you need is a conjunction of man and circumstances.[28]

The Neustadt injunction that power-maximizing individuals are necessary if we want the presidency to function properly is now questioned in some quarters. For example, a theme in Henry Fairlie's provocative, if overstated, *The Kennedy Promise* is that Americans who were once so sure that strong leadership (of the Neustadt type) was necessarily wholesome leadership no longer hold that belief as axiomatic.[29] Fairlie has nice words for FDR, but he saves most of his applause for Eisenhower. James David Barber's notable study of presidential character is another attempt to amend the Neustadt formula. He concludes, for example, that a strong power-maximizing president is not automatically a good president. Barber, of course, had the Johnson experience much in mind. But he broadened his account and his scope and in the end he urges us to look at much more than just an individual's power-maximizing qualities. Thus, he says, look at whether a would-be president is result-oriented, does he actively shape his environment, or is he passively made by it? But also ask: Is his effort in life and in politics a burden to be endured or an opportunity for personal enjoyment?[30] Barber's analysis extends and clarifies certain themes, which were underdeveloped or even misleading in *Presidential Power.* Doris Kearns's book on Lyndon Johnson attempts to blend the Neustadt and Barber perspectives for a richer understanding of an undeniably complex president.[31] New research on the Eisenhower presidency also challenges certain aspects of Neustadt's criticism of Ike.[32]

Another body of post-Neustadt research stresses that however important the president may be, he is not the only person critically involved in the nation's policymaking processes. Neustadt of course recognized this. But he sometimes wrote as if the primary thing that mattered was how the president could control and dominate the others — the advisory circles and so on — at the upper reaches of the government. This was an unfortunate impression to leave, for plainly political science has an obligation to think and write also about the quality of the policymaking process as a whole and not to just assume that what is wholesome for a president will necessarily be good or in the best interests of a thoughtful policy-formulation process. I do not think it was Neustadt's intent to leave this impression. Rather, his near-exclusive concentration on how to help presidents help themselves caused this impression of indifference to the advisory process. Fortunately, several scholars have looked beyond the president and explored ways in which the country might be better served by alterations in how a president obtains and processes advice and information.[33]

Some readers will be disappointed by Neustadt's explanation of Lyndon Johnson's failings in his Vietnam War leadership. There are those, for example, who will say that how a president behaves and acts in office depends not only on his character (on what is in him, i.e., his fears and insecurities, etc.) and his feel for power but also and perhaps even especially *on what others expect him to do.* To be more specific, there are many analysts who contend that our tragic participation in Vietnam was neither a mistake nor a series of miscalculated gambles. No, Vietnam was a presidential war that arose almost inevitably out of this nation's commitment to South Vietnam that went back at least to 1949. The key question was not why Johnson failed but why this commitment was made and reaffirmed and expanded by a succession of five postwar American presidents.[34] The root causes of this presidential commitment and America's unusual grant to the post–World War II presidency to command the national security establishment and rule "the free world" are not given the attention they cry out for in these reflections on Johnson and Nixon. Then again, these are only reflections, an addendum to an earlier book, and not a major treatise on the Johnson and Nixon period. But it seems clear that much of what a president does or does not do is shaped significantly by such compelling factors as a nation's economic needs, its domestic politics, the prevailing climate of public opinion, prevailing elite values, ideology, and so on, quite apart from a president's sensitivity to his power stakes or his capacity to persuade. (Of course, Neustadt did talk somewhat about policy expectations being a major constraint on the presidency.)

Ultimately Neustadt is a realist. For those who cherish more open and more participatory forms of governmental arrangements and for those who like to view Congress as the *people's branch*, the *seat* of republican government, and the agency of *popular action*, his message is unpleasant — at times even chilling. He knows that so much depends on clever leadership in the White House. He knows, too, how to help those presidents whom we want to succeed, although ironically his analysis and prescriptions are just as available to those presidents we wish to constrain. His optimism about the presidency may be a bit too comforting. Thus he dwells in his discussions of Nixon and Johnson on *their* deficiencies as men and seldom on the possibility that the presidency itself or our political arrangements could have contributed to each man's downfall. We need more attention to the persistence of the conditions that encouraged the imperial presidency. Have that many things changed in the past ten or fifteen years? Could it not happen again?

One further reservation. Much of what Neustadt advises a president to do makes considerable sense. The only problem is that taken collectively his admonitions and prescriptions, especially all the suggestions about going into business as your own political intelligence officer, constant backward mapping, and so on, add one more set of improbable expectations to an already crushing set of expectations by which we judge our presidents. Few students who have read Neustadt believe it is possible for a president to do all the calculating, persuading, and bargaining Neustadt insists upon. Neustadt, of course, is merely suggesting the ideal set of circumstances, the ideal kind of performance. If taken too literally, however, his advice may well produce communications overload and a paralysis of information.

However valuable his book is, Neustadt has not said the last word on this subject, nor is his analysis altogether satisfying as the nation tries, or at least should be trying, to find answers to the question: How can the presidency be made more effective and more accountable at the same time? Neustadt seems too little concerned, too willing to opt for the Walter Lippmann answer.

Taken together, Neustadt's 1960 and 1976 essays on presidential power are, nevertheless, among the best analytical treatments we have. Those who find fault with them do so primarily because they wish he had significantly broadened his scope. Undoubtedly, too, they rest uncomfortably with his realistic, rather than idealistic, frame of reference. He did not dream about how to fashion a more democratic presidency. He has not outlined the "just society" our presidents should help us to achieve. Rather, he has treated, as best he could, the realities of Washington politics and brilliantly described for us how presidents might just possibly be able to make something of their increasingly no-win situation.

Does Neustadt's model help us understand the contemporary presidency? Definitely. His 1976 introductory reflections on Johnson and Nixon add substantially to the earlier work. The 1976 essay nicely reviews some of the confusions or criticized emphases of the early work and thereby strengthens an already lasting contribution.[35]

MORE POWER TO THE PRESIDENCY:
AN ENDURING THEME

What about the prevailing attitudes toward the presidency today? Are they following the Neustadt line or are new models available? Even as the presidency was being soundly criticized for the abuse of power in the late 1960s and early 1970s, it was simultaneously portrayed by many people as alarmingly weakened by Vietnam and Watergate. The ranks of the defenders of presidential government may have been temporarily thinned in mid-1970s, but as of 1980 Neustadt's view, only slightly modified, is alive and well.

There are compelling indications that the experiment of trying to curb presidential power and relying more on Congress for national leadership has been canceled. Americans may have lost their confidence in their leaders, but they have not lost hope in the efficacy of strong purposive leadership. Thanks to Gerald Ford and Jimmy Carter, the fears of another Watergate presidency have disappeared. All the revelations about the crimes of Watergate and the dramatic resignation of a president lulled people into believing, perhaps, that "the system worked," that checks checked and balances balanced. Perhaps the very cataloging of the misuses of presidential powers, solved, or seemed to solve, the problem. The very revelations may have appeared the same as remedies. By 1980 people are asking "Whatever happened to the imperial presidency?" As the new decade dawns, observers are more likely to complain of an imperial judiciary, an imperial bureaucracy, or an imperial Congress.

If the nation had once worried about an imperial presidency, it worried also — alas even feared — about an imperial or reckless Congress. Few could object to efforts to streamline, democratize, or better staff Congress. But few informed people wished to rely only, or even primarily, on Congress for national leadership.

In the wake of the wounded or imperiled presidency of the Watergate era, could Congress furnish the leadership necessary to govern the country? Most post-Watergate scholars and writers said no. The conventional answer heard in the late 1970s was that "we will need a presidency of substantial power" if we are to get on top of the energy problem and maintain our position in foreign affairs.

Defenders of a powerful presidency, such as Samuel Huntington and others, wondered how a government could conduct a coherent foreign policy if legislative ascendancy really meant the development of a Congress into a second United States government. Could the United States afford to have two foreign policies? A nation cannot retain for long a leadership role in the world unless it is both clear and decisive. In the absence of those cherished Hamiltonian virtues chaos would reign. They feared, too, that in establishing its foreign-policy decisions congressional government would operate almost entirely on the basis of domestic politics, a purview that limits its competence in the field of foreign affairs.

More specifically, some charged that Congress, by its headline-hunting investigations, had destroyed the Central Intelligence Agency as an effective means of national policy for the United States. Others claimed Congress had served notice that the president of the United States cannot conduct the foreign policy of his country to confront Soviet expansionism.

Political scientist Huntington, writing in 1975, urges readers to recognize the legitimacy and the necessity "of hierarchy, coercion, discipline, secrecy, and deception — all of which are, in some measure, inescapable attributes of the process of government." "When the President is unable to exercise authority . . ." writes Huntington, "no one else has been able to supply comparable purpose and initiative. To the extent that the United States has been governed on a national basis, it has been governed by the President." [36]

The same verdict is heard from those who yearn for strong creative leadership in domestic or economic matters. Thus, Arthur Schlesinger, Jr., even as he condemns the imperial presidency, says that "history has shown the presidency to be the most effective instrumentality of government for justice and progress." [37]

Time and again, people caution against overreacting to Watergate. Do not be ahistorical, they say. Quoting Harold Laski, they say, "Great power makes great leadership possible."

Supporters of a strong, powerful presidency worry also about the effect of congressional assertion because they believe a president has too little power today — and has all along despite the talk of an imperial presidency — to tackle economic and energy-resource problems effectively. For example, he has very little influence over the Federal Reserve Board's policies on credit and money. He has few tools for effective, long-range economic planning. As President Carter learned, his authority over government reorganization is puny compared to expectations of him as the so-called Chief Executive.

Further, they contend that a president is no longer aided by his party because parties are virtually meaningless and virtually go out of business between elections. They point also to the decentralization of power in Congress and the growing difficulty of putting coalitions together there.

As almost always during the twentieth century, advocates of a strong presidency continue to lament that presidential powers are not stronger. They lament as well, along with Neustadt, that recent presidents have not been effective seekers and wielders of influence. The presidency, they still contend, is America's strongest weapon against such banes of progress as sectionalism, selfish or overly concentrated corporate power, and totalitarianism abroad.

Americans still long for dynamic, reassuring, and strong leadership. Watergate notwithstanding, we still celebrate the gutsy, aggressive presidents — even if many of them did violate the legal and constitutional niceties of our separation-of-powers ideal. We remember fondly the Kennedy command of press conferences and the Lyndon Johnson mastery of Congress. The day of the strong president is here to stay. People want it that way. The great presidents are the men who built the presidency and made a practice of kicking the Congress around. The feeling persists that Ford was "too nice a guy" and that Carter was not forceful enough.

Many experienced politics watchers think the nation in the mid-1970s entered a period of overreaction to Watergate, Vietnam, and the Nixon presidency. Some rebalancing was needed, but many in Congress and some reformers embarked upon a course that endangered the effectiveness of the presidency. Those who hold to this "overreaction thesis" say the White House today is enmeshed in a complex web of constraints that hobbles presidents, constraints that would have prevented an FDR or a Lincoln from providing vital leadership. Finally, adherents of this overreaction point of view say fears of presidential dictatorship are much exaggerated. It is unfortunate, they say, that people dwell so much on Richard Nixon and his abuse of the presidency. The Nixon presidency, they contend, was one of a kind and it was dealt with reasonably effectively by the impeachment provisions of the Constitution.

The central challenge, then, is not to reduce the president's power to lead, to govern, and to persuade but to ensure that the means to lead, to govern, and to persuade is not corrupted. Such is the neo- or modified-Neustadt conception today.

How you stand on the question of how strong the presidency should be depends usually on what policies you favor and how these policies are advanced or hampered by the president or by Congress. It matters too, of course, whether you like the person who is in the White House. If you approve of the president and most of his policies, the tendency is to believe that the president should be, in Woodrow Wilson's words, "free to be as big a man as he can be."

The cycle theory of presidential-congressional relations has long been a fashionable one. This holds that there will be periods of presidential ascendancy followed by periods of congressional reaction and reassertiveness. Usually these have been periods of a decade or more, often a generation in length. A modest but brief congressional assertion took place in the immediate post-Watergate years.[38] But the responsibilities of the presidency in this modern era, coupled with the complexities of foreign and economic policy, did not really permit any weakening of the presidency. Setbacks in foreign policy also reinforced the call for more presidential strength. As Republican Senator Howard Baker of Tennessee put it in 1979, with Carter's brand of leadership "there is a growing view that America is a patsy and we never retaliate." [39]

These same circumstances apparently discouraged any major revisionism in our scholarship and writings on the presidency. Congress has tried to offer constraints to curb the misuse and abuse of power — but it has not really weakened the presidency.

The American presidency — as an institution — is still strong. Its powers are such that the country will rally behind a president if the nation's vital interests are threatened. A post-Watergate president has a greater obilgation to communicate more persuasively than in the past about when and why the national security is threatened.[40] When persuasive presidential leadership is linked with purpose, Congress and the people are prepared to follow.

NOTES

1. Edwin S. Corwin, *The President: Office and Powers,* rev. ed. (New York University Press, 1957).

2. Alexis de Tocqueville, *Democracy in America* (Anchor, 1969 edition), p. 126.

3. Lyndon Johnson to Richard Nixon, quoted in Bobby Baker, with Larry King, *Wheeling and Dealing* (Norton, 1978), p. 265.

4. Richard E. Neustadt, *Presidential Power: The Politics of Leadership: With Reflections on Johnson and Nixon* (Wiley & Sons, 1976).

5. *Ibid.,* p. 229.

6. *Ibid.,* p. 230.

7. *Ibid.,* p. 239.

8. *Ibid.,* p. 33.

9. *Ibid.,* p. 241.

10. *Ibid.,* p. 246.

11. *Ibid.,* pp. 226–27.

12. *Ibid.,* p. 231.

13. *Ibid.,* pp. 1–2.

14. *Ibid.,* p. 27.

15. James David Barber, *The Presidential Character* (Prentice-Hall, 1972).

16. Neustadt, *op. cit.,* p. 33.

17. *Ibid.,* p. 41.

18. *Ibid.,* p. 50.

19. *Ibid.,* pp. 21–22.

20. *Ibid.,* p. 68.

21. See Morris Fiorina, *Congress: Keystone of the Washington Establishment* (Yale University Press, 1977).

22. John Hart, "Presidential Power Revisited," *Political Studies,* March 1977, p. 56.

23. *Ibid.*

24. Bruce Miroff, *Pragmatic Illusions* (McKay, 1976).

25. President Jimmy Carter, at the White House, 30 June 1978, *Weekly Compilation of Presidential Documents,* 3 July 1978, p. 1211.

26. Quoted in Henry Etzkowitz and Peter Schwab, eds., *Is America Necessary?* (West Publishing, 1976), p. 579.

27. C. Vann Woodward, "Populism and Intellectuals," in R. J. Cunningham, ed., *The Populists in Historical Perspective* (D. C. Heath, 1968), pp. 61–62.

28. Richard E. Neustadt, "We're Fresh Out of Heroes," *U.S. News & World Report,* 26 June 1978, p. 29.

29. Henry Fairlie, *The Kennedy Promise* (Doubleday, 1973).

30. Barber, *op. cit.*

31. Doris Kearns, *Lyndon Johnson and the American Dream* (Harper & Row, 1976).

32. See Vincent De Santia, "Eisenhower Revisionism." *Review of Politics,* 38 (1976): 190–207; Fred I. Greenstein, "Presidential Activism Eisenhower-Style: A Reassessment Based on Archival Evidence," *Political Science Quarterly* (Winter, 1979); and, Fred I. Greenstein, "A Tory Theory of the Presidency: Eisenhower's Leadership Reexamined," paper delivered at the 1979 annual meeting of the American Political Science Association, Washington, D.C., Sept. 1979.

33. Five studies deserve mention in this connection: Alexander George, *Presidential Decision Making in Foreign Policy* (Westview Press, 1979); Irving Janis, *Victims of Groupthink* (Houghton Mifflin, 1972); Joel Primack and Frank von Hippel, *Advice and Dissent: Scientists in the Political Arena* (Basic Books, 1974); Thomas Wolanin, *Presidential Advisory Commissions* (University of Wisconsin Press, 1975); and Stephen Hess, *Organizing the Presidency* (Brookings Institution, 1976).

34. Daniel Ellsberg and others argue that the major consideration in Vietnam decision making in the 1960s was a conscious desire to avoid being charged with the loss of Indochina to Communism and that this was a direct legacy from the Joseph McCarthy era and the charge that the Truman administration had "lost" China. Ells-

berg claims that the *Pentagon Papers* show that all the presidents who were involved had more than ample intelligence reports indicating the enormity of the task and that they each opted to do just enough to keep things afloat until after the next election.

35. Unfortunately, however, Neustadt's publisher places his "Reflections on Johnson and Nixon" at the front rather than at the end of the new edition. This makes little sense because, for most readers, especially students, the original book is a prerequisite for reading the material on the 1960s and 1970s.

36. Samuel P. Huntington, "The Democratic Distemper," in Nathan Glazer and Irving Kristol, eds., *The American Commonwealth* (Basic Books), p. 24.

37. Arthur M. Schlesinger, Jr., *The Imperial Presidency* (Houghton Mifflin, 1973), p. 404. For a similar post-Watergate reaffirmation of the presidency see Theodore C. Sorensen, *Watchmen in the Night: Presidential Accountability After Watergate* (M.I.T. Press, 1975).

38. For the view that Congress has really not reasserted itself effectively and that the root causes of the imperial presidency are still with us, see Philip B. Kurland, *Watergate and the Constitution* (University of Chicago Press, 1978).

39. Quoted in Hedrick Smith, "More Than a Feeling That You Can't Push America Around," *New York Times*, 25 February 1979, p. 4E.

40. Daniel Yankelovich, "Farewell to 'President Knows Best,'" *Foreign Affairs — America and the World, 1978*, Special Issue, 1979, pp. 670–93.

CHAPTER 5

THE PRESIDENTIAL JOB DESCRIPTION

And people talk about the powers of a President, all the powers that a Chief Executive has, and what he can do. Let me tell you something — from experience!

The President may have a great many powers given to him in the constitution and may have certain powers under certain laws which are given to him by the Congress of the United States; but the principal power that the President has is to bring people in and try to persuade them to do what they ought to do without persuasion. That's what the powers of the President amount to.

— Harry S. Truman, *Public Papers of the Presidents of the United States* (U.S. Government Printing Office, 1949), p. 247.

I find that when things go badly, it becomes our business. When the stock market goes down, letters are addressed to the White House. When it goes up, we get comparatively few letters of appreciation. But when you have high unemployment, it is because the President hasn't gotten the country moving again.

— John F. Kennedy, quoted in H. W. Chase and A. H. Lerman, eds., *Kennedy and the Press* (Crowell, 1965), pp. 426–27.

All Presidents start out pretending to run a crusade, but after a couple of years they find they are running something much less heroic, much more intractable: namely the Presidency.

— Alistair Cooke, quoted in Douglass Cater, *Power in Washington* (Vintage, 1965), p. 72.

The presidential job description as outlined in the Constitution was a medley of compromises. We wanted a presidency strong enough to do what was asked of it and yet not one that would use governmental authority for selfish ends or contrary to the general welfare. In almost every instance presidential powers were shared powers. Perhaps only the pardon power was a truly imperial grant of power that allowed presidents alone to monopolize an area of policymaking.

Despite the administrative, diplomatic, commander in chief, and veto powers granted the president, presidents found that they had to act within a set of strong constitutional, political, and social restraints. They had to be sensitive to the dominant elites, the cultural "rules of the game," and, of course, the threat of being impeached or turned out of office at the next election.

Nowadays a president is asked to be countless things that are not spelled out with any clarity in the Constitution. We want him to be a national renewer of morale as well as an international peacemaker, a moral leader as well as the nation's chief economic manager, a politician in chief, and a unifying representative of all the people. We want every new president to be everything — at least of virtue — all our great presidents have been. No matter that the great presidents were not as great as we think they were. Rightly or wrongly, we believe our greatest presidents were men of talent, tenacity and optimism, men who could clarify the vital issues of the day and mobilize the nation for action. We like to think our great presidents were transforming leaders who could not only move the enterprise forward but could summon the highest kinds of moral commitment from the American people. This chapter describes the kinds of leadership we now demand of our presidents.

The textbook or storybook view that presidential leadership consists primarily of a confrontation between the character of a larger-than-life heroic president and that of a national problem is a fallacy that over-emphasizes the role of presidential personality and style. "The modern Presidency is not primarily a machine for self-expression" writes historian Bert Cochran. "Caught in a swirl of conflicting tides, the President maneuvers and manipulates, grants concessions to this bloc, to maintain a social equilibrium, working within the confines of basic laws, institutions, and dispensations. . . ."[1]

Rarely is a president a free agent. He nearly always mirrors the fundamental forces of society: the values, the myths, the quest for order and stability, and the vast, inert, and usually conservative forces that maintain the existing balance of interests. Ours is a system decidedly weighted against radical leadership, a system that encourages most presidents, most of the time, to respond to the powerful, organized, and already represented interests at the expanse of the unrepresented. Moreover, a president today must preside over a highly specialized and sprawling bureaucracy of his own. A president can easily find himself sitting at the

White House, "overworked and making the best of a bad situation, while all around him he has princes and serfs doing and undoing in thousands of actions the work of his administration without his having a clue." [2]

Recent presidents have often grown publicly frustrated in the job. Carter once likened it to an endless multiple choice exam. They nearly always conclude that their responsibilities exceed their meager powers. Lyndon Johnson commented on his frustrations in achieving domestic progress this way: "Power? The only power I've got is nuclear . . . and I can't use that." [3]

Discussions about the presidency, about whether it is too strong or too weak, healthy or diseased, accountable or irresponsible, suffer from an almost constant shifting about among policy areas and from disjointed leaps from one kind of decisional activity to others substantially different. Of course, a president can be imperial and nearly dictatorial in some aspects of his job, whereas in others he may be hedged in on all sides. Often, too, the same act by two different incumbents evokes markedly different degrees of acceptance, because of the nature of the times or of the political climate. Thus, when President Hoover suggested that what the nation really needed was a restoration of confidence, he was answered with bitter laughter. When Franklin Roosevelt, only weeks later, declared that "the only thing we have to fear is fear itself," virtually the same message, the nation was thrilled and its spirit rallied.

Until recently, it has been fashionable to say that a president wears many hats — a commander-in-chief hat, a chief-legislator hat, a chief-of-state hat, and so on. This simple metaphor of presidential hats belongs to a simpler past. Several years ago a prominent political scientist wrote that "the United States has one President, but it has two presidencies; one presidency is for domestic affairs, and the other is concerned with defense and foreign policy." Further, he added that presidents have "had much greater success in controlling the nation's defense and foreign policies than in dominating its domestic policies." [4]

By the 1980s, reality, as well as expectations, has expanded and recast the presidency, organized it around three major interrelated policy areas that we may call subpresidencies: (1) foreign affairs and national security, (2) aggregate economics, and (3) domestic policy, or "quality of life," issues. The president's time is absorbed by one or another of these competing policy spheres, and his staff and cabinet have come to be organized around these three substantive areas.

THE FOREIGN-AFFAIRS PRESIDENCY

Modern presidents concentrate on foreign and national security policy, often at the expense of the two other policy areas. To be sure, an exclusively foreign, economic, or domestic problem is a rarity, and many issues are blurred, because they intersect all three areas. Critical problems such as trade, inflation, energy development, drug abuse, or environmental problems — not to mention war — require planning and policy leadership that cut across the three presidencies. Still, a close examination of how presidents have spent their time in the past forty years suggests that foreign-policy matters (often crises) have driven out domestic-policy matters. Economic matters usually come in second.

The founding politicians never intended a president to be the dominant agent in national policymaking, but they did expect the president to be the major influence in the field of foreign affairs. In the eighteenth century, foreign affairs were generally thought to be an executive matter. The first task for a national leader is the nation's survival and national defense. Today, especially in the nuclear age, foreign-policy responsibilities cannot be delegated; they are executive in character and presidential by constitutional tradition or interpretation. After the Bay of Pigs tragedy, President Kennedy vividly emphasized the central importance of foreign policy: "It really is true," he told a visiting Richard Nixon, "that foreign affairs is the only important issue for a President to handle . . . I mean, who gives a shit if the minimum wage is $1.15 or $1.25, in comparison to something like this [The Bay of Pigs]?" [5]

Kennedy frequently said the difference between domestic and foreign policy was the difference between a bill being defeated and the country being wiped out. Both Kennedy and Nixon were personally more fascinated with foreign policy than with domestic or economic policy. Both wanted history to record that they had laid the foundation for peace not only in their own time but also for generations to come. President Carter spent more time on the Middle East issue than on any other matter during his first three years in office. Panama Canal politics and relations with the Soviet Union and China were preoccupations as well. He confessed he liked dealing with foreign policy because his capacity to act unilaterally seemed much greater in the foreign than in the domestic realm.

White House advisers from all the recent administrations agree that a president spends a half to two-thirds of his time on foreign-policy or national-security deliberations. In some instances, this emphasis on foreign policy and national security has occurred by choice, most notably for President Nixon, who said, "I've always thought this country could run itself domestically — without a President; all you need is a competent Cabinet to run the country at home. You need a President for foreign policy; no Secretary of State is really important; the President makes foreign policy." [6] President Johnson, on the other hand, although strongly disposed by experience toward domestic programs, was unable to prevent his presidency from being consumed by military affairs. Aides, friends, and biographers all report, that President Kennedy became far more engulfed by foreign-policy matters than even he liked. "The President estimates that eighty percent of his first year in office was spent mulling over foreign policy." [7] After ten days in the White House, he talked as if he was overwhelmed by the flood of international crises and the ever-present possibilities of nuclear war:

> No man entering upon this office, regardless of his party, regardless of his previous service in Washington, could fail to be staggered upon learning — even in this brief ten-day period — the harsh enormity of the trials through which we must pass in the next four years. Each day the crises multiply. Each day their solutions grow more difficult. Each day we draw nearer the hour of maximum danger, as weapons spread and hostile forces grow stronger. I feel I must inform the Congress that our analyses over the last ten days make it clear that — in each of the principal areas of crisis — the tide of events has been running out and time has not been our friend.[8]

Presidents devote substantially more of their State of the Union addresses to national-security matters than to any other topic. Through a quantitative analysis of these addresses, one scholar found "this policy is clearly the prime presidential concern . . . [and] that greater attention to international affairs results from the experience of being president. Attention to this policy area grows over time . . . in a pattern that can be related to the election cycle." Special focus on national security matters "mounts during the first, second and third years, then drops as a president faces re-election. During a president's second term, concern with international involvement grows again . . . substantially higher [in fact] than . . . during the first term." [9] Other scholars persuasively attribute this accentuated attention to more formal presidential powers in the national-security area, better sources of information, and the weakness of Congress in this sphere.

In addition, presidents naturally work hardest where they see both hope of success and leeway for significant personal impact. Well-organized interest groups are less likely to differ with presidential intentions in foreign-policy matters, and vice versa: most special interests want the nation well protected and want to stop the spread of communism and make the world safe for American trade and travel. Former Nixon counsel Leonard Garment pointed to yet another reason when he explained Nixon's preference for foreign policy in this way to Theodore White: "In foreign policy, you get drama, triumph, resolution — crisis and resolution so that in foreign policy Nixon can give the sense of leadership. But in domestic policy, there you have to deal with the whole jungle of human problems." [10]

In any case, it is vastly more "presidential" to be concerned with national security and world peace than with domestic problems. One notion holds that a president should be involved in areas that allow him to make dramatic global choices. International travels and summit meetings with foreign leaders generate favorable publicity and confer stature on an incumbent, whereas at home he may be criticized as just another time-serving politician. International excursions are intertwined, of course, with domestic politics; they may even be undertaken to attract news coverage away from unsuccessful or embarrassing domestic initiatives. At home a president may be hamstrung by an opposition-dominated Congress, by a narrow electoral margin, by a hostile press, or by a scandal in his administration; but 12 miles offshore a president virtually *is* the United States, and few people qualify their loyalty under such circumstances. The purpose of many presidential trips is largely symbolic, but the American people are tolerantly disposed. When the president uses the powers of his office to bring about better chances for peace, it is hard to resent his powers even if he does not succeed. The president will be rewarded in the opinion polls for trying.

The risks for the president who allows national security matters to divert him from unresolved domestic problems are highlighted aptly by David Broder:

> The Panamanians, the Palestinians, and the Politburo may look easier to deal with than the tax lobbyists, the energy conferees or the unemployed, but they are not easily managed either.
>
> [Also], Presidents, and especially Democratic Presidents, tend to be judged by the voters on their record in domestic affairs. You can stack the treaties as high as the Washington Monument and they won't be as convincing to voters as a healthy economy, with more jobs and better pay.[11]

THE ECONOMIC PRESIDENCY

The second-largest portion of presidential policy time is spent on aggregate economic, or macroeconomic, policy. *Aggregate economics* refers here to monetary and fiscal policy, trade and tariff policy, inflation, unemployment, the stability of the dollar, and the health of the stock market, as opposed to the more explicitly domestic concerns of education, ecology, health, housing, welfare, social justice, the civil-service system, and, more generally, the quality of life in the United States.

Since the passage of the landmark Employment Act of 1946, the health of the economy has been a major issue in presidential politics. In that act, Congress mandated each president to prepare an annual economic report. The Council of Economic Advisers was also established in that year to help the president to serve, in effect, as the chief economic manager for the nation. The 1970 Economic Stabilization Act added more specific responsibilities to the presidential economic-policy portfolio.

A president can scarcely hide from the hard, visible quantitative economic indicators: unemployment rates, consumer-price indexes, the gross national product, interest and mortgage rates, commodity prices, oil import price levels and stock-market averages. These figures are available to everyone, and the American people increasingly judge their president on whether he can cope aggressively with recession and inflation, whether he can offer effective economic game plans (preferably without tax increases), and whether he can use the nation's budget as an instrument for ensuring a healthy and growing economy. The issues of tax reform and income redistribution, irritating and complex though they may be, are always on the agenda of national politics.

But a president's statutory responsibilities for maintaining full employment and pursuing stabilization policies are not matched by political resources or available expertise. In most areas of our economy the consumers are relatively weak or unorganized, but an uneven performance by the economy will call down on a president immediate pressure from wealthy businessmen, unions, and farmers, and from their large delegations of friends in Congress. Moreover, when the economy enters a period such as the recession-inflation configurations of 1974 or 1979 (or "stagflation" as it is called by some), pressures from the voting public become large as well. When the crunch is on, workers want jobs, even if they must come at the expense of the environment. Bread-and-butter pocketbook issues are nearly always more salient to the working class than the quality-of-life issues; the latter often are of more concern to the well educated.

Every president since Truman has faced inflation as a critical problem and has had to devise some kind of wage-price policy for its solution. Presidential "jawboning" to achieve price stability has been used in varying degrees by every president in recent years. Occasionally, when traditional monetary and fiscal policies have failed to halt inflation, presidents (Truman and Nixon, for example) have established wage and price controls as a direct means of economic management.[12]

Throughout the Nixon administration, the supremacy of economic over domestic policy was clear. The remarks of the press secretary on the occasion of, the establishment of the Council on Economic Policy were typical: "Let me simply conclude by saying that President Nixon feels that, with the single exception of national security and defense, he has no higher obligation to the American people than that of providing the leadership to insure a healthy, prosperous economy." [13]

A measurement factor also adds to the incentives for preoccupation with international and economic concerns. It is easier to judge whether large-scale United States corporate interests abroad are being nationalized or unemployment has increased significantly than to judge whether the criminal justice system has been improved, civil liberties have been enhanced, or poor children are learning or eating better.

THE DOMESTIC PRESIDENCY

Presidents concentrate on those areas in which they feel they can make the greatest impact, in which the approval of interest groups and the public can be most easily rallied. Getting involved in domestic policy is costly both financially and politically. Moreover, newly elected presidents find that budgets are virtually fixed for the next year and a half and that in domestic matters they are very dependent on Congress, specialized bureaucracies, professions, and state and local officialdom. Is it surprising, then, that the implementation of domestic policy has become the orphan of presidential attention? Is it possible presidents rationalize that they must concern themselves with foreign and macroeconomic policy as they lose heart with the complicated, hard-to-affect, divisive domestic problems?

From Roosevelt through Carter, all our recent presidents have complained that progress on the domestic front was more difficult than they had imagined it would be. They complain also that there are greater limits upon their ability to bring about favorable results in the domestic sphere than they had imagined.

Thus, the same John Kennedy who in many ways inspired the country was once moved to quip about a relatively low-priority project, the architectual remodeling of Lafayette Square across from the White House, "Let's stay with it. Hell, this may be the only thing I'll ever really get done." [14] Lyndon Johnson was always disappointed by the slow pace of progress in first passing and then implementing his Great Society programs. He often thought that a significant portion of the programs he had fought so hard to pass had been sabotaged by indifferent or even disloyal bureaucrats. Nixon's contempt for the domestic bureaucracy was well known. His replacement of every one of his original cabinet officers from his first term is further evidence of his frustration with dealing with his executive branch "colleagues."

Jimmy Carter learned early and often about the limits of his domestic leadership powers. One hilarious example of this lesson concerned a mouse that had climbed inside a wall of the Oval Office and died. The odor became offensive one day just as Carter was about to greet a visiting diplomat. An emergency call went out to the General Service Administration (the agency that maintains and oversees federal property), but GSA refused to respond, insisting that it had already exterminated all the mice in the White House. The dead mouse, the GSA officials reasoned, had obviously come in from outside of the building and was therefore the responsibility of the Department of the Interior. However, Interior officials objected; they contended that the mouse was not their concern because it was now inside the White House. An exasperated Carter finally ordered officials from both agencies to his office where he angrily told them, "I can't even get a damn mouse out of my office. . . ." A special task force representing the two agencies was established and they proceeded to get rid of the mouse!

Of course, the presidential litany about powerlessness can be self-serving: it can be conveniently used to suggest that presidents personally are more or less blameless for not seriously undertaking the painful domestic fights that need to be fought. It is also part of the rationalization for "going abroad," that is, for switching from exacting home-repairman tasks to the more glamorous role of world statesman.

National domestic policy has been changing in character. No longer is the federal government merely constructing interstate canals or highways, building veterans' hospitals, or writing social security checks. Federal social and regulatory programs now try to change how people think and how local institutions behave. Few of the new programs of the 1960s and 1970s were or are now administered directly from Washington: most are run in concert with a maze of state, regional, and local governments, professions, and interest groups. Local leaders and interest groups insist on having discretion over the disbursement of federal funds, especially those for problems of race, poverty, urban decay, and environmental pollution. Reference to distinct presidential policy or Washington guidelines is minimal. Presidential intentions invariably become compromised. As Martha Derthick points out: "[The federal government] gets them to carry out its purposes by offering incentives in the form of aid, which they may accept or not, and by attaching conditions to the aid. To achieve results, federal officials must have enough knowledge of local politics to perceive what incentives are necessary; they must direct the incentives to those holders of local power whose support is required to achieve the federal purpose. In short, they must intervene successfully in local politics." [15]

The administrative side of the presidency is the least glamorous and least envied aspect for presidents and public alike. Presidents too often appear to gain control over the routines and loyalties of the government only to find themselves later defending the appearances rather than acknowledging the illusions. Franklin Roosevelt came to the White House belittling the managerial tasks of the presidency. But by 1937, under fire for creating so many new agencies and with Congress threatening to move in, Roosevelt acknowledged that his preoccupation with emergency programs during his first term had caused him to give administration less than the consideration it deserved. He despaired that "the President's task has become impossible for me or any other man. A man in this position will not be able to survive White House service unless it is simplified." [16] After a time a president usually chooses to spend his scarce political capital on new policy initiatives rather than on implemental or management strategies.

A question that arises constantly within the White House is how to organize the executive office to ensure presidential priorities are carried out. The strategy of executive organization most often celebrated in traditional public-administration textbooks is that of hierarchy. The assumption is that the president's values should prevail: the White House sets policy and executive-branch subordinates obey policy directions and accept budgetary levels as sent down by the White House. To this end, a strong and effective presidency requires a strong cabinet that is responsible for the actual operation of programs and reports directly to the president.

But the federal executive branch does not function as a unidirectional hierarchical system. In the American political system, program goals are not spelled out clearly, complex problems must be dealt with incrementally, and presidential authority is constantly "leaking" away. Departmental personnel at bureau or division levels often believe they know best how to run their own programs. Some cabinet positions are weak; some departments are even celebrated for their deviance from White House goals. Field personnel feel themselves closer to the problems and to the local people and often believe they must adapt federal programs to local conditions. Career professionals in government service do not believe that a president's generalist lieutenants possess the expertise they often, in fact, do. Special interest groups constantly press for separate agencies or departments to represent their areas of concern. And, over time, the White House begins to distrust even its own cabinet.

Presidential leadership has become less a matter of authority flowing downward and more a question of the extent to which loyalty extends upward. The mix of pressures on a typical bureau chief — from Congress, from his department, from his program's constituency, and from politics at his own level — makes it difficult for him to respond solely to White House intentions, even if these are communicated thoroughly and consistently. And frequently they are not. David Brinkley once rendered this verdict:

This town is sort of like a great big steamboat that keeps going its own way regardless of which way the wind blows, or how elections go, or how the current goes; it keeps going, and it might move one degree in one direction, but it essentially keeps going the same direction. It goes on grinding out paper, spending money, hiring people, getting bigger and bigger and more troublesome all the time, and nothing seems to affect it. Presidents don't affect it. Every president I've known or know of has complained about the fantastically cumbersome size of this establishment here. As far back as Harry Truman, I was covering the White

House and Truman said, "I thought I was the President, but when it comes to these bureaucracies, I can't make 'em do a damn thing.[17]

POLICY SUBPRESIDENCIES AND PRESIDENTIAL EFFECTIVENESS

Presidential scholars traditionally have believed that presidents enjoy more success in foreign- and defense-policy matters than in domestic matters. The great urgency of national-security matters in an age of nuclear weapons is generally credited as the reason foreign policy tends to drive out domestic-policy concerns. Further, the president is thought to have more and better sources of information in the national security area.

But Vietnam and the questioning of presidential competence that it encouraged have changed the way presidents become involved in foreign policy. By the late 1970s Congress had become more involved. Congress set up its own rival institution to gather foreign-policy intelligence. And the general public became at least a little more skeptical of presidents who wanted to get the United States more involved in international ventures. Not suprisingly, then, presidential initiatives to Congress met with lower rates of approval. More specifically, presidential foreign and defense proposals were approved only about 55 percent of the time in the 1965–75 time period, compared to a handsome 70 percent presidential proposal rate in the 1948–64 period.[18] Approval rates for foreign and defense policies are still higher than for domestic policies, but the differences have diminished. The Democratically controlled Congress presented Republicans Nixon and Ford with a series of foreign-policy defeats. But Lyndon Johnson and Jimmy Carter also had their share of setbacks. Still, Carter has generally enjoyed more success in foreign than in domestic policy. His B-1 bomber, Panama Canal, plane sales to the Middle East, and a high percentage of his defense appropriation measures have won backing, whereas his tax-reform, welfare, and health-reform packages, to name just a few, have suffered repeated defeats in Congress. Two students of presidential-congressional relations summed up the recent experience this way:

> Presidents still engage in high level diplomacy, make executive agreements, and shape American foreign policy. Carter's success with the Panama Canal Treaties is just one more small indication that in spite of changes in the past decade, a President's power in foreign affairs seems different than his power in domestic affairs. . . .
>
> Congress may slash the defense budget, outrage other nations, hold up treaties, cut foreign aid but there is no congressional substitute for the President's role in the SALT talks, fostering a negotiated peace in the Mideast, taking international tours, reassuring allies, or making an imme-

diate response to a threat or a crisis. . . . In the sphere of defense and foreign policy, Congress has increased its checks, but there will never be a balance with the executive.[19]

Recent presidents have increasingly organized and differentiated their staffs and cabinets around these three policy areas — foreign, economic, and domestic — but such compartmentalization ignores relations fundamental to the health and security of the nation. What may be differentiated for organizational convenience cannot be completely separated when considering policy and political implications.

> In the future, there is likely to be an increasing emphasis on nondefense foreign policy issues, most of which will have a great impact on *domestic* politics and a great attraction for domestic interest groups. Problems with the monetary system, trade deficits and surpluses, energy policy, and the import and export of things such as inflation, unemployment, technology, and pollution will consume more and more of the foreign policy effort. This will occur, not merely because the prominence of security issues may be declining relatively with the evolution of détente, but because these nondefense issues will have a larger absolute impact on American society.[20]

Moreover, the ability of the United States to assist in solving world problems derives in large measure from its ability to solve its own domestic and social problems. Time and again, however, specialized staffs set up in the presidential establishment treat new problems as if they were solely foreign or economic or domestic. A presidency that overspecializes and overcompartmentalizes its staff and its information-gathering apparatus will doubtless be a presidency unable to provide what should be the essential presidential contribution: the capacity to integrate, synthesize, and comprehend diverse policies and their costs, their liabilities, and their effects, not only singly but also in relation to one another.

THE JOB DESCRIPTION OF THE MODERN PRESIDENCY

Within each of these three presidencies or policy subpresidencies, a president is asked to provide functional leadership in seven activity areas: *crisis management, symbolic leadership, priority setting and program design, recruitment of advisers, administrators, and so on, legislative and political coalition building, program implementation and evaluation, and oversight of government routines and early warning of problems areas.* These are not compartmentalized, unrelated functions, but rather a dynamic, seamless assortment of tasks and responsibilities. This job description does not exhaust all presidential activity; rather, the examples in Table 5.1 attempt to classify the major functional as well as substantive

TABLE 5.1   THE PRESIDENTIAL JOB DESCRIPTION

	The Subpresidencies		
Types of Activity	Foreign Policy and National Security (A)	Aggregate Economics (B)	Domestic Policy and Programs (C)
Crisis Management	Wartime leadership; missile crisis, 1962	Coping with recessions	Confronting coal strikes of 1978
Symbolic and Morale-building Leadership	Presidential state visit to Middle East or to China	Boosting confidence in the dollar	Visiting disaster victims and morale building among government workers
Priority Setting and Program Design	Balancing pro-Israel policies with need for Arab oil	Choosing means of dealing with inflation, unemployment	Designing a new welfare program
Recruitment Leadership (advisers, administrators, judges, ambassadors, etc.)	Selection of Secretary of Defense, U.N. Ambassador	Selection of Secretary of Treasury, Federal Reserve Board Governors	Nomination of federal judges
Legislative and Political Coalition Building	Selling Panama or SALT treaties to Senate for approval	Lobbying for energy-legislation package	Winning public support for transportation deregulation
Program Implementation and Evaluation	Encouraging negotiations between Israel and Egypt	Implementing tax cuts or fuel rationing	Improving quality health care, welfare retraining programs
Oversight of Government Routines and Establishment of an Early-Warning System for Future Problem Areas	Overseeing U.S. bases abroad; ensuring that foreign-aid programs work effectively	Overseeing the IRS or the Small Business Administration	Overseeing National Science Foundation or Environmental Protection Agency

responsibilities of the office. Of course, political activity solely for personal enhancement (such as reelection) should be acknowledged as a presidential preoccupation just as staying elected is a prime objective for most legislators.

In practice, no president can divide his job into tidy compartments. Instead, he must see to it that questions are not ignored simply because they fall between or cut across jurisdictional lines. Presidents must act alternately, and often simultaneously, as crisis managers and as symbolic, priority-setting, coalition-building, and managerial leaders. Ultimately, all his responsibilities mix with one another. Being president is a little like being a juggler who is already juggling too many balls and, at the most frustrating moments, is forever having more balls tossed at him.

Crisis Management

When crises and national emergencies occur, we instinctively turn to the president. Presidents are asked during a time of crisis to provide not only political and executive leadership but also the appearance of confident, responsible control, the show of a steady hand at the helm. Popular demand and public necessity force presidents nowadays to do what Lincoln and Franklin Roosevelt once did during the national emergencies of their day, namely, to do what is required to protect the union, to safeguard the nation, and to preserve vital American interests.

The most significant factor in the swelling of the presidential establishment in the post-1939 era has been the accretion of new presidential roles during national emergencies, when Congress and the public have looked to the president for decisive responses. The Constitution neither authorized presidents to meet emergencies nor did it forbid them to do so. All strong presidents have taken advantage of this omission. The Great Depression and World War II in particular caused sizable increases in presidential staffs. After the Russians orbited Sputnik in 1957, President Eisenhower added science advisers; and after the Bay of Pigs in 1961, President Kennedy enlarged his national security staff. The cold-war commitments as President Kennedy enumerated them in his Inaugural Address, to "pay any price, bear any burden, meet any hardship, support any friend, oppose any foe," and the presence of nuclear weapons fostered the argument that only presidents could move with sufficient quickness and intelligence in national-security matters. When major crises occur, Congress traditionally holds debates but just as predictably delegates vast authority to a president, charging him to take whatever actions are necessary to restore order or regain control over the situation.

Primary factors underlying the transformation of the presidency of the Constitution to the modern crisis management presidency are the invention of nuclear weapons, the permanence of large standing armies, and the interdependent role of the United States in the world economy. An almost permanent crisis in national security has dominated American thinking since 1940. Such crises include the Japanese bombing of Pearl Harbor in 1941, the North Korean invasion of South Korea in 1950, the Russian launching of Sputnik in 1957, the offensive missiles placed in Cuba by the Russians in 1962, the Viet Cong offensives in South Vietnam in the mid and late 1960s, the various Middle East wars of the 1960s and 1970s.

A greater share of crises in the past few decades may seem to have fallen within the national security or macroeconomic subpresidencies than within the domestic-policy subpresidencies. But it may be subtly deceiving to think that most crises occur in foreign policy or in the economic realm, for the cult of the textbook presidency seems to encourage the notion that presidents should be involved in areas where dramatic global choices must be made. Kennedy's Cuban-missile blockade, Nixon's historic trip to China, and Carter's Camp David summit meetings splendidly suit the public's expectation and the presidential image. Do presidents consciously take stronger stands and give a promotional "hype" to foreign confrontations and deliberately evade vital domestic matters? Some analysts think so.[21] Certain observers joked that Nixon encouraged crises or at least the appearance of foreign crises to divert attention from his Watergate problems at home: "A crisis a day keeps impeachment away."

In crisis-management activities, however, a president is often little more than the victim of the interplay of events and institutions and economic forces. The phrase "overtaken by events" describes much of the presidential position when he is required to respond to crises. Very often he really is surprised and truly placed on the defensive. He cannot enjoy the luxury of time to plan carefully and to initiate new departures in public policy; he must react to public and congressional demands for action, to journalistic and academic analyses, and to criticism from opposition party leaders. The 1962 episode involving James Meredith and Mississippi Governor Ross Barnett illustrates an issue that had to be confronted despite the deep reluctance of modern presidents to exercise federal police power against other levels of government, even in the face of blatant violation of federal law. Certainly, President Kennedy did not encourage Meredith to enroll in the University of Mississippi. Meredith and his supporters chose an approach that was delicate and that carried high risks, both to him personally and to a president already in an awkward situation. Kennedy, through his brother Robert, the attorney general, tried desperately to avoid dramatic intervention and to compromise with Barnett. Only when these efforts failed did Kennedy finally send the twenty-three thousand federal marshals into Mississippi. Robert Kennedy's book

Thirteen Days also demonstrates most effectively, in the context of the Cuban-missile crisis, how a crisis can cast aside nearly all other presidential responsibilities.

Symbolic and Morale-Building Leadership

A president is the nation's number-one celebrity, and almost anything he does is news. Merely by going fishing or to someone's wedding, a president commands attention. By his actions, a president can arouse a sense of hope, honor, or despair. The tasks of symbolic leadership of the nation — generating confidence and a sense of national purpose — are, for the most part, beyond partisanship and are some of the more easily performed and more pleasant presidential responsibilities. Acting in behalf of semi-sacred traditional American beliefs and values is often a much more enjoyable way to spend time than trying to win support for a party's program, cajoling reluctant senators to confirm a controversial judicial nominee, or overseeing and overhauling the nation's farm-subsidy programs.

Politics is the act of governing not intellectuals or rationalists but people. Politics is not simply a series of rational actions. Political leadership, at its best, symbolizes the nation's traditions, purposes, and aspirations. Whether he likes it or not a president becomes a kind of high priest of a nation. He is not merely an executive officer but a carrier of meaning, a symbol.

No matter how enlightened, rational, pragmatic, or even cynical we consider ourselves, all of us respond in some ways to symbols and rituals and all of us have our own cherished myths about what our society is or should be. The way we react to politicians and political issues is closely tied to the symbolic light in which they are seen.

To lead by example is not enough to gain popular support and to demonstrate that he is a leader; a president has to dramatize the image of a man of action, a man of decisiveness who is in control and able to lead in a crisis. He must symbolize toughness and rugged individualism, as well as compassion and forgiveness.

The Nixon campaign of 1968 was an example of the importance of symbols and images in politics. This realization shaped campaign strategy. In a now-famous 1967 memo that discussed prospects for the coming election, Nixon aide Raymond Price wrote:

> Politics is much more emotional than it is rational, and this is particularly true of Presidential politics. . . . Selection of the President has to be an act of faith. . . . This isn't achieved by reason; it's achieved by a feeling of trust that can't be argued or reasoned, but that comes across in those silences that surround the words. The words are important but less for what they actually say than for the sense they convey, for the impression they give of the man himself, his hopes, his standards, his

competence, his intelligence, his essential humanness, and the direction of history he represents.[22]

The Nixon entourage heeded this advice and often concentrated on symbolism. At the heart of the Nixon "middle America" strategy was also an effort to portray Nixon as the symbol of the traditional values of the American civil religion.

Symbolic politics can never be a substitute for effective substantive leadership. The success of Nixon's symbolic campaigns eventually came to a crashing end as the invasion of neutral Cambodia, the bombing of nonmilitary targets in Vietnam, and his Watergate scandal destroyed his claims that the war was a "moral" war or that his presidency was a competent, professional one.

Probably no presidency has employed symbolic politics in as undisguised a way as the Carter White House. After the Nixon-Watergate debacle it was clear that the strength of the moral symbol of the presidency had been undermined. It was also evident from polls that American voters wished for a reaffirmation of these values. Carter's strategists seized on this and made the need for honesty ("I will not lie to you"), compassion, and justice the central theme of his 1976 campaign.

> We have been shaken by a tragic war and by scandals and broken promises. Our people are seeking new voices, new ideas and new leaders. . . .
>   We have lost some precious things that historically have bound our people and our government together. We feel the moral decay that has weakened this country. We feel that we have been crippled by a lack of goals and values, and that our public officials have lost faith in us. We want to have faith again! We want to be proud again! We just want the truth again! . . .[23]

Carter's symbolic campaign may not have pleased those who yearned for "issue oriented" politics, but it temporarily struck a responsive chord among voters. The country was impressed and heartened when Jimmy Carter jumped out of his limousine on his way back from the Inaugural and marched hand in hand with his wife and daughter to the White House. And, at least initially, people admired how Carter retired the limousines and the trumpeters, went on a radio call-in show, wore a cardigan sweater during a fireside chat, and slept overnight with families when he went to participate in local "town meeting" sessions around the country. However, Carter's depomping of the presidency either went too far or didn't work. Some saw the "aw-shucks, small-town, friendly neighbor act" as boring and bush league. Others felt Carter's efforts to bend over backward to deny the imperial stereotype conveyed the image that he was weakening the office and was becoming something akin to "a city manager in the White House."

Carter was right in trying to cut back on some of the White House frills. He was right in trying to curb the size of the swollen White House establishment. He was right also in restoring personal modesty to the Oval Office and in trying to stay human in the very job that has inflated too many too much. But his success was ironically met by resounding pleas for Carter to assert more control and to display more decisiveness. In an effort to make the president look more authoritative, he began to veto bills, discipline his staff and cabinet, and take stronger stands. Advised one political scientist: "It is one thing to win an election because of a reaction to the imperial, abusive Presidency. But it is quite another to gut the Presidency of its important source of influence and power and prestige. If President Carter is to ever successfully convince the public, the politicians, and world leaders that he does fit the job, he is going to have to accept the symbols that have traditionally grown up with the role." [24]

Many people view the job of the president as symbolic, that is, as the performance of ceremonial duties as the chief of state. To be sure, he is expected to review parades, receive foreign dignitaries, buy Easter seals, press buttons to begin power projects, and perform countless other gestures of national unification. Occasionally someone complains that these duties take too much time from more important responsibilities. [25] Actually, the purely ceremonial duties do not burden a president. Ceremonial and chief-of-state functions actually enhance a president's authority and give him added status. No president in his right mind is going to surrender one of the few aspects of his job that allows him to be a national unifier, accentuating our past traditions and emphasizing our common assets.

A president also performs a variety of semi-religious functions. These are sometimes ceremonial or pastoral responsibilities. For example, he issues proclamations for national religious observances. He participates in events such as a national prayer breakfast and communicates regularly with major denomination leaders. Persons like the late Cardinal Spellman or the influential Billy Graham develop friendships with presidents. The archives of presidential libraries indicate that each week a president receives hundreds of letters from citizens who offer him their religious advice or who request favors for their religious interests. [26] Few presidents overlook the public-relations aspect when they lend their prestige to a religious group. Despite popular conceptions about separation of church and state, presidents play a definite religious role and the public has come to expect it.

But the symbolic job of a president involves much more than just ceremonial or quasi-pastoral duties. Presidential leadership, at its finest, radiates authority and confidence and fortifies the nation's morale. Especially in periods of doubt or premature self-defeat, a president as morale builder is called upon to be renewer of values, an articulate definer of purposes, a person who will help us to overcome stagnation by fixing our sights on the possible and the desirable. Our best leaders have been able to provide this special and often intangible element. Perhaps it can be called morale revitalization or purposive renewal. It defies easy definition. But we know that Washington, Lincoln, and Franklin Roosevelt were all able to provide it, and we know all too well that it is not something that the Constitution confers or something conveniently closeted in the White House for the use of each new occupant. In contrasting ways, Eisenhower and John F. Kennedy also radiated confidence and hope.

Finally, there is an undeniably monarchical aspect to the American presidency. Michael Novak has written that "royalty, the human heart ceaselessly reinvents it" and so it is.[27] Washington is our great pilgrimage city, and the White House one of our cherished symbols, a near shrine in the heart of the Capital city. It is the only historic and majestic building in that city in which someone dwells. Ten thousand persons march through that American shrine every day. Most Americans are inclined to agree with the Roosevelts that the presidency is a bully pulpit and preeminently a position of moral leadership. We may disagree heatedly over what constitutes the "moral" position on an issue, but as journalist James Reston writes, the White House is the "pulpit of the nation and the president is its chaplain." If this inflated sense of moral leadership sometimes invites strained or pious religiosity from some presidents, this is nonetheless a part of the dilemma of appearing presidential.

Presidents apparently have to respond as moral and quasi-spiritual leaders because of our remarkable sense of mission. We are told that all great nations have blasphemously identified their mission with a divine purpose. So our own streak of messianism should not be surprising. Herman Melville wrote that "we Americans are the peculiar chosen people . . . the Israel of our time." We were to be like "a city set upon a hill," a colony whose duty was to establish a pattern for all Christendom so that the reformation might be fulfilled. So it was that a Woodrow Wilson would claim that "the heart of the [American] people is pure" and that we would exert our moral and spiritual energy to spread and protect our values.

Much of this sense of messianism or providential destiny is illusion. Mindless patriotism can cause fatal problems. No nation is "saved." We have motives and interests that are selfish, even squalid, as well as idealistic. Providence has not set us apart from lesser breeds. We too are part of history's seamless web.[28]

Priority Setting and Program Design

Presidents, by custom, have become responsible for proposing new initiatives in the areas of foreign policy, economic growth and stability, and the quality of life in America. This was not always the case. But beginning with Woodrow Wilson and particularly since the New Deal, a president is expected to promote peace, prevent depressions, and formulate domestic programs to resolve countless societal problems.

Much of the growth in the presidency, especially since World War II, has been brought about by the belief that critical societal problems require "wise men" be assigned to the White House to advise the president on appropriate solutions and to serve as the agents for implementing them. Congress has often acted on the basis of this belief; it has approved legislation creating the National Security Council, the Council of Economic Advisers, and the Council on Environmental Quality. Congress has also increased the president's chores by giving him statutory responsibility to prepare more and more reports on what are regarded as critical social areas, for example, annual economic and manpower reports and a biennial report on national growth.

But why aren't national priorities set as a result of presidential elections? Many people assume presidents come into office knowing what they want to accomplish. Such, however, is seldom the case. Campaigns commonly offer little more than a chance to trace out broad policy directions. American elections rarely help with policy clarification. In many instances, elections do not offer meaningful choices. On other occasions presidents break their campaign pledges. On still other occasions, circumstances change. One only has to recall, for example, that the "peace candidate" won in 1916, 1940, and 1964. The important point is that rarely are explicit policy choices made during a campaign. For the candidates a campaign is a fight to win office not an intellectual exercise in program development. So it is a president must spend enormous amounts of his time — after he has become president — considering policy options and deciding how much he can budget for his new priorities.

Presidents are invariably criticized for not being programmatic enough, for not being more passionately committed. The fact is presidents, by force of habit, are almost always wanting to extend their personal influence, not their ideology, over people and programs. They are generally suspicious of long-range planning. Politicians inherently fear being in advance of their time. They enjoy flexible processes and eschew explicit platforms forever visited on them by well-meaning expert advisers. Presidents are constantly being asked to plan, to forecast, to prevent us from going down the path to policy disasters, yet their instinct is "to leave their options open."

Presidents spend considerable amounts of time early in their administrations trying to fashion better advisory and priority-setting processes. Students of advisory processes agree that what works for one president may not work for another. Even the best of formal arrangements guarantees very little, for sometimes the most unlikely sources provide the most useful advice. The most systematic advisory apparatus may fail to provide essential advice when a president needs it.[29]

Democratic presidents seem to have a penchant to set up brain-trust groups and task forces or presidential advisory commissions that will help them set priorities and formulate an activist legislative program. Republican presidents have shown somewhat less interest in initiating in this kind of domestic-policy advice procedure. Still, Hoover's social-trends studies, Eisenhower's goals for America program, and certain of Nixon's attempts to promote national growth and population policies and national-goal studies suggest that Republicans, too, have often groped for mechanisms that would help the nation plan better for future needs.[30]

Too much advice can sometimes paralyze. Harry Truman once became upset with an economic adviser who insisted on always giving him the "on the one hand and yet on the other hand" type of advice. Finally Truman bluntly exclaimed: "Get me a one-armed economist!" As a politician, of course, a president must constantly be engaged in bargaining and compromising — in the art of the possible — and as such he is forced to act as an incrementalist, a pragmatist, and an experimenter. Comprehensive programs seldom pass, as Carter found out.

The essence of the modern presidency lies in its potential capability to resolve societal problems. To be sure, a president much of the time may try to avoid, duck, or delay controversial decisions. But presidential leadership at its best knows where the followers are. Lincoln did not invent or lead the antislavery movement; nor did Roosevelt start the depression. Kennedy and Johnson did not begin or lead the civil-rights movement in the 1960s. But all of these presidents, in their respective times, became embroiled in these controversies, for a president cannot ignore for long what divides the nation.

The effective president will attempt to clarify many of the major issues of the day, define what is possible, and harness the governmental structure so that new initiatives are possible. A president — with the cooperation of Congress — can set national goals and propose legislation. Close inspection indicates that in many instances a president's so-called new initiatives are measures that are or have been under consideration in Congress. Thus many of Carter's initiatives were new attempts at old compromises or revivals of previously unsuccessful measures.

Recruitment Leadership

A president's most strategic formal resource is the ability to recruit able people who share his convictions to fill high-level positions in both the executive and judical branches. According to what might be called the good-person theory, a presidency is only as good as its staffs, cabinet, and counselors. Quality and loyalty are what is wanted. In practice, the notion that a president dominates the recruitment and appointment process is misleading. Many mistakes are made in recruitment and seldom is enough time given to it. One Kennedy aide said, in retrospect, "Our recruitment effort was pretty accidental and backward. . . ." Nixon aides reported that their patronage and recruitment efforts verged on the disastrous during the first two years.

After running for the presidency for several years the successful candidate often finds that the people he courted during the campaign — delegates, press, financial contributors, machine leaders, advance men, or political strategists — do not have the skills needed to manage the executive branch. Kennedy repeatedly complained, "People, people, people! I don't know any people [for the cabinet and other top posts]. I only know voters! How am I going to fill these 1,200 jobs?" [31] Almost half of Kennedy's eventual cabinet appointees were unknown to him. Carter supposedly had about three thousand posts to fill, but in an effort to restore dignity to his cabinet officers he permitted them to allocate a large portion of the vacancies.

In the postelection rush many appointments are made on the basis of subjective judgments or ethnic or geographical representation and from too limited a field of candidates. Ironically, at the time when a president has the largest number of jobs to fill and enjoys his greatest drawing power, he has less time and information available to take advantage of this major prerogative than at any other point in his administration. Later in his term, he has fewer vacancies and usually less prestige; candidates from outside the government are wary about being saddled with troubled programs and recognize that little can be accomplished in an administration's last year or two. During the postelection rush there is also the need to deflect an avalanche of unsolicited job requests — many from local campaign persons — without giving offense.

Too frequently appointees are not carefully related to policy. Many subcabinet appointments, for example, are made by subordinates, with the president hardly aware of whether the appointee is matched with the position. Just after election the views of the president and of his appointees are in a state of evolution. Once in office many appointees adopt new attitudes as a result of new institutionalized responsibilities; or some, perhaps ill-suited for institutional management, may become rigidly wedded to the views of the interest groups with which they most frequently interact.

Presidential appointments may and often do err in the opposite direction as well: a president can be surrounded by such like-minded appointees that an amiability and conformity in thinking can develop all too easily. Social psychologist Irving Janis points out that when this occurs there is a dangerous inclination to resort to seeking concurrence and groupthink at the expense of critical judgment. [32] The cult of loyalty to President Nixon doubtless encouraged the suspension of critical and objective thinking on the part of many of the people involved in the Watergate affair.

Many other circumstances limit the presidential appointment prerogative. The chief limit, of course, is that the members of Congress (primarily the Senate) usually view the recruitment process, especially the appointment of key policymaking officials (about 150 a year) as a power presidents must share with them. They increasingly have viewed the selections of these officials as decisions with important political and policy implication. They often try, consequently, to influence these choices. They often also have candidates of their own. This is especially the case in recent years, for as the staffs of Congress have expanded to over twenty-five thousand, there are more and more aides to members of Congress who seek top executive-branch appointments.

Some potential appointees just do not want to live or even be near Washington, D.C. Others balk at the idea of having to disclose their financial background and income. (The 1977 Bert Lance affair highlighted this problem.) Involvement with past administrators or too close an association with past scandals or major industries connected with a new assignment may be enough to occasion congressional hostility to a presidential nomination. Nelson Rockefeller's wealth and personal gifts became an obstacle in his nomination for vice president. Several former Nixon aides, such as Peter Flanigan who was nominated by Ford as ambassador to Spain, were unable to overcome senatorial opposition and subsequently Ford withdrew these nominations. Congress is somewhat more sensitive these days to any kind of potential conflict of interest, especially when it will directly affect American consumers. Carter had to withdraw a number of his nominees to regulatory agencies and his first choice for head of the CIA, Theodore Sorensen, withdrew under pressure. In short, then, the pool of available appointees is often smaller than people assume.

Presidents also nominate federal judges. They are appointed for life. Here the Justice Department, the American Bar Association, and the members of the U.S. Senate play a large role. ABA rankings and evaluations are weighed heavily in most administrations. The tradition of "senatorial courtesy" — the right of a senator to veto a candidate from his home state for purely personal reasons — tremendously constrains the president's appointment of federal district judges.

The selection of Supreme Court justices who have a constitutionally prescribed independence from the executive, as distinct from appointments nominally under a president's line of authority, can also lead to major disappointments. Historically, for example, the Senate has rejected nearly 20 percent of the presidential nominees to the Supreme Court, most recently including one each in 1968, 1969, and 1970. Political scientist Robert Scigliano suggests that one Supreme Court justice in four consistently rules quite differently from what the president who appointed him expected and that numerous other justices fail to conform to expectations in cases of particular importance.[33] Some presidents apparently thought that the people they appointed held views different from those they actually held. In other instances, the liberating conditions of court office — life tenure, high salary, and responsibility to the Constitution and legal tradition — may have altered the views of justices.

Harry Truman is alleged to have said that his appointment of Tom Clark to the Supreme Court was one of his biggest mistakes. It is known that Eisenhower was retrospectively displeased that his appointees, Earl Warren and William J. Brennan, created a Supreme Court libertarian majority. An Eisenhower contemporary wrote:

> Eisenhower felt increasing disappointment at Warren's increasing show of finding law for libertarian political doctrine where there was none in the books, and at the support of this practice by his first Democratic appointee to the Court, Justice Brennan. The President told his friends that Chief Judge Arthur Vanderbilt of New Jersey, who had an enviable reputation for decisions based on the law of the cases, had assured him that Brennan had the same "ideal judicial concept," and said the President, "he had got the same mistaken impression of Brennan in a conversation prior to the appointment." [34]

Justice Byron White has voted more conservatively than Kennedy forces had expected. But the Kennedy difficulties were greater in the selection of federal circuit and district judges in the South. In large part these choices "were the products of the preexisting judicial selection system which the Kennedys inherited and more or less perpetuated without much question. . . ." [35] As is traditional, of course, regional senators had offered nominations for these regional posts. With a slim working majority in Congress, Kennedy was constantly aware that his legislative program could suffer at the hands of disgruntled southerners. Accordingly, the Kennedy brothers learned that "you have to play ball with the senators and do the best you can." But it seems clear in retrospect that no one aspect of the Kennedy performance in the civil-rights area is more vulnerable to criticism than the exercise of the appointment prerogative. Simply stated, they gave in too readily, for the Kennedys bypassed civil-rights legislation in favor of litigation yet turned right around and appointed individuals dedicated to frustrating that very litigation. "[One result was that] the Kennedy Justice Department was forced to devote thousands of dollars, untold energy, imagination and brilliance, all to counteract the obstructionist tactics of its appointees, five of whom decided over one hundred cases against the Negro, the Civil Rights Division, and the Constitution. . . ." [36]

Nixon, of course, had considerable trouble trying to appoint a southern conservative to the bench. Twice he was thwarted and only after appointing two northerners was he able to succeed with his nomination of Justice Powell, a moderate Virginian and an esteemed past president of the American Bar Association.

Patronage factors enter more into appointments in the federal regional and field offices of domestic departments than into those in Washington. Patronage concerns often are accentuated in new and controversial program areas, presumably because of the need for political support. In many such instances congressmen and interest groups seek appointments for their nominees to advance their own interests in regional and regulatory areas. An entire spectrum of traditional patronage posts — judgeships, United States marshals and attorneys, collectors of the customs, members of selective-service boards, and regional white-collar jobs — are claimed by congressmen, governors, or state party leaders as a matter of right. Presidential resistance invites disloyalty and disaffection. Some important administrative positions are the private preserve of congressional committees, well-organized interest groups, or professions. The liabilities of the appointment prerogative are recalled by the political maxim "Filling a political job creates nine enemies and one ingrate."

AFL-CIO officials have often dictated top Labor Department appointments. Nixon's second secretary of labor, James D. Hodgson, complained after being forced to resign in 1972 that AFL-CIO President George Meany insisted on a cabinet member who would be "100% for labor's point of view regardless of how the Secretary himself feels as a member of the President's Cabinet." Hodgson added that "what Meany really wanted was for me to be the Earl Butz for organized labor." [37] During the Johnson administration, the AFL-CIO was able to keep favored a few subcabinet members in their posts despite the wishes of the president and cabinet secretary. Similarly, the American Medical Association has enjoyed a special voice in the selection of high-level federal health officials, especially under Republican administrations. The absence of lateral-entry opportunities in certain government services also works to limit the scope of presidential appointment; for example, appointees for the chairmanship of the Joint Chiefs of Staff must be designated from among a select few of the senior career military officers.

An effective president shrewdly uses his recruitment resource not only as a means of rewarding campaign supporters and enhancing his ties to Congress but also as a vital form of communicating the priorities and policy directions of his administration. One student of the appointment process describes the importance of this function:

> A President's nominees are the primary link between him and the millions of men and women in the federal bureaucracy. Most of these men and women are located in the executive branch of the government and technically they work for the President. But he has little power to hire and fire them, he cannot control their political loyalties, and he lacks the time and resources to supervise their activities. His executive appointees must act as his surrogates in dealing with the federal bureaucracy. The quality and the character of the people he chooses to serve in

executive positions will have a major impact on the ability of his tran-
sient administration to control the permanent government.[38]

Even when presidents have recruited able and loyal persons to their
administration they run the risk of high turnover. The average cabinet
member has stayed in his post for only about two and a half years. Vietnam
and Watergate motivated more resignations and premature departures than
would have otherwise been the case. It takes at least a year for most
cabinet-level administrators to make positive contributions, which is why
Carter insisted on a commitment of four years from most of his senior
appointees (though a number of them were terminated in the third year).

> Admittedly, a four-year commitment would be a deterrent to enter-
> ing government for some people; however, it is worth the price to build
> some stability into government leadership, limit the wasteful startup
> periods for new appointees, and ensure knowledgeable management from
> sincere people dedicated to making government work.[39]

Legislative and Political Coalition Building

An effective president is an effective politician. Although the public may
often say it wants the president to be above politics, the job nevertheless
requires him to be a political mobilizer, a salesman for his programs, a
lobbyist and a politician in chief. We have so designed our system with
checks and balances and dispersed powers that no change is possible without a skilled coalition builder in the White House. As discussed in earlier
chapters, a president can rarely command; he must spend most of his
time persuading people to join, help, or vote with him. Although many
of our presidents have been great persuaders, most people most of the
time think of their own interests and objectives.

Perhaps the rarest of presidential talents in this century has been
the capacity to galvanize and sustain a political party in order to realize
program objectives. The office does not guarantee political leadership;
it merely offers its incumbents an invitation to lead politically. It is in
this sense that those best suited to the job are those who can creatively
shape their political environment and savor the rough-and-tumble give-
and-take of political life.

Many presidents become timid about using the resources of the presidency for partisan leadership. The reason for this, of course, is that a
president wants above all to be president of all the people, and yet even
an outstanding performance as a symbolic chief of state cannot relieve a
president from the responsibility of educating his party about his objectives. A president is obliged to respond to the interests and expectations
of the party that nominated and elected him. Having made pledges for
which both he and his party will be held to account in future elections,
a president must try to win support for his definition of what must be

done. The paradox here is that he has to be both a national unifier and, as party leader, a divider of the people.

With rare exceptions, presidents have substantial difficulty in getting Congress to pass their programs. In President Nixon's first term only 35 percent of his publicly requested programs were approved; and in about the same time in office, President Kennedy, with 40 percent approval, fared little better. Part of the problem is that during the first year, which is the best year for him to entreat Congress to act upon his programs, much of a president's time must be spent in organizing his own household and studying policy recommedations. As President Johnson, who was able to get about 57 percent of his programs approved by Congress, noted: "You've got to give it all you can, that first year. . . . Doesn't matter what kind of a majority you come in with. You've got just one year when they treat you right, and before they start worrying about themselves. The third year, you lose votes. . . . The fourth year's all politics. You can't put anything through when half the Congress is thinking how to beat you." [40]

A president's proposals may be arrested by a Congress even fresh on the heels of a triumphant election. Franklin Roosevelt, after his election in 1936 by the largest plurality in electoral history, suffered his most embarrassing congressional rebuff in the defeat of his bill to enlarge the Supreme Court. For a different set of reasons, immediately following his electoral landslide in 1972, President Nixon experienced a strikingly similar congressional stubbornness. Congress opposed Nixon more often in 1973 than it had opposed any president in the previous twenty years.

The skills and resources requisite for winning office are not necessarily those useful in dealing with legislators. John Kennedy, in spite of fourteen years in Congress, had little taste for effectively courting Congress. From the perspective of the presidency, he saw the collective power of Congress as a bloc far stronger than he had thought when a senator:

> It is very easy to defeat a bill in the Congress. It is much more difficult to pass one. To go through a subcommittee . . . and get a majority vote, the full committee and get a majority vote, go to the Rules Committee and get a rule, go to the Floor of the House and get a majority, start over again in the Senate, subcommittee and full committee, and in the Senate there is unlimited debate, so you can never bring a matter to a vote if there is enough determination on the part of the opponents, even if they are a minority, to go through the Senate with the bill. And then unanimously get a conference between the House and Senate to adjust the bill, or if one member objects, to have it go back through the Rules Committee, back through the Congress, and have this done on a controversial piece of legislation where powerful groups are opposing it, that is an extremely difficult task. [41]

One of the misleading indications of presidential power or success is the so-called presidential box score used by the *Congressional Quarterly* to indicate successes and failures in legislative programs. If Congress has approved a majority of a president's legislative program, the *Congressional Quarterly* may headline their story "Congress Acts Favorably on President X's Requests." The impression often given is that a president is not only devoted to high principle but has also given independent, creative, galvanizing impetus to legislative progress. It is as if the president is the chief legislator; the Congress is mainly passive and has yielded its legislative authority.

However, these scores must be regarded cautiously. In the first instance, they are often deceptive because legislative measures are by no means equal in importance. Such box scores, moreover, fail to distinguish between measures that were central and those peripheral to presidential priorities. In addition, they were skewed by the high percentage of presidential requests in the areas of defense and foreign policy, which Congress approves somewhat more readily than other matters. They show nothing of those programs a president wanted but, recognizing the overwhelming likelihood of defeat, never requested at all. Much of what a president does not achieve consists of what he never requested, rather than of what he proposes but does not get passed. Finally, sometimes a president merely anticipates what is going to pass Congress and adds his endorsement at a late stage in its legislative development. Table 5.2 and Figure 5.1 offer two different ways in which the *Congressional Quarterly* displays a president's legislative box score.

The relationship between president and Congress is designed as much for conflict as for cooperation. Congress enjoys substantial authority over confirmations and program authorizations. The quality of the congressional staff has increased impressively in the past thirty years. More than twenty-five thousand employees now serve Congress. Moreover, more professionals and professional organizations now render assistance to Congress as well as to the executive branch: "The nation's corps of expert professionals . . . has long given primary allegiance to the executive branch, and has often been scornful of Congress. But today even that pendulum has begun to swing. Former State Department and Presidential advisors are seeking congressional outlets for their services in unprecedented number. Ex-ambassadors, analysts and White House staffers abound on Capitol Hill. The powerful staff of the Senate Foreign Relations Committee consists almost entirely of refugees from the Foreign Service." [42]

Congress may not be the fountainhead of reformist and redistributive leadership; but, when it wants to be, it can play a relatively active role in determining or thwarting particular policies. It has clearly played such a role in tax matters, in policies determining freedom of information, and in the procurement, development, and evaluation of weapons systems.

Textbooks tend to emphasize the legislative triumphs of Wilson, Roosevelt, and Lyndon Johnson. But a closer examination of these presi-

TABLE 5.2   PRESIDENTIAL PROGRAMS
ENACTED INTO LAW, 1954–1978

Year	Proposals Submitted	Approved by Congress	Percent Approved
1954	232	150	65%
1955	207	96	46
1956	225	103	46
1957	206	76	37
1958	234	110	47
1959	228	93	41
1960	183	56	31
1961	355	172	48
1962	298	133	45
1963	401	109	27
1964	217	125	58
1965	469	323	69
1966	371	207	56
1967	431	205	48
1968	414	231	56
1969	171	55	32
1970	210	97	46
1971	202	40	20
1972	116	51	44
1973	183	57	31
1974 (Nixon)	97	33	34
1974 (Ford)	64	23	36
1975	110	30	27

Source: Congress and the Nation (Washington, D.C.: The Congressional Quarterly, 1969), vol. 2, p. 625 and as updated in the *Congressional Almanacs,* 1970–1979. By permission. The Congressional Quarterly decided to discontinue this kind of analysis in 1976, apparently because it was open to the criticisms outlined on page 170.

dential efforts suggests that they occurred usually during brief periods (1913–1915, 1933–1935, 1964–1965). A development just as important, but seldom given as much attention, has been the rise and frequent importance of the conservative coalition in Congress, which refers to the tendency of southerners or conservative Democrats to join with Republican colleagues in Congress in resisting social and economic reform measures proposed by the White House. Since 1936 this coalition has been an important political force in tempering White House leadership efforts. All of our recent presidents, including Nixon, Ford, and Carter, have had programs undermined, if not buried, by the conservative coalition. The conservative coalition has taken especially heavy tolls on Carter's program.

FIGURE 5.1
PRESIDENTIAL SUCCESS ON MEASURES ON WHICH PRESIDENTS
TOOK A POSITION, 1953–1978

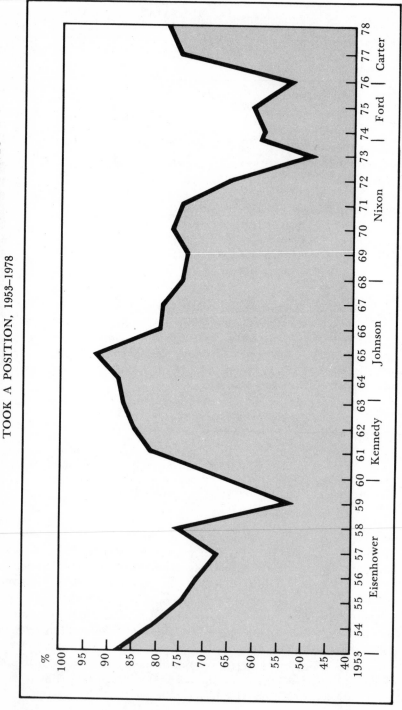

Source: 1978 Almanac Quarterly, 95th Congress (Washington, D.C.: The Congressional Quarterly, 1979), vol. 34, p. 23c. By permission.

Congressional barriers to presidential initiatives are particularly apparent in the important areas of budget and tax policies, both of which must be approved by Congress. Timely presidential fiscal initiatives, particularly countercyclical fiscal actions, become difficult to carry through because Congress generally resists any raising of taxes and, at the same time, any cutting of spending for federal programs. Even the threat of the latter brings an avalanche of protests from interest groups inside and outside the government. Thus, for example, tax cuts passed in 1964, 1969, and 1971 were coupled with actual expansions of existing programs, which sharply reduced federal revenue receipts and strongly braked the ability of either the president or Congress to launch significant new social-action programs.

Another area in which Congress influences presidential initiatives is in the shaping of legislation. Much of the recent writing about the presidency suggests that Congress merely delays and amends and is basically incapable of creating legislation or formulating policy. In actuality, however, Congress sometimes plays the dominant role in initiating legislation; the formulation as well as the enactment of virtually all major legislation relating to domestic and economic policy is the result of extensive conversations between the presidency and Congress and between both of these institutions and pivotal interest groups.

Much of the policy presidents supposedly formulate and propose as their own is derived directly from traditional party priorities, from previous presidents, or from Congress. Just as the celebrated New Deal legislation had a fairly well-defined prenatal history extending back several years before its espousal by FDR, so also recent investigations into the origins and enactment of most of the New Frontier and Great Society legislative programs — for example, broader medical-care programs, federal aid to education, and the more activist stance on civil rights — indicate they too were the fruition of past recommendations by the Democratic party.

A president has three major resources with which he can enhance his political coalition and legislative lobbying roles. First, he can achieve a closer contact with the American public than any other politician in the country. The president can and often does appeal directly to the people for their support. This does not always work, but when a president can define an issue and rally the public's concern, Congress and other power centers usually will take careful note.

A second resource is his use of patronage. Patronage today refers not only to jobs and favors rendered but also to campaign trips into districts and states, invitations to the White House, and countless considerations that a president can exchange in an effort to win friends and influence votes. The president's congressional liaison office, with a staff of sometimes up to twenty in recent years, works full time trying to employ these possibilities for maximum advantage.

The third resource is a president's role in his political party. A president has no formal position in the party structure, but his influence over national policies and appointments and his celebrity status commands respect from party leaders. A president needs the party's support to enact his program. However, a president has virtually no influence over his party in Congress. He cannot select its leaders and he cannot select the people who run for House and Senate seats. A president finds, consequently, that he has to bargain and negotiate with party leaders in his own party just as he does with other independent power brokers. Because national parties have declined in importance, most recent presidents often fall back on the personal network that originally enabled him to gain the presidential nomination.

President Carter, even more than others, has found the job of political coalition builder an exacting one. Why has this been the case? One of his greatest handicaps is that he came to the White House at a time when people were seriously questioning both the power of the presidency and the scope of government itself. The toothful southerner had come to office to make programs work better, not to preside over diminution of presidential powers and federal programs. But the mood of the country had become fixed, or so it seemed, and Carter's pleadings for new, multiple comprehensive programs fell on indifferent if not hostile ears.

Although Carter was willing to make accommodations with power brokers and leading congressmen, he would move out aggressively on a project without first exploring the political minefields to see what traps and opposition he would encounter. "And when he discovered that he did not have the necessary support, he would have to back down in public — with a consequent loss of personal and public prestige. His compromises, in short, came later in the game after damage had been done to his political reputation and his relationship with politically powerful others." [43] That was his problem in dealing with the Georgia state legislature and it continued to cause him problems in Washington.

Carter's coalition-building leadership was further complicated by new congressional rules and especially by the power diffusion in the House of Representatives. As of 1975 Congress was a much more democratic institution than it had been. A presidential "leadership breakfast" with congressional leaders no longer meant as much as it did in the mid-1960s or late 1950s. By 1977 the president literally needed to "do business" and "horse-trade" with hundreds of members.

Moreover, few Democrats in Congress felt dependent in any way on Carter. Just about all the members of Congress ran well ahead of Carter in their districts or states. Whereas Lyndon Johnson definitely helped several dozen congressmen and senators in their election or reelection bids in

1964, and consequently reaped an obligation due, Carter ran behind them. This, together with other changing aspects of congressional campaigns, has added further distance between the president and members of his own party.[44] For example, incumbent members of Congress now have such an armament of campaign tools (including countless trips home, the free franking mailings, low-cost television productions, enlarged staffs in Washington and mobile-van offices in their districts) that they are less in need of the president's goodwill. It has also been realized, by both presidents and congressmen, that there is not much a president can do to punish members of Congress who fail to vote for the administration's programs.

> Attempting to coerce members of Congress into voting along with the White House has never been a productive strategy for Presidents; any threats made by the President will be perceived as quite empty, simply because he has few if any sanctions to use in retaliation against an uncooperative Congressman. The appeal to a member's constituency, however, has been a more useful one for the White House. If the President or his staff could convince the Congressman that the President's program was also something desired by the member's constituents . . . perhaps the President could get a member previously in opposition to vote with the White House. With more and more members now adopting non-issue-based representation stories, however, such an appeal also becomes more problematic for the President. If the member feels that he will be re-elected on the basis of constituency service activities, regardless of how he votes on issues with the exception of issues such as abortion in which positions are held especially intensely), he will not be especially responsive to arguments from the President's men that it will be good politics back home for him to support the White House. Since the President cannot coerce the member, and since appeals to the member's constituency are increasingly less effective, what remains is for the President to convince the Congressman on the merits of the issue. Such convincing is, of course, often more difficult than an appeal to the member's self-interest.[45]

Many of the techniques, therefore, that were available to presidents such as Lyndon Johnson are not as available or as usable for Carter.

Finally, Carter, for reasons that are not altogether clear, did not project an image as a forceful mobilizer and lobbyist. He very early became portrayed as a soft-spoken and almost lonely man. He was so effectively "cool" and calm on television that he seldom stirred people to any action other than switching channels. It often appeared he simply lacked the improvising and parrying coalition-builder skills needed to lead his party and Congress. Some wondered whether Carter really had intellectual commitments for which he was willing to fight. Perhaps he was really just a process president, someone who merely wanted to make programs work better.

Policy Implementation and Evaluation

Implementation, the carrying out and realization of presidential goals, is a crucial part of a president's job. The provisions made within the executive office to ensure presidential control over implementation simply do not guarantee this happens. Repeatedly, federal programs fail to accomplish desired goals. When such failures occur, it is relatively easy to blame the original legislation rather than examine what happened after a bill became a law. Of course, poorly written legislation can yield poor results. But students of national policymaking now realize even the best legislation can fail owing to problems encountered during implementation. Sometimes these problems can lead to the outright failure of a program; more often, however, they mean excessive delay, underachievements of desired goals, or costs way above those originally expected.

Implementation can be viewed as a process involving a long chain of decision points all of which need to be cleared before a program can be successfully carried out. At each decision point is a public official or community leader who holds power to advance — or delay — the program. The more decision points a program needs to clear, the greater the chance of failure or delay. Special problems result if the successful implementation of a national program depends on the cooperation of state and local officials. The state or locality may be eager to help; another might be opposed to a program and try to stop it. The advent of new federalism and the vast growth in the number and scope of federal grant-in-aid programs have added to the problem of implementation.[46]

If anything has been learned by students of the presidency during the past twenty years, it is that policymaking does not end once a law is passed (or when a court decision or presidential executive order is handed down). The implementation of such laws, especially the development of specific guidelines and regulations, can have just as great an impact on public policy as the law itself. The ultimate responsibility for the implementation of the nation's governmental decisions rests with the president. "Implementing a public policy may include a wide variety of actions including issuing directives, enforcing directives, disbursing funds, making loans, awarding grants, making contracts, collecting information, disseminating information, assigning personnel, hiring personnel, and creating organizational units. Rarely are policies self-executing, i.e., implemented by their mere statement such as a policy not to recognize a certain government. Most policies require some positive action." [47]

We generally elect politicians as our presidents and then, almost as an afterthought, we hope they will be competent executives. Executive skills are not the highest priorities people seek in their preferred presidential candidates. More often than not our presidents come from the legislatures and law practices that may prepare them well for passing laws but ill prepare them for policy-implementation leadership.

Presidential decisions transmitted to the bureaucracy often have a way of getting watered down or ignored. The routines of governmental bureaucracies are geared to maintaining the status quo. That's fine if a president merely wants to maintain the status quo. But most presidents want to change at least some policies. Yet policies persist from one administration to the next remarkably unchanged. Resistance to change is reinforced by several factors, chief of which are (1) inadequate communication and determination by a president, (2) the alliances between bureaucrats and the appropriate special interests and congressmen, and (3) inadequate information and evaluation processes.

A president has to be extraordinarily clear in his policy directives and persuasion efforts for lack of clarity is a prime excuse for officials — even appointed political officials — to go their own way. An aide to Franklin D. Roosevelt emphasized how even cabinet members ignore a president's requests: "Half of a President's suggestions, which theoretically carry the weight of orders, can be safely forgotten by a Cabinet member. And if the President asks about a suggestion a second time, he can be told that it is being investigated. If he asks a third time a wise cabinet officer will give him at least part of what he suggests. But only occasionally, except about the most important matters, do Presidents ever get around to asking three times." [48]

Time and again all our recent presidents have been astonished at instances of noncompliance with their suggestions for implementation. But seldom is it a problem of outright defiance. Typically, it is because of red tape and cautious, slow-moving officials who believe they know how to do their jobs. Sometimes, of course, this does involve differing policy preferences.

Too often the White House underestimates the importance of clear communications at the outset of an administration and later to overestimate the uncooperativeness of career public servants. Caution is needed not to breed a we/they relationship or to breed hostility and disloyalty where none exists. Too often, also, the White House accepts the size and complexity of the large bureaucracies of the permanent government as insuperable and nonadaptive obstacles. What is needed is a White House strategy that consciously recognizes presidential dependency on the federal bureaus and field operations and takes into account the fact that presidential policy objectives will continue to lose clarity between the stages of legislation and implementation. What is also needed are innovative outreach and feedback strategies designed to keep organizations well informed of presidential intent, motivated to carry out such intents, and accountable for performance. These, of course, are far easier to talk about than to achieve.

Another major factor minimizing presidential influence in the implementation stage is the fact executive-branch departments are more the creation of Congress than the White House. Special-interest groups often effectively capture administrative as well as legislative officials and succeed in fragmenting the organization to their own ends. Former Secretary of Health, Education and Welfare John W. Gardner told the Senate Government Operations Committee:

> As everyone in this room knows but few people outside of Washington understand, questions of public policy nominally lodged with the Secretary are often decided far beyond the Secretary's reach by a trinity consisting of (1) representatives of an outside body, (2) middle level bureaucrats and (3), selected members of Congress, particularly those concerned with appropriations. In a given field these people may have collaborated for years. They have a durable alliance that cranks out legislation and appropriations in behalf of their special interest. Participants in such durable alliances do not want the Department Secretaries strengthened. The outside special interests are particularly resistant to such change. It took them years to dig their particular tunnel into the public vault, and they don't want the vault moved.[49]

Congress, even when it is dominated by the president's party, often does not want to increase presidential discretion within executive agencies. The congressional committee structure in large measure parallels executive-branch organization, and what often appear to be structural absurdities in the executive branch may persist because of long-standing jurisdictional disputes within the Congress. Citing their responsibility of administrative review, these committees jealously protect what they consider to be their prerogative to determine how the departments and agencies they oversee are to be restructured. In addition, congressmen guard those areas in which they have developed expertise and close relations with government officials and extragovernmental clientele. A committee reorganization could diminish a member's sources of campaign finance or even jeopardize his chances for reelection.

Congressional opposition, no doubt mirroring labor and agricultural interest groups who feared losing functional representation and symbolic status, helped doom Johnson's attempt to abolish the Labor Department in 1967 and Nixon's 1971 attempt to restructure the executive departments. Influential congressmen have undermined repeated attempts to shift the civil functions of the Army Corps of Engineers to the Interior Department. Influential members of Congress also blocked the establishment of Nixon's proposed Department of Community Development in 1972, even though it had been reported out favorably by the House Government Operations Committee. Time and again, duplication, inefficiency, and anomalies in the executive-branch organization chart have been allowed to persist because particular committees have demanded programs remain in departments under their control.

Presidential policy implementation requires accurate information and evaluations of how programs are doing. But a president often does not have the staff resources to perform these functions effectively. Existing arrangements for program development rely heavily on ad hoc efforts by collections of executive-office aides and part-time outside advisers. Moreover, quantitative indicators of performance, especially in domestic programs, are difficult to obtain, and the measurements that are available often are not transmitted swiftly or accurately to the White House. Until recently, most domestic bureaus and agencies have assessed their programs in such a way as to praise them rather than analyze them.

Another difficulty is departments and agencies have routinely "measured" their own performance by adding up program inputs, that is, the number of dollars spent, the number of people employed, or the number of local projects in operation. Departmental officials until recently seldom were trained or required to view their programs in terms of outcomes, that is, as performance results or as comparisons of one program with that of others. Program-evaluation reports coming from departmental bureaus are still suspect, however, because to a considerable extent the success of the programs they administer puts their own performance on the line. As Victor Navasky points out: "It is an unwritten law of annual report writing in the federal bureaucracy that every agency's statistics are better than those of the previous year and far better than those of the previous administration, so the statistics trotted out at such moments prove nothing." [50] Agencies and bureaus such as the FBI annually must show increased activity in their areas if their funding is to be raised accordingly.

Not only are available statistical indicators crude but the political implications of the available data must also be gauged. Evaluation is never entirely apolitical; it will be used by one party or branch of government against another, and evaluators may become passionate advocates of programs that their analyses support, thereby risking their neutrality. But statistical information on young pilot programs must be interpreted cautiously; ambiguity must be confronted with a sense of balanced perspective; short- and long-term effects may appear contradictory. These are complex assignments for both social scientists and public officials. A former commissioner of the Bureau of Labor Statistics, Arthur Ross, explained that officials can easily deceive themselves with statistics of impeccable quality:

> The trouble is that the unmeasured, or unmeasurable aspects of a problem may be vastly more important than those that have been, or can be, measured. And even with measurements that are known to reflect on the core of a problem, the rate of change in the United States has become so swift that "good" statistics, intelligently used in decision-making, may be rendered irrelevant or obsolete by the time action results from an official decision.

> These margins for misjudgment are not always stressed to the policy-maker. Attracted by the appearance of objectivity and precision, he keeps

his eyes fixed on charts and tables that may be incomplete, obsolete, or both. Eventually he may come to believe that poverty really is a condition of having less than the current cut-off point of $3,335 in annual income, that full employment really is a situation where the national unemployment rate is 4 percent or less, and that Vietnam really is a matter of body counts and kill ratios.[51]

There are, of course, additional obstacles that thwart effective policy implementation. Some observers suggest that presidents have ignored the managerial side of their responsibilities because there were so few incentives or rewards for trying to make headway there. In the words of one public administration expert, "No President has been able to identify any significant political capital that might be made out of efforts to improve management except for the conservative purpose of economizing or reducing costs." [52] Others feel that the way in which our civil-service system is organized encourages bureaucratic reluctance or resistance.[53] Still others remind us that the president frequently lacks authority to issue directions to operating departments. "The President's title as Chief Executive is misleading; there is very little that he can or does execute. . . . The work of the executive branch is carried out by operating departments granted specific powers and responsibilities by Act of Congress, and not by Presidential delegation." [54] Joseph Califano, a former White House aide and HEW cabinet secretary, sums up the frustrations of the implementation function:

> The President's power to achieve his goals is remarkably limited. In the budgetary area, he can propose Federal expenditures and tax policies, but it is the Congress that must enact them if they are to become national policy and the law of the land. . . .
>
> Smaller agencies respond to Presidential leadership only in the minds of the most naive students of government administration. Under the myth of reporting to the President, more often than not these agencies operate as independent fiefdoms. . . .
>
> No President, no matter how hard and long he works, can hope to have more than a superficial knowledge and control of the enormous bureaucracy over which he presides.[55]

In sum, the array of formal powers and accumulated "chief executive" prerogatives that we commonly associate with the modern presidency do not, in fact, guarantee the achievement of very much.

Oversight and Early-Warning System

Still another part of the job of the modern president is the design of oversight and early-warning systems and putting these to effective use. Very often, little presidential time or stamina remains for inquiring into those routine activities that make up the great bulk of federal governmental work. Unfortunately, routine activities that are neglected or improperly monitored and evaluated can escalate to crisis proportion. But, for the most part, a president must delegate large amounts of discretion to political subordinates and career professionals, and his influence over routine activities is indirect: through appointees, budgetary examinations, or legislative clearance. A president may view these activities as self-executing, or he may even attempt to dissociate himself from them, but much of the administrative and executive burden of the presidency consists of imaginative supervision of program implementation. The functional task of a president in the leadership of federal implementation activities is much more than merely issuing directives to the cabinet. It entails compromise, coalition building, education, and political leadership just as much as does the winning of congressional or public support. The quality of bread-and-butter service and assistance programs is important to the average American; and a president, like it or not, is held responsible for the general quality of governmental performance.

Progress in both implementation and oversight areas requires leadership at many levels of society. Effective leadership in the future will be provided very often by teams of individuals who possess the skills of power brokers and yet have the patience to work in a context of federalism and complexity. A former cabinet member speaks to this development as follows:

> The old hierarchical model is useless. Our top leaders have a crucial role in helping us to achieve a sense of direction, to aid us in sifting priorities and clarifying values. But less and less can they make the system work without the help of many others throughout the organization of society. We can't expect top leaders, working alone, to "make the thing go." "The thing" won't respond to their command any more because it's no longer "a thing." It's a great many things — innumerable subsystems loosely related in ever-changing configurations.[56]

Only through the skillful monitoring of routine governmental activities can a president know whether citizens are getting a fair return on their taxes. Only by a more imaginative use of presidential resources in overseeing these activities can they be prevented from becoming sources of crises themselves. To be sure, supervision and reform must come not only from presidents but also from other quarters as well. But how effective a president is in fashioning an executive oversight and review system is crucial. On the one hand, he must be able to delegate vast responsibilities to talented managers; on the other hand, he must have an early-warning system that alerts him through, among other means, his managers about inadequate government performance, about experimentation that yields negative results, and about progress in research and development that could provide corrective feedback.

In short, a proper management system would ensure that governmental activities concerned with implementation and routine would be brought to a president's attention when necessary and as they affected priority-setting and political-leadership tasks instead of only when they become matters of crisis management. Interior and transportation officials, for example, should detect evidence of impending fuel shortages sufficiently in advance to permit a president to commission studies and devise remedial strategies before the crisis occurs. White House supervision should have uncovered the extent and scope of illegal CIA domestic spying long before it was discovered by the press. Similarly, data from government-run or -funded experiments or from program evaluations should be processed by the White House in order to find more desirable or workable priorities. If one of the purposes of presidential power is to execute federal laws faithfully and to help avert costly crises, the presidency must be organized systematically as a learning agency, capable of anticipating and preventing system overload, communications failures, and corruption or ineptness in the operations of the executive branch.

CONCLUSIONS

Several underlying incentives help to shape the performance of the presidential job. As they have operated in the recent past, these incentives ensure that certain responsibilities get special attention, whereas others become neglected. Preoccupation with problems of national security and macroeconomics leaves little time for leadership in the area of domestic policy. Crisis management, symbolic leadership, and priority setting also crowd out the tasks of lobbying and program implementation and supervision. Creative follow-through is seldom adequate; the routines of government often go neglected. Program evaluation and the imaginative recruitment of program managers for appropriate tasks never receive the sustained attention they merit. On balance, the White House is caught running around doing either what is easy to do or what it perceives as urgent, sometimes to the neglect of doing what is important.

Doing what is easy or what appears to be more "presidential" seems to make sense because it is rewarded and is rewarded because it seems to make sense. These incentives accentuate certain responsibilities over others and have consequences for the balance and quality of national policymaking. Presidents have tended to assert themselves aggressively in those tasks and functions in the upper left-hand portions of figure 5.1. In these areas the restraints of the three-branch governmental system occur with less force. Political parties, too, are largely irrelevant in this regard, especially on questions of national security and international economic policy.

These tasks get pulled into the White House and treated as personal responsibilities of the president and his senior lieutenants.

Presidents have concentrated in recent years on selected areas of the presidential job. In part, this is because we have created a nearly impossible presidential job description. We give our presidents too much to do and too little time in which to do it. In part, however, recent presidents have also been, or so it would appear, lulled into responding to those parts of their job that are more glamorous, more prominent.

Presidential activity in symbolic, priority-setting, and crisis contexts often conveys an image of strength, vigor, and rigor. Presidents often do appear virile and effective in these areas of the presidential job. But measuring presidential strength or evaluating presidential leadership requires a more comprehensive look at what a president is doing and what he can achieve not only in the three substantive subpresidencies but also in the seven functional leadership categories outlined above. Of course the true measure of a president's effectiveness is his capacity to integrate where necessary his multiple responsibilities in order to avoid having initiatives in one area compound problems in another or having problems go unattended merely because they defy the usual organizational boundaries. Another challenge of presidential leadership is the intricate relating of each aspect of the presidential job to the others. A close examination of presidential performance in recent years relative to the whole matrix of the job suggests that presidents are strong in some areas, weak in others, and that the overarching job of synthesis and integration is seldom performed adequately.

We are not likely to reformulate or redefine in any measurable way the presidential job description, although altering our expectations of the office could help. Nor will structural, institutional reforms that seek to make the presidency more efficient and manageable be able to resolve entirely the paradoxes and dilemmas compounding the job of the presidency, for almost all of the complexities of the presidential condition in America revolve around political problems and the diversity of American values. Those who devise structural solutions to what are essentially political questions are likely to be disappointed. In the end we shall get improved presidential performances when we have a clearer idea of what we want to do as a nation and when we understand better the mix of incentives that now shape the way presidents respond to their political and executive duties. New and different incentives, rewards, and sanctions may be needed. New and different kinds of pressure politics will be needed as well. New and different forms of leadership are needed in positions throughout society as well as in top national government positions.

For the present, a marked imbalance characterizes how presidents perform their job. Existing incentives doubtless lead almost anyone in that job to credibility gaps and tempt the adoption of manipulative coping strategies. What might be done to fashion a presidency that could realistically perform those tasks assigned it and still, as an institution, enhance our democratic system? We can begin to tackle this question by gaining a better appreciation of presidential-congressional relations and of how the White House and the cabinet are organized to assist the president, which are treated in the next chapters.

NOTES

1. Bert Cochran, *Harry Truman and the Crisis Presidency* (Funk & Wagnalls, 1973), p. 120.

2. William Carey, "Presidential Staffing in the Sixties and Seventies," *Public Administration Reviews,* September-October 1969, p. 453.

3. Lyndon Johnson, quoted in Hugh Sidey, *A Very Personal Presidency* (Atheneum, 1978), p. 260.

4. Aaron Wildavsky, "The Two Presidencies," *Trans-Action,* December 1966, in Wildavsky, ed., *Perspectives on the Presidency* (Little, Brown, 1975), p. 448.

5. John F. Kennedy, quoted in Richard Nixon, *RN: Memoirs of Richard Nixon* (Grosset & Dunlap, 1978), p. 235.

6. Richard Nixon, quoted in Theodore White, *The Making of the President 1968* (Atheneum, 1969), p. 147.

7. William Manchester, based on an interview with John F. Kennedy, quoted in Manchester, *Portrait of a President* (Macfadden Books, 1962), p. 33. Manchester also quotes a Kennedy family member as saying, "Of course he's preoccupied [with foreign policy]. It would be a miracle if he weren't. Saigon, Germany, fifty-megaton bombs — that's why he can't get to sleep until two or three in the morning" (p. 33).

8. John F. Kennedy, State of the Union Address, 30 January 1962, *Public Papers of the Presidents of the United States* (U.S. Government Printing Office, 1962), pp. 22–23.

9. John H. Kessel, "The Parameters of Presidential Politics" (Paper presented at the 1972 Annual Meeting of the American Political Science Association; processed), pp. 8–9. Later published in *Social Science Quarterly,* June 1974, pp. 8–24.

10. Leonard Garment, quoted in Theodore H. White, *The Making of the President 1972* (Atheneum, 1973), p. 52.

11. David S. Broder, "To Lose at Home Is to Lose," *Boston Globe,* January 1978, p. A7.

12. For an excellent comparative study of presidential antiinflation efforts, see Cranford D. Goodwin, ed., *Exhortation and Controls: The Search for Wage-Price Controls, 1945–1971* (Brookings Institution, 1975).

13. Presidential press secretary Ronald Ziegler, 1 December 1972, *Weekly Compilation of Presidential Documents* (U.S. Government Printing Office, 4 December 1972) 8:49:1711–12.

14. John F. Kennedy, quoted in Richard Rovere, "Letter from Washington," *New Yorker,* 30 November 1963, p. 53.

15. Martha Derthick, *New Towns In-Town* (Urban Institute, 1972), p. 84.

16. Franklin D. Roosevelt, quoted by Herbert Emmerich, *Federal Organizations and Administrative Management* (University of Alabama Press, 1971), p. 207.

17. David Brinkley, during a television interview, *Thirty Minutes With . . .* (Public Broadcasting Service), 13 July 1971.

18. Lance T. Leloup and Steven A. Shull, "Congress Versus the Executive: The 'Two Presidencies' Revisited" *Social Science Quarterly,* March, 1979.

19. *Ibid.,* pp. 717, 718.

20. Donald A. Peppers, "The Two Presidencies: Eight Years Later," in Aaron Wildavsky, ed., *Perspectives on the Presidency* (Little, Brown, 1975), pp. 463–64.

21. Broder, *op. cit.*

22. Quoted in Joe McGinness, *The Selling of the President, 1969* (Trident Press, 1969), pp. 190–92.

23. Jimmy Carter, Acceptance Speech to the Democratic Convention, 15 July 1976, *New York Times,* 16 July 1976.

24. A perceptive essay on this topic is Harold Barger, "Carter and the Desymbolizing of the Presidency" (Paper delivered at the 1978 Annual Meeting of the Southwestern Political Science Association, Houston, Texas, April 1978), p. 36.

25. Representative Henry S. Reuss proposed that we create a separate Head of State Office in 1975. See *Congressional Record,* 21 July 1975, H. 7158–H. 7163, for his views and his proposed constitutional amendment. Michael Novak also proposes some form of chief of state or royal office for the United States, *Choosing Our King* (Macmillan, 1974). None of these proposals has ever won any support.

26. See Merlin Gustavson, "The Religious Role of the President," *Midwest Journal of Political Science,* November 1970, p. 709.

27. Novak, *op. cit.*

28. See Arthur M. Schlesinger, Jr., "America: Experiment or Destiny?" *American Historical Review,* June 1977, pp. 505–30.

29. For analyses of the way presidents obtain advice see Thomas E. Cronin and Sanford Greenberg, eds., *The Presidential Advisory System* (Harper & Row, 1969) and Norman C. Thomas, "Presidential Advice and Information" in N. C. Thomas, ed., *The Presidency in Contemporary Context* (Dodd, Mead, 1975), pp. 160–92.

30. For different views of how much centralized national planning is desirable in the United States, see Otis L. Graham, Jr., *Toward a Planned Society* (Oxford University Press, 1976), and Sanford Weiner and Aaron Wildavsky, "The Prophylactic Presidency," *Public Interest,* Summer 1978, pp. 3–19.

31. Quoted in Arthur M. Schlesinger, Jr., *A Thousand Days* (Houghton Mifflin, 1965), p. 127.

32. See Irving L. Janis, *Victims of Groupthink* (Houghton Mifflin, 1972).

33. See Robert Scigliano, *The Supreme Court and the Presidency* (Free Press, 1971), pp. 96–99, 146–58. The author shows persuasively that both partisanship and the timing of appointments are critical factors, especially in combination. See also Harold Chase, *Federal Judges: The Appointing Process* (University of Minnesota, 1972), and Henry Abraham, *Justices and Presidents* (Oxford University Press, 1974).

34. Arthur Krock, *Memoirs* (Popular Library, 1968), p. 282.

35. Victor Navasky, *Kennedy Justice* (Atheneum, 1971), p. 256.

36. *Ibid.,* p. 245.

37. James D. Hodgson, interview in the *Los Angeles Times,* 30 November 1972.

38. G. Calvin Mackenzie, "The Politics of the Appointment Process" (mimeo, 1977), pp. 66–67. See also F. V. Malek, *Washington's Hidden Tragedy* (Free Press, 1978), chap. 4, and Kenneth Prewitt and William McAllister, "Changes in the American Executive Elite, 1930–1970," in Heinz Eulau and Moshe Czudnowski, eds., *Elite Recruitment in Democratic Polities* (Sage, 1976), pp. 105–32.

39. Malek, *op. cit.,* pp. 88–89.

40. Lyndon Johnson, quoted in Harry McPherson, *A Political Education* (Atlantic-Little, Brown, 1972), p. 268.

41. John F. Kennedy, television interview, *Public Papers of the Presidents of the United States* (U.S. Government Printing Office, 1963), pp. 892, 894.

42. Alton Frye, "Congress: The Virtues of Its Vices," *Foreign Policy*, Summer 1971, p. 109.

43. Betty Glad, "The Governor and The General Assembly: Prologue to the Presidency" (Paper delivered at International Society of Political Psychology, New York City, 3 September 1978), p. 23.

44. On the changing nature of congressional campaigns see David Mayhew, *The Electoral Convention* (Yale University Press, 1974), and Morris Fiorina, *Congress: The Keystone of the Washington Establishment* (Yale University Press, 1977).

45. Eric L. Davis, "What Can Jimmy Carter Learn About Congress From Previous Presidents?" (Paper delivered at American Political Science Association Annual Meeting, New York City, 2 September 1978), pp. 21–22.

46. Two of the most useful studies of implementation are Jeffrey Pressman and Aaron Wildavsky, *Implementation* (University of California Press, 1973), and Eugene Bardach, *The Implementation Game* (M.I.T. Press, 1977).

47. An excellent review of the problems a president encounters in implementing policy decisions is found in George C. Edwards III, "Presidential Policy Implementation: The Critical Variable" (Paper prepared for the Annual Meeting of the Midwest Political Science Association, Chicago, Ill., 20–22, April 1978), p. 1. See also George C. Edwards III and Ira Sharkansky, *The Policy Predicament* (W. H. Freeman, 1978).

48. Jonathan Daniels, *Frontiers on the Potomac* (Macmillan, 1946), pp. 31–32.

49. John W. Gardner, testimony, Senate Government Operations Committee, *Congressional Record*, 92nd Cong., 1st sess., 3 June 1971, S. 8140.

50. Navasky, *op. cit.*, p. 443.

51. Arthur M. Ross, "The Data Game," in C. Peter and T. Adams, eds., *Inside the System* (Praeger, 1970), pp. 259–60. See also Ewan Clague, *The Bureau of Labor Statistics* (Praeger, 1968).

52. Marver Bernstein, "The Presidency and Management Improvement," *Law and Contemporary Problems*, Summer 1970, p. 516. See also Otis L. Graham, Jr., *Toward a Planned Society: From Roosevelt to Nixon* (Oxford University Press, 1976).

53. Hugh Heclo, *A Government of Strangers* (Brookings Institution, 1977).

54. Richard Rose, *Managing Presidential Objectives* (Free Press, 1976), p. 147.

55. Joseph A. Califano, *Reorganization of Executive Departments*, Hearings before a subcommittee of the Committee on Government Operations, House of Representatives, 92 Cong., 1st sess., 14 June 1971, pp. 392–93.

56. John W. Gardner, former secretary of Health, Education and Welfare, personal communication, 17 October 1978.

CHAPTER 6

PRESIDENTIAL-CONGRESSIONAL RELATIONS

We want a strong and intelligent President, but he has to bear one thing in mind — we got elected too.

> — Congressman John Brademas, House Majority Whip,
> *Boston Globe,* 20 June 1974, p. 14.

The "Imperial President" was a straw man created by defensive congressmen and by disillusioned liberals who in the days of FDR and John Kennedy had idolized the ideal of a strong presidency. Now that they have had a strong President who was a Republican — and Richard Nixon at that — they were having second thoughts and prescribing re-establishment of congressional power as the tonic that was needed to revitalize the Republic.

> — Richard Nixon, *RN: The Memoirs of Richard Nixon*
> (Grosset & Dunlap, 1978), p. 771.

Surely, [Carter] is aware that the power of the presidency lies largely in the public's perception of his leadership capabilities. The electorate may be willing to accept an austere budget but not a weak-appearing commander-in-chief. . . . If the public views Carter as a President who is incapable of responding adequately to international challenges and is even hard put to settle differences among his Cabinet members, he may not have to worry about 1980. The decision whether to seek reelection may be taken out of his hands.

> — Dom Bonafede, "Bad News From Abroad,"
> *National Journal,* 24 February 1979, p. 318.

"If you don't like the weather around here," goes an old Maine saying, "just wait a few days and it's sure to change." Attitudes toward the American presidency also fluctuate. The *imperial* presidency was much condemned in the early 1970s, but an *imperiled* presidency or presidential incapacity was what most distressed the American public in the late 1970s. This chapter examines the imperial presidency of the late 1960s and early 1970s and assesses why the concerns about it diminished so rapidly, and especially during the Carter presidency. In treating this topic, I shall analyze in particular presidential-congressional relations during the past two decades.

On paper, or in theory, Congress is much the more powerful branch. The Constitution grants the Congress a whole range of powers — to make the laws, to declare war, to confirm the appointment of almost all the important officials, to have the power of the purse, to impeach, and so on. As a unified and ruthless body, there is virtually no way a Congress can be outmatched by a president. But Congress, of course, is seldom a unified body. Seldom, too, has it been a ruthless branch. Countless developments, many of them discussed in earlier chapters, have contributed to the growth of presidential powers. Most of these have to do with the emerging position of the United States as a significant world power and the related enlargement of the role of the president as commander in chief. The mystique of the presidential mandate, the wide support since the 1930s for the idea of the "strong" presidency, and the comparative advantages of the single executive were all additional factors in the swelling of the presidential role.

The *imperial presidency* means many things to many people. But it especially suggests the abuse and misuse of presidential powers. By the year 1973 it became an accepted term to describe presidential deceptions, lying, and transgressions against cherished notions of the separation of powers. A deep-seated skepticism set in as an increasing number of Americans lost confidence in President Nixon.

As has been discussed in earlier chapters, citizen trust in the president had been high during the New Deal and post–New Deal periods. Historians, political scientists, and journalists had generally held that a strong presidency was a necessity.[1] Too many checks and balances would paralyze the capacity for leadership. In a way, they were saying the absence of power can also corrupt.

But then came Watergate. It was a subversion and corruption of the political process. Nixon did not invent the tactics so much as extend and refine them, for he inherited most of the shortcuts and the growing reliance on secrecy and deceit from several of his predecessors. But, unlike them, he was caught.

In the wake of Watergate the easy optimism that once characterized popular attitudes toward presidents rapidly disappeared.

A disciple of Confucius once asked his master, "What are the basic ingredients of good government?" Confucius answered, "Weapons, food, and the confidence of the people."

"But," continued the disciple, "suppose you had to dispense with one of these three things — which would you forgo?" "Weapons," replied the master.

The disciple persisted. "Suppose you were forced to choose between the two that are left. Which would you then forgo?"

"Food," Confucius said. "From of old, death has been the lot of all men, but a people that no longer trusts its rulers is lost, indeed."

These words of the ancient Chinese philosopher have a special meaning and a ring of wisdom in our day, all the more so because our republic was explicitly founded on the principle of the consent of the governed.

During the early and mid-1970s, the American public's attitudes toward the government took on a deep, almost estranged cynicism. This loss of faith was doubtless caused by a variety of events, among which were political assassinations, civil disorders, rising crime rates, illegal wiretapping, recession, soaring inflation, and high unemployment — and especially the deep divisions in the country over Vietnam and then Watergate.

As one of my students put it: "As one crisis has succeeded another, the wellsprings of American optimism have seemed to dry up, and the effervescent American spirit seemed to tire." And he added, "Through all of this, political leaders appeared impotent at best and criminals at worst. People who had expected them to solve the nation's problems were sorely disappointed. People who had expected that they would listen to the popular will found they ignored it instead. It was therefore hardly surprising that the American people drew from the course of our times a simple lesson: they think their government is not to be trusted."

THE EFFECT OF WATERGATE

Reaction to Watergate took at least two forms. Critics said here was irrefutable evidence that the presidency was isolated, autocratic, and imperial. They charged too that the deceptions during Vietnam and the corruptions of Watergate occurred because our checks and balances were inadequate and too much power had been given to the presidency.

Defenders of the presidency argued that Vietnam and Watergate exemplified not so much the *excess* of power as the *abuse* of power. Moreover, supporters of the American system of dispersed powers saw at least some evidence that the system was working — that is, they felt the courts, the press, and even Congress had asserted themselves when put to a critical test.

The Watergate disclosures and the first forced resignation of a president in our history aroused public concern about the role of Congress. Certainly in the mid-1970s the public wanted Congress to become a more coequal branch of government, more assertive and alert, more jealous of its own powers.

The change in public attitudes is well documented by polls taken before and after Vietnam and Watergate. In 1959, social scientists at the University of Michigan asked, "Some people say the president is in the best position to see what the country needs. Other people think the president may have good ideas about what the country needs, but it is up to the Congress to decide what ought to be done. How do you feel about this?" Sixty-one percent of those polled chose the president and 17 percent chose Congress (the remainder said about equal or were undecided).[2] In 1977 the *New York Times* asked virtually the same question: "In general, who do you think *should* have the most say in the way our government is run, the Congress or the President?" Fifty-eight percent chose Congress and only 26 percent the president (the remainder said about equal or were undecided).[3]

What form has congressional reassertion taken? Has Congress effectively addressed the charges made against the "imperial presidency"? Could a vast new array of checks and balances cripple the presidency and undermine its potential for creative leadership?

THE IMPERIAL-PRESIDENCY ARGUMENT

In his book *The Imperial Presidency,* historian Arthur M. Schlesinger, Jr., contends that presidential power had become so expanded and abused by 1972 that it threatened our constitutional system. This imperial presidency, he says, was created primarily as a result of America's wars, particularly Vietnam.[4]

Schlesinger explores two critical instuments that gave rise to the abuse of power by presidents: the war power and secrecy. In discussing the evolution of war power, he points out the troubling constitutional ambiguity in the president's power as commander in chief: it is an undefined *office,* not a *function,* the only constitutional office a president is given. Schlesinger makes what he believes to be a critical distinction between the *abuse* and the *usurpation* of power. Abraham Lincoln, FDR, and Harry Truman temporarily *usurped* power in wartime, knowing they would be held accountable when the wartime emergency ended. Lyndon Johnson and Richard Nixon, however, *abused* power, even in peacetime, claiming a near-absolute power to be the permanent prerogative of the presidency.

Schlesinger's second central theme is the evolution of secrecy as a weapon to protect and preserve the president's national-security power. He notes that until President Eisenhower, the presumption was that Congress would get the information it sought from the executive branch and that instances of secrecy were to be rare exceptions. Obviously, he adds, a Congress that knows only what the executive wants it to know is not an independent body

Schlesinger says that the notion of a bipartisan foreign policy was a bad one. It had the effect, the longer it ran, of stifling debate. "And it gave the Presidency a powerful new peacetime weapon by refurbishing the wartime theory of 'national security' as the end to which other values could be properly sacrificed in times of crisis." [5]

Schlesinger devotes much of his attention to the Nixon presidency, arguing that under Nixon the office became not only fully imperial but also revolutionary; that is, Nixon, in effect, tried to carry out a revolution against the separation of powers and the American Constitution. For instance, in authorizing the plumbers group, Nixon became the first president in our history to establish an extralegal investigative force, subsidized by the taxpayers but unknown to Congress and accountable to no one but himself. Other misuses of intelligence agencies and authorized breaking and entering meant that Nixon became the only American president in peacetime who had ever supervised blatantly lawless actions. Moreover, the White House ignored, lied to, and spied on Congress.

Schlesinger's book is a useful point of departure for a review of the general charges of a too-powerful presidency. The chief complaints will now be specifically examined.

Presidential War Making

Over the years it had become obvious that the presidency needed the power to respond to sudden attacks and to protect the rights and property of American citizens. But just how much power did a president have to conduct undeclared war?

The Department of State in a 1966 legal memorandum summed up some of this enlarged mandate this way:

> In the twentieth century the world has grown much smaller. An attack on a country far from its shores can impinge directly on the nation's security. . . . The Constitution leaves to the President the judgment to determine whether the circumstances of a particular armed attack are so urgent and the potential consequences so threatening to the security of the U.S. that he should act without formally consulting the Congress.[6]

Legal advisers to Presidents Johnson and Nixon insisted that although the framers of the Constitution rejected the traditional power of kings to commit unwilling nations to war, they nevertheless recognized the need for quick executive response to rapidly developing international situations. This apparently encouraged these presidents to become exceedingly inventive in circumventing the congressional war-making power.

Congress became especially upset at President Johnson because in 1964 he succeeded in getting the Gulf of Tonkin resolution passed on information that subsequently proved to be highly misleading. (Congress in 1971 repealed that resolution.) Later, a secret air war in Cambodia was waged in 1969 and 1970 with no formal congressional authorization or knowledge. Also, the U.S. military operated in Laos without any formal notification to the Congress.

Our founding politicians, in giving to Congress, and not to the president, the power to declare war, intended to prevent just such occurrences as these. They sought to create a permanent institutional safeguard against unilateral presidential war making. What happened in Indochina was the result, many members in Congress believed, of a disregard by the White House of the Constitution. But many members of Congress agreed too that presidential excess in these matters came about because Congress either agreed with presidential policies or silently did nothing to stop them. Others pointed out that Congress has declared war on only five occasions despite some two hundred instances of United States use of force overseas.

Too Many Emergency Powers

Since the Great Depression of the early 1930s, Congress has passed about five hundred federal statutes that give a president extraordinary powers. Once a state of emergency is declared, for example, a president may seize property, organize and control the means of production, seize commodities, assign military forces abroad, institute martial law, control all transportation and communications, restrict travel, regulate the operations of private enterprise, call up all military reserves, and in countless other ways control all aspects of our lives.[7]

Abuses of presidential power under these vast emergency laws included the detention of Japanese aliens and Americans of Japanese descent during World War II and the suspension of the federal law requiring the publishing of official documents in the *Federal Register*. This latter practice allowed President Nixon to cover up the bombings in Cambodia and his directives to the FBI for domestic surveillance and intelligence work.

"If the President were to make use of all of the power available to him under the emergency statutes on the books, he could conduct a government without reference to usual constitutional processes," declared Idaho Democrat Senator Frank Church. "These powers taken together could form a basis for one-man rule." [8]

Too Much Diplomacy by Executive Agreement

Treaty ratification procedures require that diplomatic agreements receive the consent of two-thirds of the Senate, but executive agreements permit a president to enter into secret and highly sensitive arrangements with a foreign nation without congressional approval. Many members of Congress feel that the subversion of the treaty ratification process of the Constitution was an important element in the growth of the imperial presidency.

Executive agreements have been recognized as distinct from treaties since George Washington's days, and their use by the executive has been upheld by the courts. But what irked Congress in the 1960s and 1970s was that although the Senate was asked to ratify international accords on trivial matters, the White House arranged critically important mutual-aid and military-base agreements without even informing Congress. Walter F. Mondale, as a senator, put the complaint this way:

> During the 1960s and 1970s, the Senate disposed by treaty of such "crucial" issues as the preservation of archeological artifacts in Mexico, a protocol relating to an amendment to the International Civil Aviation agreement, the Locarno Agreement establishing an international classification for industrial designs, a treaty relating to international classification of goods and services to which trademarks are applied, revisions of international radio regulations, and an international agreement regarding maintenance of certain lights in the Red Sea.
>
> Yet Congress was not informed about the secret agreements or understandings pledging American assistance that President Nixon apparently entered into with former South Vietnamese President Thieu in 1973, at the time of the signing of the Paris Peace Accords. And the Senate subcommittee involved with such matters had no knowledge of vital executive agreements in 1960 with Ethiopia, in 1963 with Laos, in 1964 with Thailand, in 1966 with Korea, and in 1967 with Thailand.[9]

It was argued that these practices were an insult to Congress and a violation of the Constitution's clear intent that Congress share in the making of foreign policy. Members of Congress began to probe for ways to limit the president's authority to make executive agreements. "The executive branch should welcome this opportunity to share with the Congress the weighty responsibility of reaching agreements with other nations," said Texas Democrat Senator Lloyd Bentsen, "agreements which reflect our national priorities and which lie at the very heart of the foreign policy process." [10]

Presidential Secrecy and
Executive Privilege

The Founding Fathers did not intend that the president should decide what information Congress and the American people needed to know. They were aware of the maxim that he who controls the flow of information rules our destinies. Moreover, without information, Congress cannot oversee the execution of its laws, and if it cannot do that, it is scarcely in a position to legislate at all.

The difficulty arises because constitutional scholars, the courts, and Congress concede that a president does have the right to withhold certain diplomatic and military information when it is vital to the national security. Thus during World War II the executive properly kept secret the time and place of the Normandy Beach invasion.

Several presidents have invoked a prerogative that has come to be called executive privilege, a claim based on the Constitutional separation of powers, to the effect that the executive branch may withhold information from Congress. It was invoked about thirty-four times prior to the Nixon presidency. During Nixon's first term, executive privilege was invoked three times on matters that included military assistance and five-year plans and foreign aid for Cambodia.

It was only with the spectacular Watergate disclosures after the 1972 election, when the Senate investigating committee began to request documents, tapes, and testimony, that executive privilege became a cause célèbre. It was then Nixon and his lawyers, in a brief before Judge John Sirica, claimed executive privilege is an inherent and absolute power, and that although Congress and the courts may request information from a president, the separation of powers directs that disclosure cannot be forced.[11]

Legal historian Raoul Berger, on the other hand, contends executive privilege is "a myth, without constitutional basis, and the best evidence that can be mustered for it is a series of self-serving presidential assertions of a power to withhold information." [12]

Most people and most members of Congress felt the truth seemed to lie somewhere between the views of Richard Nixon and those of Raoul Berger. Senator Sam J. Ervin, Jr., accused the executive branch of "contempt of Congress" for refusing to cooperate by sharing information. In fact, Ervin supervised a study of refusals by the executive branch to provide information to Congress, and he found that there were nearly three hundred instances of withheld information during the 1964–73 period. An exasperated Ervin complained:

> The actions of public officials whether elected or appointed to deny the Congress the information it requires in its legislative functions, or unilaterally to decide what information will be provided or which witnesses will appeal, are clear encroachments upon the powers of Con-

gress. Yet a study of the findings of the survey will reveal a full range of devices, subterfuges, preposterous extensions and assumptions of authority, and outright evasiveness used by the bureaucracy to thwart Congress in its legitimate inquiries.[13]

Presidential Policy — Impoundment

The extraconstitutional power of impoundment allows the executive to refuse to spend funds that have been appropriated by Congress. Impoundment is a complicated practice because it can take — and has taken — so many forms. Refusals to spend have occurred in the past to effect savings because of either a change in events (i.e., a war is over and funds are no longer needed) or for managerial reasons (i.e., a project can be carried out in a more efficient way).

Before President Nixon, impoundments were rather infrequent, usually temporary, and generally involved insignificant amounts of money. Only occasionally were earlier impoundments controversial. Still, the precedent was set for the future. Nixon stretched the use of impoundment to limits previously not attained. Altogether he impounded funds appropriated by Congress in the amount of approximately $18 billion.

What bothered Congress about Nixon's impoundments of funds for water-pollution control, urban aid, the emergency loan program of the Farmers Home Administration, and others was that he used impoundment to set policy and reorder the nation's priorities. Congress felt it was one thing for a president to delay funds for purposes of efficiency, but quite another for him to engage in extensive policymaking or priority setting by impoundment.

Congress responded to Nixon's frequent impoundment of its appropriations in a relatively united manner. Drawing strength from the constitutional clause "No money shall be drawn from the Treasury, but in consequence of appropriations made by law," Congress decided it had the final voice in fiscal policymaking. Members of Congress complained that by refusing to spend appropriated funds the executive was, in effect, exercising an *item veto*, thereby avoiding the potential embarrassment of a public veto message and the risk of a congressional override. Nixon's impoundment practices, they added, were merely a means whereby the White House reallocated national resources in violation of congressional dictates. It was a question of which branch should decide how to allocate the public funds.[14]

A Monarchical Presidential Pardon Power

President Gerald Ford's pardon of former President Nixon called public and congressional attention to a little-appreciated, but sometimes very controversial, presidential power — the power to pardon. During his confirmation hearings for the vice-presidency, Ford indicated that if a pardon situation arose, he would not pardon Richard Nixon. When it, in fact, did arise, he pardoned the former president. Many people believed, rightly or wrongly, that a secret deal had been made between the two men and a substantial public uproar ensued.

Unlike most presidential powers, the power to pardon is absolute. A president can grant clemency to any of thousands of federal felons and virtually answer to no one, save, of course, the voters at the next election. Most scholars have agreed that the errors that occur in the administration of justice provide a sufficient reason for the existence of the pardoning power.[15]

Still, the Ford pardon of Richard Nixon struck several members of Congress as the ultimate Watergate cover-up. They viewed it, too, as the ultimate injustice, telling the public, in essence, that some people are more equal than others. Some members of Congress subsequently called for a limitation or at least a review process on controversial political pardons. An irritated Walter Mondale, then a United States senator from Minnesota, called for a provision whereby a two-thirds vote of both houses of Congress could overrule a presidential pardon. Mondale reasoned that "Our system is carefully designed with numerous checks and balances to keep power controlled. In my opinion, the pardon power needs a check." [16] President Ford obviously disagreed with this suggestion, as did most members of Congress, but Ford did sense that the public alarm was great enough to warrant an unprecedented presidential appearance before a congressional committee to try to explain his pardon action. Ford insisted to this committee that the Nixon pardon was granted solely to change our national focus, to shift our attention from the pursuit of a fallen president to the pursuit of the urgent needs of the nation.

CONGRESS TRIES TO
REASSERT ITSELF:
1972–1980

The role of Congress in helping to end the war in Vietnam and then in the impeachment hearings against President Nixon gave the legislative branch some much needed new vigor. The public looked to Congress for leadership. Congress set out to recover lost authority and discover new ways to participate more fully in national policymaking. In doing so it has clearly tried to reassert itself. But even the most ardent supporter of Congress realizes that many of the so-called post-Watergate reforms are provisional. It is one thing to enact new curbs, but it is another to put them into practice and enforce them rigorously — especially in the face of United States setbacks abroad. It is not clear that presidential powers are really constrained very much by what Congress has done since 1972 — although it may be constrained for other reasons. Examples of congressional reassertion are discussed below to illustrate the ambiguity of the enterprise.

The War Powers Resolution of 1973

In an attempt to redress the balance, Congress in 1973 took an unprecedented step when it enacted the War Powers Resolution. Nixon vetoed the resolution, calling it an unconstitutional intrusion into the president's constitutional authority and an action that seriously undermines this nation's ability to act decisively and convincingly in times of international crisis. Congress overrode the veto, however, and by law declared that henceforth the president can commit the armed forces of the United States pursuant only to (1) a declaration of war by Congress, (2) specific statutory authorization, or (3) in a national emergency created by an attack on the United States or its armed forces. After committing the armed forces under this third condition, the president is to report immediately to Congress; and within sixty days, unless Congress has declared war, the troop commitment is to be terminated, with the proviso that the president may be allowed another thirty days if he certifies to Congress that unavoidable military necessity for the safety of United States forces requires their continued use. Ninety days having elapsed, the resolution then permits Congress, by concurrent resolution not subject to presidential veto, to direct the president to disengage the troops. A president is also obligated by this resolution to consult Congress "in every possible instance" before committing troops to battle.

Not everyone was pleased by the passage of the War Powers Resolution. Some members of Congress supported President Nixon's stand. Still another group in Congress as well as some scholars felt the resolution granted a president *more power* than he already had, perhaps even to the extent of encouraging short-term interventions. Whether or not this resolution will make any difference, it symbolizes a determination by Congress in 1973 to try to control the president's formerly unlimited discretion to decide when and where and under what conditions American troops may be engaged. Any future president who remembers the reaction of Congress and the nation to Vietnam and the 1973 War Powers Resolution will know that a commitment of American troops to foreign combat is subject to the approval of Congress.

Whether the intensity of this reaction will last much longer than the disenchantment over Indochina remains an open question. Congress certainly has the constitutional authority to intervene whenever it has the will to do so. But will it have the courage to resist being stampeded into granting power whenever a president waves the flag and says there is urgent crisis? This emphasis on "will" or "courage" strikes some observers as naive or hazy. They feel that, under most circumstances, whenever a president takes a foreign-policy initiative, he is likely to have most of the country behind him, including influential business leaders, the communications media, and the bulk of the public. The history of presidential actions in wartime suggests that presidents in the future will not have much difficulty in doing what they please. The Constitution, as Chief Justice Hughes once said, is a "fighting Constitution." Nothing in it then or. now will prevent a president from winning a war that is truly vital to our national survival. Legal niceties will be given little attention. The Lincoln example will doubtless be followed; national survival will always be the ultimate value. Only after the war initiative is shown "not to work" — that is, after the death tolls and inflation become unbearable — will popular support begin to flag and only then will Congress begin to reflect the popular feeling.

The National Emergencies Act of 1976

Enacted in September of 1976, the National Emergencies Act terminated as of September 1978 the extensive powers and authorities possessed by the president as a result of the continuing state of emergency the nation had been in since the mid-1930s. It also established authority for the declaration of future emergencies in a manner that will clearly define the powers of the president and provide for regular congressional review.

The National Emergencies Act of 1976 also calls upon the president to inform Congress in advance and identify those laws he plans to use when he declares a national emergency. An emergency would automatically end after six months, although a president could then declare it again for another six months. But Congress is obligated to review the declaration of emergency powers at least every six months. A significant section of the new law states that a majority vote in both Senate and House can end the emergency at any time. President Ford called this section unconstitutional and hinted that future presidents might go to court to fight this provision if Congress chose to act upon it.

Congress hopes that this legislation will ensure that emergency powers can be utilized only when legitimate emergencies actually exist, and then only under safeguards of legislative review. As Connecticut Democrat Senator Abraham Ribicoff reported to the Congress:

> Reliance on emergency authority, intended for use in crisis situations would no longer be available in non-crisis situations. At a time when governments throughout the world are turning with increasing desperation to an all-powerful executive, this legislation is designed to insure that the United States travels a road marked by carefully constructed legal safeguards.[17]

The Case Act
(on Executive Agreements)
of 1972

The Case Act, named after one of its major sponsors, New Jersey Republican Clifford P. Case, requires the secretary of state to submit to the U.S. Senate within sixty days the final text of any international agreement made by executive agreement. Executive agreements having sensitive national-security implications may be submitted to the Senate Foreign Relations Committee and the House Foreign Affairs Committee on a classified basis.

Presidents still negotiate executive agreements, however, and sometimes fail to comply with the Case Act's relatively mild provisions. Even when executive agreements are reported to the appropriate committees of Congress, there is no provision for any congressional response. Some efforts were made in the mid-1970s to enact a stronger law that would permit Congress an opportunity to review and to disapprove executive agreements. In 1974 the Senate actually passed such a measure, but the House failed to act on it. Later attempts also failed, but the following initiatives have won some congressional support.

A Senate-sponsored bill requiring that executive agreements be submitted only to the Senate, such agreements to take effect at the end of sixty days unless the Senate disapproves them by simple resolution.

A House-sponsored bill requiring that executive agreements be submitted to Congress, such agreements to take effect in sixty days unless both houses adopt a concurrent resolution disapproving them.

Another Senate-sponsored bill providing that if either house decides an international agreement is sufficiently important to require congressional approval, it must be approved through regular legislative procedures or as a treaty.[18]

Congress and the Intelligence Agencies

Abuse of the intelligence and spying agencies was also a central contention of the imperial-presidency argument. The Central Intelligence Agency was established in 1947 at a time when the perceived threat of "world communism" encouraged a vast arsenal of national-security instruments, including covert political operations overseas and espionage. When the CIA was established, Congress recognized the dangers to a free society inherent in a secret organization not accountable in the ordinary way for what it does. It was consequently stipulated that the CIA *was not to engage in any police work or to perform operations within the United States.*

But from 1947 to the mid-1970s, no aspect of national policymaking was more removed from congressional involvement than CIA operations. In many instances Congress acted as if it really didn't want to know what was going on. Said one senator: "It is not a question of reluctance on the part of CIA officials to speak to us. Instead it is a question of our reluctance, if you will, to seek information and knowledge on subjects which I personally, as a Member of Congress and as a citizen, would rather not have." [19] The evidence is substantial that Congress declined to use its resources to participate in intelligence policymaking.

Congress has tried in recent years to amend this. In 1975 the Senate established a temporary committee of inquiry chaired by Idaho Democrat Senator Frank Church. This committee found widespread abuses of power and violations of the rights of American citizens in the conduct of both foreign and domestic intelligence operations. The Church committee recommended that Congress bring all the intelligence operations within the framework of congressional oversight.

The Senate then voted to create a permanent Select Committee on Intelligence with legislative and budgetary authority over the CIA and other intelligence agencies. The House subsequently also voted to set up a similar panel. But since we now know that even presidents have had difficulty getting a handle on the CIA, there is some doubt about whether Congress will have any better luck. Yet, in an unprecedented exercise of its power over the intelligence budget, Congress in 1976 amended the Defense Appropriations bill to terminate American covert intervention in Angola. "The inevitable public disclosure of a secret operation served, in this instance, the will of Congress; and in the short run the Angola controversy was a warning that the executive should proceed with caution." [20]

How likely is it that Congress will be effective in regulating the CIA? People differ widely in their answers to this question. Halperin, Berman, Borosage, and Marwick conclude their study, *The Lawless State: The Crimes of the U.S. Intelligence Agencies* (Penguin, 1976), by saying, "To date, only a few patchwork elements of reform have been put into effect. At every turn the executive branch continues to fight any major changes and, instead, offers 'reforms' that end up authorizing for the future the abuses of the past." Some say the Senate Committee should spell out a charter that would limit the CIA to foreign operations, severely restrict and control all covert activities, require written approval for any major field operations, and shut down the political intelligence work of the FBI. Others feel that a full disclosure of the intelligence community's budget is necessary.

A long-range view suggests that the intensity and direction of congressional interest in these matters depend on the movement of larger political forces. That is, when a national consensus supports a president and his foreign-policy initiatives, as it plainly did in the early years of the cold war, Congress and the general public are likely to go along. But in the absence of such a consensus a more assertive Congress may try to find a more realistic system of accountability for the CIA and related intelligence activities as a substitute for the public scrutiny that normally is given major governmental operations. It is worth recalling that already established committees in Congress to oversee intelligence agencies simply did not do their job.

The Budget and Impoundment Control Act of 1974

"Congress has seen its control over the federal purse-strings ebb away over the past 50 years because of its inability to get a grip on the overall budget, while the Office of Management and Budget in the executive branch has increased its power and influence," said Maine Democrat Senator Edmund S. Muskie in 1974.[21]

Congress had become too dependent on the president's budget proposals and had no budget system of its own — only a lot of separate actions and decisions coming at various intervals throughout the year with little or no connection among them.

Muskie was one of the chief authors of the 1974 Congressional Budget and Impoundment Control Act, which was designed to encourage Congress to evaluate the nation's fiscal situation and program spending priorities in a comprehensive way. It was also hoped that in a period of high inflation Congress could help put a lid on unnecessary spending.

The act creates a permanent Budget Committee for each chamber. The House committee of twenty-five members includes: five members from the Ways and Means Committee, five from the Appropriations Committee, thirteen from other legislative committees, and one member each from the majority and minority leadership. The Senate committee is a sixteen-member committee appointed in the usual fashion.

Under this law, Congress also established a Congressional Budget Office (CBO). It provides budgetary and fiscal experts and computer services and gives Congress technical assistance on the president's budgetary proposals. Some members of Congress hoped CBO would provide hard, practical economic data to guide the drafting of spending legislation. Others viewed it as a potential "think tank" that might provide Congress with a more philosophical approach to spending that would help reorder national priorities. In fact, CBO is most frequently used to provide routine cost estimates for spending and tax bills and to keep track of the overall budget level.

Optimists feel that the budget reform act will force Congress into more systematic and timely action on budgetary legislation by tying its separate spending decisions to fiscal-policy objectives. Its new budgetary timetable gives Congress three additional months to consider the president's budget recommendations. By May 15 of each year, Congress, after receiving reports from its Budget committees and its Budget Office, adopts an initial tentative budget that sets target totals for spending and taxes. This target is then broken down by category and serves as a guide for the various committees and subcommittees considering detailed appropriation measures. By September 15, Congress is required to adopt a second concurrent resolution that will either affirm or revise the earlier targets. If necessary to attain compliance with the final budget-resolution totals, this resolution must also dictate any required changes in expenditures and revenues.

How has it worked? The new budget process has clearly stimulated increased congressional participation in the fiscal policymaking process. Using these new powers of the purse, Congress seemed somewhat better able to contribute to budget making in the Carter era. The budget resolutions provide a vehicle for debate on key macroeconomic issues, and the newly created House and Senate committees are able to challenge the president's dominance in initiating fiscal proposals. The long-term success of the experiment will depend on whether the new committees are powerful enough to induce cooperation with their target and ceiling resolutions.

The impoundment-control provisions of this new law have not worked out as well, but here again Congress has put the executive branch on the defensive. Presidents are obligated to report delays in spending to Congress; either house may veto presidential decisions to defer spending; and both the Senate and the House must approve any presidential request to eliminate a project that Congress has funded. If the comptroller general of the General Accounting Office finds in behalf of Congress that impoundments have been made without proper reports to Congress, he may report these delays and Congress may act to force release of the funds. Should a president fail to comply with a congressional action overruling an impoundment, the Congress may go to court for an order requiring the funds be spent.

There have been many complaints about the new impoundment law. It is vague. It creates a vast amount of paperwork. Too many reports must be sent Congress even when executive-branch officials have saved a few thousand dollars for managerial and efficiency purposes. Other complaints stem from the vagueness of the impoundment law's provisions. There will no doubt be further changes in the law designed to meet these additional objections.

The Legislative Veto

In recent years Congress has turned the so-called congressional veto into an instrument of policymaking. The Constitution stipulates that every bill, order, resolution, or vote to which the concurrence of the Senate and House may be necessary shall be presented to the president for his approval or veto. But concurrent resolutions in contrast to joint resolutions by convention do not have to be submitted to the president. In the past this made little difference because concurrent resolutions were used merely to express congressional sentiments and had no force of law.

Then in 1932 Congress passed a joint resolution allowing President Hoover to reorganize the executive agencies but stipulated that his proposed reorganizations would not take effect for ninety days during which time either house of Congress by a simple resolution could veto the regulation. Since then the congressional veto has come to be a frequently used statutory provision through which Congress either disapproves a measure by vetoing it or approves it by affirmative action, generally within sixty or ninety days, retaining the authority to approve or disapprove part of the program before final implementation. The legislative veto may take the form of a concurrent resolution, a simple resolution passed by either house, or a committee veto.

Since 1932 hundreds of pieces of legislation have carried some form of legislative veto, most of those since 1972. Significant statutes with legislative-veto provisions include the Budget and Impoundment Control Act of 1974, the Trade Act of 1974, and the Energy Policy and Conservation Act of 1975. In 1976 the House fell only two votes short of passing a bill that would have required federal agencies to submit all new regulations to Congress for sixty legislative days. If during that time one house acted to disapprove, the regulations would not go into effect unless the decision was reversed within thirty days.

Congressional spokesmen favor the legislative veto and contend that it is the most effective device Congress has to ensure that the president and federal bureaucrats issue regulations that conform to the intent of Congress. They also argue that without the use of the legislative veto the president could use his veto to prevent Congress from terminating powers previously delegated to him by the Congress. Democratic Representative Elliott Levitas of Georgia reflects the sentiment in Congress in favor of a veto on administrative rules and regulations. He complains that the bureaucracy is infringing on Congress's right to make laws by putting out "a thick tangle of regulations that carry the force of law without benefit of legislative consideration." To back up his point he cites statistics showing that in 1974 Congress passed 404 public laws, whereas sixty-seven agencies adopted 7,496 regulations.[22]

Most supporters of the presidency consider the legislative veto a violation of the doctrine of separation of powers and an unconstitutional intrusion into the executive branch.[23] They also argue that it gives lobbyists more influence on government. Critics of the legislative veto contend too that Congress is already overworked now and cannot oversee adequately each regulatory action. Consideration of each regulation would doubtless be left to only a few members. John Bolton, a Washington lawyer, writes that the legislative veto "eliminates the president from the law making function by not presenting him with 'legislation' that he can veto. It allows Congress to change its mind an unlimited number of times about what a statute is intended to do after passage of the statute — in effect, amending the statute. . . . The President's administrative authority — his duty to 'take care that the laws be faithfully executed' — is impinged because he is prevented from implementing regulations he deems suitable and consistent with the enabling legislation." [24]

Assistant Attorney General Antonin Scalia presented the executive-branch brief in opposition to the expanded use of the legislative veto. Testifying before a congressional committee in late 1975 he argued:

> As our system operates Congress makes the laws, in as much detail as it desires; the President executes those laws, with due regard for the congressional intent; and the judiciary determines the President's execution, including issuance of regulations, to be of no effect when it is inconsistent with the laws or the Constitution.
>
> This rough division of government power is what the doctrine of separation of powers is all about.
>
> Both of the present bills (under discussion before the House Committee on the Judiciary) disrupt this system in one way or another, depending upon how the ambiguities discussed earlier are resolved. If they envision Congress setting regulations aside on the basis of its own notions as to what constitutes desirable enforcement policy, they intrude upon the executive's functions.
>
> If, on the other hand, they mean only to permit congressional review of the executive's compliance with statutory intent, they intrude upon the province of the judiciary. Either way, they carry Congress beyond its proper function of making laws under Article I of the Constitution." [25]

Presidents Ford and Carter both assailed the legislative veto as an unconstitutional intrusion on presidential authority. They have also urged judicial review of this device. The Supreme Court, however, continues to decline a review of the legislative-veto process, thus, in effect, sustaining the legislative veto without giving it official sanction. Meanwhile, Congress keeps adding veto language to new legislation. Members of Congress say the veto provisions merely ensure that executive and regulatory officials carry out the intent behind a law.

Whatever its merits, and whatever the eventual court rulings on the process, Congress has surely used the legislative veto to make life more difficult for presidents and other executive-branch leaders. The courts may someday modify this relatively new and now significant feature of presidential-congressional relations — but that may be sometime in the future.[26]

Other Actions
Successful and Unsuccessful

Congress has also become more involved in foreign policy. Shaking off years of inertia, Congress cut off aid to Vietnam, called a halt to bombing in Cambodia, and restrained the Ford administration from getting involved in Portugal and Angola. Led by Senate Democrat Henry Jackson of Washington, Congress refused to permit the White House to grant the Soviet Union the "most-favored nation" treatment allowed for in the Trade Reform Act of 1974. This was clearly a case in which Congress imposed its goals on the executive. Congress also demanded and won a greater role in arms sales abroad and in determining United States aid to Turkey.[27]

The maintenance of democratic controls over foreign and military policy has become increasingly difficult in the cold war and in the nuclear age. Secrecy is at the heart of the problem. All recent presidents have said that successful diplomacy without secrecy is impossible. Carter, for example, told members of Congress that he felt excessive restraints were keeping him from reacting to a Cuban-assisted invasion of Zaire. See Figure 6.1, 206–209 for additional curbs on the president's foreign policy-making.

But executive secrecy is subject to abuses, as Watergate dramatically illustrated. People could understand, even if they might oppose, the use of secrecy in the president's negotiations with China or in his diplomatic initiatives with Middle Eastern nations. But most people found it difficult to understand the need for it in dealing with congressional leaders. Tapping telephones to prevent security leaks, breaking into offices — these are the tactics not of politics but of *war*. These practices may be appropriate in dealing with enemies but they are not appropriate when dealing with domestic political opponents.

The question is how to prevent the use of secrecy to cover up obstructions of justice while permitting its legitimate use for diplomatic purposes. Many Americans feel that a greater power sharing with Congress over foreign policy is needed even at the risk of a less effective policy. Some indeed have doubts whether presidential exclusiveness is more likely than congressional sharing to produce good policy.

Among congressional-reassertion proposals was former Senator Sam Ervin's surprising proposal to remove the Department of Justice from the ex-

TABLE 6.1   CONGRESS'S TOOLS TO IMPOSE ITS WILL ON THE PRESIDENT'S FOREIGN POLICY OPTIONS

Congress has used its constitutional control of the nation's "purse strings" to influence U.S. foreign policy — sometimes in broad and general ways, such as paying for the Marshall Plan, other times in a more specific fashion, such as restricting money for the invasion of Cambodia. There are now more than 70 "constraints" on the books that impose the will of Congress on the President's foreign policy options, from insisting that no U.S. aid be spent on abortions to protecting the interests of American property abroad. Following is a summary of the major provisions affecting the President and when they originated.

ARMS EXPORT CONTROL ACT
(22 USC 2751 *et seq*)

Sec. 2753—No defense articles and services shall be sold unless they strengthen U.S. security; the recipient agrees not to transfer them without consent of the President and the recipient agrees to maintain the articles transferred. (Originally adopted as part of the Foreign Military Sales Act of 1968.)

Sec. 2753—No credits may be extended or cash sales on deliveries made to countries that use defense articles in "substantial" violation of agreements for purposes not authorized, by transferring the articles without presidential consent or by failing to maintain security of the articles. "Substantial" is not defined in the law. (Originally adopted in 1973.)

Sec. 2753—The President may not consent to third-party transfers unless he reports to Congress and until Congress has 30 days to consider a concurrent resolution of disapproval. However, the section includes a presidential determination waiver clause that allows immediate transfer without congressional action. (Adopted in 1976.)

Sec. 2754—Foreign military forces receiving U.S. arms should not be maintained or established solely for civil action; funds should not be used in connection with any

sales of sophisticated weapons systems to underdeveloped countries — with exceptions. The President may waive these restrictions for national security reasons. (Adopted in 1968.)

Sec. 2755—No sales, credits or guarantees should be provided to countries that discriminate against Americans. (Adopted in 1976.)

Sec. 2321 (i)—U.S. military advisers may not perform combatant duties outside the United States. (Adopted in 1976.)

Sec. 2772—Export-Import Bank of the U.S. credits shall not be extended for defense articles and services to less developed countries. (Adopted in 1968.)

Sec. 2773 (b)—Total military assistance for Africa shall not exceed $40 million in each fiscal year, subject to a presidential national security waiver. (Adopted in 1968.)

Sec. 2775—Less developed countries that divert resources to unnecessary military expenditures shall be ineligible for further sales and guarantees, as determined by the President. (Adopted in 1968.)

Sec. 2776—The President shall submit a certification to Congress on letters of offer to sell defense articles and services of $25 million or more, or major defense equipment of $7 million or more. Congress can prevent the issue of a letter of offer if it adopts a concurrent resolution within 30 days, although the President can waive this in the interests of national security. This section involved Congress in the proposed jet warplanes sale to Israel, Saudi Arabia and Egypt this spring. (Adopted in 1974.)

Sec. 2778—No license may be issued for major defense equipment worth more than $25 million to non-NATO countries, with exceptions. (Adopted in 1976.)

Sec. 2751—No funds under this act or the Foreign Assistance Act may be used to aid any country that gives or receives nuclear enrichment or reprocessing equipment, materials or technology, unless it enters into certain safeguard agreements. A limited presidential waiver is provided,

TABLE 6.1 *(cont.)*

with reporting to Congress. (Adopted in 1976 and 1977.)

FOREIGN ASSISTANCE ACT
(22 USC 2151 *et seq*)

Sec. 2302—Military assistance shall be furnished solely for internal security and for legitimate self-defense and other purposes. Foreign military forces aided by this act should not be maintained or established solely for civil action. (Adopted in 1961.)

Sec. 2304—No security assistance may be provided to countries whose governments engage in consistent patterns of gross violations of internationally recognized human rights. (Adopted in 1976.)

Sec. 2321 (f)—No military assistance is authorized after June 30, 1972 for Thailand, after June 30, 1974 for Laos and after June 30, 1976 for South Vietnam unless authorized by Congress. (Adopted in 1971.)

Sec. 2370 (x)—No arms may be sold to Turkey until "substantial progress" is made toward settlement of the Cyprus dispute with Greece. The embargo became law in 1974 and took effect in 1975. President Carter has requested its repeal and the House International Relations Committee voted this year to go along, 18–17. The Senate Foreign Relations Committee, however, voted, 8–4, against repeal.

Sec. 2151 (l)—Economic assistance may not be used for abortions or involuntary sterilizations. (Abortion ban adopted in 1973; sterilization ban, in 1977.)

Sec. 2151 (m)—Development assistance may not go to countries receiving security supporting assistance, with exceptions, and unless Congress specifically authorizes such use. (Adopted in 1974 after development funds were reprogrammed for Vietnam.)

Sec. 2151 (n)—No economic aid may be given to any country that engages in a consistent pattern of gross violations of human rights, but the President may use a "needy poeple" waiver if he reports to Congress. (Adopted in 1975.)

Sec. 2161—Development loans are limited to 20 countries in any fiscal year, but the limitation does not apply to Latin America or regional programs. (Adopted in 1966.)

Sec. 2221 (b)—Contributions to the United Nations Development Program may not be used in Cuba. (Adopted in 1966.)

Sec. 2221 (h)—Contributions to the United Nations Educational, Scientific and Cultural Organization are prohibited until it changes its policies towards Israel. (Adopted in 1974.)

Sec. 2370 (a)—Economic assistance to Cuba is prohibited, but the President may waive the ban. (Adopted in 1960.)

Sec. 2370 (b)—No economic assistance may go to any country dominated or controlled by the international Communist movement. (Adopted in 1961.)

Sec. 2370 (c)—No economic aid may go to any country indebted to a U.S. citizen and not taking steps to pay the debt, but the President may waive this for national security reasons. (Adopted in 1961.)

Sec. 2370 (d)—Development loan assistance may not be granted for any productive enterprise abroad that will compete with U.S. enterprises, unless the recipient country agrees to limit exports of the product to no more than 20 per cent of its annual production during the life of the loan. The President may institute import controls if the recipient country fails to honor this agreement, but he may also waive the limit for reasons of national security. (Adopted in 1961.)

Sec. 2370 (e)—Economic assistance is denied to any country that has expropriated U.S. property without adequate compensation, but the provision may be waived by the President in the national interest if his exception is reported to Congress. (Adopted in 1962. Waiver authority was added in 1973.)

Sec. 2370 (f)—Economic assistance may not be given to any Communist country, but the President may waive the ban for national security reasons. (Adopted in 1962.)

TABLE 6.1 *(cont.)*

Sec. 2370 (g)—No economic aid may be granted to any country that will use the aid to compensate owners for expropriated property. (Adopted in 1962.)

Sec. 2370 (h)—The President must adopt regulations and procedures assuring that U.S. aid is not used in a manner contrary to the best interests of the United States by promoting or assisting foreign aid projects of Communist countries. (Adopted in 1962 in an effort to prevent "commingling" of U.S. and Communist-bloc aid.)

Sec. 2370 (i)—Economic assistance to any country engaged in or preparing for aggressive military efforts is prohibited, but the President may waive this provision. (Adopted in 1963.)

Sec. 2370 (k)—A $100 million limit on economic aid is set for any productive enterprise and a $100 million limit on military aid to any country, with certain exceptions, but with no presidential waiver. (Adopted in 1963 to forestall aid for construction of the Bokaro steel plant in India; the military aid limit was added in 1966.)

Sec. 2370 (m)—Economic aid shall be denied any country capable of sustaining its own defense burden and economic growth. (Adopted in 1963.)

Sec. 2370 (o)—Consideration shall be given to denying assistance to any country that seizes or penalizes U.S. fishing vessels. (Adopted in 1965.)

Sec. 2370 (q)—Economic aid shall be denied any country that is in default on a loan obligation to the United States, but this may be waived by the President for national security reasons with a report to Congress. (Adopted in 1966.)

Sec. 2370 (t)—No economic assistance may go to any country that severs diplomatic relations with the United States. (Adopted in 1967.)

Sec. 2371—Assistance is prohibited for one year to any country that harbors international terrorists, but the President may waive this for national security reasons with a report to Congress. (Adopted in 1976.)

Sec. 2372—Military or security supporting assistance may not go to Argentina, effective next September. (Adopted in 1977.)

Sec. 2415—As of 1975, no funds in excess of $377 million may be appropriated for Cambodia. (Adopted in 1971.)

Sec. 2419—No assistance may be given to a country with a U.S.-supported military base if U.S. reporters are denied access. (Adopted in 1974.)

Sec. 2420—Foreign aid funds may be used to train police and other law enforcement forces for foreign governments only for narcotics control and crimes unlawful under U.S. law. (Adopted in 1973.)

Sec. 2422—In peacetime, no funds under any act can be spent for CIA operations — other than intelligence gathering — in foreign countries unless the President finds each such operation important to U.S. national security and reports his finding to the appropriate congressional committees in a timely fashion. (Adopted in 1974.)

Sec. 2466—No funds may be granted for economic development assistance to any country that objects to the presence of U.S. aid employees on the grounds of race, religion, national origin or sex. (Adopted in 1975.)

1976 INTERNATIONAL SECURITY ASSISTANCE ACT (90 Stat 729)

Sec. 404—No aid may be given to conduct military or paramilitary operations in Angola unless Congress specifically authorizes such assistance by law. This does not prohibit assistance provided solely for humanitarian purposes.

Sec. 406—Military assistance, training and foreign military sales to Chile are banned.

1977 INTERNATIONAL DEVELOPMENT ACT (91 Stat 533)

Sec. 132—No assistance may be given to Vietnam, Cambodia, Laos or Cuba.

TABLE 6.1   *(cont.)*

1977 INTERNATIONAL SECURITY ASSISTANCE ACT (91 Stat 614)

Sec. 25—No aid under this act in fiscal 1978 may be used for military or paramilitary operations in Zaire unless the President determines such aid is in the U.S. national security interests and so certifies to Congress. A certification was made to Congress by President Carter on May 18, 1978.

1978 FOREIGN AID APPROPRIATIONS ACT (91 Stat 1230)

(These prohibitions expire after Sept. 30, 1978 unless they relate to past funds authorized to remain available until expended.)

Title I—No appropriated funds may be used to provide international military education and training to Argentina.

Sec. 105—No funds may be used to pay arrearages or dues of any United Nations member.

Sec. 107—No appropriations may finance directly any assistance to Uganda, Cambodia, Laos or Vietnam.

Sec. 112—No funds other than those for "international organizations and programs" may be used to finance the export of nuclear materials or to pay for nuclear-related training.

Sec. 114—No appropriated funds may finance directly any assistance to Mozambique or Angola.

Sec. 503—No assistance may go to a country that is in default for more than a year in repayment of a loan from the United States, with exceptions.

Sec. 503A—No funds may be used to provide military assistance, international military education and training or military credit sales to Ethiopia or Uruguay.

Sec. 503B—No funds may be used to finance foreign military credit sales to Argentina, Brazil, El Salvador or Guatemala.

Sec. 503C—Foreign military credit sales are limited to $1,850,000 and military education and training to $7,000,000 for the Philippines.

Sec. 506—No funds may be used for any form of direct aid or trade with Cuba.

Source: From *National Journal,* vol. 15 (July 1978), pp. 1120–1121. Reprinted by permission of the Government Research Company, Washington, D.C.

ecutive branch. He felt that this was necessary to separate the vital justice and prosecution functions from the contamination of partisan politics and undue White House influence, but he failed to persuade many members of Congress. Another variation of the Ervin proposal was to call for the establishment of a permanent office of special prosecutor, independent of the executive branch. Democratic Representative Henry Reuss of Wisconsin championed a constitutional amendment to provide a vote of no-confidence that would permit Congress to call for new elections when it believed a president had become incompetent or had lost the support needed to govern effectively. Others proposed a constitutional amendment to limit the president to a single six-year term. Another proposal provided for an American "question hour" in which cabinet members or even the president would regularly go before the Congress to respond to questions and participate in a dialogue on major policy questions. Finally, some members of Congress wanted to establish ceilings on the number of White House aides and involve Congress in overseeing the policymaking powers of the unconfirmed White House staff. This measure always fails, in part because of the president's claim of separation of powers and in part because Congress does not like to call attention to burgeoning staffs, since theirs has grown even more substantially in recent years.

THE IMPERIAL
PRESIDENCY RECONSIDERED

"Who would have thought five years ago that we would today be calling for new measures to strengthen the American presidency?" That is how activist liberal friends of mine put it in some meetings a year ago in Washington, D.C. A mere six years after Watergate there is again an intensified call for vigorous presidential leadership. If our two most recent presidents have been a welcome relief from the profound tragedies of the Watergate period, they have nonetheless not really lived up to our expectations of presidential leadership. It is appropriate to ask about the presidency in general. How is it doing since Watergate and Richard Nixon's inglorious departure? Have post-Vietnam and post-Watergate "reforms," such as they are, really weakened the presidency? Are the problems Gerald Ford and Jimmy Carter have had with Congress problems of their own making or those of institutional weakness?

Ford and Carter have been sensitive to most of the complaints Americans had about how the presidency was run in the late 1960s and early 1970s. For example, students of the presidency kept saying things would be well if only we had a president who didn't have an enemies list. Or things would be well if we could finally get this war over and no American boys were dying overseas. Or things would be well if only our presidents regularly met with the press, regularly met with their cabinets, and if only they would treat their vice presidents humanely. There was also, of course, a widespread feeling that presidents should "depomp" or "deroyalize" the ceremonies and status symbols at the White House. During the Nixon and Ford years we heard repeatedly that presidential-congressional relations would be much improved if only these two branches were under the control of the same political party.

All these things have come to pass. The war is over. The era of the manipulative and imperial presidency has thankfully passed. Ford and Carter have upgraded the status of the cabinet and appointed reasonably strong activist persons to the vice-presidency. If anything, these two presidents have bent over backward in an effort to restore as much integrity and openness to the office as possible. They have, to their credit, achieved most of the objectives that critics had called for eight and ten years ago.

But save for President Carter's Panama Canal treaty and achievement in arranging for and helping to achieve the Middle East peace accords, both Ford and Carter have had very rough troubles with Congress. The seeming inability of both men to get Congress to pass much of their programs has contributed to a general impression of ineffectiveness. Why then have they been ineffective — or at least appeared ineffective? No single explanation will suffice. Clearly, Congress has strengthened itself in some respects, and it is enjoying asserting itself in both policy-making and policy-thwarting activities.

Congress may have reorganized and revitalized itself in many ways, but many of its reforms have also had the effect of diluting the ability of congressional leaders to obtain action. Power in the Congress has been decidedly decentralized. Also, fringe benefits for members of Congress have had the effect of making it easier for members to engage in constituency services and spend more time on reelection chores — developments that make members of Congress less dependent on presidential patronage or election support.

Several "system" factors are doubtless also at work. Thus our national and international problems are more complex than they used to be. Our economy is vastly more interdependent with those of other leading nations around the world. Our dependence on imported raw materials is much greater now than a decade or two ago. We used to concern ourselves almost exclusively with the *demand* side of the economic equation, whereas now we have to worry about the *supply* side of the equation.[28]

To determine the derivation of the other problems that have plagued Ford and Carter, we will take a close look at their relations with Congress.

PRESIDENT FORD AND CONGRESS

"I do not want a honeymoon with you. I want a good marriage," said Ford to the Congress as he started his presidency. "As President I intend to listen . . ." Ford said his relations with Congress would be characterized not by confrontation but by "communication, conciliation, compromise and cooperation." But his hoped for holy wedlock soured and an unholy deadlock set in as he proceeded to veto sixty-nine legislative measures.

Congress did give Ford a hard time. Having shaken off years of inertia, Congress took advantage of an appointed president to regain some of its own lost authority. They consequently rejected some of his nominations, took four months to confirm Nelson Rockefeller, rejected his foreign-aid bill, trimmed his defense appropriations, curtailed military aid to Turkey, denied him the means to conduct open or covert operations in Angola, and so on.

Some of Ford's aides warned of a new period of congressional government. Ford himself said:

Frankly, I believe that Congress recently has gone too far in trying to take over the powers that belong to the President and the executive branch.

This probably is a natural reaction to the steady growth of executive branch power over the past forty years. I'm sure it is a reaction to Watergate and Vietnam. And the fact that I came to this office through a Constitutional process and not by election also may have something to do with current efforts by the Democratic Congress to take away some of the powers of the President.

As a member of Congress for twenty-five years, I clearly understand the powers and obligations of the Senate and House under our Constitution. But as President for eighteen months, I also understand that Congress is trying to go too far in some areas.[29]

Why did Ford have such troubled relations with Congress? Aside from the reaction to Vietnam and Watergate, which obviously played a role in his difficulties, he had to contend with a Congress that had reorganized itself in several ways. It was a more democratic institution, with power more noticeably dispersed among its members. It had streamlined some of its procedures and was more conscious of its responsibility to the people. But perhaps the major problem was that Ford was decidedly more conservative than the Congress. This should have come as no surprise; as a member of Congress, he had voted against medicare, opposed the creation of the Office of Economic Opportunity, opposed aid to education, and opposed federal help for state water-pollution projects. He had, however, always been a strong supporter of Defense Department spending.

Moreover, he was an appointed president. As our first Twenty-fifth Amendment President he also bore the stigma of illegitimacy. He had absolutely no mandate from the people. He had to deal with a Democrat-controlled Congress. He came to office right in the midst of a midterm congressional election. At the State Department he had the always-secretive Henry Kissinger, who had by then acquired strong opponents in both parties. He had to contend with a strong attack from the right wing (the Reagan wing) of his own minority party. The Ford presidency experienced additional troubles because it came during the seventh and eighth years of the Nixon-Ford administrations. Their top people were tired and had run out of imaginative ideas and solutions. Ford suffered too from the disillusionment that invariably sets in toward the end of an eight-year hold on the presidency. The same thing had happened in 1960 and 1968.

Actually, however, the Ford presidency was neither as weak nor constrained as it wanted people to believe (the White House liked to convey the impression that the press, the courts, and Congress were literally undermining presidential powers). Ford was vulnerable, and the office itself was constrained as it often is after a strong president. Still, the major powers of the office were still available to the president even if the mood in Congress and among the general public doubtlessly indicated that a respite from an overly assertive presidency was desired. Effective use of presidential powers would require shrewd use and especially clear communication of intent — as well as circumstances that called for their use.

PRESIDENT CARTER AND CONGRESS

Carter's relations with Congress were often strained, not turbulent. He suffered setbacks on his energy package, welfare reform, election reforms, Korean strategy, proposed consumer-protection agency, and countless other measures. He scored some victories (i.e., on the B-1 bomber and the Panama Canal), but these seemed to be the exception to the rule, and even the victories seemed to anger or divide Congress. Actually Carter's overall record was not as weak as the late Nixon or the Gerald Ford years — but the impression was left, mostly accurate, that Carter fared poorly with Congress.

Carter's difficulties with Congress were partially due to the post-Watergate efforts to constrain the American presidency — but *only partially*. To be sure, Congress did not want to become a rubber stamp for a Democratic president. Congress was enjoying its struggle to reassert itself. Also, the dispersion of influence (i.e., power to the subcommittees and subcommittee chairmen) in the House of Representatives made it more difficult for a president to deal with Congress. Gone were the days when the White House could deal with a handful of "whales" who really ran the show. But Carter's difficulties stemmed from a number of other factors as well.

Carter's Campaign "Washington Is the Problem" Bred Resentment

Carter ran for the White House as a Mr. Pure, a Mr. Integrity as well as an outsider. He sold himself to the public almost like a detergent who could be sent to Washington to clean and scrub things up. His campaign slogans were often seen as a "put down" to Congress. He talked often of the mess in Washington. He said Congress was "inherently incapable of leadership" and added that "in the absence of strong presidential leadership . . . there is no leadership." One of his slogans was "Leaders for a Change."

His personal style of campaigning stressed confrontation with Washington elites rather than negotiation. "I am not from Washington, I'm not a lawyer and I will not lie to you" was a basic appeal. It was as if nearly everyone in Washington lies. In short, he seemed too righteous. He implied that his administration would be guided by only the highest morals. He knew he had a good theme, but he overdid it. As one of his supporters put it, "I wish he was just a little less righteous." And another said, "Next time, I'd like someone who doesn't talk as high and mighty before he gets in and does more of a job after he's elected." Hence, when the Bert Lance affair occurred, and when Carter's own loan and bank transactions became the center of various investigations, Carter found himself all the more critically judged by the Washingtonians.

Carter's Base Within the Democratic Party Was Fragile to Begin With

Much was made of the idea that most of the problems in presidential-congressional relations could be overcome if only both branches were held by the Democrats. That came to pass as Carter came to the White House, but the promised harmony did not ensue, partly because the Democratic party is in many ways several parties in one. Any party with a militant Ron Dellums on one hand and a James Eastland on the other is split and strained. Moreover, Carter really had no viable political base within the Democratic party. He is not really a southern old-boy conservative. Some have suggested he is more of a Yankee puritan.[30] In many ways, the mere fact that he is a southerner in the White House makes him a novelty. Ironically, although Carter enjoys his highest popularity in the southeastern section of the nation, the members of Congress from that region consistently give him low rates of support for his programs in Congress. Southern pride didn't produce policy support.

His election coalition had built-in instabilities, for it contained urban blacks and southern small-town whites, northern liberals and southern conservatives, frost-belt states and sun-belt states. Organized labor never was close to him; they didn't really know him and didn't really trust him. He never had any real support in the West, and he never commanded the respect of the foreign-policy establishment. Further, he was not popular among governors, a natural peer group, and he ran well behind most members of Congress in his 1976 election.

Carter himself was not unaware of these circumstances. He knew that his coalition was fragile at best. His pollsters kept warning of this. He knew that he would have to take special pains to weld together a more lasting coalition. For awhile it appeared he might have some success. His celebrated town meetings in various parts of the country, his staying overnight with average Americans in their own homes, his frequent press conferences, and varied other activities showed that Carter was trying.

But Carter's coalition came apart, especially after Edward Kennedy's challenge.

Activist Without Mandate

Carter is an activist who wants to achieve countless comprehensive policy and process changes, but he had no mandate to do so from either the 1976 or 1978 elections. Forty-seven percent of the voters stayed at home in 1976 and even more in the congressional elections of 1978. Carter lost nearly 30 points in the polls between August and election day as his election campaign stumbled haphazardly to a narrow victory. White voters, even white southerners, preferred Ford over Carter. Further, the 1976 election was hardly an election fought over issues. His election seemed to be due more to the public's lack of confidence in Gerald Ford than to any program pledges Carter put forth.

Yet Carter in office often acted as if he had some direct mandates to reshape domestic and foreign policy. Although not a populist by any stretch of the imagination, he tried nonetheless to be assertive, innovative, and purposeful. At least initially, he was in the don't-just-stand-there-do-something tradition. Although he seldom succeeded, he did seek to set standards, establish new guidelines, deregulate transportation industries, spearhead human-rights crusades, and push for serious energy conservation. If he did not exactly display a "take-charge-guy" approach, he nevertheless time and again tried to offer a sense of direction.

So much did he propose in the first two years that Congress complained he was asking too much of them. Perhaps this was a camouflage for the fact he was proposing programs they didn't like. Sometimes he would outline programs but not push for their funding — as with health insurance or aid to the cities. In other cases, Carter's problems with the Hill arose either because he was in advance of his times or because he was unable to communicate why his so-called comprehensive policy changes were needed.

Carter Wasn't Political Enough

Some of Carter's early difficulties stemmed from the fact that he did not enjoy the politics of dealing with members of Congress. He gave the impression that he was the rational man and that Congress should deal with him and his programs completely on their merits. The idea that deals would be made and favors would be dispensed seemed quite alien to Carter. However, deals and horse-trading must go on, at least to some extent, with various interest group leaders. That may be how politics works, but Carter set out, often in vain, to establish a new model.

It was often as if the realities of political life just didn't occur to Carter and his top White House aides. Said Wisconsin congressman Henry Reuss, "the high minded approach is fine, but something more is needed. It need not be low minded. . . . They still haven't learned horse-trading." He added, "Sometimes, it only requires a very small horse. . . . They should do nice little things and not wait until they're asking for a vote." [31]

Reporters covering his trips around the country during his first year or so said he was almost incapable of saying nice things about members of Congress even as he traveled among their constituents. One United States senator's office had arranged for Carter to say a few words of endorsement for the senator when Carter was in the senator's home state. Expensive television and video machinery had been rented and set up to capture Carter's few words of praise, hoping that they might be usable in the 1978 election race. But Carter came and talked and went but never uttered the expected words of praise. Washington was full of such anecdotes. It was as if he didn't like politics, and yearned to be above both politics and politicians.

Members of Congress complained too that he did not consult them enough. Unlike Lyndon Johnson, he seldom invited them in to go over the drafts of prospective bills. Carter seemed often to prefer a government by surprise. He also had a penchant for bypassing Congress and going to the country. Of course, most presidents do this, but his style of doing it, coupled with his reputation as an "outsider," came back to weaken his ties to Congress.

One scholar who has studied Carter's legislative-relations staffs offers an additional explanation that since Carter won the nomination and then the presidency itself largely without having to build coalitions with the left, right, and center of the Democratic party, so also his congressional-relations teams did not build these needed coalitions to get things passed. Political scientist Eric Davis puts it this way:

> Since they did not have to engage in bargaining to get the nomination or to win the election, they would not have to engage in bargaining or exchange to get their programs passed on Capitol Hill. Because they did not recognize the importance of coalition-building through brokerage, they did not, at the very outset of the Administration, make an effort to establish cooperative lobbying relationships with the other important participants in the legislative process. . . . Since these relationships were not established, the White House had to rely on its own resources to obtain legislative successes. Therefore, legislative defeats resulted. And these defeats fed upon themselves, creating the image of ineptitude on the part of the White House. This image of ineptitude, in turn, has led to members of Congress being less willing to rely on White House judgments and to accept White House analyses of issues.[32]

By the middle of his third year in office, Carter began to acknowledge some of his personal inadequacies as a politician. Speaking to a meeting of the Democratic National Committee he allowed that his failings with Congress were to a major degree his own fault. Then he said, "Maybe if I was a better politician, I would have gotten these bills through the Congress." [33]

Different National Mood

In the early 1960s the mood of the country embodied a seemingly boundless self-confidence in itself and in what its government could achieve. The mood was one of feeling we could go anywhere and do anything from conquering outer space to effecting land reform in Latin America and political reforms in Indochina. We believed government could end poverty in America and achieve countless other things.

John Kennedy became our president during this era of good feelings, this era of confident and sometimes reckless adventuresomeness. Optimism and idealism aided both him and Lyndon Johnson in their efforts to deal with Congress.

That era is over. Today we dwell on the scarcity of our resources. We say we overextended ourselves abroad. We salute the slogan of "Small Is Beautiful" and read study after study predicting the limits to growth.

President Carter would doubtless have liked to provide leadership of the Roosevelt, Wilson, and Kennedy kind, but he didn't have the appropriate climate of expectations. There was neither the trauma of a depression nor the crusading spirit of a world war nor the buoyant national optimism of the early 1960s.

The presidency is obviously hedged in by the national mood. The mood today is one of disillusionment with federal programs. Moreover, this is certainly not the age of the hero. We may long for leadership, but we are skeptical of our leaders.

So Carter had his problems with Congress, but many of his problems were due to factors other than the post-Vietnam, post-Watergate, anti-imperial presidency reforms.[34]

WHATEVER HAPPENED TO THE IMPERIAL PRESIDENCY?

Americans want strength in their presidency and in their presidents, but they do not want the powers of the presidency used for selfish ends or to corrupt the nation's political processes. Thus we acted, although not swiftly, to strengthen the checks and balances. Other institutions rose to the challenge — Congress, courts, the press, and the general public gradually developed a questioning approach to presidential requests, to presidential action. No single act or assertion or reassertion stands out so much as a gradual welling up of a sense of consciousness that we had allowed certain presidents to go too far. The end result, often intangible and defying measurement, was more a political response than structural or constitutional.

Perhaps more than anything else the appointment of Gerald Ford and election of Jimmy Carter ended the fears about the imperial presidency. Ford bent over backward to place distance between himself and Nixon's strategies and practices. Jimmy Carter built his campaign around honesty, open government, and rectitude. For a good while, Carter received a welcome response to this approach.

But even as the nation went about trying to remove the causes of imperial presidency or merely trying to forget about presidential abuses of power, growing numbers of thoughtful Americans worried about whether the presidency was strong enough to carry on the responsibilities of that office. After debating the merits of congressional reassertion, most Americans realized that our choices are few. We could really weaken the presidency even to the point of crippling it, or we could leave it pretty much alone, or we could try to regulate it so as to make sure that its powers were used for only those purposes the public wanted it used. Because few people wanted to weaken it, the debate revolved around the second and third options.

To weaken the presidency, upon closer inspection, really meant that the bureaucracy and special interests would be strengthened. A weakening of the presidency would not mean turning power back to Congress and the people. A weakening of the presidency would also weaken the ability of the United States to negotiate and conduct an effective foreign policy. Michael Novak once perceptively suggested that the Right worries about the imperial presidency at home and the Left worries about the imperial presidency in foreign-policy matters. What he did not suggest, but which is equally appropriate, is that many on the Right actually want a near-imperial presidency abroad and much of the Left wants something approaching an imperial presidency at home. That is, the Right is concerned about national security as a prime consideration of the health of the nation and they know well that the Hamiltonian energies of a single executive are not only desirable but essential. The Left generally favors more planning at home, wars on poverty, public jobs, and creative social regulation that might advance the ends of equality, justice, and humanity. Here again, the energies and commitments of a leader in the Franklin Roosevelt image is wanted — save even more so.

In short, large numbers of Americans for a large number of often differing reasons rallied around the proposition that our presidency should not be weakened — and, in particular, it should not be in any way diminished at the altar of an imperial Congress or an imperial public. The president's primacy, they would add, has been founded in the necessities of the modern American condition. We live in a continuous state of emergency, where instant nuclear warfare could destroy the country in a matter of minutes and where global competition of an extraordinary sort now highlights the need for swiftness, efficiency, and unity in our government. Some would add another characteristic, secrecy. Further, today's social, urban, and environmental problems require a persistent display of creative presidential leadership. Thus, any reduction in the powers of the president might leave us naked to our enemies, to the forces of inflation and depression at home, and to the forces of unrest and aggression abroad.

Without strong presidential leadership, many feared that parochialism in Congress might become unremitting. The old saw about the district-preoccupied congressman, "I regret that I have but one country to give to my congressional district," summed up the fears of those who preferred that the presidency rather than the Congress be the primary leadership institution.

Both Ford and Carter were found lacking according to the postimperial standards of the late 1970s. Public putdowns — often verging on the cruel — were echoed around the country. On Ford: "He would have made a fine mayor of Grand Rapids — in a quiet year." On Carter: "The President has a case of terminal meekness." Carter and Ford tried to maintain the necessary strength in that office. But their efforts were frequently in vain.

Congress tried to reassert itself vis-à-vis the presidency. Congress has the constitutional authority and it also has most of the tools to become a reasonably effective partner in shaping most national policies. Whether it chooses to use them, however, is another matter. However much the public may have wanted Congress to be a major coequal partner with the president, the public's support for Congress as an institution is always subject to deterioration. The presidency is favored as the leader of the nation by most Americans most of the time. They would agree with Harvard Law Professor Larry Tribe when he writes:

> To be reminded that it was not meant to be so — that the Framers envisioned a vastly more modest chief executive — is only to recall that, had the blueprint been incapable of expanding beyond the Framers' designs, the Nation could not have persisted through two centuries of turmoil. No act of the imagination, constitutional or otherwise, can recapture the Presidency's past. We are, and must remain, a society led by three equal branches, with one permanently "more equal" than the others: as the Supreme Court and Congress are preeminent in constitutional theory, so the President is preeminent in constitutional fact.[35]

Or they would agree with James Sundquist who writes:

Ask the people who the great Presidents were, and they don't name any weak Presidents; they name the strong Presidents. They name Jackson, and Lincoln, Jefferson and Washington, Franklin Roosevelt and Teddy Roosevelt. They were the men who built the Presidency and made a practice of kicking the Congress around. . . . I don't mean to be happy about this, but I think that is realistically what the situation is.[36]

Many will continue to worry about future imperial presidents and about the kinds of policy impulses that give rise to the imperial presidency. Many of the underlying causes are still present. Those who are concerned about these persisting realities will not content themselves — nor should they — with the existing safeguards against future misuses of presidential power. The difficulty is (as shall be discussed further in Chapter 10 of this book) that few of the yet untried safeguards suggested by the reformers seem to be politically acceptable or practicable. It is not easy to contrive devices that will check the president who would misuse powers without hamstringing the president who would use the same powers for democratically acceptable ends. We are again back to that now familiar paradox.

In the end, both the president and Congress have to recognize that they are not two sides out to "win" but two parts of the same government, both elected to pursue together the interests of the American people. Too much was made for too long — both by presidents and scholars — of that partial truth that only presidents represent all the people. If there is an overriding lesson to be learned from our brush with the imperial presidency, it is that the American people refuse to be governed by one branch of government alone. If history is any teacher, rebalancing efforts such as the congressional reassertion of the mid-1970s will be needed again — after the next experience with abuses. What is past is often prologue.

NOTES

1. See chapter 3.
2. Roberta S. Sigel, "Image of the American Presidency: Part II of an Exploration into Popular Views of Presidential Power," in Aaron Wildavsky, ed., *The Presidency* (Little, Brown, 1969), p. 300.
3. *New York Times*/CBS Poll, April 1977.
4. Arthur M. Schlesinger, Jr., *The Imperial Presidency* (Houghton Mifflin, 1973).
5. *Ibid.*, pp. 129–30.
6. See Leonard C. Meeker, "The Legality of U.S. Participation in the Defense of Vietnam," *Department of State Bulletin*, 28 March 1966, pp. 484–85.
7. See J. Malcolm Smith and Cornelius P. Cotter, *Powers of the President During Crisis (Public Affairs Press*, 1960), and see also Harold C. Relyea, "Declaring and Terminating a State of Emergency," *Presidential Studies Quarterly*, Fall 1976, pp. 36–42.
8. Quoted in "The President Versus Congress," *National Journal*, 29 May 1976, p. 736. See also *Emergency Powers Statutes*, Report of the Special Committee on the Termination of the National Emergency, U.S. Senate, 19 November 1973.

9. Walter F. Mondale, *The Accountability of Power* (McKay, 1975), pp. 114–15.

10. Lloyd Bentsen, testimony, *Congressional Oversight of Executive Agreements — 1975*, Hearings Before the Subcommittee on Separation of Powers of the Committee on the Judiciary, U.S. Senate, 94th Cong. (U.S. Government Printing Office, 1975), p. 79.

11. See his own account in Richard Nixon, *RN: Memoirs of Richard Nixon* (Grosset & Dunlap, 1978), pp. 896–910. See also Leon Jaworski, *The Right and The Power* (Pocket Books, 1977), chap. 10.

12. Raoul Berger, "The Grand Inquest of the Nation," *Harper's*, October 1973, p. 12. See also his *Executive Privilege: A Constitutional Myth* (Harvard University Press, 1974).

13. Sam J. Ervin, Jr., quoted in *Separation of Powers Annual Report*, Report of the Committee on the Judiciary, U.S. Senate, Subcommittee on Separation of Powers, 19 July 1976, p. 9. See also, *Refusals by the Executive Branch to Provide Information to the Congress, 1964–1973*, issued by the same committee, 93rd Cong., November 1974. Note that these instances of withheld information or refusals to share information with Congress are not the same as formal White House use of the "executive privilege" practice. More often than not these were delays and long drawn-out instances of non-cooperation, often by subcabinet or bureau chiefs or agency heads and not necessarily by cabinet officers or White House aides.

14. The best source on impoundment is Louis Fisher, *Presidential Spending Power* (Princeton University Press, 1975).

15. The standard work on the pardon power is W. H. Humbert, *The Pardoning Power of the President* (American Council on Public Affairs, 1941).

16. Walter F. Mondale, "Harnessing the President's Pardon Power," *American Bar Association Journal*, January 1975, p. 108.

17. Quoted, *National Emergencies Act*, Report of the Committee on Government Operations, U.S. Senate, 1976, p. 2.

18. See *Congressional Oversight of Executive Agreements — 1975, op. cit.*

19. Leverett Saltonstall (R. Mass.), quoted in Henry Howe Ransom, *The Intelligence Establishment* (Harvard University Press, 1970), p. 169.

20. John T. Elliff, "Congress and the Intelligence Community," in Larry Dodd and Bruce I. Oppenheimer, eds., *Congress Reconsidered* (Praeger, 1977), pp. 193–206.

21. Quoted in *National Journal*, 29 May 1976, p. 742.

22. Quoted in Mary Russell, "Bill to Give Congress Veto Power Is Defeated," *Washington Post*, 22 September 1976.

23. For President Carter's message on his opposition to certain legislative vetoes, see "Legislative Vetoes: Message to Congress, June 21, 1978," in *Weekly Compilation of Presidential Documents*, 26 June 1978, p. 1146.

24. John R. Bolton, *The Legislative Veto: Unseparating the Powers* (American Enterprise Institute, 1977), pp. 31–32. For a balanced view, see Louis Fisher, "A Political Context for Legislative Vetoes," *Political Science Quarterly*, Summer 1978, pp. 241–53.

25. Antonin Scalia, Assistant Attorney General, in testimony, *Hearings before the Subcommittee on Administrative Law and Governmental Relations*, House of Representatives, October and November 1975, p. 377.

26. For useful discussions on the legislative veto from a variety of viewpoints, see Harold H. Bruff and Ernest Gellhorn, "Congressional Control of Administrative Regulation: A Study of Legislative Vetoes," *Harvard Law Review*, May 1977, pp. 1369–1440; Arthur S. Miller and George M. Knapp, "The Congressional Veto: Preserving the Constitutional Framework," *Indiana Law Journal*, Winter 1977, pp. 367–95; and Louis Fisher, *The Constitution Between Friends* (St. Martin's Press, 1978), chap. 4.

27. William J. Lanouette, "Who's Setting Foreign Policy — Carter or Congress?" *National Journal*, 15 July 1978, pp. 1116–23.

28. Thomas E. Cronin, "The Imperiled Presidency," *Society Magazine,* Nov.–Dec. 1978, pp. 57–64. I have drawn on this previously published essay in this discussion.

29. Ford, in a written reply to a *New York Times* query, quoted in Philip Shabecoff, "Appraising Presidential Power," in Thomas E. Cronin and Rexford G. Tugwell, eds., *The Presidency Reappraised,* 2nd ed. (Praeger, 1977), p. 37. Ford expanded on this theme in his memoir: Gerald R. Ford, *A Time to Heal* (Harper & Row/Reader's Digest, 1979), Ch. 4.

30. See the well-written account by William Lee Miller, *Yankee From Georgia: The Emergence of Jimmy Carter* (Times Books, 1978).

31. Henry S. Reuss, quoted in Shirley Elder, "The Cabinet's Ambassadors to Capitol Hill," *National Journal,* 29 July 1978, p. 1200.

32. Eric L. Davis, "Legislative Liaison in the Carter Administration" unpublished paper delivered at 1978 Annual Meeting of the Midwest Political Science Association, Chicago, Ill., 20–22 April 1978, pp. 30–31.

33. Jimmy Carter, quoted in Richard E. Cohen, "The President's Problems," *National Journal,* 2 June 1979, p. 918.

34. Additional constraints along these lines are discussed in Thomas E. Cronin, "President and Party: The Strained Relationship," in Gerald Pomper, ed., *Party Renewal in America* (Praeger, 1980).

35. Larry Tribe, *American Constitutional Law* (Foundation Press, 1978), p. 157.

36. James L. Sundquist, "What Happened to Our Checks and Balances," in C. Roberts, ed., *Has the President Too Much Power?* (Harper's, 1974), pp. 107–08.

CHAPTER 7

PRESIDENTIAL-DEPARTMENTAL RELATIONS

Everybody believes in democracy until he gets to the White House and then you begin to believe in dictatorship, because it's so hard to get things done. Everytime you turn around, people resist you and even resist their own job.

> — A Kennedy aide, 1970,
> personal interview with the author.

We have no discipline in this bureaucracy. We never fire anybody. We never reprimand anybody. We never demote anybody. We always promote the sons-of-bitches that kick us in the ass. . . .

> — Richard Nixon to John Ehrlichman, Presidential Transcripts,
> published in *Washington Star-News*, 20 July 1974.

It would be good if the President fired a few people around here . . . [people in the Administration who have been disloyal or incompetent].

> — A senior Carter White House aide, 1978,
> personal interview with author.

Every White House has problems with the departments and agencies that make up the bulk of the executive branch. It is difficult to overestimate the degree of frustration and resentment that White House aides develop about the seeming indifference of the permanent government toward presidential policy. This chapter and the next examine the contrasting perspectives during the 1960–1980 era of White House aides and their counterparts in departmental officialdom. This chapter focuses on the role of White House staffers as middlemen charged with winning departmental compliance. Chapter 8 focuses on the diverse roles of cabinet members as advocates and as advisers to the White House.

The relationship between presidential staff and departmental officials has been shown to be almost inevitably adverse in character and typified by considerable conflict. A president has only a few years to devise his priorities and set them in motion, whereas the federal bureaucracy is already well set in the routines of managing on-going programs, has well-established patterns of interest and interaction with Congress and groups outside government, and will outlive the new president and his particular directives. The primary loyalties of most career government officials are not to presidential lieutenants but to the professional norms and bureau activities to which they owe their livelihood and to which they have given years of work. Cabinet secretaries may be interest-group brokers from the beginning, and in any case they tend to become absorbed quickly by the relatively narrow objectives and politics of their particular fiefdoms. As department officials respond sluggishly to White House budget-cutting ideas or legislative strategies that may promote other interests at the expense of theirs, the president may perceive these weaknesses in his cabinet and reject the body as a continuing adviser in policy matters.

All of these tensions, all of the pulling and hauling, are a part of the informal but continuous power struggles within the executive branch. Presidential government is by no stretch of the imagination a pyramid-like structure with a single pinnacle.

PRESIDENTIALISTS VERSUS DEPARTMENTALISTS

Just as there are those who argued in the mid-1970s for a revitalized Congress that would reassert itself in presidential-legislative relations, so also there are some who urge that the cabinet and the departments need to be strengthened in relation to the White House staff. The textbook orthodoxy holds that the presidency should be the strongest partner in all executive-branch relations. The reason behind the creation of the Executive Office of the President in 1939 was to equip the presidency with the tools of management and with the authority commensurate with its responsibilities. What was needed, people thought, was a strong single executive to provide unity and direction on the one hand and to be held openly accountable for the administration of the national government on the other.

The basic premise was that the requisite unity and energy for the political system could only come from a strong, well-staffed, vigorous presidency. This is the great office, the only truly national office in the whole system, say the textbooks. The presidency, the advocates of strength insisted, must be the central tower of strength and the articulator of the forward thrust in every sphere of policy, not because it was the ideal institution but because there was no alternative to it.

Opposed to the presidential view are departmentalists, who hold that the success or failure of federal programs rests almost entirely on the quality of the executive departments. Their underlying premise is that most federal laws deliberately allow discretion in many areas, and thus authority must be vested largely in departmental and bureau leaders. Appointed and career executives should have leeway to apply standards, modify regulations, and interpret legislative intent as they deem appropriate to fit specific situations. The involvement of the White House should be highly selective; moreover, Congress is as much a chief administrator as a president. After all, it creates the agencies and departments, it confirms the cabinet officers, it enacts the laws, and it also funds the programs. Certain departmental officials, for example, deplored the considerable White House involvement in clearing AID grants and in HUD model-city selections, Department of Education desegregation proceedings, and price supports for the dairy industry.

Presidentialists feel that only the presidency can provide the needed orchestration of complex, functionally interdependent federal programs. Only the president should have discretion over budget choices and the administration of federal policies. He is the one charged with faithfully executing the laws. These advocates assume that a strong presidency makes a major difference in the way government works, and that this difference will be in the direction of a more constructive (desirable) set of policy outcomes. They pledge allegiance to Alexander Hamilton: "A feeble Executive implies a feeble execution of the government. A feeble execution is but another phrase for a bad execution; and a goverment ill-executed, whatever it may be in theory, must be, in practice bad government." [1]

Presidentialists invariably argue that the presidency is not adequately staffed or funded. The presidency needs not just more help but a major infusion of skills, talent, tools, and loyalty if it is to gain control over the permanent federal departments. Implicitly, if not explicitly, their slogan is "more power to the White House!" Presidentialists argue that, because so many previous presidents have set up their own agencies in order to bypass the bureaucracy, and because of the sheer size and diversity of the executive branch, the White House too often serves at the pleasure of the bureaucracy rather than vice versa. McGeorge Bundy spoke for many of this school of thought when he observed that the executive branch in many areas "more nearly resembles a collection of badly separated principalities than a single instrument of executive action." [2] What is needed, presidentialists imply, is more hierarchy: if a president is to be held accountable for program performance, he must have adequate control over the executive departments.

Ill-concealed within the presidentialist point of view is a contempt for the federal bureaucracy and a skepticism about the utility of the cabinet as an administrative tool. Presidentialists never completely trust civil servants; they frequently mistrust political appointees as well. Whatever of importance needs doing ought to be done directly from the White House; otherwise, the departmental people will temper or undermine the desired intentions of policy. As former Kennedy staffer Arthur Schlesinger, Jr., explained:

> At the start we all felt free to "meddle" when we thought we had a good idea or someone else a poor one. But, as the ice began to form again over the government, freewheeling became increasingly difficult and dangerous . . . our real trouble was that we had capitulated too much to the existing bureaucracy. Wherever we have gone wrong . . . has been because we have not had sufficient confidence in the New Frontier approach to impose it on the government. Every important mistake has been the consequence of excessive deference to the permanent government. . . . The problem of moving forward seemed in great part the problem of making the permanent government responsive to the policies of the presidential government.[3]

The presidency is a prime target of reform for presidentialists, who see it as lacking in adequate staff and resources for interdepartmental coordination and program evaluation, and who see presidents as the recipients of endless special-interest pleas and narrow-minded agitation, even from many of their own cabinet members. In its crudest form, their goal is *to presidentialize* the executive branch. Toward that end there are catalogs of reform proposals: "The strong Presidency will depend upon the Chief Executive's capacity to control and direct the vast bureaucracy of national administration. Ideally, the President should possess administrative powers comparable to those of business executives. What the President needs most can be simply formulated: a power over personnel policy, planning, accounting, and the administration of the executive branch that approaches his power over the executive budget." [4] Other variations on this theme call for better policy-evaluation and program-management staffs

within the executive office. Presidentialists with a narrow policy interest
are always asking that the formulation and administration of this particular interest be brought more intimately into the presidential orbit "much
along the lines of the Council of Economic Advisers." Others would
place within the presidential establishment field agents or expediters —
federal domestic-program "czars" — located in federal regional offices or
large metropolitan areas to ensure that presidential priorities are being
carried out properly at the grass-roots level.

The Departmental Loyalists

The departmentalist view has varying degrees of support among professional civil servants, several former cabinet officers, and even some
former White House staff assistants. Often it is also supported by congressmen who disagree with presidential objectives. Moreover, an increasing number of skeptics have been persuaded that a larger presidency with
greater resources or a greater institutionalization of the presidency is not
a realistic answer to the problem of creating and then managing a more
responsive federal government. Career public servants point to the abuses
of White House powers in the events surrounding the 1972 election as
evidence of how presidential aides can misuse their positions to influence
officials of the IRS, CIA, FBI, and State and Justice departments.

Some departmentalists claim that in recent years the White House
staff has become too much a center for operations management and less
an overseer or chief executive institution. Presidents, they say, should be
involved in broad policy questions, not in the nuts-and-bolts concerns of
program operation. As David Truman has written:

> [The president] cannot take a position on every major controversy
> over administrative policy, not merely because his time and energies are
> limited, but equally because of the positive requirements of his position.
> He cannot take sides in any dispute without giving offense in some quar-
> ters. He may intervene where the unity of his supporters will be threat-
> ened by inaction; he may even, by full use of the resources of his office,
> so dramatize his action as to augment the influence he commands. But he
> cannot "go to the country" too often, lest the tactic become familiar and
> his public jaded. Rather than force an administrative issue, he may
> choose to save his resources for a legislative effort. . . . [For effective-
> ness he] must preserve some of the detachment of a constitutional mon-
> arch.[5]

But even if the president remains detached from the day-to-day operations of
the federal government, communicating and delegating authority only
indirectly through his close lieutenants, cabinet officials want both relative
independence and a vote of confidence with which to carry on their work.

They feel they should have the right of direct access to the president. They insist that the White House staff members should not have authority to issue directives independent of the president. They feel rather strongly that the swelling of the White House staffs has caused an isolation as well as an obstacle to the free exchange and examination of ideas and alternatives.

The more the White House usurps responsibilities from their proper home in the departments, the more the White House undermines the goal of competent departmental management. A cabinet member ignored or bypassed by the president is made to look weak in front of relevant congressional and client support groups as well as his or her subordinates. Departmental officials who must fight hard to maintain access to, and rapport with, the White House have correspondingly less time and energy for internal departmental management. The takeover by White House staff of certain departmental functions also diminishes the capacity of the department to streamline these functions in the future. Imaginative professional people will not long remain in departmental positions if they are underused or misused consistently.

Departmentalists believe that White House meddling in department affairs is often disadvantageous for everyone involved — except perhaps for the White House aide who has to look busy. George Reedy noted that "there is, on the part of the White House assistants, a tendency to bring to the White House problems which should not properly be there, frequently to the disadvantage of the president." [6] His view is echoed loudly by a senior State Department official: "Part of the problem is endemic to the White House. It's Parkinsonian; unless the White House staff see problems, they'll become underemployed. So, naturally, they will see all sorts of problems. . . . White House staff have to find something to do, so they will see or even invent a need to modify this, or change that, intervene here, and so forth — otherwise there is no employment for them." Carter Attorney General Griffin Bell bluntly said, "I would place a severe restriction on the staff allocated to the President. . . ." [7] Robert Wood, a professional urbanologist and former secretary of HUD, offered this sober evaluation:

> The longer one examines the awesome burdens and limited resources of those who help the president from within his immediate circle, the more skeptical one becomes of a strategy for overseeing government by "running" it from 1600 Pennsylvania Avenue. The semiheroic, semihopeless posture has been captured many times in several administrations: dedicated men, of great intelligence and energy, working selflessly through weekends and holidays to master an endlessly increasing array of detail on complex subjects beyond their understanding on which decisions must be made "here" because a resolution elsewhere is not to be trusted. They persevere, taking their stand against "the bureaucrats," pushing programs

through against sullen, hidden resistance from the departments. Committees are abolished, agencies rejuggled, staff reviews simplified, new reporting forms introduced, all in the effort to assure that more and more decisions are, or can be, presidential. Yet, in the end, after thirty years, the effort to help the president in making government work has not succeeded.[8]

Conflicting Perspectives of Roles

A characteristic difference that distinguishes White House staff from department leaders often emerges from a difference in recruitment patterns. In its early months every administration makes an exhaustive effort to plant loyal friends in top departmental positions, but presidents and their chief patronage headhunters often find that the number of their qualified as well as trusted acquaintances is far smaller than that of available department positions. An increasing number of presidential campaign aides are assigned to the White House — as, for example, were Kenneth O'Donnell, Lawrence O'Brien, Theodore Sorensen, Bill Moyers, George Reedy, Jack Valenti, H. R. Haldeman, John Ehrlichman, Hamilton Jordan, Jody Powell, and Stuart Eizenstat. On the other hand, most of the cabinet and more important subcabinet officers are recruited from among persons with previous governmental experience or from among the professional and business elite in the relevant subject area — as, for example, were Dean Rusk, Douglas Dillon, Robert McNamara, John Gardner, Clark Clifford, Elliot Richardson, Cyrus Vance, and Harold Brown. The selection of cabinet officials is also influenced by considerations of geography, ethnicity, religion, and party balance.

The White House aides generally reflect a concern for loyalty to the president, teamwork, interdepartmental coordination, follow-through on the president's priorities, and protection of the president's image. They see themselves as charged with keeping options open, with leaning against the wind rather than advocating fixed positions and yet being able to end discussions and act when decisions can no longer wait. They seldom trust departmental aides enough to delegate such tasks. White House aides spend much of their time engaged in building alliances within the executive branch. They are concerned with how best to communicate what the president wants done; how to give the departmental leaders a sense of involvement in presidential decisions; how politely but firmly to tell them of the president's dissatisfaction with department performance; how to motivate them to give added energy to get presidential programs moving; how to extricate the operation of a program from what the aides consider to be a nearly impossible group of people.

Senior departmental officials such as assistant secretaries, bureau chiefs, and the like are no less involved in exchanges with the presidential staff. Some are temporary political appointees; many are career civil servants with long experience in dealing with the presidency, especially with the budget officials in the executive office. Although wanting to cooperate with the objectives of the current presidential team, they are concerned at the same time with attending to departmental priorities and integrity. White House requests are usually honored; pressures and arrogant communications are always resented. Their day-to-day concerns are how to get White House endorsement and increased budget approvals for departmental initiatives; how to get the White House to side with them in a jurisdictional matter; how to make an end run around an unsympathetic and amateur White House aide and make sure the president hears about a new idea; when, if at all, they should notify the White House of some emerging and potentially embarrassing outside advisory report; whether they should supply a potentially credit-winning news announcement to the White House or use it to gain publicity for their own cabinet officer and department; in short, how to deal with the White House when it can help them but otherwise preserve their autonomy.

More contention exists within the executive branch over the priorities and tempo of federal activity than over the basic ends or legitimacy of the government. In this sense the executive branch operates much like a trading arena in which different participants hope that their preferences will prevail. (Few on either side of the White House-departmental exchange are easily pleased.) Both sides have needs and expectations and often even illusions about what the other will give. White House aides usually come in expecting that people in the departments will do what they are told, whether out of respect, fear, or ambition. As one Johnson aide reported: "The president, and vicariously his staff, were thought to vibrate power. . . . The enormous panoply of office that surrounded us — the jets and helicopters, the limousines, the communications system, the ubiquitous guards, the train of press — all contributed to the idea. It was exaggerated. I never tested presidential power and authority over others without discovering that anew."[9] Ford chief of staff Richard Cheney echoed a similar refrain:

> There is a tendency before you get to the White House or when you're just observing it from the outside to say, "Gee, that's a powerful position that person has." The fact of the matter is that while you're here trying to do things, you are far more aware of the constraints than you are of the power. You spend most of your time trying to overcome obstacles getting what the President wants done.[10]

One of the realities in Washington, however, is that the government needs a sense of purpose, a sense of leadership, and a sense of coherence; and often it needs to be told which way to go. Hence, the president and the White House aides must go about their job of asking tough questions, making hard decisions, and prodding people to do a better job. Shaping the issues, and shaping them in such a way that they can be resolved, become critically important. But such tasks, especially if performed rigorously, breed tension. Some of the relationships within the White House-departmental exchange system are sketched briefly in Richard Neustadt's comment: "Agencies need decisions, delegations, and support, along with bargaining arenas and a court of last resort, so organized as to assure that their advice is always heard and often taken. A president needs timely information, early warning, close surveillance, organized to yield him the controlling judgment, with his options open, his intent enforced. In practice these two sets of needs have proved quite incompatible; presidential organizations rarely serve one well without disservice to the other." [11]

Whether the tension inherent in these relationships will be constructive and tolerable depends on many factors, the most important of which is the attitude of the participants. If an aide such as Henry Kissinger (before he became secretary of state) goes around saying, "First of all, you have to weaken the bureaucracy! . . . They all want to do what I'm doing! So the problem becomes: how do you get them to push paper around, spin their wheels, so that you can get your work done," [12] a hostile relationship inevitably will evolve. Predictably, such acid attitudes toward the permanent government are countered by the evaluation of most White House aides as amateurish, arrogant, and ill-informed nuisances who serve the presidency poorly. By extension, it becomes conventional wisdom among veteran officials in the departments that the presidency actually needs to be protected against these presidential aides, these part-timers or temporaries who often seem to be serving their own short-term interests at the expense of both presidency and nation.

Perhaps the most compelling concern is that the swelling of the presidency and the White House usurpation of operational responsibilities normally belonging in the departments might undermine what Aaron Wildavsky saw as "the one quality above all others which the White House staff must have if it is directly and dispassionately to serve the chief executive: the ability to view problems from the broad perspective of the presidency. . . ." [13]

CONFLICT AS PERCEIVED BY THE
WHITE HOUSE STAFF

The eighty aides and former aides the author interviewed during the 1970s were asked whether they experienced major difficulties in working with the executive departments: "Can you give your view of this? Is this really a problem?" Conflict was widely acknowledged: considerable conflict in

White House-departmental exchanges was felt by 66 percent, 25 percent felt only moderate conflict; and only 8 percent felt an insignificant amount. Some aides talked of conflicts within the executive branch as the single greatest problem in contemporary government. One man who had worked for both Presidents Kennedy and Johnson said that "it was an absolutely terrible problem. . . . There are major problems with cabinet members and civil servants alike. Even the great members like McNamara and Secretary of Agriculture Orville Freeman were terrible in evading their share of many of our efforts." A senior Johnson-administration counselor observed that "the separation of governments is not so great between Congress and the president as between a president and those people like subcabinet and bureau officials who become locked into their own special subsystem of self-interested policy cencerns." Others talked about the increasing defiance of department personnel toward the White House:

> It's a terrible problem and it's getting worse, particularly with the State Department. The major problem is the lack of any identification [on their part] with the president's program priorities. At State they try to humor the president but hope he will not interfere in their complex matters and responsibilities. It is equally a problem with civil servants and cabinet types. It is amazing how soon the cabinet people get captured by the permanent staffs. Secretary _____ under Nixon, for example, was captured within days . . . and Nixon's staff didn't even try to improve things. They just assumed there was a great problem. Personally, I think you can't expect too much from the bureaucracy. It is too much to expect that they will see things the president's way.

Some aides noted that conflicts varied with different departments and with different cabinet members: for example, "Yes, there are certainly many problems, but it differs from area to area and from president to president. I think the amount of friction is related to the role of the White House staff and what they undertake and what presidents let them do." A more tempered assessment of the existence of conflict comes from a congressional-relations aide in the Kennedy-Johnson White House: "Oh, yes, there are problems to an extent. There is deep suspicion around the whole government toward the new president when he comes into power. . . . But the fights you get in are different all around town. . . . We had some excellent men around town, and some boobs. The important thing for a president to do is to get good men and then decentralize the responsibility. Let the department people do their job and don't let your [White House] staff interfere too much."

A few aides who had less involvement with the departments acknowledged little if any serious conflict. One speechwriter observed that "on my level this really isn't a problem. You have to remember that I wasn't in a straight policy role. When I had contact with department people, it was mainly to get facts and statistics for speeches, etc. . . . and I always had plenty of help. . . . 'They' would even stay after 5 o'clock if you emphasized that this stuff was for the president."

Conflicts in White House-departmental relations can be attributed to both *subjective* factors, such as differing allegiances, differing definitions of priorities and roles, personality clashes, or personal ambitions, and to *objective* factors, such as the size of the federal effort, time and communications restrictions, budget limitations, knowledge gaps, and the centrifugal pulls inherent in federalism and in the functionally independent department. White House staff members stressed as sources of conflict the subjective differences and the ill effects of the disjunction of presidential and departmental perspectives.

White House Sources of Conflict

White House staffers suggested that their own definition of their roles and the pressures under which they had to work often exacerbated relations with cabinet and department officials. Presidents and their staffs arrive at the White House charged up to produce results, to make good on the pledges of their campaign. The postelection euphoria and the simplification of issues during the campaign contribute to overextended and insensitive strategies:

> Well, a Kennedy staff hallmark was to seize power from around town. In retrospect I think they often were insensitive to the channels of the existing government. They came in after the campaign with a pretentious "know-it-all" attitude, and they hurt their case by this stance. For example, I think the White House staffers often called people low in the departments and deliberately undercut cabinet people too much in the early years. . . . In retrospect, I don't think you can coordinate much from the White House. You just can't evaluate all that much [not to mention managing it].

No etiquette manual is available to help White House aides avoid antagonizing department officials; for newly appointed aides, the pressure-cooker, goldfish-bowl atmosphere is an invitation to problems. Hatchet men for the opposition party abound, as do columnists in search of conflicts of interest. Often, White House aides feel that as they try desperately to get faster results for their president from securely tenured department officials, they are either damned for becoming arrogant or rendered totally ineffective to the president. One Kennedy lieutenant concluded that "part of our problem was that we were too arrogant, and really for the most part we were all amateurs too." According to another former aide, many eager staffers "if they had the option between (1) giving an order to the bureaucracy or (2) trying to win their cooperation, would always settle quickly for issuing orders."

Many White House aides were ambivalent about staff insensitivity. They talked somewhat contemptuously of the need for more care and feeding of cabinet members, as though some members of the cabinet were merely symbols, kept simply for window dressing, but they also insisted that they had to be aggressive to get anything accomplished. For example:

> I think most of the problem lies in the disregard of some White House aides of the rank, and age, and positional dignity or status of cabinet members and agency heads. Three little words can give a White House aide a lot of power, "the President wants." You need to combine a proper sense of firmness with deference . . . but you have to know the danger traps and the mine fields and always have to keep in mind the question, "How can I serve the President?"
>
> I'll tell you exactly how to deal with this problem: you use two plans. Plan A: get in touch with the cabinet or department head and say "the President is anxious to have your judgment on X matter." If they squirm or delay or fail to comply, then you use Plan B: "Damn it, Mr. Secretary, the President wants it by 3 this afternoon!" You have to be tough in this business.

Yet insensitivity may also be a direct product of personal arrogance, as reported by a former assistant to an HEW secretary about his first encounter with Daniel P. Moynihan:

> "This report you sent me . . ." [Moynihan] said, interrupting. "It's a hell of a lot better than the usual junk I get from those goddam educators at the Office of Education."
>
> I must have beamed.
>
> "But it's barely good enough, goddamit! And good enough won't do. Don't forget, Moffett. You're not writing for some newspaper." He looked me straight in the eye and pointed a finger toward my face. "You're writing for smart people. Like *me*, Moffett." [14]

Some of the aides' most instructive commentary concerned communications within the executive branch. Numerous aides mentioned that the basic reason for conflict was the lack of communications. Often, the problem is not that department officials fail to respond to White House policy directives, but rather that those directives are too hazy and inadequately communicated — or that the president and his aides really have not made up their minds. Sometimes different White House aides send out contradictory messages: for example, the domestic legislative development staff might press department officials for new ideas at the same time the budget director and his staff are warning the same officials of the need to reduce activities. Moynihan, in a pep talk to the Nixon cabinet, said:

> It is necessary for members of the Administration to be far more attentive to what it is the President has said and proposed. Time and again

the President has said things of startling insight, taken positions of great political courage and intellectual daring, only to be greeted with silence or incomprehension within our own ranks. . . . Nixon's initial thrusts have rarely been followed up with a sustained, reasoned, reliable second and third order of advocacy. Deliberately or no, the impression was allowed to arise with respect to the widest range of Presidential initiative that the President wasn't really behind them.[15]

Yet the capacity of the departments to understand what the president means and to believe that he really means it should never be taken for granted. The president may have multiple audiences in mind when preparing his remarks, which handicaps a forceful, direct communication of his views to the departments. Said one Kennedy aide: "Often people don't know what the president really wants. Words sound different depending on where you sit. Professional civil servants feel they must protect their rational objective interests from White House interference — they regard most White House influence upon their activity as very degrading. The presidential voice has to make itself clear, heard and understood throughout Washington."

The sheer size of the federal enterprise also affects communications. A former Johnson aide gave the analogy that the dinosaur became extinct partly because signals were not transmitted from brain to foot or from foot to brain rapidly or accurately enough to create a picture of reality on which the dinosaur could act. More important is the view that stubborn opposition to the White House from the departments often has no other basis than the complaining question: "Why wasn't I consulted?"

Some aides stressed that the always delicate distinction between staff or advisory roles at the White House and operational, administrative line responsibilities in the cabinet departments became blurred during the 1960s and 1970s. Too many of the staff came to give orders rather than transmit requests. One Kennedy staffer became jokingly referred to as the "Over-Secretary" of certain cabinet departments because of the way he would give orders to some cabinet members. "His problem was that he was just too directive oriented and also too brusque!"

Under recent presidents the presidential establishment has taken over many policymaking functions from the cabinet and has also absorbed a multitude of concrete operational activities. Kennedy's postmaster general noted: "After the first two or three meetings, one had the distinct impression that the President felt that decisions on major matters were not made — or even influenced at Cabinet sessions, and that discussion there was a waste of time. . . . When members spoke up to suggest or to discuss major administration policy, the President would listen with thinly disguised impatience and then postpone or otherwise bypass the question." [16] A major Johnson aide said that "after awhile he [Johnson] never even bothered to sit down with most of the domestic cabinet members even to discuss their major problems and program possibilities." Because of the war and because he had grown used to leaning on his own staff so heavily, "Johnson became lazy and wound up using some of the staff as both line managers as well as staff and, I think in retrospect, *it frequently* didn't work out!" In 1971 Senator Ernest Hollings noted: "It used to be that if I had a problem with food stamps, I went to see the Secretary of Agriculture, whose department had jurisdiction over that problem. Not any more. Now, if I want to learn the policy, I must go to the White House to consult [a special assistant]. If I want the latest on textiles, I won't get it from the Secretary of Commerce, who has the authority and responsibility. No, I am forced to go to the White House and see Mr. Peter Flanigan. I shouldn't feel too badly. Secretary [of Commerce Maurice] Stans has to do the same thing." [17]

Nearly one-third of the White House aides felt that their administrations tried to do too much too fast. A Carter aide told me: "I think we have asked too much of Congress and the government — all of these comprehensive programs are too much, too sweeping and they overload the system. We have got to cut back and have just a few major pushes at a time if we are to get going and have some winners." Even President Johnson was quoted to this effect in the last days of his presidential term. The Great Society programs were seldom ill conceived, merely insufficiently planned or ill managed. One veteran budget counselor to presidents explained his view of the conflict:

> Too much was attempted under LBJ. We didn't ask ourselves enough questions about whether we could do these things. Expectations outran the capability to work things out. There were too many other demands or problems in the mid- and late 1960s, Vietnam, inadequately trained manpower at all levels of government, and the structure of intergovernmental relations was inadequate. The space and missile programs had the backing of the people, but public support was terribly splintered over the War on Poverty, etc. . . . It was like a Tower of Babel, with no one interested in the other people's programs.

Another aide said, "You soon forget about programs that were started earlier, even programs begun earlier by your own administration," and "The burden of the presidency is to get things started. The presidency is not an executive agency with clout to carry out the goals of a president. Perhaps it ought to have been, but we did not have time for it, we just didn't work that way." A veteran budget adviser put it a slightly different way: "By and large, the presidency is in the retail business when it comes to policy formulation. It reacts, responds, modifies, and tinkers with departmental policy in program suggestions, but it does not wholesale public policy in the sense of recasting priorities and evaluating the relationship of crude commitments to long-term goals." Several idealistic aides, convinced that their foremost priority was to fashion a sweeping legislative record, accepted the Johnson rationalization of spending the first term putting the laws on the books. His second elected term, they presumed, would be used to streamline the executive branch and make things work.

Departmental Sources of Conflict

Securing the cooperation of the departmental bureaucracies is never simple. But White House aides seem to differ on precisely what the source of the problem is. Some, as mentioned, felt it was as much a matter of how the White House conducted itself as what the bureaucrats or political executives in the departments did. Still, many White House aides held a sinister opinion of the bureaucrats. One Nixon aide reported that "there are many of my colleagues who, like General Al Haig, hold almost a conspiracy view of this problem. They actually believe people out there are malevolent towards White House requests." The more perceptive presidential staffers recognized that there were just a lot of intrinsic problems, structurally built in, that inhibited cordial and frank relations between the White House and the bureaucracy. A Nixon aide summed up this perspective:

> We over here in the Executive Office of the President only have one constituent — the President. If the President makes a clear statement of his preferences, then we know what to do and where to go. But over in the bureaucracy — in the departments and agencies — they not only have the president as a constituent, but they also have Congress, their civil servants, outside pressure groups, etc. . . . The difference in constituency is important. The difference especially in relationship to Congress is very different and intrinsically different. Also, there is just the bureaucratic problem inherent in a large, complex organization. Over here we serve the President, but down the line, like the Secretary of HEW, he has to spend some of his political currency heeding the qualms and wishes of the bureaucracy.

About half the White House aides mentioned a seeming inability of many government workers to adopt the presidential perspective. This capacious point of view, always ill defined, seems to include concern for the public interest, responsiveness to the electorate, maturity of judgment, and all manner of other virtues and wisdom. Whatever it is, many White House policy assistants were convinced that department people either did not understand it or resisted it: "Mostly, the bureaucrats are unresponsive; they view themselves as 'the professionals' and see your [White House] impact as purely political. They don't fight you openly, but they don't cooperate if they can help it!" Said another, "We tried to have department officials over to the White House for drinks and give them pep talks about our programs . . . but it was a band-aid operation, and at best it retarded their loyalties away from the [opposite] direction they otherwise would have gone. After six to twelve months even the political appointees in the departments get captured and taken in by the agencies."

One aide explained, with satirical insight, that some subcabinet officials come into office with great energy and much promise. Soon after they arrive, however, the permanent department staffs convince them that they must go out into the field "to see our extensive field operations." The permanent staff also makes sure that its new boss is kept out of his office and on an exhausting circuit of out-of-town speaking engagements. Meanwhile, back in the agency or bureau, the permanent staffers busily reorganize the office to serve their own priorities and promote themselves, their friends, and, of course, their pet programs. The overworked, travel-weary political appointee has so little time to learn what is going on within his office that he becomes dependent on his subordinates in, for example, testimony before congressional committees or in encounters with the departmental secretary and White House aides. This version of what happens may be an exaggeration, but it expresses the frustrations of being a White House staff aide and of being a subcabinet officer.

Vice President Mondale, speaking more as a senior White House aide than as vice president, said that one of his biggest frustrations was how big the government was and how hard it was to deal with it. The key problem was the number of people in policymaking jobs in the executive branch who could, and often did, revise and even reverse the policies of the White House. What to do about it? Mondale replied: "I think when a President is elected, it ought to be his shop, and he ought to be responsible and accountable to the American people. I'm for civil service, but I think that those positions in Government that are responsible for implementing public policy ought to be held by people who are totally responsible to the President, so that we get a single, coherent implementation of the President's policy. Today the President often gets blamed for things he can't control." [18]

Another way White House aides explain departmental sources of conflict is by questioning the competence or loyalty of an individual cabinet member. A cabinet member is faulted for being too much of an individualist, too aloof, too stubborn, and sometimes for not being a take-charge type. The frequent complaint that cabinet members are captured by narrow special interests was to some the major problem. Said one person: "Often times we appointed weak cabinet people to start with. ——— at Commerce was very weak. And ——— chickened out after he came aboard and saw the mess which he was supposed to administer — so he merely presided over it temporarily while he began making plans to leave and run for a U.S. Senate seat." Another felt that: "It all comes down to people, some people do a great job, like ———. They really run their show and get great people to help them and don't need White House interference. Rusk and McNamara were talented and loyal, but ——— was very weak and had loyalties mainly to his department's interests. Even ——— became seduced by special interests much faster than anyone predicted. And ——— was terrible. He saw himself as Labor's representative to the president rather than as part of the president's cabinet. He even out-Meanyed George Meany a few times." And a Nixon staffer observed:

> After a man is secretary in a department over an appreciable time, too often there is a tendency for him to act as though this is "my department," "my program," "my men." This takes about a year or so. . . . After a while he forgets he serves at the pleasure of the president. Working for Nixon, for example, I occasionally would come up against a man who said that the President had goofed terribly in this or that, or the President didn't understand what was going on, etc. . . . and I had to stress to these individuals that they had better rethink exactly what they were saying because they serve at the pleasure of the President and should know that it is the President's intentions and the President's program that count and not what some cabinet member or undersecretary thinks. So, occasionally a White House aide like myself has to readjust the compasses of political appointees.

A significant factor in promoting conflict between the departments and the presidential staff is their different perspectives on time. A president and his staff think in terms of two- and four-year frames, at the most. They strive to fulfill campaign pledges and related priorities with a sense of urgency, seeking always to build a respectable image for forthcoming election campaigns. The haste with which different programs were announced, such as LBJ's Model Cities, Ford's "Whip Inflation Now," and Carter's early human-rights initiatives, may well have damaged the chances for the effective design and launching of these programs. Career civil servants, on the other hand, are around after the elections regardless of the outcome; and, more important, they usually feel very accountable to the General Accounting Office, the Office of Management and Budget, or to congressional investigating committees for the way federal programs are administered (and for any mistakes that might be made). The work incentives for most careerists are slanted toward doing a thorough, consistent, and even cautious job, rather than toward any hurried dancing to the current tunes of the White House staff. The time frames of sub-cabinet officials fall in between: some seek to impress the president; others, the agency's permanent interest groups, congressional committees, and department professionals.

Conflict and strain also arise because the departments often disagree about priorities and implementation strategies. Most presidents are willing to leave departments alone as long as they are doing a reasonably good job. But the White House is inevitably drawn into departmental matters when two or more departments are feuding with one another. Or when departments are refusing to work with one another — an all too common problem. Indeed, the growth of the White House staff is in part a direct response to the increased number of intradepartmental controversies. Thus, Eisenhower's White House chief of staff, Sherman Adams, allegedly told two cabinet members who could not resolve a matter of mutual concern: "Either make up your mind or else . . . I will do it [for you]. We must not bother the President with this. He is trying to keep the world from war." [19] Kennedy, Johnson, and Nixon all turned more and more to their White House staffs for coordination and particularly for help in resolving jurisdictional disputes between executive agencies.

The same was the case in the Carter administration. After initially giving wide latitude to his cabinet officials in the first year of his term, Carter strengthened his White House staff units, especially those involved in domestic and economic planning. Stuart Eizenstat and various executive-office officials were frequently turned to by Carter when he felt there was too much departmental squabbling. The White House aides were charged with coordination of the president's program and coordination obviously involves being involved and occasionally differing with departmental views. Said Eizenstat: "I don't consider myself an ideologue but we have a political perspective. We have tried to insure that the constituents who elected us will feel we are representing their interests." [20] In effect, he acknowledges that the White House sees things from different perspectives than even the president's own personnel in the departments.

Another Carter White House aide told me, in an exasperated mood, of an Agriculture Department political appointee who had just been caught virtually writing sugar legislation up on Capitol Hill, legislation that was in direct opposition to the President's program. "One of our own men! He said he had always done it for them in years past in his previous capacities and he was just helping them out. The same things have happened in some other departments. The problem is that there is no fear of the White House. People out there are just doing whatever they want to do." The aide then went on to say that people should be fired or somehow disciplined to put a little needed "fear of the White House" into them.

About a year later President Carter apparently arrived at the same view. After several leaks of disclosures that brought into question policy decisions he had made, he brought in a score or more top State Department officials for a dressing down. As pieced together by veteran *New Republic* reporter John Osborne, Carter's awkward confrontation with top State Department officials went like this:

Carter, tense and discernibly trying to contain himself and his anger, opened with a tribute to Secretary Vance. The President said he'd read up on all previous secretaries of state and Vance was the greatest. After saying this he said he called them in because he wanted to talk to them about a problem that he had. He said then with an intensity that burned into the memories of his hearers: YOU ARE THE CAUSE OF THE PROBLEM. The problem was that presidents always get conflicting advice; he did; they have to make choices, and people whose advice is rejected or about to be rejected might try to promote the ideas through the media. You folks (he said) are bright people, maybe some of the brightest in town. But you can't know everything. I understand that some of you go out on the cocktail circuit. I don't know anything about the cocktail circuit, but I can understand that some people might want to make themselves look more important than they are. I've been in this business long enough to know that the press doesn't just make these stories up. You're very good but I'm going to tell you that this leaking has got to stop and what I am going to do is this. If there are any leaks out of your area, wherever the area may be, I AM GOING TO FIRE YOU.[21]

Thus Carter felt the same frustrations prior presidents had encountered. And like many of them, he tried vainly to resolve them as best he could.

Conflict from Complexity

Nearly all the comments by White House aides on executive-branch conflict could be traced at least in part to the size of government and the complexity of the problem being attacked. Eisenhower aide Emmet J. Hughes suggested: "The sheer size and intricacy of government conspire to taunt and to thwart all brisk pretensions to set sensationally new directions. The vast machinery of national leadership — the tens of thousands of levers and switches and gears — simply do not respond to the impatient jab of a finger or the angry pounding of a fist." [22]

President Johnson made an effort to improve civil-rights opportunities for departmental personnel and within programs administered by the departments. Although the president made occasional references to this in cabinet meetings, he could not spend much time on the effort, so he designated an aide to carry it out. That aide soon found out that most of the cabinet members themselves lacked the time to think through a logical strategy for action; some even bluntly disagreed with the effort, denying its importance as a priority. Moreover, "many of them have great internal problems and actually have little leeway to get things done with their subordinates. You cannot assume a cabinet member is in good control over his department. Sometimes it is a matter of geography — his department is spread all over Washington and perhaps in twelve or more regions around the country." Not surprisingly, the aide soon concluded that "you have to do their work for them; that is, you have to know their internal situation and be able to come up with the alternatives." This aide appeared to be decidedly pessimistic about his job:

> You can't really be an administrator at the White House. You have to get top personnel to carry things out — and that is literally impossible to do with this venal Civil Service system. Frankly, I would abolish it and rather live with a spoils system. You need to be able to make far more appointees than you can now. Civil Service officials can play very tough politics with their senior friends in Congress, and they can resist the White House constantly. . . . Another thing is that departments are so big that it is difficult for anyone to get "the message" around even when they want to do something about it.

A certain amount of conflict and confusion arise too because the White House staff itself is confused about what should be done in a certain policy area or because White House aides are feuding among themselves about what the president really wants done. President Ford's press secretary confides in his memoir that Ford himself was partly to blame for the staff fighting that persisted throughout his presidency. "He was too much Mr. Nice Guy," writes Ron Nessen. Nessen's book is full of staff feuding, staff leaks, and staff efforts to undermine certain cabinet members. Why didn't Ford do something about all this? Nessen quotes Ford as admitting that "I'm probably too easygoing on people that work for me. . . . I tend to overlook. . . . I don't get angry and stomp my feet and swear at people. Some people take that to mean that I'm too easygoing. . . ." [23]

From the cabinet member's point of view, things are even worse. The cabinet officer usually comes into an on-going enterprise with a cast of thousands — thousands of strangers who may or may not share the views of the new administration. Treasury Secretary W. Michael Blumenthal, a Carter cabinet member, put it this way:

> Out of 120,000 people in the Treasury, I was able to select twenty-five, maybe. The other 119,975 are outside my control. And not only are they outside my control in terms of hiring and firing — they're also virtually outside my control in terms of transferring.
>
> So it's hard to talk about running something. If you wish to make substantive changes, policy changes, and the department employees don't like what you're doing, they have ways of frustrating you, or stopping you, that do not exist in private industry. The main method they have is the Congress. If I say I want to shut down a particular unit or transfer the function of one area to another, there are ways of going to the Congress, and in fact using friends in the Congress to block the move. [24]

Conflict between the White House staff and the departments may arise from substantive or ideological differences, sometimes reflecting political party positions, but more often they arise from differences about the role of the federal government in solving local or international problems. A typical controversial goal is that of pushing the government to new levels of commitment and compassion, an aim enunciated during heated campaigns or in major policy addresses. Prime ingredients for confused communication with a large bureaucracy include the failure of the White House to choose among intense and competing values, the naive effort to make every problem the first order of attention, and the inability to distinguish between what the federal government can and cannot do. The continual need to reset priorities and rethink program objectives is separated from organizational and implementation decisions only at substantial cost.

THE SWELLING OF THE PRESIDENCY

The number of employees working directly under the president has been growing steadily since New Deal days when only a few dozen people served in the White House entourage. President Carter sought, with some success, to cut the size of the White House staff, but he most assuredly did not much reduce the importance of the White House and executive office staffs.

The most disturbing aspect of the expansion of the presidential establishment, as it is often called, is that it has often become a powerful inner sanctum of government, isolated from traditional, constitutional checks and balances. Under some presidents it was common practice for anonymous, unelected, and unratified aides to negotiate sensitive international commitments by means of executive agreements that are free from congressional oversight. Other aides in the presidential orbit were able to wield fiscal authority over billions of dollars that Congress had appropriated but a president had refused to spend, or that Congress had assigned for one purpose and the administration had redirected to another — all with no semblance of public scrutiny. Such exercises of power pose an important question of governmental philosophy: Should a political system that has made a virtue of periodic electoral accountability accord an ever-increasing policymaking role to White House counselors who are neither confirmed by the U.S. Senate nor, because of the doctrine of executive privilege, subject to questioning by Congress?

As the presidential establishment has taken over policymaking and even some operational functions from the cabinet departments, the departments have been undercut continuously and the cost has been heavy. These intrusions can cripple the capacity of cabinet officials to present policy alternatives, and they diminish self-confidence, morale, and initiative within the departments. George Ball, a former undersecretary of state, noted the effects on the State Department: "Able men, with proper pride in their professional skills, will not long tolerate such votes of no-confidence, so it should be no surprise that they are leaving the career service, and making way for mediocrity with the result that, as time goes on, it may be hopelessly difficult to restore the Department. . . ." [25]

The irony of this accretion of numbers and functions to the presidential establishment is that the presidency found itself increasingly afflicted with the very ills of the traditional departments that the expansions were often intended to remedy. The presidency has become a large, complex bureaucracy itself, rapidly acquiring the many dubious characteristics of large bureaucracies in the process: layering, overspecialization, communication gaps, interoffice rivalries, inadequate coordination, and an impulse to become consumed with short-term, urgent operational concerns at the expense of thinking systematically about the consequences of varying sets of policies and priorities and about important long-range problems.

Another toll of the burgeoning presidential establishment is that White House aides, in assuming more and more responsibility for the management of government programs, inevitably lose the detachment and objectivity that is so essential for evaluating new ideas. Can a lieutenant vigorously engaged in implementing the presidential will admit the possibility that what the president wants is wrong or not working? Yet a president is increasingly dependent on the judgment of these same staff members, because he seldom sees many of his cabinet members.

Why has the presidency grown bigger and bigger? There is no single villain or systematically organized conspiracy promoting this expansion. Among the variety of factors at work the most significant is the expansion of the role of the presidency itself — an expansion that for the most part has taken place during national emergencies. The reason for this is that the public and Congress in recent decades have both tended to look to the president for the decisive responses that were needed in those emergencies. The Great Depression and World War II in particular brought sizable increases in presidential staffs. Once in place, many stayed on, even after the emergencies that brought them had faded. Smaller national crises have occasioned expansion in the White House entourage, too. After the Russians successfully orbited Sputnik in 1957, President Eisenhower added several science advisers. After the Bay of Pigs, President Kennedy enlarged his national-security staff. After the oil and inflation problems of the 1970s went to the top of the national agenda Presidents Nixon, Ford, and Carter enlarged staffs in these areas.

Considerable growth in the presidential establishment, especially in the post–World War II years, stems directly from the belief that critical societal problems require that wise men be assigned to the White House to alert the president to appropriate solutions and to serve as the agents for implementing these solutions. Congress has frequently acted on the basis of this belief, legislating the creation of the National Security Council, the Council of Economic Advisers, and the Council on Environmental Quality, among others. Congress has also increased the chores of the presidency by making it a statutory responsibility for the president to prepare more and more reports associated with what are regarded as critical social areas — annual economic and manpower reports, a biennial report on national growth, and so on.

Another reason for the growth of the presidential establishment is that occupants of the White House frequently distrust members of the permanent government. Nixon aides, for example, have viewed most civil servants not only as Democratic but as wholly unsympathetic to such objectives of the Nixon administration as decentralization, revenue sharing, and the curtailment of several Great Society programs. Departmental bureaucracies are often viewed from the White House as independent, unresponsive, unfamiliar, and inaccessible. They are suspected again and again of placing their own, congressional, or special-interest priorities ahead of those communicated to them from the White House.

Still another reason that more and more portfolios have been given to the presidency is that new federal programs frequently concern more than one federal agency, and it seems reasonable that someone at a higher level is required to fashion a consistent policy and to reconcile conflicts. Attempts by cabinet members themselves to solve sensitive jurisdictional questions frequently result in bitter squabbling. At times, too, cabinet members themselves have recommended that these multidepartmental issues be settled at the White House.

The presidential establishment has also been enlarged by the representation of interest groups within its fold. Even a partial listing of staff specializations that have been grafted onto the White House in recent years reveals how interest-group brokerage has become added to the more traditional staff activities of counseling and administration. These specializations form a veritable index of American society: budget and management, national security, economics, congressional matters, science and technology, drug-abuse prevention, telecommunications, consumers, national goals, intergovernmental relations, environment, domestic policy, international economics, military affairs, civil rights, disarmament, labor relations, District of Columbia, cultural affairs, education, foreign trade and tariffs, the aged, health and nutrition, physical fitness, volunteerism, intellectuals, blacks, youth, women, Wall Street, governors, mayors, "ethnics," regulatory agencies and related industry, state party chairmen, Mexican-Americans.

Both Presidents Ford and Carter, in their efforts to "keep the doors of the White House open," maintained a fairly large staff called the Public Liaison Office. William Baroody, Jr., ran Ford's office. Margaret

"Midge" Costanza was for a two-year period Carter's top aide for this operation. She reported that she and her staff met constantly with ethnic groups and special-interest organizations — with everyone from poet Allen Ginsberg, who wanted to discuss his philosophy on food, to groups who wanted to discuss opposition to the B-1 bomber. Critics contend that this kind of White House activity is unnecessary, too much of an on-going campaign unit or merely a staff that engages in "stroking" people or groups who want to say they have taken their cause to the White House. White House aides, of course, claim that these staffs, which ensure access to the White House for nearly every interest, are a requirement of an open and effective coalition-building presidency.

One of the more fascinating elements in the growth of the presidential establishment is the development, particularly during the past few administrations, of a huge public-relations apparatus. More than one hundred presidential aides are now engaged in various forms of press-agentry or public relations, busily selling and reselling the president. Although this activity — sometimes cynically called the politics of symbolism — is devoted to the particular occupant of the White House, it inevitably affects the presidency itself by expanding public expectations about the job to be done.

Last, but by no means least, Congress itself, which has grown increasingly critical of the burgeoning power of the presidency, must take some blame for the expansion of the White House. Divided within itself and often ill equipped or simply disinclined to make some of the nation's toughest political decisions in recent decades, Congress has abdicated significant authority to the presidency. In late 1972 Congress almost passed a grant of authority to the president that would have given him the right to determine which programs to cut whenever the budget went beyond a $250 billion ceiling limit — a bill that, in effect, would have handed over to the president some of Congress's long-cherished "power of the purse." Fortunately, Congress could not agree on how to yield this precious power to the executive.

The important point here is that as the White House grew, communications became more difficult with many of the departments. Moreover, White House aides were constantly drumming up new business for themselves, business that often belonged in the departments or perhaps in some instances belonged nowhere at all. President after president in recent years has come to the White House pledging to keep the White House staff from growing too big or too powerful. In many respects the problem is not so much the size of the White House staff as it is the purposes to which they are put. Are they really helping the president and helping to strengthen the positions of the cabinet members and other governmental officials who must carry out the business of the government? Are they going into business for themselves and playing president? Are they aware of

their own biases and do they understand the incentive systems that motivate those working in the executive departments? These are some of the
important questions that presidents and top White House aides constantly
need to monitor.

One of President Ford's top White House staffers, later Secretary
of Defense Donald Rumsfeld once tried to spell out some do's and don'ts
for White House aides. Although they may strike the reader as mere
common sense or even trivial, they nevertheless remain a challenge to
most White House aides. A few of them are:

Promptly learn how to say "I don't know." If used when appropriate, it
will be used often.

Keep your sense of humor. Don't forget General Stilwell's motto, "the
higher a monkey climbs, the more you see of his behind."

It is easier to get into something than it is to get out of it.

Don't play president; you're not. The Constitution provides for only one.

Don't begin to believe you are indispensable or infallible.

Never say "the White House wants" — buildings don't want.

Make sure that the president, cabinet, and top staffers are constantly aware
of all important problems. If they are out of the flow of information,
decisions will either be poorly made or not made — each is dangerous.

You will need the support of each member of the House and Senate, regardless of philosophy or party, on some issue at some time.

Members of Congress are not there by accident. Each managed to get there
for a reason. Discover it, and you have learned something valuable about
our country.

Don't become (or let the President or White House personnel) become
obsessed or paranoid about the press, the Congress, the other party,
opponents, or leaks.

Don't blindly obey directions from the president with which you disagree
or where you feel he hasn't weighed all sides without first contesting
it with him.

Work to reduce the size of the White House staff and of the executive
office of the President from your first day to your last. All the pressures
are to the contrary. Fight them, and the president and the country will
be better served.[26]

Pithy and corny, but not a bad list for any White House.

REALITIES AND IMPERATIVES

White House aides often become arrogant and insensitive because they are
asked to do too much in too short a time. They breathe down the necks of
cabinet and department leaders because presidents become impatient for

answers and results. Departments appear inert or unresponsive because they have difficulty in pulling together diverse specialists to work on complex questions. Cabinet members give the impression of being weak (and sometimes are) because they must preside over huge holding companies of diverse, functionally specialized enterprises. Departmentalism — the constant clamor by departmental spokesmen for more money, more presidential support, or more autonomy from other agencies or priorities — thrusts itself ceaselessly on a president. White House aides are disappointed by the lack of coordination both within and among departments. Communications problems exist because many people are involved in administering programs throughout the country and are working within an environment of constantly shifting priorities and circumstances. Legislative or executive intent, or the General Accounting Office and Office of Personnel Management rules and regulations, even if they could be memorized, do not provide sufficient guidance to the relationship of one complex problem to another.

Listening to White House aides' views of these conflicts heightens appreciation for the responsibilities of the chief executive. The president has to act, even in the face of uncertainties, complexity, opposition, and division among his own advisers. Eventually, the consequences of inaction may outweigh the results of even an ill-designed initiative. As the general public expects more and more of presidents, and as the responsibilities become greater, the institution finds itself in the midst of a disillusioning squeeze.

It is tempting for a president to rely on a small brigade of handpicked and personally loyal White House aides. Often, however, he will find that such a strategy will only exacerbate his situation. As Irving Janis and others have suggested, a consensus mind-set easily takes hold, an artificial sense of conviviality and team-player mentality can set in that encourages a view that can falsify reports, denigrate alternatives that deserve consideration, and in general keep unfavorable information from reaching a president.[27] Every president sooner or later will find himself surrounded by unremitting problems of complexity, diversity, jurisdictional disputes, and bureaucratic recalcitrance. But the essence of presidential leadership is, in one sense, the capacity to deal with complexity and to manage conflict. The president must be able to ask the right questions, preside over compromises, and engage in the art of making the difficult possible.

That the constraints on directing an effective application of presidentially interpreted policies to problems are enormous does not mean that the presidency should be removed or elevated from bureaucratic or societal conflicts. Resolving conflicts is a strategic occasion for exercising leadership. Information and evaluation are the prime needs. An open presidency capable of listening as well as giving orders is imperative. An open presidency that holds a proper regard for the positive aspects of conflict is needed as well.

Conflict and competition do not inevitably indicate weakness in an administration. Adversary relationships may provide a salutary jolt toward the adapting and renewal of systems. Lewis Coser's suggestions are relevant: "Conflict prevents the ossification of social systems by exerting pressures for innovation and creativity; it prevents habitual accommodations from freezing into rigid molds and hence progressively impoverishing the ability to react creatively to novel circumstances."[28] Several former members of recent administrations have made the case that certain policies and practices with which they were involved suffered not from too much conflict but from too little.[29] Certainly the history of the illegal plans and activities of the Watergate conspiracies of 1971–74 illustrate a series of episodes that might have been halted or avoided had more adversary deliberations taken place.

Conflict and heated argument do not necessarily upset every president, although most presidents generally grow to dislike it. John F. Kennedy, for example, once made the point to two aides in the midst of a heated debate that "the last thing I want around here is a mutual admiration society. . . . When you people stop arguing, I'll start worrying."[30] Yet, Kennedy himself was criticized by a shrewd if caustic British observer, Henry Fairlie, who cautioned appropriately that

> . . . to the end of his days of power, the politician must believe that he has defective eyesight. He must seek the help, witting and unwitting, not only of a thousand pairs of eyes, but of eyes which see in a thousand different ways, eyes that flash at him, eyes that are suspicious, eyes that seem to sleep, eyes that are open, eyes that tell him nothing and, in doing so, tell him all which he needs to know. John Kennedy had the same object as Franklin Roosevelt, the accumulation of power to the Presidency; he had genuine political ability, as did many of those around him; but he and they saw, with few exceptions, with a single pair of eyes; that was how he wished it.[31]

Breathing and thinking space must be guaranteed by careful staffing, delegation, and use of presidential time; not by isolation, arrogance, or palace guards permitted to become egregiously antagonistic toward the permanent government and cabinet. Both sides — presidential staff and the bureaucracy — are needed to perform the functions of the executive branch; each wants certain types of help from the other; each usually seeks to avoid overt antagonism toward the other. Although White House staff members can be the creative connective tissue linking a president with the complex network of administration officials, bringing in the necessary information and sending out word of presidential intentions, it is clear that operational and managerial activities should be delegated beyond his immediate entourage.

Presidents and most of their staff usually are aware that cooperation from the permanent federal departments must be earned rather than taken for granted. Loyalty and support, as well as crucially needed expertise, usually are eagerly sought from the departments; for a basic premise in White House-departmental relations is that department officials, especially civil servants, play — or can play — an all-important role in implementing (or subverting) presidential goals. But how to arrange proper administrative leadership remains a question. Can the cabinet be vivified and recast to do the job? Could a strengthened cabinet of counselors who are strong administrators be delegated authority to perform the managerial duties that people are constantly visiting on presidents? Can the presidency and the cabinet be strengthened at the same time?

To summarize, most presidents want an easy exchange of information. They want objective, neutral analysis as opposed to special pleading. Invariably, half the cabinet, or more, become staunch advocates of fairly fixed viewpoints and hence, in the president's eyes, they become special pleaders. It is clear that many of the cabinet posts have lost authority, usually to a more centralized and personalized White House staff. Nearly every recent president has tried to enhance the role and status of his cabinet members, frequently pledging, too, that he will hold regular cabinet meetings and use the collective wisdom of his cabinet. In practice, however, the cabinet is usually a pallid institution as will be discussed in the next chapter.

Richard Neustadt cautions that our equivalent to the British cabinet is not our formal cabinet but rather "an informal, shifting aggregation of key individuals — the influentials at both ends of Pennsylvania Avenue. Some of them may sit in what we call the cabinet as department heads; others sit in back rows there as senior White House aides; still others have no place there. Collectively these men share no responsibility nor any meeting ground. Individually, however, each is linked to all the others through the person of the president. . . ." [32] Thus, the whole notion of what a cabinet is needs rethinking. We have built up a counterpart to the British cabinet, but it is only in part drawn from our cabinet. We rely heavily, as Neustadt has demostrated, on "in-and-outers." People like Clark Clifford, David Rockefeller, McGeorge Bundy, Averell Harriman, William Scranton, and George Meany, despite their absence from the formal cabinet, are often far more influential in shaping presidential policy decisions than cabinet officers. Sometimes members of Congress or even members of the press serve a president in the role of policy counselor. These developments have occurred, or so it has seemed, at the expense of securing talented cabinet officers.

Benjamin Cohen, a wise New Dealer, once outlined the problem this way:

> In recent times it has not been unusual for cabinet members to be directed rather than consulted even in regard to policies within their own departments. There has been a growing tendency for the president

to gather about himself a small elite group of advisers and assistants, generally with little political experience or standing in their own right, personally devoted to the president, eager to help him but reluctant to press their objections to a suggested course of action once they sense that the president is favorably inclined towards it. This elite group is not subject to confirmation but is chosen because of their aptitude to work easily and on the same wave length with the president.[33]

At the same time, however, a president needs able cabinet officers and, indeed, presidents should value the diversity of their views and the fact that certain information perhaps can only come from the cabinet officer, who reflects such organized interests as agriculture, the transportation industry, health professionals, and labor. To be sure, most cabinet officers after a while become more parochial and narrow gauged than the White House view. But a president who is to offer national leadership needs to be able to listen and weld together the myriad of contending factions, both the organized and unorganized.

Plainly, the role of the contemporary cabinet needs reappraisal. How should it function? Should it be larger or smaller? Should it act under certain conditions as a collective council for policy formulation and program coordination? What should be the relationship of the cabinet to the congressional leadership? What can be done to improve White House-cabinet relations?

NOTES

1. Alexander Hamilton, *The Federalist,* No. 70 (Modern Library, 1937), p. 455.

2. McGeorge Bundy, *The Strength of Government* (Harvard University Press, 1968), p. 37. See also his entire chap. 2.

3. Arthur M. Schlesinger, Jr., *A Thousand Days* (Houghton Mifflin, 1965), p. 683.

4. Louis W. Koenig, *The Chief Executive* (Harcourt, Brace and World, 1968), p. 417.

5. David Truman, *The Governmental Process* (Knopf, 1951), pp. 407–08. See also Stephen Hess, *Organizing the Presidency* (Brookings Institution, 1976).

6. George Reedy, *The Twilight of the Presidency* (World, 1970), p. 94.

7. Attorney General Griffin B. Bell, lecture (mimeo), University of Kansas, 25 January 1979, p. 6.

8. Robert C. Wood, "When Government Works," *Public Interest,* Winter 1970, p. 45.

9. Harry C. McPherson, *A Political Education* (Atlantic–Little Brown, 1972), p. 286.

10. Quoted in Stephen J. Wayne, "Working in the White House: Psychological Dimensions of the Job" (Paper delivered at the 1977 Annual Meeting of the Southern Political Science Association, New Orleans, 3 November 1977, mimeo. p. 10).

11. Richard E. Neustadt, "Politicians and Bureaucrats," in David Truman, ed., *The Congress and America's Future* (Prentice-Hall, 1965), p. 113.

12. Henry Kissinger, quoted in *Newsweek,* 21 August 1972, p. 19. See also *The White House Years* (Little, Brown, 1979).

13. Aaron Wildavsky, "Salvation by Staff: Reform of the Presidential Office," in Aaron Wildavsky, ed., *The Presidency* (Little, Brown, 1969), p. 697.

14. Toby Moffett, *The Participation Put-On* (Delta, 1971), p. 201. Both Moffett and Moynihan are now members of Congress.

15. Moynihan (White House press release, processed), 21 December 1970.

16. J. Edward Day, *My Appointed Rounds: 929 Days as Postmaster General* (Holt, Rinehart and Winston, 1965), p. 98.

17. Quoted in Dom Bonafede, "Ehrlichman Acts as Policy Broker in Nixon's Formalized Domestic Council," *National Journal,* 12 June 1971, p. 1240.

18. Walter F. Mondale, interview, *U.S. News & World Report,* 28 March 1977, p. 64.

19. Sherman Adams, quoted in Robert J. Donovan, *Eisenhower: The Inside Story* (Harper and Bros., 1956), p. 71.

20. Quoted in "Eizenstat Is Helping to Fill a Vacuum," *New York Times,* 3 December 1978, p. 13F.

21. John Osborne, "Under Pressure," *New Republic,* 3 March 1979, p. 11.

22. Emmet J. Hughes, *The Ordeal of Power* (Dell, 1962), pp. 53–55.

23. Ron Nessen, *It Sure Looks Different from the Inside* (Playboy Press, 1978), pp. 161–62. For similar accounts of infighting in the Carter administration, see James Fallows "The Passionless Presidency," *Atlantic,* a two part series, May and June 1979. Also see Timothy B. Clark, "The Power Vacuum Outside the Oval Office," *National Journal,* 24 February 1979, pp. 296–300. See also, on the difficulty of arriving at firm presidential objectives, Richard Rose, *Managing Presidential Objectives* (Free Press, 1976).

24. W. Michael Blumenthal, former Secretary of Treasury, "Candid Reflections of a Businessman in Washington," *Fortune,* 29 January 1979, p. 39. For additional evidence on this point, see Joel D. Aberbach and Bert A. Rockman, "Clashing Beliefs Within the Executive Branch," *American Political Science Review,* June 1976, and Hugh Heclo, *A Government of Strangers* (Brookings Institution, 1977).

25. George Ball, "Is This Trip Necessary?" *New York Times Magazine,* 13 February 1972, p. 55.

26. These do's and don'ts come from a superb essay column by Alan L. Otten, "Rumsfeld's Rules," *Wall Street Journal,* 9 December 1976. editorial page.

27. Irving Janis, *Victims of Groupthink* (Houghton Mifflin, 1972). See also Alexander L. George, "The Case for Multiple Advocacy in Making Foreign Policy," *American Political Science Review,* September 1972, pp. 751–85.

28. Lewis A. Coser, "Conflict — Sociological Aspects," in David Sills, ed., *International Encyclopedia of Social Sciences* (Free Press-Macmillan, 1968), p. 235.

29. This case is made by, among others, Charles Frankel, *High on Foggy Bottom* (Harper & Row, 1968); Roger Hilsman, *To Move a Nation* (Doubleday, 1967); Daniel P. Moynihan, *Maximum Feasible Misunderstanding* (Free Press, 1969); and George Reedy, *The Twilight of the Presidency* (World, 1970).

30. John Kennedy, quoted in Pierre Salinger, *With Kennedy* (Doubleday, 1966), p. 64.

31. Henry Fairlie, *The Kennedy Promise* (Doubleday, 1973), p. 159.

32. Richard Neustadt, "White House and Whitehall," *Public Interest,* Winter 1966, pp. 65–66.

33. Benjamin Cohen, "Presidential Responsibility and American Democracy" (a Royer Lecture delivered at the University of California, Berkeley, processed 23 May 1974), pp. 7–8.

CHAPTER 8

THE PRESIDENT'S CABINET

A good cabinet ought to be a place where the large outlines of policy can be hammered out in common, where the essential strategy is decided upon, where the President knows that he will hear, both in affirmation and in doubt, even in negation, most of what can be said about the direction he proposes to follow.

— Harold J. Laski, *The American Presidency: An Interpretation* (Harper and Brothers, 1940), pp. 257–58.

Cabinet meetings in the United States, despite occasional efforts to make them into significant decision-making occasions, have, at least in this century, been characterized as vapid non-events in which there has been a deliberate non-exchange of information as part of a process of mutual nonconsultation.

— Edward Weisband and Thomas M. Frank, *Resignation in Protest* (Penguin, 1975), p. 139.

Two of Carter's biggest mistakes have been his idea of "Cabinet Government" and his drive to reduce the size and power of the White House staff. Frankly, the power of the cabinet secretaries in the first year of this administration badly hurt us.

— A Carter White House aide, personal interview with the author.

The president's cabinet is a continual battleground of strong egos, and pulls and tugs over political and policy matters. The cabinet in America is also a much misunderstood institution. This is so in part because the cabinet in many parliamentary systems has substantial power as a policy-making body. Perhaps because a cabinet room is adjacent to the Oval Office it is assumed that frequent and important cabinet sessions take place there to hammer out the major positions of an administration.

The cabinet as an institution weathered some especially tough years in the 1960s and 1970s. Most of our recent presidents have been perplexed with the question of how best to use their cabinet members and their cabinets. The way the cabinet is used and the value of the cabinet to a president obviously fluctuates according to the personality and the needs of the president and changing national conditions. After reviewing the origins of the cabinet and how cabinet members are selected, this chapter will assess how presidents and cabinet members have viewed the role of the cabinet.

The Founding Fathers discussed at length the possibility of creating some form of executive council that would be comprised of the president, heads of the departments, and the chief justice of the Supreme Court; but they decided to leave things flexible. The Constitution made no specific provision for a cabinet. It merely implies there are to be principal officers and executive departments. The first Congress passed statutes that provided for the creation of three principal departments, State, War, and Treasury, and an attorney general who would be a part-time adviser, not the head of a department.

From the outset of our new government President George Washington regarded the principal officers as assistants and advisers. "He began the practice of assembling his principal officers in council. And this practice became in the course of time a settled custom. The simple truth is that the cabinet is a customary, not a statutory body." [1] The term *cabinet* was probably first used in 1793, but mention of it in statutory language did not occur until 1907. Presidents over the course of our almost two-hundred-year history have used the cabinet in greatly differing ways. Thus President Andrew Jackson did not even convene his cabinet in joint session during his first two years in office, whereas President James Polk held at least 350 cabinet sessions during his four years. Lyndon Johnson told his cabinet secretary that the thing that bothered him most about cabinet meetings was they were so dull; he said, "I just don't want them falling asleep at the damned [cabinet] table." [2] On the other hand, Carter held more than sixty cabinet meetings during his first two years in office, no doubt hoping frequent cabinet meetings might help him overcome his lack of previous Washington experience. He also hoped strengthened and more visible cabinet members might help reduce the charges of an "imperial presidency" and "palace guard government." Plainly, the cabinet exists by custom, and if a president desires to dispense with it, he does so.

PRESIDENTIAL CABINET MAKING

Presidents are often thought to have a completely free hand in choosing their cabinet members but this is seldom so. In addition to administrative competence and experience, loyalty and congeniality are basic considerations as a president goes about selecting his cabinet. But several other factors are at work as well. Party rivals often have to be disarmed and placated either with appointments to the cabinet or selection as the vice-presidential running mate. The selection of Lyndon Johnson by John Kennedy and the nomination of Nelson Rockefeller by Gerald Ford are illustrative. Regional, ethnic, and geographical considerations are almost always important. Nowadays, for example, it is a custom to have at least one woman, one black, one westerner, and one southerner in the cabinet. It is politically prudent to have at least one former governor, a former member of Congress, a Jew, an Italian, a prominent businessman or banker, and either a labor leader or someone especially approved by the leaders of major labor unions. After capturing the presidency, a president usually goes about selecting his cabinet in such a way as to try to win the confidence of major sections and sectors of the nation. "I knew," writes Richard Nixon, "that some of my choices for Cabinet posts would have to serve, even if only symbolically, to unite the country and 'bring us together.' " [3]

President Carter and his top campaign aides said he was going to appoint a crop of fresh faces from a new generation, not from the generation that had already served in high posts for previous administrations. As it turned out, however, most of Carter's cabinet recruits were either veterans of the Johnson and Kennedy administrations or prominent businessmen and lawyers who served on the IBM board of directors and were associates of David Rockefeller's elite Trilateral Commission (a group of business, academic, and political leaders trying to establish better ties with Japan and Western democracies).[4]

Carter was no doubt quite earnest when he said he wanted to bring in fresh faces to help him govern the nation. But his attitude on this matter runs counter to a theory held by those who feel that to be effective in Washington you should have had extensive earlier experience learning the ropes there. Clark Clifford puts the case this way:

> I have another theory, and that is the first time a man serves in government, he's only reasonably effective, the second time he serves in government, he's infinitely more effective, and maybe the third time, then he's that rare fellow who makes a unique and outstanding contribution.

> There's an enormous advantage in having experience with our government. You begin to understand how wheels mesh, you know where the centers of power are, you know how to get things accomplished. Some of the most unfortunate results we've had in government have been the result of individuals who have held top positions in the business community with no previous acquaintanceship with government. And when they come in, they're given a Cabinet position, and it could be a calamity.[5]

In theory, a president can nominate anyone for a cabinet post. In practice, the constraints are many. President Carter, for example, may have had as many as ten individuals decline to have their names considered for cabinet positions at the outset of his administration. First, each of the cabinet members has to be confirmed by a majority of the members in the U.S. Senate. This automatically precludes some persons who will not submit to this process. Governor Stanley Hathaway of Wyoming, selected as secretary of the interior by Ford, suffered a nervous breakdown soon after a grueling confirmation process in the summer of 1975. Some are unwilling to give up their much higher salaries and fringe benefits. Some are unwilling to join the cabinet because it would mean having to give up a seat in the U.S. Senate or it would hinder their own chances of running for a national leadership position. Still others sometimes pose conditions under which they would accept nomination — conditions that sometimes are not acceptable to the president.[6] Others may be put off by the conflict-of-interest regulations that recent presidents have imposed on all top appointees. Carter, for example, asked his top officials to make a full public disclosure of their financial net worth and to pledge not to return to Washington for at least one year after leaving the government to lobby for pay before the agency or department in which they would serve. He also asked that officials divest themselves of financial holdings that were likely to be affected by their official acts or that would be broadly affected by government monetary and budgetary policy.

A president has to select certain cabinet officers because of the needed expertise they will bring to the administration and the policy needs of certain departments. Typically, for example, the secretary of defense is someone who has worked closely with that department in some previous capacity. The labor secretary will usually be someone like Arthur Goldberg, John Dunlop, or Ray Marshall, who has had extensive negotiating background as well as advisory ties to the AFL-CIO leadership. A treasury secretary is traditionally viewed as the financial community's representative in the cabinet. In selecting a treasury secretary a president-elect usually wants someone who can simultaneously serve as a "spokesman" to the financial world as well as a "spokesman" for these interests.

Generalists are often appointed to head up some of the domestic departments such as Commerce, Transportation, and HUD. Politicians especially close to clientele groups are often appointed head of Agriculture and Interior. These patterns vary somewhat from one president to the next, but similar constraints and considerations shape cabinet making over time. Political scientist Nelson Polsby examined the Nixon and Carter cabinet selections and found a trend away from selecting experts or clientele-oriented cabinet secretaries and a trend toward selecting generalists who might work more cooperatively with the White House. In looking at the Nixon cabinet experience, Polsby writes:

> After beginning with a politically diverse and reasonably visible group of cabinet appointees, Nixon increasingly appointed people of no independent public standing, and with no constituencies of their own. In this shift we can read a distinctive change in the fundamental political goals and strategies of the Nixon administration, once Mr. Nixon's re-election was assured, with centralizing power in the White House.[7]

For a different set of reasons Carter appointed cabinet members who were also less likely to carry messages from interest groups or traditional party constituencies to the White House. His second round of cabinet appointees continued this pattern. Polsby reasons that this advantages the White House over the bureaucracy in the short run, but in the longer run the bureaucrats acting independently of their own cabinet secretaries may seek to form their own alliances with clientele groups and congressional committees.

THE JOB OF THE CABINET MEMBER

Defining the job of the cabinet member depends on one's vantage point. Members of Congress believe a cabinet officer should communicate often and well with Congress, and be responsive to legislators' requests. Reporters want a cabinet officer to be accessible, to make news; they applaud style and flair as well as substance. Interest groups want a cabinet member who can speak out for their interests and carry their messages to the White House. Civil servants in a department are generally looking for a cabinet leader who will boost departmental morale and appropriations. White House aides are as keenly concerned about a cabinet officer's loyalty to the president as they are about ability. A president wants a cabinet member who will conserve his freedom of action and enhance his administration's reputation without overshadowing him.

What is a good cabinet officer? In 1978 a Carter White House aide summarized how he and White House co-workers viewed the cabinet job:

> First, he should be clearly in charge of the department. Everyone in the department should know that he is in charge and know what he and the

department are doing. Second, he should be very sensitive to the department's interest groups and have access to them and fully understand their views. But, third, he should also at the same time be able to distinguish the president's interests and political needs from the department's clientele interests. He should be able to say that this is what they want but it is or is not compatible with your interests. Fourth, the effective cabinet officer is one who can work on most of his congressional relations problems without running to the president for help. Finally, he should be able to follow-through on presidential policies, that is, to see that they don't get watered down, or lost in the shuffle.

Presidents and their aides repeatedly say the last thing they want to see is a cabinet member who has become a special pleader at the White House for some of the special-interest groups that are strong in their departments. As a former White House aide wrote, "The Cabinet officer must certainly be attentive to his departmental business, and he should seek to ensure that the President has timely notice of the impact of other policies on his department's specific interests. . . . But a Secretary should never choose his departmental interest as against the wider interest of the Presidency." [8]

The greatest test of cabinet members arises from the fact they are tied as closely to Congress as they are to a president. In the perpetual tug of war between these two branches, the cabinet officer is often like the knot in the rope. Bradley Patterson, a longtime civil servant and a staff aide in the Eisenhower White House, sums up this strain on a cabinet member's loyalties:

A Cabinet officer is tied to the President: appointed by him, usually after some personal search, and as an expression of the President's highest confidence. The Secretary serves at the President's pleasure, is removable by the President at any time. Even when an incumbent President is re-elected, the Cabinet submit their resignations at the beginning of the new Presidential term. A Cabinet officer is part of the Executive Branch; Article II makes clear that the power a Cabinet officer exercises (whether by statute or delegation) is the President's power. A Cabinet officer meets with the President frequently, counsels him on any matter he asks, sends the President and his staff a stream of information and recommendations, receives and acts on Presidential instructions and decisions. A Cabinet member's budget is part of the President's budget, his or her legislative proposals are shaped to conform to the President's program, the noncareer personnel appointments in his or her Department are themselves either Presidential nominations or are cleared with the White House.

But every Cabinet officer is also tied to the Congress. His or her appointment is subject to Senate confirmation. Every power a Cabinet officer exercises is derived from some Act of Congress; every penny he or she expends must be appropriated by the Congress; every new statutory change the Cabinet officer desires must be submitted to the Congress and defended there. A Cabinet officer's every act is subject to oversight by one or more regular or special Congressional committees, much of his or her time is accordingly spent at the Capitol and with few exceptions, most of the documents in his or her whole Department are subject to being produced at Congressional request.[9]

Presidents, and supporters of the presidency, feel cabinet members all serve as servants of the president who do not make decisions independent of the president. On the contrary, when a president makes a decision the cabinet officer is expected to carry it out faithfully. But that is almost a textbook view of how it is *supposed* to happen. In fact, it is inevitable that after a person has been in the cabinet for a period of time and has become enmeshed in the activities and interests of a department, he or she develops certain independent policy views. After a cabinet officer has been in a department for a year a certain hardening of views sets in as the cabinet secretary gets pushed by subordinates, interest-group leaders, or others in a direction that makes it likely he or she will come into conflict with the president. When this happens, the White House typically complains that the cabinet member has "gone native," meaning that he or she has been captured by the interests native to that department. Very often, this means the cabinet officer wants to extract more money out of the president's budget for his department. This is why an old-time budget director once complained that "cabinet members are vice presidents in charge of spending, and as such they are the natural enemies of the presidents." [10] This is why Richard Nixon once bellyached about an independent cabinet member that "rather than running the bureaucracy, the bureaucracy runs him." [11]

"Marrying the natives" is usually a gross oversimplification of what actually happens. A useful instance of the complexity involved is illustrated by President Ford's well-regarded secretary of labor. In late 1975 John Dunlop had talked Ford into backing a longtime union proposal to legalize broader construction-union picketing rights. In return, union leaders pledged support for another bill that Dunlop had drafted, which would set up a construction-bargaining monitoring agency. But as Congress took action on the legislation, President Ford found himself decidedly vulnerable to attacks from his own party's vocal right wing, especially from Ronald Reagan supporters. Also, the construction industries, with whom Dunlop had thought he had a deal to give their backing to the legislation, backed down. Meanwhile Ford's support wavered. Ford's political advisers persuaded him to break his promise and veto the measure. One White House aide rationalized later that "Dunlop got way out ahead of Ford. He sold Ford on a deal without the extensive debates and evaluations of other considerations that should have taken place on a measure like this. Dunlop really let the President down — he thought he had a deal, but in the end contractors weren't on board." Even as he vetoed it in January 1976, Ford acknowledged that he had promised Dunlop he would sign it. Moreover, he publicly urged Dunlop to stay on in the cabinet. But Dunlop felt sufficiently compromised and labor's anger at the Ford administration became so intense that Dunlop, of his own doing, resigned. Dunlop, it can be argued, was no more to blame than Ford. He had been caught between labor and the politically vulnerable White House. In a very real sense, Ford's political fortunes had changed from the time he had pledged his support to the time he felt he had to veto the legislation. In the end, he lost a cabinet member and he also motivated labor leadership to go all out in support of his Democratic rival in the 1976 elections (in 1972, labor leadership had not supported the Democrat).

THE WHITE HOUSE WANTS LOYALTY
ALONG WITH COMPETENCE

In reflecting upon his old cabinet, former President Lyndon Johnson once blurted out that "I'll always love Dean Rusk, bless his heart. He stayed with me when nobody else did." [12] Though they might not always admit it, those at the White House judge cabinet officers by a formula that weighs ability as primary but ranks loyalty to the president and to the president's political future as a very close second. For some White House aides loyalty to the boss even outweighs competence. Definitions of loyalty not surprisingly vary depending on where you sit. Outsiders often complain that loyalty in the top reaches of the executive branch can too easily lead to mindless servility and a cabinet of "yes-men." Friends and supporters of a president insist a president needs and is entitled to loyalty from cabinet members and staff. A president's own authority, his very capacity for leadership, and his being taken seriously can be jeopardized by disloyalty and independence of cabinet members. Some presidencies, John Adams' for one, were undermined by cabinet disruptions. Jealousies, political ambitions, rivalries, turf fights, and tactical differences can tear an administration apart and can leave considerable doubt in the public's mind as to who is really in charge. Persons with the president's point of view in mind often say that loyalty can just as easily be undervalued as overvalued, adding that true loyalty should include the willingness to argue vigorously and speak one's mind — at least within reasonable bounds. Taking both ability and loyalty into account, we can construct a simple fourfold matrix with some examples that illustrate how some recent cabinet members have been viewed by the White House (Fig. 8.1). Keep in mind that these rankings are *relative* rankings. Most of these cabinet officers were viewed as reasonably able and loyal. Yet interviews with White House aides and an examination of presidential memoirs and administration oral histories indicate some were viewed as abler than others, some more loyal and some

FIGURE 8.1
ILLUSTRATIVE WHITE HOUSE ASSESSMENTS
OF CABINET OFFICERS

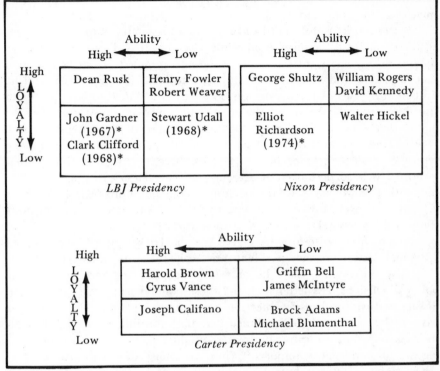

	Ability			Ability	
	High ⟷ Low			High ⟷ Low	
High					
↑	Dean Rusk	Henry Fowler Robert Weaver	George Shultz	William Rogers David Kennedy	
L O Y A L T Y	John Gardner (1967)* Clark Clifford (1968)*	Stewart Udall (1968)*	Elliot Richardson (1974)*	Walter Hickel	
↓ **Low**					
	LBJ Presidency		*Nixon Presidency*		

	Ability	
	High ⟷ Low	
High		
↑	Harold Brown Cyrus Vance	Griffin Bell James McIntyre
L O Y A L T Y	Joseph Califano	Brock Adams Michael Blumenthal
↓ **Low**	*Carter Presidency*	

* Note that these Low Loyalty rankings were sometimes temporary and that the years are indicated. (Earlier these cabinet offices often were ranked in the *High* category.)

less loyal. Still, even as impressionistic rankings, these can suggest the two-fold standard used by most White House aides, and no doubt by presidents as well, as they pass judgment on cabinet-member performance.

Firing cabinet members is the last thing presidents like to do. They do it, of course, but usually only after it is long "overdue." And they do it at the risk of considerable political backlash. President Andrew Johnson's removal of Secretary of War Stanton led to Johnson's impeachment. President Nixon's removal of special prosecutor Archibald Cox and the related resignations of Attorney General Elliot Richardson and Deputy Attorney General William Ruckelshaus badly damaged what remained of Nixon's credibility. To fire a cabinet member is to acknowledge you made a poor administrative decision in the first place. It is to acknowledge that you were unable to create a balanced atmosphere in your cabinet of forthright disagreement and constructive congeniality. Sometimes the fired cabinet officer becomes a media celebrity, or joins the political opposition on either partisan or substantive issues, or both. Sometimes the fired cabinet member has inside information that would be politically damaging if revealed, or is sufficiently hurt by the removal to write a critical book about the inadequacies of the administration.

For example, Gerald Ford did not enjoy his relationship with Defense Secretary James Schlesinger even while vice-president. Ford considered removing Schlesinger right away after he became president. Later he regretted that he hadn't and he eventually did have to fire Schlesinger. Why did he wait so long? Part of the reason was because Ford wanted to have a smooth transition from the trauma of Watergate to his own administration. Legend has it that Ford finally fired Schlesinger because of the toplofty Schlesinger's condescending rather than deferential manner. According to one report, Schlesinger seldom deigned to look directly at Ford during cabinet meetings. Instead he looked at Secretary of State Henry Kissinger, as if to imply that his remarks would be lost on the bumbling Mr. Ford. This version may overstate the case, but the former president's own memoirs confirm the chilly relations between these two.

Nixon fired Interior Secretary Walter Hickel after a celebrated "personal letter" to the president was leaked to the press. Hickel was especially frustrated because he only saw the president once or twice for policy discussions. His letter included those pointed sentences: "Permit me to suggest that you consider meeting, on an individual and conversational basis, with members of your Cabinet. Perhaps," continued Hickel, "through such conversations we can gain greater insight into the problems confronting us all, and most important, into solutions of these problems." [13] Hickel soon left the cabinet. They say he left in the same manner he came — fired with enthusiasm.

Late in his presidency, President Johnson became particularly upset at several of his domestic cabinet members. Oral interview tapes at the Lyndon B. Johnson presidential library in Austin, Texas, indicate that several cabinet members were in his dog house for crossing him on some program or another, or for failure to support the Vietnam war effort enough. More often than not, his chief domestic aide, Joseph Califano (who later, as Secretary of HEW, would be fired by Jimmy Carter for lack of cabinet member loyalty) was ordered to win compliance and greater cooperation from the particular cabinet member in question. Illustrative of Johnson's disappointment with some of his cabinet is his sharp denunciation of his former Attorney General, Ramsey Clark: "You know ol' Harry Truman said his biggest mistake was appointing Tom Clark to the Supreme Court. Well, my biggest mistake was appointing Tom's son, Ramsey, as my Attorney General. He couldn't make up his mind about a fish fry." Johnson continued. "Ramsey wanted to go around preachin' bleeding-heart stuff, but he never did a damn thing. I heard Dick Nixon made a campaign speech against Ramsey Clark one night and I had to sit on my hands so I wouldn't cheer it." [14]

From the perspective of the White House, these are the questions asked about a cabinet member. Has he managed the department well? Has he recruited talenated officials to the department? Has he been loyal to the President? Has he "handled" the interest groups associated with that department? Has he brought prestige to the department and to the administration? Does his presence in the administration boost confidence in it? Does he help politically as the next election nears? Has he handled his relationships with Congress and the press effectively? Has he come up with bright new ideas? Has he been able to implement the administration's programs in his department? Note too that a cabinet level official sometimes can be both loyal and competent, and still be viewed as a political liability. Former President Ford, for example, acknowledged in his memoir that Rockefeller was absolutely loyal and did whatever was asked of him. But Ford's aides convinced him that Rockefeller's perceived liberalism as well as his age made Rockefeller a burden rather than an asset as the 1976 primaries approached.

THE ROLE OF THE CABINET

In practice, the cabinet is used as a forum for information exchange, as an occasion for a president to boost morale and highlight his priorities, to review major issues that cut across all departments, to go over how members can help push for congressional approval of the president's program, and to discuss ways to improve implementation of major programs. It is, of course, also used as a feedback device through which presidents can obtain political and professional advice on how things are (or are not) working.

The idealization of the mythical American cabinet that never was is in part encouraged by presidents themselves. Kennedy, Nixon, and Carter all emphasized the importance of their cabinets when they picked their original teams. This is part of the postelection euphoria and one of the first manifestations of the presidential honeymoon. Harry Truman said that "the cabinet is not merely a collection of executives administering different governmental functions. It is a body whose combined judgment the president uses to formulate the fundamental policies of the administration." But one of Truman's biographers argues that "while President Truman claimed that he used his cabinet to formulate decisions, in practice, many important decisions were made by ad hoc groups containing cabinet officers and others. He did not wish to create a cabinet secretariat and to formalize the meetings." [15]

A consistent pattern seems to characterize White House-cabinet relations over time. Just as a president enjoys a distinctive honeymoon with the press and partisan critics, so also White House-cabinet ties are usually the most cordial and cooperative during the first year of an adminstration. The newly staffed executive branch, busily recasting the federal policy agenda, seems to bubble over with new possibilities, daring ideas, and imminent breakthroughs. White House ceremonies feature the installation and self-congratulatory ritual of welcoming the recently anointed cabinet chieftains. Ironically, the White House staff, which soon will outstrip most of the cabinet in power and influence, receives less publicity at this time. In the immediate postinaugural months, the Washington political community, and the executive branch in particular, becomes a merry-go-round of cheerful open doors for the new team of cabinet leaders. One Kennedy cabinet member, recalling those early days, noted that Kennedy told his cabinet that frequent cabinet meetings would be held and that individual cabinet officers should telephone him or Vice President Lyndon Johnson about anything of importance; when in doubt, they should "err on the side of referring too much" on policy matters.[16] Even silly or trivial proposals by cabinet members are entertained at this time by a deferential White House staff and a happily elected president.

Domestic crises and critical international developments, however, soon begin to monopolize the presidential schedule. As the president has less time for personal contacts, cabinet members become disinclined to exhaust their personal political credit with him. The president's program becomes fixed as priorities are set, and budget ceilings produce some new rules of the game. Ambitious, expansionist cabinet officers become painfully familiar with various refrains from executive office staff, usually to the effect that there just isn't any more money available for programs of that magnitude; or that budget projections for the next two or three years just can't absorb that type of increment; and, perhaps harshest of all, that a proposal is excellent but will just have to wait until the next term.

A high policy aide during Nixon's first term nicely captured the complex entanglements of time, presidential priorities, and interactions of people in the following passage:

> Everything depends on what you do in program formulation during the first six or seven months. I have watched three presidencies and I am increasingly convinced of that. Time goes by so fast. During the first six months or so, the White House staff is not hated by the cabinet, there is a period of friendship and cooperation and excitement. There is some animal energy going for you in those first six to eight months, especially if people perceive things in the same light. If that exists and so long as that exists you can get a lot done. You only have a year at the most for new initiatives, a time when you can establish some programs as your own, in contrast to what has gone on before. After that, after priorities are set, and after a president finds he doesn't have time

to talk with cabinet members, that's when the problems set in, and the White House aides close off access to cabinet members and others.

Jeb Stuart Magruder, a former Nixon aide, attested to the subsequent hostile White House treatment of the Nixon cabinet when he wrote: "From our perspective in the White House, the cabinet officials were useful spokesmen when we wanted to push a particular line — on Cambodia, on Carswell, or whatever. From their perspective, however, it was often a rude awakening to have Jeb Magruder or Chuck Colson calling up and announcing, 'Mr. Secretary, we're sending over this speech that we'd like you to deliver.' But that was how it was. Virtually all the cabinet members had to accept that they lacked access to the president and that their dealings would be with Haldeman and his various minions." [17]

A senior Kennedy staffer once told me an experience with one cabinet officer: "He kept calling and calling [for an appointment with the president], and so finally about the forty-third time — after I had told him over and over again that this wasn't the type of problem the president wanted to discuss with cabinet members — I finally relented and scheduled an appointment. Immediately after the secretary had completed his appointment and left, Kennedy stormed into my office and [in emphatic language] chewed me out for letting him in!" In his witty and somewhat bitter memoir, J. Edward Day, Kennedy's postmaster general, suggested that the president had neither the time nor the inclination to use the collective judgment of his cabinet. He also hinted that Kennedy hardly made use of several of the cabinet members even in their roles as departmental leaders.

> President Kennedy had never had the experience of being an executive among lesser but by no means subservient executives; he had been served by a fanatically devoted band of men of his own creation. His Cabinet was a different run of shad. Each member was independent and quick to express his views, perhaps too much so to the President's taste. . . .
>
> The atmosphere at Cabinet meetings should have been right for free-and-easy, frank discussion. At the outset it had been only natural to assume that such discussion would be encouraged. . . . The setting may have been right, but. . . .
>
> The impression was created that the President preferred smaller meetings with those Cabinet members concerned with a specific problem. *But his absorption with politics, publicity, and foreign policy allowed him little time to be concerned about the domestic departments,* unless they had an immediate political aspect. For the domestic Cabinet, *personal meetings with the President became fewer and farther between,* and more than one member grew increasingly unhappy because it was so difficult to see the President. [Emphasis added][18]

President Kennedy regarded the idea of the cabinet as a collective consultative body largely as an anachronism and often told close friends this in blunt terms. He felt that the nature of a problem should determine the group with which he met. He noted that the historical custom of the cabinet should carry with it no special claim on his time. He believed that there were few subjects that warranted bringing together, for example, the postmaster general, the secretary of agriculture, and the secretary of defense. As Kennedy aide Theodore Sorensen recalls:

> [Kennedy] had appointed his Cabinet members because he regarded them as individuals capable of holding down very difficult positions of responsibility. He did not want to have them sit through lengthy Cabinet sessions, listening to subjects which were not of interest to them, not of importance to them, at least not of an interest to their primary duties and their primary skills. So he called Cabinet meetings as infrequently as possible. . . .[19]

Richard Nixon had sat through countless formal cabinet meetings during the Eisenhower years. In his memoirs he recalls that "most of them were unnecessary and boring. On the few issues that cut across all departments . . . group discussions would sometimes be informative. But the day had long since passed when it was useful to take an hour and a half to have the Secretary of Defense and Secretary of State discuss the Secretary of Transportation's new highway proposal." [20]

If Nixon found them boring in the Eisenhower period, Elliot Richardson found them the same way in the Nixon years. He writes that cabinet meetings in both the Nixon and Ford administrations "ordinarily focused on bland common denominators like the economic outlook, displays of budgetary breakdowns, or reviews of the status of administrative proposals." Richardson adds, sarcastically, that "in the Nixon Cabinet, as a special treat, Vice President Spiro T. Agnew would occasionally give us a travelogue." [21]

The point is that most of the recent presidents have found it neither comfortable nor efficient to meet frequently with their cabinets as a whole. When they have, it seems to have been as much for purposes of publicity, symbolic reassurance, or appearance of activity as for substantive debate or learning. In the words of one Johnson White House lieutenant: "The cabinet became a joke; it was never used for anything near what would be called presidential listening or consultation." A Johnson cabinet officer complained that "cabinet meetings under L.B.J. were really perfunctory. They served two purposes: to let Dean Rusk brief us on the state of foreign affairs and let the President give us some occasional new political or personnel marching orders."

Cabinet members who went to President Johnson with requests were often asked to do favors in return, an added factor that kept some of them at a distance. One cabinet member noted that most domestic department heads tried not to bother the president because of his Vietnam war burdens: "But even at that, it was known that the president would welcome visits by domestic cabinet members on Saturday mornings. In retrospect, several of us regret that we did not make greater and better use of those opportunities. But part of the reason we didn't was because Johnson had an uncanny way of asking favors of you or giving you a number of political chores to do that you knew you didn't want and often couldn't carry out." This suggests, in part, that some cabinet members do not want too close a presidential relationship — surely an unconventional perspective, although in certain contexts understandable.

By the time of mid-term elections, the White House expects cabinet members to campaign for the administration, celebrating the administrative and legislative record of the past two years. Cabinet members come to be judged by the White House on their capacity to generate favorable publicity and to proclaim the virtues of the recent White House achievements. Strong-willed men of independence — those who might be praised as "men of distinguished excellence in an open administration" — can hardly be expected to be enthusiastic about performing public-relations tasks assigned to them by White House political counselors.

As time passes, cabinet members grow bitter about being left out of White House decisions, though they seldom make their opinions public.[22] Some exceptions exist, of course, and many cabinet officers will talk about the problem privately. The case of Nixon's first secretary of the interior, Walter Hickel, who had had only two or three private meetings with his president in the two years before his public protest and subsequent firing, is perhaps extreme. Most cabinet officers have more frequent contact with their president, but few of the domestic cabinet members have been wholly pleased by the quantity or quality of these meetings. A former secretary of commerce in the 1970s once joked of his infrequent ties to the White House by saying that his president "should have warned him that he was being appointed to a secret mission." Michael Blumenthal and Brock Adams (Carter's first secretaries of treasury and transportation) both felt bypassed by White House staff aides. Blumenthal, for example, was furious in 1978 when the President announced the designation of Robert Strauss as an anti-inflation czar. Not only was Blumenthal not informed of this move until the last minute, but he had been told earlier it wouldn't happen.

Nixon's increasing centralization of power in the White House was an apparent vote of no confidence in most of his cabinet members, although in naming his original cabinet in Deccember 1968, Nixon claimed to have appointed men who had the potential for great leadership, men with "an extra dimension which is the difference between good leadership and superior or even great leadership." Five years later he had a totally new cabinet. Nixon ran through cabinet members faster than any president in recent history. During one period of about eighteen months he had five attorneys general.

Nixon paid a price for keeping his cabinet officers at such a distance. Some of them were so often undercut that they sometimes purposely acted on their own just to show themselves, their departments, and the press that they were capable of independent action. Occasionally this made for a divided administration. At other times, as Nixon himself now admits in his memoirs, it threatened to undercut the administration's credibility with foreign countries. More important, Nixon's disuse and downgrading of the cabinet increased his isolation from responsible sources of political and professional advice. An already insecure man — a man who needed friendship and peers — removed himself from a potential source of support.

Why are more spirited and substantive discussions absent from the modern-day cabinet? First, the number attending cabinet sessions is too large. President Ford sometimes had thirty people in attendance. Most cabinet members are unlikely to talk about their troubles or highly sensitive topics in a group that large. A Roosevelt cabinet officer summed up the problem when he said: "My principal reason for not having a great deal to say at Cabinet meetings was that there was no one at the table who could be of help to me except the President, and when I needed to consult him, I did not choose a Cabinet meeting to do so." [23] Moreover, all the cabinet members are competitors for the president's support, all compete also for scarce funds. "Knowing that his fellow Cabinet officers have no real voice in the affairs of his own department, a Cabinet member is often reluctant to bring before a Cabinet meeting any still unresolved issue that he really cares about. . . ." [24]

One of the president's dilemmas is that a fundamental separation of policy formulation and its implementation can develop. Whereas most major policy decisions are made by the president and a small number of his personal aides, the responsibility for enacting these programs rests, for the most part, with the cabinet officers and their departments. The gap between these two functions of the executive has been widening, a result of the transference of power from the more public institution of the cabinet to the relatively hidden offices of the White House staff. The result has been a divorce of the exercise of power from accountability for that exercise, a situation many people believe threatens the effectiveness of the presidency.

The very nature of the cabinet — a body with no constitutional standing, members with no independent political base of their own and no requirement that the president seek or follow their advice — helps contribute to its lack of influence as a collective body. Ultimately, the influence of the cabinet rests solely on the role that a president desires for it. Most presidents, particularly those since Eisenhower, have made that role an increasingly limited one.

To some extent, this downgrading of the cabinet was imminent from the late 1930s when Roosevelt first began to place top-level advisers in the White House itself. Roosevelt often relied on braintrusters scattered throughout the government in positions other than cabinet posts. Easy and frequent access to the president is an important determinant of an adviser's influence. As Daniel Moynihan aptly put it, "Never underestimate the power of proximity." But perhaps more importantly, presidents tend to view many of their cabinet officers as parochial and narrow in their outlook, playing only an advocacy role for their own departments. White House aides and Executive Office advisors, on the other hand, lend the appearance of being more impartial arbiters between the competing departmental interests. These impressions, coupled with presidential perceptions of the departments as slow-moving bureaucracies consistently opposed to innovation at a pace that the president desired, led to the transfer of domestic- and economic-policy decisionmaking to the White House.

The result has been that policy has been determined by presidential aides who often have little understanding about what can be effectively implemented through the departments. Because they are neither accountable to anyone other than the president nor responsible for the implementation of policy, there is little incentive to devise an inherently workable policy and no place to afix the blame or revise a program when it fails.

Ironically, the presidential view of cabinet members as advocates for their departments often has proved to be a self-fulfilling prophecy. Not only have presidents, as a result, tended to use their cabinets to appease interest groups with a spokesman at the head of their relevant department, the limitations a president places on the time he spends with each member forces them to use that precious time to push for their department's needs first. Paradoxically some presidents render the departments less effective in implementing their policies by denying them a say in program development. There is less incentive for a cabinet officer or his department to implement a program efficiently if they feel they have no real stake or say in it.

THE EISENHOWER AND CARTER "CABINET ADMINISTRATIONS"

Historical experience suggests three basic ways presidents can use the cabinet as a group.

1. For discussing issues and problems in an informal and unfocused manner, primarily to exchange information back and forth.

2. For focused, regular consideration of specific issues, set forth in papers authored by cabinet members and circulated ahead of time, aided by agendas, concise records of action, and a small secretariat.
3. For summit discussions of issue papers, which have been through a searching prior interdepartmental review, with dissents identified and alternative language proposed.[25]

By general consensus the first format was used by Truman, Kennedy, Johnson, Nixon, and Ford, at least when they were willing to hold cabinet meetings. Eisenhower, however, followed the second alternative. Carter began with aspirations to the second format but his patience wore thin, as I shall discuss. Probably no president has ever used his full cabinet according to format three, although Truman and Eisenhower sometimes did employ their National Security councils in approximately this manner.

Eisenhower was one of the most enthusiastic proponents of an up-graded cabinet. It was as though he didn't want to believe that by the well-established law of politics secretaries of the great executive departments must serve several masters simultaneously. He hoped that each cabinet member in his administration would be a broad-gauged adviser, taking into account the total national welfare, not merely the clientele or congressional committees to which their departments traditionally had been beholden. Milton Eisenhower, the president's brother and close confidant, sums up the hopes Dwight Eisenhower entertained:

> General Eisenhower was determined to have the Cabinet become a major policy and program force in his administration. . . . [He] felt it imperative that the men and women who headed the major executive establishments should be consulted constantly in policy formation, for then they would more intelligently and enthusiastically carry out the agreed-upon policies and programs. Further, he did not want cabinet meetings to become merely a compromise of the preconceptions if its members. He wanted policies and programs of consequence to be analyzed and discussed thoroughly and candidly, with evidence and views based on careful research, reserving to himself, of course, the making of final decisions.[26]

Eisenhower created a cabinet secretariat and charged it with the explicit duty not only of preparing for the cabinet meetings, often held on a weekly basis, but also of following up to ensure that every decision was carried into action. Eisenhower also expanded the cabinet to include a handful of presidential assistants and directors of important government agencies whom he recognized as the equivalent of cabinet rank and status. The Eisenhower cabinet meetings often included up to two dozen officials, including the ambassador to the United Nations, the budget bureau director, a director of defense mobilization, a director of mutual security, a national security affairs assistant, with assorted top White

House aides sitting around the wall. Eisenhower raised some of these posts to the same rank as department heads so that they could work among the top-level officers of the government where they properly belonged.

From every indication, Eisenhower did try to make the cabinet work as something more than just a body of advisers to the president. Issues of great diversity and importance were on the cabinet agenda. He did, within certain limits, encourage his cabinet members to take an independent line of their own and argue it out within the cabinet session. Eisenhower appreciated the limits of a cabinet system but seemed motivated to use the cabinet sessions both as a means to keep himself informed and as a way to prevent the personality conflicts, throat cutting, and end running that had characterized the history of past administrations.

The Eisenhower cabinet did not, however, decide policy nor did it really formulate policy, but it came about as close to the ideal of an upgraded or European-style cabinet as we have witnessed in the United States.

One can only speculate about why Eisenhower chose to treat the cabinet in this atypical way. Perhaps in his career as a military and Pentagon official he simply had acquired a patience and a high tolerance of staff and management meetings. It is probable, too, that Eisenhower was more secure, politically and personally, and thus more permissive of free interchange from stronger cabinet members. Still another factor may have been his notion of policy leadership, which, in short, was to move slowly, cautiously, and only after public opinion, Congress, or the courts had already taken a stand. In this sense, Eisenhower viewed himself as more of a manager and a moral leader than as a catalyst for initiating progressive change.

If the Eisenhower use of the cabinet was an exception to the general practice, it is nonetheless still true that even in his administration congeries of functional cabinets with reduced and appropriate membership were often relied on. By all odds Eisenhower's favorite policy-review group was the National Security Council. The NSC meetings were much smaller and the issues were of more personal interest to him. "More and more, we find that the central body in making policy is the N.S.C. Its sessions are long, bitter and tough. Out of that sort of discussion we're trying to hammer policy." [27] Moreover, close observers concluded that Eisenhower was bored more often than not with nonnational security matters, especially with the business of the departments of Agriculture, Commerce, Labor, and Health, Education and Welfare.

If the Nixon administration epitomized the extreme concentration of power and executive authority in the White House and the virtual eclipse of the cabinet, the early Carter presidency typified an experimentation in cabinet revitalization. Ford had begun to upgrade the pattern. He met with his cabinet about once a month, encouraged individual cabinet members to meet with him privately whenever they wished, and generally used cabinet meetings as a discussion group dealing with the issues that cut across departmental boundaries. But Ford's cabinet suffered almost as much turnover as Nixon's. He fired one member. One resigned on principle. One, Earl Butz, had to resign after embarrassing the administration with racist and ethnic jokes (jokes told privately but later widely published in the press). Another suffered a nervous breakdown. His vice president came late (it took nearly four months to get Rockfeller confirmed) and, for all practical purposes withdrew from running for renomination early. Then, too, Ford's term was a peculiarly short one.

Carter came to office pledging that his cabinet would meet regularly and would play a major role in setting policy in his administration. He also said: "There will never be an instance while I am president when the members of the White House staff dominate or act in a superior position to the members of our cabinet." [28] Early on, he talked naively about having open press-covered cabinet sessions and about having cabinet members represent the president in scheduled and televised public interrogation sessions with the full bodies of Congress.

Although the notion of "cabinet government" to refer to the early Carter experience would be a misnomer, he did allow his cabinet officers a reasonably freer hand in selecting their subordinates and in setting many of the initial priorities in their departmental policy areas. "We were really too free," said one. Physical access to Carter was easy during his first two years in office — so much so that White House aides frequently complained that Carter was bending over backward too far in his attempts to signal an end of the distasteful Nixon practices.

Carter, however, really did not use the cabinet as a policy-setting collegium. The policy contribution of the cabinet members came principally through their participation on task forces associated with the National Security Council, the domestic policy staff, or other such groups. Each of these task forces is headed by a cabinet officer or a White House aide. The purpose is to coordinate policy planning and to develop policy options. In the end the task forces reported to the president who served as the ultimate arbiter.

Still Carter believed he could fashion some kind of "cabinet administration." His two-hour meetings with the full cabinet practically every Monday morning at nine o'clock for his first year and a half demonstrated his keen interest. However, even his cabinet members felt he went overboard with these sessions. One said the meetings "were tedious, boring and virtually a waste of time." Another said there were two or three times as many as were really needed. Most of the cabinet meetings had no agendas. The president merely raised issues that were on his mind and elicited their views, one by one, on his comments or on matters they felt should be raised. Many meetings sounded like an adult version of a first-grade Show and Tell session.[29]

Carter's White House aides were surprisingly hostile to his "cabinet administration" efforts. "It was one of his biggest mistakes," one told me. Another said, "Carter was naive about how the government works. He really believes all this stuff. He is an optimist and an idealist when it comes to working with people. He doesn't think people are evil or capable of disloyalty. In effect, he trusts people too much. He has an army manager's sense of thinking." These and other Carter aides stressed that Carter had given his cabinet too much freedom. "He should discipline some of them," they said. One White House lawyer surveyed the first year and a half of Carter's cabinet administration this way:

> All of our problems are aggravated by the so-called "cabinet government" efforts. . . . People took it too literally — including the White House staff. But you can't run the government that way — from 10 different locations. It is just too difficult to get government together. There are so many agencies involved in one issue. People don't understand that 5 agencies all going in different directions creates chaos. There needed to be a coordinating place. There had to be a legislative package prepared by the Administration. . . . It took us most of the first year to figure this out and to begin to iron it out. . . .

Jack Watson, a Carter aide assigned to cabinet liaison duties, defended Carter's use of the cabinet. He said the meetings stimulated a collegial atmosphere between the cabinet and the president. The president, he felt, learned more about the intensity of a cabinet member's feelings by talking with him directly. "Two hours a week is not an inordinate amount of time for the leaders of government to be together and talk about important issues." [30] Carter eventually did cut them back to one or two a month.

Midway in his second year, Carter let it be known that more coordination from the White House would be necessary. Thus he was especially upset when Treasury Secretary W. Michael Blumenthal spoke out favoring limited tax changes when he (Carter) favored more sweeping and comprehensive tax reform. He was somewhat upset that HEW Secretary Joseph Califano may have been too public in his opposition to the Carter-endorsed idea of a new Department of Education. He also decried the countless instances when the cabinet or subcabinet spoke out in criticism of either each other or of White House policy directions. Carter was having serious doubts about his experiment with cabinet revitalization. Perhaps he had gone a little too far; perhaps there were liabilities he had underestimated.

A year later in mid-July 1979, Carter fired two of his cabinet members and dramatically accepted the doubtlessly forced resignations of two others. His "cabinet purge" was unprecedented in recent times and surely ended his romantic illusions of cabinet administration. He wanted more unity, more loyalty and more of a team effort. He designated his top political strategist, Hamilton Jordan, as a White House chief of staff. Although disclaiming he was in any way weakening his cabinet or limiting their access to him, there was little doubt that Carter was disillusioned with the idea of independent cabinet members making end runs around the White House.

It was as if as his political troubles grew he needed more loyalty and more control over his own team. He had earnestly hoped to retain his cabinet intact for four years. "He had a thing about keeping his cabinet together" said his first Attorney General, Griffin B. Bell. Carter no doubt wanted to prove his managerial competence by making the cabinet work. He wanted to defy the turnover rates that plagued Nixon and Ford. So much did he want to have his use of the cabinet praised that he excessively boasted (even up to a few months before his 1979 cabinet purge) that he was very pleased with his superb cabinet, and that if he had it to do all over again, he would appoint all the same individuals. But under this veneer of public relations gloss tensions were growing and ego-frictions were escalating. Moreover, Carter was continually criticized for not being tough enough. His cabinet purge was, by most accounts, an effort to demonstrate toughness and an effort to gain more control over the sprawling executive branch. But this firing of the most outspoken and independent members of his cabinet was widely criticized as cover for weakening the cabinet and strengthening the White House staff.

A CABINET OF UNEQUALS

Cabinet roles and influence with the White House differ markedly according to personalities, the department, and the times. Each cabinet usually has one or two members who become the dominant personalities. Herbert Hoover's performance as secretary of commerce under Harding was of this type. George Marshall's performance in both State and Defense under Truman was similar. George Humphrey of the Treasury and John Foster Dulles of State clearly towered over others in the Eisenhower cabinet. Robert McNamara enjoyed especially close ties with both Kennedy and Johnson. His reputation as manager of a large, complex organization and his performance in a similar capacity at Defense virtually mesmerized both presidents and most of the White House staff, few of whom had ever managed any organization except temporary campaign staffs. Both Kennedy and Johnson repeatedly pointed to McNamara and the Defense Department as models for other departments to imitate, conspicuously congratulating their Planning, Programming and Budgeting System (PPBS), cost reduction, and cost-effectiveness operations. McNamara's capacity to present his own case before the presidents seemingly made it unnecessary for White House aides to serve as intermediaries; for example, he personally carried his annual budgetary requests directly to the president, and the president granted the budget director the opportunity for selective appeals or disagreements. George Shultz's early influence with President Nixon substantially exceeded the power inherent in the Labor Department, leading to his reassignment, first as director of the Office of Management and Budget, then as secretary of the treasury.

Certain departments and their secretaries gained prominence in recent decades because every president has been deeply involved with their priorities and missions — Defense and State in the cold war as well as in the so-called détente years, for example. The Acheson-Dulles-Rusk-Kissinger-Vance tradition of close and cordial ties with their presidents were founded in an era of continuous international tension during which diplomatic and alliance strategy loomed large. Other departments may become important temporarily in the president's eyes, sometimes because of a prominent cabinet secretary who is working in an area in which the president wants to effect breakthroughs: for example, John Kennedy's Justice Department headed by his brother Robert. HEW sometimes was thought to be developing into a presidential department during the mid-1960s when under John W. Gardner it was growing rapidly in order to manage Johnson's major educational and health programs. The Department of Energy enjoyed special considerations in the early Carter years for similar reasons.

Much White House-cabinet estrangement undoubtedly arises because presidents simply lack the time to spend with all cabinet officers, let alone the leaders of independent agencies or major bureau chiefs. Most of a president's schedule is consumed with national-security and foreign-policy matters. One recent cabinet member complained: "In retrospect, all of the past three presidents have spent too much time on foreign affairs. They all felt that's where the action is and that's how they would be judged in the history books!"

Vast differences exist in the scope and importance of cabinet-level departments. The three million-person Defense Department and the six-teen-thousand-person or so departments of Labor or Housing and Urban Development are not similar. Certain agencies not of cabinet rank — the Central Intelligence Agency, the National Space and Aeronautics Administration, the Veterans Administration, and the Environmental Protection Agency — may be more important, at least for certain periods of time, than cabinet-level departments. Conventional rankings of the departments are based on their longevity, annual expenditures, and number of personnel. Rankings according to these indicators can be seen in the first three columns of Table 8.2. Even a casual comparison of these columns reveals unexpected characteristics. Thus, although the State Department is about 190 years older than some of the newer departments, its expenditures are the lowest of all. On the other hand, the Department of Human Services, formerly the Department of Health, Education and Welfare, officially only about thirty years old, ranks first in expenditures and second only to Defense in personnel.

The contemporary cabinet can be differentiated also into inner and outer cabinets, as shown in table 8.1. This classification, derived from extensive interviews, indicates how White House aides and cabinet officers view the departments and their access to the president. The inner cabinet includes the secretaries of state, defense, and treasury and the attorney general. The occupants of these cabinet positions generally have maintained a role as counselor to the president; the departments all include broad-ranging, multiple interests. The explicitly domestic-policy departments with the exception of justice, have made up the outer cabinet. By custom, if not by designation, these cabinet officers assume a relatively straightforward advocacy orientation that overshadows their counseling role.

THE INNER CABINET

A pattern in the past few administrations suggests strongly that the inner, or counseling, cabinet positions are vested with high-priority responsi-

TABLE 8.1   WAYS OF LOOKING AT
THE EXECUTIVE DEPARTMENTS

A. BY RANK-ORDER

Seniority	Expenditures (1980)	Personnel (1980)	Real Political Power and Impact (Alsop's assessment) (1968)
1. State	1. HHS	1. Defense	1. Defense
2. Treasury	2. Defense	2. HHS	2. State
3. War/Defense	3. Treasury	3. Treasury	3. Treasury
4. Interior	4. Labor	4. Agriculture	4. Justice
5. Justice	5. Agriculture	5. Transportation	5. Interior
6. Agriculture	6. Transportation	6. Justice	6. HEW
7. Commerce	7. Education	7. Interior	7. Labor
8. Labor	8. HUD	8. Commerce	8. Agriculture
9. HHS	9. Energy	9. State	9. Commerce
10. HUD	10. Interior	10. Labor	10. HUD
11. Transportation	11. Commerce	11. Energy	11. Transportation
12. Energy	12. Justice	12. Education	
13. Education	13. State	13. HUD	

TABLE 8.1 *(cont.)*

B. BY ORGANIZATION

Inner and Outer Clusterings [a]	Nixon's 1971 Proposals	Carter Staff Suggestions, 1979 [b]	Supercabinet Plan A [c]
Inner:	State	State	National security
State	Defense	Defense	Economic stability
Defense	Treasury	Treasury	and growth
Treasury	Justice	Justice	Domestic policy
Justice	Human resources	HEW	
Outer:	Natural resources	Energy	
Agriculture	Economic	Transportation	
Interior	development	Labor	
Transportation	Community	Natural Resources	
HHS	development	Development	
HUD		Assistance	
Labor		Food and	
Commerce		Nutrition	
Energy		Trade,	
Education		Technology	
		and Industry	
		Education	

Source: Expenditures from estimated budget outlays of the executive departments in 1980; personnel from *The Budget of the United States Government, Fiscal Year 1980*, pp. 524 and 529 respectively; Alsop's assessment from Stewart Alsop, *The Center* (Harper & Row, 1968), p. 254; Nixon's proposals from the State of the Union Message, January 22, 1971. Carter proposals from Carter press conferences and from Rochelle L. Stanfield, "The Best Laid Reorganization Plans Sometime Go Astray," *National Journal*, 20 January 1979, pp. 84–91.

a Genetic clustering made according to counseling-advocacy department.

b A cabinet consolidation plan proposed by some of President Carter's reorganization staff in 1979.

c The way some White House aides view aggregate departmental concerns, and the apparent priority of these concerns as viewed by recent presidents.

bilities that bring their occupants into close and collaborative relationships with presidents and their top staff. Certain White House staff counselors also have been included in the inner cabinet with increasing frequency. The secretary of defense was one of the most prominent cabinet officers during all recent administrations, for each president recognized the priority of national-security issues. Then, too, the defense budget and the DOD personnel, the latter ranging from 3 to 4 million (including the military), makes it impossible for a president to ignore a secretary of defense for very long. Despite the inclination of recent presidents to serve as "their own secretary of state," the top man at the Department of State has nevertheless had a direct and continuous relationship with contemporary presidents. Recent treasury secretaries — George Humphrey, Robert Anderson, Douglas Dillon, John Connally, George Shultz, William Simon — also have played impressive roles in presidential deliberations on financial, business, and economic policy. The position of attorney general often, though not always, has been one of the most influential in the cabinet.

The inner cabinet, as classified here, corresponds to George Washington's original foursome and to most memoirs of the Eisenhower through Carter period. Note that these inner-cabinet departments alone were immune to President Nixon's proposed overhaul of the executive branch in 1971; all others were nominated for merger. The status accorded these cabinet roles is, of course, subject to ebb and flow, for the status is rooted in a cabinet officer's performance as well as in the crises and the fashions of the day.

A NATIONAL-SECURITY CABINET

The seemingly endless series of recent international crises — Berlin, Cuba, the Congo, the Dominican Republic, Vietnam, the Middle East, and continuing strains with the USSR — have made it mandatory for recent presidents to maintain close relations with the two national-security cabinet heads. Just as George Washington met almost every day with his four cabinet members during the French crisis of 1793, so also all of our recent presidents have been likely to meet at least weekly and be in daily telephone communication with their inner cabinet of national-security advisers. One Johnson aide said it was his belief that President Johnson personally trusted only two members of his cabinet, Rusk and McNamara. Kennedy aides quote their president to the effect that his "regional assistant secretaries of state were more important officers of the government than most of the cabinet." Carter aides said Harold Brown and Cyrus Vance were probably President Carter's best appointments as well as two of his closest counselors.

Throughout recent administrations, more than a little disquiet has been engendered in the White House by the operational lethargy of the State Department. Although the secretary of state is customarily considered by the White House to be a member of the president's inner cabinet, the department itself was regarded as one of the most difficult to deal with. More than 25 percent of the White House staff interviewed cited the State Department to illustrate White House-department conflicts. They scorned the narrowness and timidity of the encrusted foreign service and complained of the custodial conservatism reflected in State Department working papers.

Some of State's problems may stem from the threats of the Joe

McCarthy era of the early 1950s, which intimidated State Department careerists into holding only the most puristic interpretations of the received policies of the day and inhibited imaginative and inventive policy. In State, more than in the other departments, the method and style of personnel, the special selection and promotion processes, and the protocol consciousness all seem farther removed from the political thinking at the White House. Although they often may be gifted and cultured, State's personnel invariably become stereotyped by White House aides as overly cautious and tradition bound.

Another source of the department's problems is the way in which recent secretaries, especially John Foster Dulles, Dean Rusk, and Henry Kissinger, have defined their job. The demands on Rusk personally were such that departmental management was hardly his major priority. John Leacacos has surmised that the priorities appeared to have been: "First, the President and his immediate desires; second, the top operations problems of the current crisis; third, public opinion as reflected in the press, radio and TV and in the vast inflow of letters from the public; fourth, Congressional opinion; fifth, Rusk's need to be aware, at least, of everything that was going on in the world; and only sixth and last, the routine of the State Department itself." [31] That the secretary of state so often serves as the president's representative abroad or before Congress is another reason so few secretaries have had the time or energy necessary for managing the department's widely scattered staff. Moreover, more than fifty federal departments, agencies, and committees are involved in some way in the administration or evaluation of United States foreign policy.

LEGAL AND ECONOMIC COUNSEL

The Justice Department is often identified as a counseling department, and its chiefs usually are associated with the inner circle of presidential advisers. That Kennedy appointed his brother, Nixon appointed his trusted campaign manager and law partner, and Carter appointed a close personal friend to be attorneys general indicates the importance of this position, although extensive politicization of the department has a long history. The Justice Department traditionally serves as the president's attorney and law office, a special obligation that brings about continuous and close professional relations between White House domestic-policy lawyers and Justice Department lawyers. The White House depends heavily and constantly on the department's lawyers for counsel on civil-rights developments, presidential veto procedures, tax prosecutions, antitrust controversies, routine presidential pardons, and the overseeing of regulatory agencies and for a continuous overview of the congressional judiciary committees. That these exchanges involve lawyers working with lawyers may explain in some measure why White House aides generally are more satisfied with transactions with Justice than with other departments. Attorney General Griffin Bell in the late 1970s was especially close to Jimmy Carter. White House aides said Bell "is powerful because he has immediate and frequent access to the President. He also has a lot of self-confidence; like many former judges he thinks pretty highly of his decisions."

The secretary of the treasury continues to be a critical presidential adviser on both domestic and international fiscal and monetary policy, but he also plays somewhat of an advocate's role as an interpreter of the nation's leading financial interests. At one time the Treasury Department included the Bureau of the Budget. With budget staff and numerous economists, particularly within the Council of Economic Advisers, now attached to the White House, however, Treasury has become a department with major institutional authority and responsibility for income and corporate tax administration, currency control, public borrowing, and counseling of the president on such questions as the price of gold and the balance of payments, the federal debt, and international trade, development, and monetary matters. In addition, Treasury's special clientele of major and central bankers has unusual influence. Although the Council of Economic Advisers and the Federal Reserve Board may enjoy greater prestige in certain economic deliberations, they are less effective as counterweights in international commerce and currency issues, in which Treasury participation is most important. The latter connection helps to draw the department's secretary into the inner circle of foreign-policy counselors to the president. Also, the treasury secretary is almost always a pivotal figure on key cabinet-level committees, such as the Cabinet Committee for Economic Growth, the Cabinet Committee on Balance of Payments, the Cabinet Committee on Economic Policy, and the Cabinet Committee on Price Stability.

The importance of the treasury secretary as a presidential counselor derives in part from the intelligence and personality of the incumbent. Dillon and Connally, for example, were influential in great part because of their self-assuredness and personal magnetism. President Eisenhower found himself responding in a similar manner to George M. Humphrey: "In Cabinet meetings, I always wait for George Humphrey to speak. I sit back and listen to the others talk while he doesn't say anything. But I know that when he speaks, he will say just what I was thinking." [32] Leonard Silk has suggested, however: "Formally, the Treasury Secretary had a mystique and power potential fully comparable to those of the Chancellor of the Exchequer in Britain or the Minister of Finance in France. The mystique may not be all that mysterious to explain; it derives from money. Power over money, in the hands of the right man, can enable a Secretary of the Treasury to move into every definite action of government — in military and foreign affairs as well as in domestic economic and social affairs." [33]

President Carter's first treasury secretary, W. Michael Blumenthal, described his cabinet role this way:

> A department like the Treasury is a conglomeration of different activities, operating under set laws about hiring and firing and the seniority system and the Civil Service employment rights. So the top man coming in has very few tools with which to influence who's hired, who's fired, and who's moved where, except for the very top. So, even though I'm technically the chief executive of the Treasury, I have little real power, effective power, to influence how the thing functions.
>
> . . . As in any organization, you have to decide where to put your energies. You learn very quickly that you do not go down in history as a good or bad Secretary in terms of how well you run the place, whether you are a good administrator or not. You're perceived to be a good Secretary in terms of whether the policies for which you are responsible are adjudged successful or not: what happens to the economy, to the budget, to inflation, and to the dollar, how well you run debt financing and international economic relations, and what the bankers and the financial community think of you. Those are the things that determine whether you are a successful Secretary.[34]

INNER CIRCLES

The inner-circle cabinet members have been noticeably more interchangeable than those of the outer cabinet. Henry Stimson, for example, alternated from Taft's secretary of war to Hoover's secretary of state and then back once more to war under FDR. Dean Acheson was undersecretary of the treasury for FDR and later secretary of state for Truman. Dillon reversed this pattern by being an Eisenhower undersecretary of state and later a Kennedy secretary of the treasury. When Kennedy was trying to lure McNamara to his new cabinet, he offered him his choice between ,Defense and Treasury. Attorney General Nicholas Katzenbach left Justice to become an undersecretary of state; Eisenhower's attorney general William Rogers became Nixon's first secretary of state; and John Connally, once a secretary of the Navy under Kennedy, became Nixon's secretary of the treasury. Within a mere four and a half years, Elliot Richardson, sometimes called "our only professional cabinet member," moved from undersecretary of state to HEW secretary to defense secretary to attorney general. He became, his unexpectedly short tenure notwithstanding, the fourteenth head of the Justice Department to have served also in another inner-cabinet position. Cyrus Vance, who had served as deputy secretary of defense for LBJ, became Carter's secretary of state. Harold Brown, LBJ's secretary of the Air Force, became Carter's secretary of defense. Occasional shifts have occurred from inner to outer cabinet, but these have been exceptions to the general pattern.

This interchangeability may result from the broad-ranging interests of the inner-cabinet positions, from the counseling style and relationship that develop in the course of an inner-cabinet secretary's tenure, or from the already close personal friendship that has often existed with the president. It may be easier for inner-cabinet than for outer-cabinet secretaries to maintain the presidential perspective; presidents certainly try to choose men they know and respect for these intimate positions.

In recent years several members of the White House staff have performed cabinet-level counselor roles. Eisenhower, for example, explicitly designated Sherman Adams to be a member of his cabinet ex officio. Kennedy looked upon Theodore Sorensen, McGeorge Bundy, and some of his economic advisers as perhaps even more vital to his decision making than most of his cabinet members. Johnson and Nixon also assigned many of their staff to cabinet-type counseling responsibilities. Carter advisor Robert Strauss performed several cabinet-level responsibilities in the late 1970's, ranging from anti-inflation matters to diplomatic negotiations.

The people to whom presidents turn for overview presentations to congressmen and cabinet gatherings are another indicator of inner-counselor status. When Kennedy wanted to brief his cabinet on his major priorities, typically he would ask Secretary Rusk to review foreign affairs, chairman of the Council of Economic Advisers Walter Heller to review questions about the economy, and Sorensen to give a status report on the domestic legislative program. When Lyndon Johnson held special seminars for gatherings of congressmen and their staffs, he would invariably call upon the secretaries of state and defense to explain national-security matters and then ask his budget director and his chairman of the Council of Economic Advisers to comment upon economic, budgetary, and domestic program matters. Nixon and Ford usually called upon Henry Kissinger, the director of the Office of Management and Budget, and one of their chief White House domestic-policy counselors.

THE OUTER CABINET

The outer-cabinet positions deal with strongly organized and more particularistic clientele, an involvement that helps to produce an advocate relationship to the White House. These departments — Health and Human Services, HUD, Labor, Commerce, Interior, Agriculture, Transportation, Energy, and Education — are the outer-cabinet departments. Because most of the president's controllable expenditures, with the exception of defense, lie in their jurisdictions, they take part in the most intensive and competitive exchanges with the White House and the Office of Management and Budget. These departments experience heavy and often conflicting pressures from clientele groups, from congressional interests, and from state and local governments, pressures that often run counter to presidential priorities. Whereas three of the four inner-cabinet departments preside over policies that usually, though often imprudently, are perceived to be largely nonpartisan or bipartisan — national security, foreign policy, and the economy — the domestic departments almost always are subject to intense crossfire between partisan and domestic interest groups.

White House aides and inner-cabinet members may be selected primarily on the basis of personal loyalty to the president; outer-cabinet members often are selected, as already mentioned, to achieve a better political, geographical, ethnic, or racial balance. In addition to owing loyalty to their president, these people must develop loyalties to the congressional committees that approved them or to those that finance their programs, to the laws and programs they administer, and to the clientele and career civil servants who serve as their most immediate jury. Johnson's HEW secretary Wilbur Cohen describes the cross-pressures vividly: "If you're the secretary of HEW, you're responsible really, in the end, to the Ways and Means Committee and the House Education and Labor Committee. And, boy, they can tell you in the White House, they can tell you in the Office of Management and Budget, and they can tell you everywhere, do this, that and the other thing. But if you come back next time to Capitol Hill, and you've violated what is their standard for their delivery system, you're not going to get what you're asking for." [35]

Advocacy Conflicts

White House aides generally view outer-cabinet executives as special pleaders for vested clientele interests over the priorities of the president. One of Franklin Roosevelt's commerce secretaries frankly acknowledged his representational and advocacy obligations when he explained: "If the Department of Commerce means anything, it means as I understand it the representation of business in the councils of the administration, at the Cabinet table, and so forth." [36] Few White House aides speak of the virtue of having a cabinet member reflect his or her constituency and how this helps, or could help, educate a president. Most White House aides speak of the cabinet as a burden and an ordeal for presidents rather than as a chance to forge coalitions and exercise leadership. For example, as one Carter aide put it: "Nobody expects Ray Marshall at Labor to be a spokesman for anything other than big labor. You just have to live with this, although Marshall does seem to be making the best out of a bad situation." Advocacy usually, though not always, is viewed in negative terms.

Because presidents have less and less time to spend with the outer-cabinet members, the advocate role becomes less flexible and more narrowly defined. Unlike senior White House aides who enjoy greater access to the president, outer-cabinet members find they have little chance to discuss new policy ideas or administrative problems with the president. They must make the most of their limited meetings:

> One basic problem lies in the fact that domestic cabinet members are so rarely with the president that when they do have a chance to see him, they have to advocate and plug their departmental program in an almost emotional style, trying to make a plea for expanded appropriations or some new departmental proposal. But precisely at such times, the senior White House aide present can adopt or strike a pose as the more objective, rational statesman taking a non-advocate and more "presidential" position — all of which leaves the domestic cabinet members appearing like a salesman or lobbyist rather than part of the president's team. But the cabinet member seldom has a chance to make his points or his case. The White House aide knows, on the other hand, that he can see the president later that day or the next, and so can afford to play a more reasonable and restrained role in such meetings. Such role-casting clearly favors the staff man while placing the cabinet member in a most uneasy position.

The interpretation of the advocate role by both the outer-cabinet member and the president may vary. It is much easier to listen to an advocate whose point of view fits with the White House philosophy than to one who continually transmits substantively different arguments or who encroaches upon other policy arenas. As departments have grown and their administration has become more exhausting, fewer of the department heads have had time to be well versed on problems beyond their domain. And as the last three columns in Table 2 suggest, White House aides and, to a lesser extent, recent presidents have come to feel that in many ways today's cabinet remains organized around problems of the past far more appropriately than the problems challenging the nation's present or future.

Interior secretary Walter Hickel complained that the performance of the adversary role alienated him from the president. Noting that President Nixon "repeatedly referred to me as an 'adversary,'" he continued:

> Initially I considered that a compliment because, to me, an adversary within an organization is a valuable asset. It was only after the President had used the term many times and with a disapproving inflection that I realized he considered an adversary an enemy. I could not understand why he would consider me an enemy.
>
> As I sensed that the conversation was about to end, I asked, "Mr. President, do you want me to leave the Administration?"
>
> He jumped up from his chair, very hurried and agitated. He said,

"That's one option we hadn't considered." He called in Ehrlichman and said: "John, I want you to handle this. Wally asked whether he should leave. That's one option we hadn't considered." [37]

Hickel's advocacy and style both differed from Nixon's and he was fired later that week. Such an occurrence is not inevitable, however: an outer-cabinet member's advocacy and adversary role can and sometimes does fit perfectly with an administration's substantive philosophy.

Outer-Cabinet Isolation

As tension builds around whether, or to what extent, domestic policy leadership rests with the departments or with the Office of Management and Budget or with the White House, and as staff and line distinctions become blurred, the estrangement between the domestic department heads and the White House staff deepens. White House aides believe they possess the more objective understanding of what the president wants to accomplish. At the same time the cabinet heads, day in and day out, must live with the responsibilities for managing their programs, with the judgment of Congress and with the multiple claims of interest groups. Outer-cabinet members often complain bitterly about the unmanageability of their departments and the many pressures on them.

Interviews with the domestic cabinet members yield abundant evidence that most of them felt removed from the White House in the Kennedy, Johnson, and Nixon years. From a Kennedy-Johnson cabinet-level administrator:

> Recent presidents have let their White House political and personal aides go much too far in pressing administrators to do things they shouldn't. Too many of them are trying to make administrators squirm. There are too many aides at the White House who are just looking for a headline for the president. You have to guard against those types. There is just too much of it and presidents are guilty of letting it continue — they don't sufficiently realize that you have to have confidence in your department administrators. Perhaps it is due to the fact that they have never been administrators — they spent all their time in the Senate.

From Nixon's first secretary of the interior:

> There was an "isolation of thought" developing [in the Nixon presidency]. In early 1970, I was conscious of a deepening malaise inside the Administration — a sense of vague uneasiness. Others in the Cabinet shared my feelings that some of the White House staff were stepping up their efforts to filter contacts between the Cabinet and the President. It appeared that an effort was being made to centralize control of all executive branch activities of the government immediately within the White House, utilizing the various departments — represented by secretaries

at the cabinet level — merely as clearing houses for White House policy, rather than as action agencies.

Should a department — for example, Interior — develop policy for those activities under its control, submit those ideas to the White House for approval or disapproval, then follow through at the administrative level? Or, as some of the White House personnel seemed to want it, should a department wait only for marching orders to be issued by the Executive Mansion? [38]

The size of the bureaucracy, distrust, and a penchant for the convenience of secrecy led most recent presidents to rely more heavily on White House staffers. The White House and executive office aides increasingly became involved not only in gathering legislative ideas but also in getting those ideas translated into laws and those laws into programs. Program coordination and supervision, although often ill managed, also became primary White House interests. To an extent, these additional responsibilities transformed the White House into an administrative rather than a staff agency. Outer-cabinet departments, understandably, began to lose the capacity to sharpen up their programs, and the department heads felt uneasy about the lack of close working relations with the president.

One of the difficulties of this tendency to pull things into the White House and exclude departmental officials is that excellent ideas or proposals that may exist lower down in the bureaus of the permanent government seldom get the attention they deserve because, according to the departmentalists, nobody asks them. As social psychologists have suggested, one group tends to develop stereotyped perspectives that not only dehumanize the outsiders but also cut off the very communications channels that might provide valuable and even vital information.

In the early 1960s Kennedy and his staff tried to get the domestic departments to come up with proposals for innovative legislation. But, according to White House aides, they usually came up with "interest-group types of claims, very parochial, more-of-the-same types of proposals." Rather than try to strengthen departmental capacities to come up with broader, more innovative proposals, White House aides, impatient for action, instead developed a wide array of advisory committees, commissions, and secret task forces.

PROPOSALS FOR IMPROVED
WHITE HOUSE-CABINET RELATIONS

White House aides perceive several sources of conflict between the White House and the executive departments; they also suggest a number of different remedies. The appropriateness of any suggested reform depends not only on the type of problem but also on which staff functions at the White House and which departments are involved. Rather than calling uniformly for a strengthened presidency, as might have been expected, White House aides support a middle way, that is, an enhanced cabinet role as well as a strong, assertive White House role.

Most White House aides acknowledge that numerous remedial efforts are needed within the White House as well as between the White House and the departments. Many former presidential aides began their discussion of reforms by pointing out that presidential styles, as well as policy preferences, differ, so "each president should organize his office more or less as he sees fit." Several recall intentions of remedying bad habits at the White House that quickly evaporated:

> Johnson would occasionally try to organize us into some better relationship to the cabinet and agencies. He would get memos on a certain day from two different White House people with two differing views or competing thoughts. He must have told me several times [after such occasions], and I know he told some of the others on the White House staff to *"organize this place!!* — organize it along more coherent lines so there won't be so much overlap." But this [when tried] wouldn't last for more than a few days, because the President himself wouldn't stick to it or honor it. In practice, the White House just does not lend itself very easily to that type of straight-line or box-like organization.

Nearly 80 percent of the domestic- and budget-policy aides interviewed offered suggestions that would strengthen White House policy planning and management capabilities. Even those who complain about the arrogance of the White House staff often conclude that presidents must have tough and aggressive staff help. The following responses from Kennedy and Carter White House staffers, suggested as remedies for reducing problems with the departments, provide some flavor of the strong "presidentialist" beliefs of many of these aides.

> The presidency has to be the activist within the very conservative federal bureaucracy. The bureaucracy is the conservative agent or the custodian of old laws and old policies. They fight against anything new suggested by the White House, hence a president has to be the destabilizing factor in the system. The inability of department institutions to be creative or to take on new responsibilities is fantastic! In my view, the most important thing for a president is to know how to *shake up* the bureaucracy! My own law is that for every new major priority you need to create a new agency — never give it to the existing department. You need a new agency to get the resources and the leadership to pull off anything that is a major departure — like getting a man to the moon.

> I think it is impossible to run the White House staff without having tough men to do the work of the president. Sorensen, Myer Feldman,

and Ralph Dungan [Kennedy aides] were of this type. They could be very tough, abrasive, and uncompromising. But they had to be tough because if they were not the people in the agencies and departments just wouldn't respect the communications that came from the White House. I think it is a fundamental dilemma that people working for a president have to be arrogant, and almost be bastards, in order to get White House work done with the departments.

There are two approaches to getting better relations with cabinet and sub-cabinet officials. First, you tell them that to lower everyone's anxieties they should all cooperate and involve the White House very early and this will help make things work more smoothly and quickly later. Second, if they don't cooperate you've got to play hardball and get the President to tell a department head to make his people cooperate with us. We've had to use both strategies.

Although considerable overlap exists between those aides who supported a presidential and an integrative perspective, the latter approach received relatively more support from among the administrative, public-relations, and national-security policy aides than from among the domestic- and budgetary-policy advisers. Integrative recommendations seemingly are based on the assumption that the White House is unlikely to have much effect on the implementation of federal programs unless it can win support and cooperation from the middle and upper echelons of the executive-branch departments. For example:

I think the basic solution to the problem of dealing with the departments is to get one or two top staff people in the office of a cabinet member or department head and have these people work closely with the White House team. This helps a lot. It has to be a two-way street between the White House and the cabinet members. It is very important for White House aides to do favors for Cabinet members when they really want to get a promotion for somebody, or get some projects done. If you don't go along with them occasionally, and do this type of thing for them, they in turn are going to be difficult to deal with for yourself. It should be a bargaining, give and take, two-way relationship.

Keep them [department officials] involved and make sure you have some subcabinet people on your side whom you can trust and keep in touch with, and let you know what's happening. For example, I had an assistant secretary in the Commerce Department who knew our [White House] view, and was fighting with us against the State Department on textile tariff matters. He would go to the meetings and keep us posted if we needed to know more about anything.

Try to make them see the potential resources as well as the reason for the existence of a White House staff man assigned to their area. (1)

Frankly, they can't cut you off because every agency needs to know what the president thinks on matters pertaining to their agency. (2) The White House staff man can help a department or agency on internal matters and often does help a department official if he [the department official] knows how to use him wisely: for example, in regard to appointments, promotions, reorganizations, etc. (3) White House staff can be effectively used on interdepartmental problems, as in communicating something from one agency to another. Of course, there are always costs to these various usages, but in my experience the benefits outweigh those costs.

About 40 percent of the former White House staff aides note that even a strong presidency cannot succeed without an executive branch characterized by strong cabinet and departmental leadership. Many of these aides felt that the president and senior staff had underestimated the importance of these factors in making the government work. One aide insisted that letting the domestic cabinet departments become so divorced from the White House was a major mistake: "One way to improve things is to have the president and the cabinet members, particularly in domestic areas, meet at least six or seven times a year and talk in great detail and in highly substantive terms about the major priorities of the administration. You have to have better communication. Basically you have to make the cabinet less insecure." Other aides criticized certain of their colleagues for having usurped operational responsibilities of the regular agencies, adding that if they accomplished anything, these aides enlarged their own importance more often than they expedited programs.

It should be noted that no White House aides and no president in recent times have favored any structural reform of the cabinet. That is, they do not favor radical proposals put forward to create several presidents or to raise the level of the cabinet member to that of a president. In the immediate aftermath of Watergate there were some such suggestions, almost always made by persons who had had little involvement with the presidency. Alexander Hamilton's brief against these notions of a plural executive remains compelling today. He argued that the restraints of public opinion would lose their efficacy if there were several executives rather than one. Whom should the people blame? Which one or which set of executives should be removed from office? Hamilton believed that trust, accountability, and responsibility might be severely impaired with a plural executive. The people, he said (*The Federalist,* No. 70), needed the opportunity of discovering with facility and clearness the misconduct of the responsible official.

The American system is not a parliamentary one, and the cabinet cannot exist as a collegial body in any formal sense. We elect the president, not the cabinet. We do not want a system in which the president is merely the first among equals. The essential question of the role of the cabinet in presidential government is an attitudinal, not a structural, one. A strong and "healthy" cabinet can exist today only because the president wants it that way. Multiple-advocacy systems that would enhance the constructive advice he might get cannot be imposed on a president. A president must find it compatible with his style. Ultimately, operating with a strong cabinet requires a president who is at ease with different and new opinions, who has high confidence in both his own personal and political position and the people he appointed. One thing remains clear: presidents will always have strained relationships with some members in their cabinets. Time and time again this has happened, even under the best of circumstances. It is inevitable.

MAKING THE BEST OF
ADVERSARIAL RELATIONS

Inner-cabinet members may enjoy close ties with the White House, and outer-department heads may have to contend with centrifugal forces that tend to dissipate the counseling relationship. Other implications of this dichotomy, however, may be less immediately obvious. Rather than re-forming the outer cabinet to approximate more closely the inner cabinet, both the White House and the inner cabinet might benefit from relating to each other in some of the ways that characterize the relationship be-tween the White House and the outer cabinet.

The cordial and frequent contact between the White House and Defense, Justice, Treasury, and the secretary of state may actually camou-flage substantive problems that should be contended and issues that should be subject to the clashing of adversary views. The United States policy in Vietnam, the Bay of Pigs episode, a persistently inadequate tax structure, and the too casual concern for rigorous criminal prosecutions exemplified by the Watergate and related scandals are among the recent sorry by-products of the handling of inner-cabinet responsibilities. The inner departments may seem so congenial and professional in comparison with the overtly advocate departments that the White House may accept their judgments too·readily, overlooking potentially divisive issues and neglecting to create an effective system for scrutinizing the substantive and operational aspects of these departments. Important debates may be foreclosed procedurally with reference to inner-cabinet policy choices. If this is so, then many of the more popular and conventional reforms — including much of what President Nixon proposed in his 1970 State of the Union message — misunderstand an important aspect of White House–executive-department relations. Efforts could be made to increase certain kinds of conflicts, critical thinking, and adversary proceedings in order to maintain a strong awareness of the values inherent in alternative policy choices. The tension between a president and his cabinet officers on the one hand are too often construed at the White House as a liability and a hindrance. But, on the contrary, they may create some of the most important of the creative confrontations that should be continuous in a democratic political system.

Presidents probably will not stop delegating the leadership and coordination of domestic-policy matters to White House aides. But White House aides too often mirror a presidential disposition to set up new White House councils or to pass new bills to the neglect of implementation or departmental management responsibilities. By doing so, the aides reinforce presidential leanings — and emotions and whims — rather than serve as an independent counterbalance. Peter Drucker, a management specialist, makes a good point: "The handling of foreign affairs, the economy, and social welfare *are* basic operations of government. Thus the President's counselors have jobs that parallel operating functions and, inevitably, they compete with and tend to undermine these functions. But no matter how he organizes his effort to get ideas, the chief executive will fail if he has a central operating staff. Anyone providing fresh ideas is, almost by definition, critical of the accepted wisdom and will therefore seem obviously disloyal. A central operating staff [in the White House] will always resent and fight him." [39]

Obviously, a president needs some aides to assist him in the White House. But they must, if they are to be helpful to the president, see themselves as part of the larger political system. They must appreciate that the department heads have to serve, both constitutionally and politically, more than one master. The White House aides of the recent past have sometimes refused to accept that cabinet heads quite naturally have a different perspective, different incentives, and different rewards than those influencing a president.

Strength in cabinet members is not an unmixed blessing. Too much independence and too much feuding can paralyze. Overall, however, a weak cabinet member is more of a liability than a strong one. A weak cabinet is also a liability. Aaron Wildavsky once concluded that "the more prominent a President's Cabinet is, the less of a target he becomes." [40] Former Eisenhower and Nixon aide Stephen Hess seems to agree when he argues that "the overblown presidential staff . . . has become counterproductive to the purposes of Presidents. Among the more glaring deficiencies of a White House-centered system is that it increasingly draws no-win problems into the Oval Office; this in turn contributes to undermining public trust in Presidents." [41]

What needs to be continually understood at the White House is that a cabinet member's authority is constantly challenged by powerful legislators, muscular interest groups, and an admixture of personnel and program mandates of a distinctly centrifugal character. If a cabinet member is going to survive and stay a few years, he or she will need to have his or her hand strengthened by the president and the White House. The strength and effectiveness of the presidency depends in no small measure on the quality of departmental leadership, especially on the effectiveness of learning through administrative feedback systems at that level.

"A good cabinet member — one who isn't just filling some political niche — can be a very excellent corrective to the White House 'hothouse' staff who are confined there and are virtually locked up fourteen hours a day. The President needs to hear from his cabinet. The president should occasionally sit down in a leisurely way with his cabinet members and listen and ask that important question: 'What do you think?' " is the way one recent cabinet officer put it. Another 1960s era cabinet member stated, without question, that more cabinet meetings should have been called:

> There are two important things that should be done through the use of the cabinet meetings. First, meetings should be held to inform the cabinet members about major developments or new priorities. Second, the president should occasionally bring some major policy issue before the cabinet and open it up for detailed discussion. He should take advantage of the broad-gauged abilities of these very able men. For example, never once was there any discussion of whether we should send more troops to Vietnam. This type of policy matter was always confined to the national security council group — but they could have benefited from our views and ideas on this type of matter, for we had less personal involvement in the earlier decisions and might have been able to give valuable added perspective or fresh appraisals.[42]

Robert Kennedy wrote his brother in March 1963 that he should pay more attention to using his cabinet:

> The best minds in Government should be utilized in finding solutions to major problems. They should be available in times other than deep crisis and emergencies as is now the case. . . . These men should be sitting down and thinking of some of the problems facing us in a broader context. I think you could get a good deal more out of what is available in Government than you are at the present time.[43]

Regardless of how organization charts are drawn, future presidential use of the cabinet and White House staff probably will give greater weight to the realities of the differentiated roles and activities of the federal departments. The cabinet as a collectivity will move farther toward oblivion with the more complete emergence of (1) a national-security cabinet, (2) an economics directorate, and (3) a domestic-policy cabinet. Each of these will be presided over by some combination of presidential counselors, from the president's staff or from the executive departments. But as this continues to happen, presidents should realize that they also need the advice of some persons who are not necessarily directly concerned with a problem. For "those who are handling a problem, however much they differ, have to establish very early a frame of reference within which they can contain their differences, and that frame of reference then becomes fixed, and those acting within it find it hard to escape." [44]

A redesigned and strengthened outer cabinet might enable the White House staff to abstain more often from the temptation to gather administrative responsibilities to itself. But reorganizational developments will not lessen the need for skillful and decisive executive-branch mediators who, with the full confidence of the president, can preside over thorny and complex claims and counterclaims by competing domestic departments, and who also can know when important elements of a debate are being seriously neglected or misrepresented within cabinet-level negotiations. White House aides need to be chosen with these abilities in mind.

To summarize, the American cabinet has had a strange and anomalous history. It is simultaneously one of the best known and least understood aspects of our governmental system. It has seldom operated as a policymaking body. Few presidents have used it as a collegium. No law or constitutional authority commands a president to consult with a collective cabinet or even to hold cabinet meetings. The job of the department head, especially in modern times, necessarily demands that department heads heed the concerns of Congress, bureaucracies, the Constitution, and various professional and ethical considerations *in addition to* the desires and demands of a president. Even the most carefully chosen cabinet member will occasionally differ, if not clash, with certain presidential wishes.

A president will seldom be wholly satisfied with the loyalty of department heads. Most cabinet members, to be sure, will aspire to a president's intimacy, and many of his inner cabinet will indeed become long-term counselors and friends, but even some of these will often break with him, frequently without realizing how serious their differing perspectives have been. A president, however, must welcome advocacy from his cabinet officers. And although open and frank discussions in cabinet meetings will sometimes limit a president's discretion, a president will generally profit from using the cabinet as a consultative body.

The historical record of the cabinet may be an ambivalent one, but the American cabinet does hold out bright promise for what it could be. Structural changes that must take place are minimal relative to the attitudinal changes that must take place on the part of a president, his staff, and cabinet members. In the end, it is the president who will determine whether that promise will remain unrealized because of ineffectual disuse or be translated into a means for futhering effective and responsible presidential leadership.

NOTES

1. Henry Barret Learned, *The President's Cabinet: Studies in the Origin, Formation and Structure of an American Institution* (Burt Franklin, 1912, reissued in 1972), p. 119. This is a useful study of the origins of the cabinet. The best study of the cabinet in the mid-twentieth century is Richard Fenno, *The President's Cabinet* (Vintage, 1959).

2. Lyndon B. Johnson, quoted in Charles Maguire, oral history (August 19, 1969), Lyndon B. Johnson Presidential Library, Austin, Texas, p. 28.

3. Richard Nixon, *RN: The Memoirs of Richard Nixon* (Grosset & Dunlap, 1978), p. 338.

4. Paradoxically, Democratic presidents in recent years often appoint members of the social and financial establishments — men like Harriman, Dillon, McNamara, Vance, and Clifford — while Republican presidents often appoint either self-made rugged individuals or Ph.D.-carrying college professors. Nixon and Ford, for example, could practically hold a faculty meeting with their cabinet of Professors Shultz, Kissinger, Schlesinger, Dunlop, Moynihan, Burns, Butz, Walker, and university presidents Hardin, Matthews and Levi. This general point is suggested in Stephen Hess, *Organizing the Presidency* (Brookings Institution, 1976), p. 185.

5. Clark M. Clifford, oral history (December 15, 1969), Lyndon B. Johnson Presidential Library, Austin, Texas, tape 6, p. 4.

6. Nixon, *op. cit.*

7. Nelson W. Polsby, "Presidential Cabinet Making: Lessons for the Political System," *Political Science Quarterly*, Spring 1978, pp. 15–16.

8. McGeorge Bundy, *The Strength of Government* (Harvard University Press, 1968), p. 39.

9. Bradley H. Patterson, Jr., *The President's Cabinet: Issues and Questions* (American Society for Public Administration, 1976), pp. 17–18.

10. Quoted in K. Gordon, "Reflections on Spending," in J. D. Montgomery and Arthur Smithies, eds., *Public Policy* (Harvard University Press, 1966), p. 15.

11. Richard M. Nixon, 27 November 1972, *New York Times* 28 November 1972, p. C40.

12. Lyndon B. Johnson, quoted in Bobby Baker, with Larry King, *Wheeling and Dealing* (Norton, 1978), p. 265.

13. Walter J. Hickel, *New York Times,* 7 May 1970, p. C18.

14. Lyndon B. Johnson, quoted in Bobby Baker, with Larry King, *op. cit.,* pp. 265–66. It should be noted that this statement was made some four years after LBJ had left the White House. There is reason to believe Johnson had soured on Clark as much for his postcabinet activities such as his trip to Hanoi in the early 1970s and his strident liberal positions on peace, criminal justice, and so forth. The record seems to indicate that Clark was a reasonably loyal and a very hardworking attorney general during the Johnson presidency. Clark differed with Johnson on some issues, but he almost always loyally carried out the Johnson decisions. Moreover, Clark often won praise for being one of the most persuasive and articulate speakers to defend the Johnson Great Society programs. It is true, however, that Clark was less than effective in selling the Johnson Safe Streets program to an increasingly "law and order" Congress in 1967 and 1968. See Thomas E. Cronin, "The War on Crime and Unsafe Streets, 1960–76," in Allan P. Sindler, ed., *America in the Seventies: Problems, Policies and Politics* (Little, Brown, 1977), pp. 208–60.

15. Harold Gosnell, Harry S. Truman (Greenwood Press, 1980).

16. J. Edward Day, *My Appointed Round: 929 Days as Postmaster General* (Holt, Rinehart and Winston, 1965), p. 97.

17. Jeb Stuart Magruder, *An American Life: One Man's Road to Watergate* (Atheneum, 1974), p. 102.

18. Day, *op. cit.*, pp. 96–98.

19. Theodore C. Sorensen (Transcript of a panel discussion at the Annual Meetings of the American Society for Public Administration, New York City, 22 March 1972), p. 22. Reprinted as "Advising the President: A Panel," *Bureaucrat*, April 1974, p. 33.

20. Nixon, *op. cit.*

21. Elliot Richardson, *The Creative Balance* (Holt, Rinehart and Winston, 1976), p. 74.

22. One Kennedy-Johnson cabinet official told me that President Johnson had an uncanny ability to intimidate the occasional dissenter within his cabinet, especially when the going became rough during the peak of public anguish over involvement in Vietnam. Apparently, or so it seemed to this cabinet member, LBJ let it be known indirectly to several of his cabinet members that should they ever decide to resign in protest and make public their opposition to his war policies, they better well know that the FBI and IRS directors would be on their heels following them right out of office. To this particular cabinet member, it did not really matter whether Johnson actually would have done this — indeed, he felt that Johnson would say this sort of thing only in weaker moments over a drink or two with his closest aides — but the very fact that on occasion he would suggest such reprisal was intimidation enough.

23. Jesse Jones, quoted in Robert J. Sickels, *Presidential Transactions* (Prentice-Hall, 1974), p. 31.

24. Richardson, *op. cit.*, p. 76.

25. Patterson, *op. cit.*, p. 113.

26. Milton S. Eisenhower, *The President Is Calling* (Doubleday, 1974), p. 257.

27. Quoted in Peter Lyon, *Eisenhower: Portrait of the Hero* (Little, Brown, 1974), pp. 503–04.

28. Carter, quoted in Joel Havemann, "The Cabinet Band," *National Journal*, 16 July 1977, p. 1104.

29. See the remarks of Cecil Andrus, Secretary of Interior, in Dom Bonafede, "A Day in the Life of a Cabinet Secretary," *National Journal* 12 May 1979, p. 791. For a series of irreverent short essays on the Carter cabinet meetings, see *Nation*, 30 September 1978.

30. Havemann, *op. cit.*, p. 1106.

31. John Leacacos, *Fires in the In-Basket* (World, 1968), p. 110.

32. Quoted in Richard H. Rovere, "Eisenhower: A Trial Balance," *The Reporter*, 21 April 1955, pp. 19–20.

33. Leonard Silk, *Nixonomics* (Praeger, 1972), p. 81.

34. W. Michael Blumenthal, "Candid Reflections of a Businessman in Washington," *Fortune*, 29 January 1978, p. 31. For the on-the-job views of an earlier Treasury Secretary see Lawrence C. Pierce, *The Politics of Fiscal Policy Formation* (Goodyear, 1971), p. 100.

35. Wilbur Cohen, former secretary of HEW under Lyndon Johnson, quoted in *National Journal*, 16 December 1972, p. 1921.

36. Jesse Jones, quoted in Richard Fenno, "President-Cabinet Relations and a Pattern and a Case Study," *American Political Science Review*, March 1958, p. 394.

37. Walter J. Hickel, *Who Owns America?* (Prentice-Hall, 1971), p. 259. In 1978 White House aide Midge Costanza resigned her job, doubtless under pressure to do so, in large part because she too had tried to play an adversarial role. As she noted in her letter of resignation: "My own approach has been largely one of advocacy. . . . There are those who suggest that I should have simply carried out your policies and not voiced my own opinions and ideas openly. But that was not my style. . . ."

Margaret Midge Costanza, 31 July 1978, *Weekly Compilation of Presidential Documents,* 2 August 1978, p. 1359.

38. Hickel, *op. cit.,* pp. 221–22.

39. Peter Drucker, "How to Make the Presidency Manageable," *Fortune,* November 1924, pp. 148–49.

40. Aaron Wildavsky, "The Past and Future Presidency," *Public Interest,* Fall 1975, p. 73.

41. Hess, *op. cit.,* p. 179.

42. Although this quote came from a personal interview with a 1960s cabinet officer, it has been repeated by several others. See also a similar view in Hubert Humphrey, *The Education of a Public Man: My Life and Politics* (Doubleday, 1976), pp. 317–27, 339.

43. Quoted in Arthur M. Schlesinger, Jr., *Robert F. Kennedy and His Times* (Houghton Mifflin, 1978), p. 624.

44. Henry Fairlie, *The Kennedy Promise* (Doubleday, 1973), p. 167.

CHAPTER 9

PRESIDENTIAL NONCRISIS POLICYMAKING: THE CASE OF A SMALL GREAT SOCIETY PROGRAM

The management of a bureaucracy comprising perhaps thousands of careerists will be, at best, nominal; the agency heads will inevitably outmaneuver a politician-secretary. Presidential orders transmitted through such channels become more mysteriously changed to suit the bureaucracy's preferences. Policies persist from one Administration to another remarkably unchanged. Resistance to change is also reinforced by the alliances between bureaucrats and the appropriate congressmen. Altogether, it requires a most sophisticated and determined President to effect any changes at all.

> Rexford G. Tugwell, "Bringing Presidents to Heel"
> in *The Presidency Reappraised,* Rexford G. Tugwell
> and Thomas E. Cronin, eds. (Praeger, 1974), p. 290.

One thing to realize is that the tests of efficiency and cost-effectiveness, which are the basic standards of business, are in government not the only — and frequently not even the major — criteria.

> W. Michael Blumenthal, former Secretary of the
> Treasury under President Carter, "Candid Reflections of a
> Businessman in Washington," *Fortune,* 29 January 1979, p. 41.

One of the enduring truths of the nation's capital is that bureaucrats *survive.* Agencies don't fold their tents and quietly fade away after their work is done. They find Something New to Do. Invariably, that Something New involves more people with more power and more paperwork — all involving more expenditures.

> Gerald R. Ford, *A Time to Heal: The Autobiography of
> Gerald R. Ford* (Harper & Row: Reader's Digest, 1979), p. 272.

This is the story of a small, well-meant, presidentially endorsed program that failed to do much of what it was supposed to but somehow survived anyway. It is also the story of an embattled program that demonstrated bureaucratic tenacity and resilience in the face of the political forces and political institutions that controlled its fate. It is of particular interest because its small size allows a close examination of what went awry, and the strength and determination of the groups antagonistic to it are representative of those that thwart high hopes in a variety of domestic-policy ventures.

The National Teacher Corps was set up to bring a new breed of teachers to schools in poverty areas. Passed as a section of the Higher Education Act of 1965 (P.L. 89–320, Title V, Part B), the enacting legislation was meant to help lay a part of the foundation of Lyndon Johnson's Great Society. It established a small program to send teams of talented college graduates to study education and to teach under the supervision of specially recruited experienced teachers. The program retained a special place in Johnson's heart, and he retired to Texas in 1969 considering it one of the successes of his administration.

In fact, however, the Teacher Corps never accomplished many of its objectives. Its history is virtually an application of Murphy's Law to politics: almost everything that could go wrong did go wrong. The program was poorly planned, hastily enacted, badly implemented, and inadequately evaluated. Debilitating local resistance, changes in mood, faulty analogies, and unexpected outcomes only dimly foreseen are all part of the story.

THE GENESIS OF
THE TEACHER CORPS

Policy proposals come to the White House in dozens of ways, but presidential commitment to policy "reform" is likely to develop (1) once a problem is widely recognized, (2) when a suggested remedy appears to be a logical extension of previous efforts, (3) when it has incubated for a time among congressional and professional constituencies, and (4) when it can earn political credit for a president.

Each of these elements was present at the time President Johnson embraced the Teacher Corps idea. Johnson and his staff had become aware that each year nearly a million children dropped out of school and that the children of as many as 5 million families in low-income areas were denied high-quality education. According to Johnson, the danger existed that a whole generation of poor children would become unskilled dropouts, unemployed, or delinquent. Everyone was aware, too, that the best teachers generally migrated to wealthy or middle-class communities. A national teacher shortage existed, and this shortage was especially pronounced in poverty-area schools.

Programs to encourage volunteers to serve in poverty areas were certainly not novel. For years, community-conscious university students had maintained small organizations that sent volunteers to settlement houses, centers for the mentally retarded, and Indian reservations. Also, the concept of a federal service corps, in the guise of the Civilian Conservation Corps of the 1930s, had been one of the most popular aspects of the New Deal.

In the early 1960s, in the light of increased attention to domestic poverty, many people suggested that if the nation sent idealistic young people to help the poor abroad, perhaps it should offer the same opportunities for service among poor people at home. President Kennedy proposed a "domestic Peace Corps" in his January 1963 State of the Union address.[1] After Kennedy's death, antipoverty legislation was passed, creating a program (VISTA) that encouraged volunteers to serve one year, working directly with social workers and local community councils. The Teacher Corps was visualized as a channel for similar commitments to educational institutions.

The notion of recruiting experienced teachers to work in hardship posts had been tried in a few places and found to be "successful," notably in Prince Edward County, Virginia, which had experienced a long and bitter struggle over public school desegregation. There, after the county board of supervisors had closed the schools for four years to avoid integrating them, the Kennedy administration took upon itself the task of securing money from foundations, corporations, and others to subsidize Prince Edward County "Free Schools" for the county's blacks (and a handful of whites who elected to come). About a hundred teachers were recruited; they set up ungraded schools where novel teaching techniques were encouraged. The experiment was judged successful, winning favorable attention in the press and among liberal members of Congress.[2]

A year or so later a noteworthy experiment in recruiting and training Peace Corps returnees for urban teaching assignments had begun at Cardozo High School in Washington, D.C. Though small, this program was distinctive: it stressed a need to have young teachers experiment with and develop curriculum materials that would be meaningful to urban youngsters, and it placed teacher training in the local public school rather than at the university school of education. It caught the attention of several members of Congress, one of whom, Senator Gaylord Nelson, was sufficiently impressed that he proposed an amendment to the Elementary and Secondary Education bill of 1965 modeled almost entirely on the Cardozo project.

Intellectual support also had been building for something like the Teacher Corps as several individuals tried their hand at prescribing remedies for the ills of the newly rediscovered "other America." An important contribution to this discussion was an article by John Kenneth Galbraith that appeared in *Harper's* in March 1964. Galbraith urged President Johnson to designate one hundred of the poorest urban and rural poverty areas as eligible for special federal funds to upgrade educational, recreational, and transportation facilities. One key to his detailed plan was the creation of an elite body of teachers "ready to serve in the most remote areas, tough enough and well-trained enough to take on the worst slums, proud to go to Harlan County or to Harlem" — a Green Beret Teacher Corps.[3]

The idea of a Teacher Corps was also politically attractive. Johnson had seen at firsthand the popularity of Roosevelt's Civilian Conservation Corps and National Youth Administration, and he was aware of the substantial political credit gained by President Kennedy for establishing the Peace Corps. He knew too that a National Teacher Corps was another way to show that he cared deeply about poor people. He liked the image of himself as a supporter of the underdog. As a former teacher and principal, the most illustrious graduate of San Marcos State Teachers College found the notion of a Teacher Corps especially appealing. Finally, political competitiveness may have encouraged him to embrace the proposal, since credit for the Teacher Corps idea would otherwise largely have accrued to a Kennedy brother.

The precise motives of Johnson were always hard to pinpoint, for as the late White House wire service reporter Merriman Smith pointed out, in Johnson's case "hypnosis, mind reading and truth serum probably could not have separated political motive from deep concern."[4] But all the elements necessary for presidential commitment to a new policy were present when Johnson decided to champion the Teacher Corps, even if in themselves they do not account for his decision: a problem existed; the federal government was already involved in similar activity; members of Congress, intellectuals, and interest groups had brought the idea to the attention of the White House; it was a variation of the already popular Peace Corps; it was politically feasible; and, finally, it would promote the president's proclaimed mission of ending poverty.

THE CONGRESSIONAL AND
PRESIDENTIAL INITIATIVES

When political scientists call the president America's "chief legislator," they imply that he can virtually write, shape, and obtain passage for legislation in which he is especially interested. But even when, as with the Teacher Corps, the president is generally successful in "putting a law on the books," members of Congress and various lobbies often exert considerable influence in shaping and altering the character of a federal program, though the program continues to be labeled "the president's."

Moreover, the president himself seldom has time for detailed involvement in the formulation of domestic policy plans and usually less time for monitoring subsequent implementation and evaluation. This circumstance is seldom the presidential preference. Rather, it is in large part due to a necessary presidential preoccupation with national security and economic policy. Concern about the crises of the moment constantly distracts the White House from critical stages of program drafting and administration. The amount of presidential-level attention that policies receive in the drafting stage plays an important role in determining their success, but presidents and their White House aides are often unaware or unappreciative of significant choices made at this level.

In the case of the Teacher Corps, the program idea was originally the brainchild of several senators, notably Edward Kennedy and Gaylord Nelson. William Spring, an aide to Senator Nelson, was impressed with the Galbraith article of 1964 and moved by what he observed at the Cardozo urban teacher training project. He was also on the lookout for meritorious legislation that his senator could sponsor. He would later recall in an interview: "Another thing that go us interested in this program was that Senator Nelson had just transferred from another Senate committee and was joining the Senate Labor and Public Welfare Committee. We, his staff aides, felt that he needed an issue to get his feet wet, an issue that would let him get deeply involved in his committee and show his interest in the committee's sphere of interest." [5] Spring took it upon himself to "touch base" with the U.S. Office of Education in HEW, with the major educational lobbies, with the people who ran Cardozo-style experiments around the country, and with a variety of education deans and school officials. With Office of Education (USOE) assistance, Spring drafted a bill for Senator Nelson.

Educational lobbies and USOE were unenthusiastic. They worried about federal control of local educational efforts and expressed concern about duplication of efforts.

At the White House, President Johnson, having completed much of the unfinished legislative agenda he had inherited from his predecessor, was impatiently setting out an even more ambitious agenda of his own. He was hungry for new ideas. As one of his aides put it, "Johnson was like a bottomless barrel; it seemed to me that we had to keep pouring ideas and proposals into him." The Great Society messages of 1965 illustrated the president's mood. Johnson had pledged to assemble the best thought and the broadest knowledge "from all over the world" to find the answers to the problems of urban decay, poverty, and inadequate housing. He had specifically singled out the classrooms of America as one of the chief sites on which the Great Society must be built.[6]

By 1965 Johnson had presided over passage of both the Economic Opportunity Act (1964) and the landmark Elementary and Secondary Education Act (1965). He was understandably delighted at his growing reputation as "the education president" but wanted further recognition that he was doing more for education and more for poor people than any other president. So Johnson now decided to follow up his earlier achievements by making sure that good teachers would be available to use these new monies. The assumption was that effective teachers were a critical part of education, hence the need for a program that would get especially able teachers to move into hardship posts.

The president's point man for education legislation was Douglass Cater, a veteran Washington reporter whom he had recruited from a research center at Wesleyan University. It became Cater's responsibility to work on educational policy matters with the major lobbies, appropriate members of Congress, and department officials. His job was to piece together ideas and proposals that came to his office, assess their merit, and bring the best to the president's attention.

Cater read Galbraith's article. Soon thereafter he was visited by staff aides to Senators Wayne Morse, Kennedy, and Nelson, all of whom were enthusiastically supporting Teacher Corps bills of one kind or another. Cater was also aware of hearings then taking place in the Senate that focused on these various ideas. About this time he was asked to draft the president's forthcoming address to the National Education Association, and Cater recalls that he decided to insert the call for a National Teacher Corps in an early version. This was one way of again bringing it to the president's attention and, if approved by him, of generating public support. Johnson readily approved.

Thus, on July 2, 1965, Johnson surprised an audience of 7,000 educators with this announcement:

> In the next few days I will propose a National Teacher Corps to enlist thousands of dedicated teachers to work alongside local teachers in city slums and in areas of rural poverty where they can really serve their Nation. They will be young people, preparing for teaching careers. They will be experienced teachers willing to give a year to the places in their country that need them most. They can bring the best in our Nation to the help of the poorest of our children.[7]

Nothing that could legitimately be called "research" had been done on the idea — at least not at the White House. Nor had the idea been subject to systematic evaluation at the staff level or in the Bureau of the Budget. The process was far more casual. It was assumed that the Teacher Corps would be a relatively modest undertaking. No new organization or new federal agency was envisaged. Indeed, it was assumed that it was no more than a variation on existing teacher fellowship programs, based on the Peace Corps model and with the purpose of injecting a sense of mission and idealism into teaching. Questions such as who would pay for it, how much it might cost during the next few years, and what its criteria of success or failure would be were given little consideration.

It may surprise some readers to discover that a president will announce new programs or that staff assistants to a president will even suggest them to him without careful scrutiny. But in politics to be deliberate is often to be indecisive. Reaching out for "new ideas" and adopting "innovations" is common practice for politicians, especially Democrats, who are constantly being asked: How are you going to solve this problem? What have you done for us lately? Why aren't you trying harder to improve things? At the time, Johnson enjoyed a working majority in Congress, and he wanted to make use of this luxury while it lasted. And Johnson personally had a voracious appetite for new legislative proposals. As one Johnson aide said, "Basically, our philosophy was to get things started. The philosophy that Lyndon Johnson had was to keep a full legislative plate before the Congress."

THE ABSENCE OF CLEAR GOALS

From the beginning the Teacher Corps program was a hybrid. Its sponsors in Congress had diverse models in mind. Little thought was given to precise objectives by the president or his staff. This was left to the subgovernment of Senate aides, USOE staff, and educational organization representatives. The Office of Education had not advocated the new program and had in fact initially questioned its merit. The resulting legislation was a compromise, a quick response to an impatient White House request for a program. The charter was drafted, modified, and eventually enacted, but Congress left the details of implementation and evaluation exceedingly vague.

The fundamental dilemma as to whether the Teacher Corps was professional or voluntary seems never to have been resolved by the White House or Congress. In the Galbraith-Edward Kennedy view the need was for experienced and highly qualified teachers who would be sent to poverty-area schools and be given higher pay, some variation of "combat pay," for going to these hardship posts. But Senator Gaylord Nelson, employing the Peace Corps analogy, adopted the philosophy that Teacher Corps personnel were really engaged in volunteer service, motivated by idealism and altruism, dedicated to learning how to teach and to "reforming" education at the same time.

Part of the reason that things were left so vague was an overeagerness to justify the program's existence before the jury of suspicious congressional committees and to capture support from added constituencies. As one politically attentive aide at the Teacher Corps recalled, "We used every argument we could when we were selling the Teacher Corps idea because we had to in order to win support. There was no other way you could do it. You had to use every bit of evidence you could, however valid or invalid, so we sold it as a manpower program to some people, and just about everything else that was related, and along the way we certainly were guilty of overpromising."

Later, as criticism mounted from Congress, educational lobbies, and local school officials, the Teacher Corps searched for additional tasks, symbols, and selling points. With the program under growing pressure to justify itself in the absence of a clear legislative intent, the corps' charter continuously expanded. A bright idea would be brought to the director's attention, would gain almost immediate acceptance, and would be hastily incorporated into the guidelines. A communication overload developed between the Washington "front office" and the local programs across the country. Here is a short list of some of the targets specified at one time or another:

to attract highly motivated people to the teaching profession
to improve the quality of education for poor children
to improve the quality of teacher training models
to help remedy the nation's teacher shortage
to reform local schools by introducing community service activities
to reform the curriculum in schools that teach poor children
to provide an opportunity for altruistic service
to encourage coordinated efforts among school, community, and university
to provide jobs for returning veterans
to improve the quality of education on Indian reservations, behind the
    walls of juvenile correction institutions, and in state prison systems
to retrain experienced educational personnel serving in local educational
    agencies

By 1970, an outside management consulting firm discovered seven broad Teacher Corps objectives embodied in the enabling legislation and some forty-five explicit goals embraced by the Washington office. Most of these were worthy goals, but a national program can plainly become so preoccupied with public-relations efforts to enhance its prestige that it neglects the less glamorous work that makes up its true purpose.

CONCEPTUAL INADEQUACIES
OF THE PROGRAM

A lack of precise objectives was not the only problem resulting from the hasty drafting of the Teacher Corps proposal. The lack of forethought behind the plan was also reflected in some serious conceptual weaknesses.

The analogy to the Peace Corps upon which the plan was based was faulty, some of the program's purposes were questionable, and its multiple goals were in partial conflict with one another.

Because the pressure for immediate action and a show of results in political areas is intense, it is often tempting to build programs by analogy, to use what appears to work in one area to generate offspring in another. As its name suggests, the immediate parent of the Teacher Corps was the Peace Corps, which had its beginning about four years earlier. The Peace Corps analogy transferred to the Teacher Corps a burden of exaggerated hope, which subsequent events were to modify for both programs, and it applied the Peace Corps model of short-haul voluntarism to a teacher-training program that hoped in contrast to produce dedicated professionals with a long-haul commitment to education of the disadvantaged. Role ambiguity often resulted: Was the Teacher Corpsman a volunteer in training or a teacher in service? But in another way, the analogy was unhappily quite appropriate: the disenchantment of host countries with Peace Corps volunteers had a close analogue in the struggle the Teacher Corps had to confront over the local autonomy of host schools and schools of education.

It would be unfair to criticize too harshly the planners who adapted the Peace Corps model for wholesale application to the quite different area of education. To do so is to forget the whole spirit of soaring enthusiasm that surrounded the beginnings of the Peace Corps, and some of the baneful results of that program could not have been foreseen. In any case, the purpose here is not so much to criticize as it is to outline the limitations that seem to be inherent in the exercise of presidential initiative.

Forecasts of a national teacher shortage also figured importantly in the case for a Teacher Corps, which was seen as one answer to the shortage. It was emphasized by the bill's sponsors that by 1965 there was an annual shortage of 118,000 teachers. In recommending to President Johnson that the Teacher Corps be tripled in size, HEW Secretary John W. Gardner in late 1966 argued that the Teacher Corps was an "ideal device" to help remedy the shortage of qualified teachers. However, two years later that shortage had become a decided surplus. Warnings that this would occur had been sounded earlier, but few officials had listened. The initial tactic of the directors of the Teacher Corps was to respond that there was no surplus of qualified teachers who knew how to work with children who have special needs in poverty areas. However, by 1973 the Teacher Corps did begin adapting to the reality of a teacher surplus by stressing that the corps would become a teacher retraining rather than teacher recruitment program (see table 9.1.).

Another assumption that influenced the Teacher Corps held that it was important to cut the high school dropout rate, which averaged about nine hundred thousand students yearly in the 1960s. Both the Kennedy and

TABLE 9.1 CORPS MEMBER DATA

Cycle	Year	No. of Interns Started	Teachers in Retraining	Ratio Interns:Teachers
1	1966	1,279	213	6:1
2	1967	930	155	6:1
3	1968	1,029	171	6:1
4	1969	1,330	222	6:1
5	1970	1,223	204	6:1
6	1971	1,385	231	6:1
7	1972	1,534	272	5.6:1
8	1973	1,358	951	1.4:1
9	1974	735	1,873	1:25
10 *	1975	220	3,770	1:17

Source: Teacher Corps, Department of Health, Education and Welfare.
   * Estimate

Johnson administrations strongly endorsed "stay in school" campaigns, and the Teacher Corps was viewed as another effort in this direction. Yet some studies show little evidence that dropouts suffer financially, emotionally, or intellectually by quitting school before graduation. Usually, their problems were as great *before* dropping out of school. Thus, it is open to question whether merely preventing students from dropping out was a valid goal.[8]

THE PROGRAM'S LOCATION AND ITS CONSEQUENCES

On occasion, a major presidential priority is given over to a new agency designed specifically to bypass existing bureaucracies. The space program was located in NASA rather than in the Air Force because it was feared that the Air Force might view the space race and the goal of getting a man on the moon as secondary to its raison d'être. No such decision was even considered with the Teacher Corps, partly no doubt because the president had already set up several new agencies (HUD, OEO, and DOT, which he was then pressing for), and partly because the Teacher Corps was viewed at the White House as complementary rather than competitive with other U.S. Office of Education responsibilities.

As noted, certain USOE veterans were skeptical about the idea of a Teacher Corps. Some believed that existing grant programs already permitted and encouraged local authorities to develop improved teacher-training programs. It was feared that a Teacher Corps might be viewed as an indictment of existing practices; many within USOE had come from institutions in the field and had helped organize and run those "existing practices." Others were wary of the political consequences of sending reform-minded young people to conventional school systems in areas represented in Washington by ever-attentive members of Congress. But even though many in the USOE opposed the Teacher Corps proposal, the office backed the president. It was hardly about to resist a president who was then dominating the national legislative process.

Educational and teacher-college lobbies urged that the corps be an Office of Education program, because they wanted to make sure they would have some control over the new venture. Once the program was lodged in the office, business-as-usual naturally prevailed, and the educational interest groups were dutifully consulted and "taken into account." The United States commissioner of education delegated Teacher Corps staff work to career bureaucrats in the USOE, who, not surprisingly, enjoyed especially close ties with the nation's schools of education. These career staff viewed themselves as educational professionals and came to this new task with the previous experience of running and staffing NDEA (National Defense Education Act) teacher fellowship and teacher-training institute programs, always, of course, in close collaboration with the schools of education.

Supporters of the Teacher Corps based many of their hopes on the belief that what was wrong with education and schools of education could be overcome by an infusion of talented liberal arts graduates with a minimum of traditional teacher training. The emphasis would be on learning and experimentation on location in poverty-area schools. However, any hope that the Teacher Corps could bypass or otherwise jolt the established schools of education was thwarted by the final legislation and by these early planning or consultation strategies. The whole approach amounted to a vote of confidence in schools of education. The legislation was patterned after existing programs and stated that "the Commissioner is authorized to . . . enter into arrangements with local educational agencies, after consultation in appropriate cases with State educational agencies and institutions of higher education. . . ." The teaching teams would be afforded time by the local educational agency "for a teacher-intern training program ' to be carried out in cooperation "with an institution of higher education." USOE officials, with a business-as-usual approach, encouraged the schools of education to make out applications and to organize local Teacher Corps programs much as they were accustomed to doing with other programs.

Most schools of education have long been in the business of preparing teachers and, to put it mildly, view themselves as the experts in the business. To them, the Teacher Corps was just a new program promising extra federal money and a chance to try "innovations," which often meant a slight shift of emphasis toward black history or urban sociology. As one observer of this early stage of implementation described it, "Office of Education officials wanted to work only with schools of education and they were very conscious of not wanting to hurt any of their friends in the education groups. The flaw was their reliance and hope that schools of education would use this money differently than they were using other funds coming from the same source. It was just another case of good money following bad money." A few years later, even the director of the Teacher Corps would conclude that he had not realized how resistant to change the schools of education would be: "Schools of education were of necessity the main people we dealt with, our contracts and contacts were with them and this turned out to be a bad decision. I didn't realize until after a couple of years how difficult they are to work with . . . unless you know that the whole school of education is going to support the program and is supportive of change and innovation, it   probably is best to stay out and save the federal money."

ENACTMENT

The Teacher Corps legislation moved briskly through Congress. It was enacted a mere eighteen weeks after President Johnson called for its passage. Johnson succeeded in winning quick passage for the Teacher Corps because he was enjoying an unusually friendly Congress, owing in large measure to the landslide of 1964 that brought dozens of new liberals to the House. Most of the educational lobbies felt obliged to go along with the president because he had so recently done so much for education. In addition, the Teacher Corps amendment was tagged onto the Higher Education legislation, soon to pass. The Teacher Corps itself was not subject to much discussion, legislative debate, or hearings. Indeed, several members of the House felt the bill was being brought up so quickly that they did not have a chance to deliberate, and that it was just another example of President Johnson's bulldozing legislative tactics.

As enacted, the purpose of the Teacher Corps was to strengthen the educational opportunities available to children in areas having concentrations of low-income families and to encourage colleges and universities to broaden their programs of teacher preparation. To do this, the Teacher Corps was mandated to attract and train inexperienced teacher-interns who were available for teaching and in-service training in teams led by an experienced teacher. School systems and universities were asked first to decide on their training plans in this area and then how the Teacher Corps could help them get from where they were to where they wanted to go. In common with countless other federal programs, they had to develop a program proposal with their plans, needs, and budgets. Ideally, members of the community, students, and diverse educators in the community would participate in the drawing up of the plans. In practice, most plans were devised by a few faculty members at schools of education in cooperation with some local school principals or a nearby school superintendent.

The plans had to be approved by the appropriate state educational agency (a perfunctory obstacle) and then submitted to the Teacher Corps, where a panel of educational consultants evaluated the proposals and made recommendations for funding of those proposals that showed the greatest promise. Most proposals were for at least a two-year period. A major objective emphasized at all stages of the program was the goal of attracting persons who would be superb in working with disadvantaged young students but who had not previously considered teaching as a career.

INITIAL IMPLEMENTATION AND THE OFFICE OF EDUCATION

The location of the Teacher Corps in USOE and the selection of its leaders explain part of the problems it was to experience in its implementation. The White House and Congress virtually forced the program on USOE. Yet it was left to the office to breathe life into the general intentions outlined by the political authorities. As it turned out, however, the office was not well endowed with special knowledge about teaching low-income students. USOE was accustomed to administering federal grant-in-aid or loan programs; few if any of these had explicit objectives that might alter the way local authorities operated. To date, the major function of the Office of Education had been to enlarge the size of the educational economic pie rather than to impose "change" programs on localities. But the Teacher Corps was different; it was intended to prod and stimulate, to create a new model. During the initial planning for the program, Office of Education officials sought counsel from outside professionals, calling several conferences with specialists from schools of education and from a few state and local systems that had shown special interest in the preparation of teachers for low-income students. These advisers opposed the idea contained in the initiating legislation of recruiting well-trained, experienced public-school teachers from one part of the country and sending them to poor school districts elsewhere. The idea of "combat pay," proposed by Galbraith and others, was rejected because teacher unions would be opposed to income disparities. The general concept of recruiting an elite corps of experienced teachers was considered problematic. How would a school system protect itself from troublemakers? Would Teacher Corps units be used to integrate southern school faculties? What about seniority? What about local control over schools? The concept of bringing in outsiders was seen as radical, upsetting, and politically unacceptable. In this way, the problems of professionalism and localism became issues even before the Teacher Corps came off the drafting boards.

Funding also proved to be an important problem. Money was appropriated only a few weeks before the program's field operations began with the training of Teacher Corps interns. Because of late and uncertain funding, the Teacher Corps had to be organized in less than two months. In this time it solicited, reviewed, and approved over forty contracts with universities and somehow selected and recruited more than twelve hundred college graduates. The administrative imperative was to get the program running, get the money to the field, and worry later about spelling out clear objectives or providing for evaluation procedures. It was perhaps an act of faith that highly motivated new people and new federal money properly mixed would somehow liberate teacher training from traditional practices.

Attracting leadership also proved difficult. The Teacher Corps went without a director for nearly a year after the legislation was passed. Then its first director, Richard A. Graham, came to the Teacher Corps as an outsider to the field. Trained as an engineer, he had previously been a public-relations specialist and an overseas country director for the Peace Corps. He had not been a teacher, held no degrees in education, and had not worked within a university. But he did have commitment and energy. Modeling himself after the Peace Corps' Sargent Shriver, he waged a tireless campaign to sell the Teacher Corps to Congress and to the public. He was to find, however, that the most difficult selling job was convincing his own associates and superiors within the USOE.

Much as Shriver had sought to differentiate Peace Corps from State Department and overseas AID personnel, so the Teacher Corps now tried to differentiate itself from the traditional USOE. Several "noneducators" were recruited to staff the Washington office. Some had been active in the Peace Corps, others enjoyed political ties to the Congress. Administrative headaches plagued them from the start. Because initial funding was late, the Washington office was not able to participate systematically in candidate selection, and many mistakes were made. Then, too, in the first year an old-boy network was at work in which seasoned USOE veterans, temporarily assigned to the Teacher Corps, alerted their friends at the schools of education that here was another federal contract they could get in line for. Late congressional funding also made it impossible for the Washington office to pay the recently recruited Teacher Corpsmen during the first several weeks of the 1966 school year, prompting an unusually high dropout rate in the first months of the program. Some 51 percent of entering Teacher Corps interns and 50 percent of the experienced teachers, or Teacher Corps team leaders, quit.

The director of the Teacher Corps resented being submerged within a bureau within an agency within a department. The program was losing its identity and, in the minds of its loyal cadre of leaders, its integrity. Major skirmishes were waged over stationery and secretarial allotments.

Teacher Corps director Graham persisted in seeking expanded legislative and executive branch commitments. He spent countless days on Capitol Hill in pursuit of votes. At the same time Graham sought out every chance to convince his own commissioner of the merits of expanding and granting greater independence to the Teacher Corps. He campaigned publicly for more status for the Teacher Corps, eventually openly supporting efforts to secede it from the USOE.

Thus in the early years the Teacher Corps staff consisted largely of two groups: the USOE old guard, moderately resistant to innovation, adept at foot-dragging, attentive to the wishes of the educational lobbies, and the young, enthusiastic, and conspicuously inexperienced new people trying to replicate the Peace Corps. The sometimes unseemly struggle between old and new people, often between those with and without education school doctorates, created image problems and made staff recruitment more difficult.

Meanwhile, what was the White House doing while one of the president's pet programs hit these snags? It did very little, if it was aware of them at all. Although the president is nominally chief administrator of the government, it is extremely difficult for an activist president to follow the operations of individual programs, as the case of the Teacher Corps illustrates. One of Johnson's aides says, "We just didn't monitor much. The White House staff can't really go out and look at programs, and even when we do we probably don't get accurate evidence. You really have to go out with a team of specialists and stay for awhile, look over the books, and get involved. And that was impossible. It might be possible to have some spot checks into trouble situations with troubleshooters but we just didn't have very much time for that either."

CONFLICT WITH LOCAL EDUCATORS

The Johnson White House assumed too readily that the Teacher Corps would be welcomed by local communities, schools of education, and local schoolmen, as other nations had welcomed the Peace Corps. But from the beginning there were critics. The name "National Teacher Corps" was changed after a year or so to "Teacher Corps," to minimize or at least try to mute the role of Washington. Several prestigious schools of education said they would work with the Teacher Corps only if they could design and run their own programs. Others were miffed if not explicitly insulted by the premise that existing programs were not accomplishing what was needed.

Perhaps the greatest shock for the Teacher Corps was its confrontation with the personnel of participating schools. Teacher Corpsmen were young, and they were mainly from liberal arts schools. They believed schools of education and most teachers had failed students in low-income areas and that "it was time for a change." Teachers and principals in most of the public schools where they served had graduated from local teachers colleges, majoring in education rather than in liberal arts. They were generally more cautious, more satisfied with the way their schools served the community. More important, they controlled the schools, so conflict was almost inevitable.

Local school systems generally favored the Teacher Corps notion in the abstract, but they often discovered that having outsiders in their midst, with different values and a decidedly youthful impulse to change the existing order (or at least complain about it) was considerably more than they had bargained for. Invariably, the Teacher Corps members worked with each other and became separated from regular teachers. Many interns, contrary to "professional" norms, identified with and befriended their students. More often than not, the Teacher Corpsmen were frustrated by the lack of support from regular teachers and blamed them for the problems of the disadvantaged. It became a vicious cycle: interns implying that the older teachers were to blame and urging sweeping reforms; older teachers saying the Teacher Corps people were troublemakers and naive about education.

A few years after the program had been in operation a visitor to Teacher Corps schools was as likely to hear deep-seated resentment as well-deserved praise. As a superintendent in southern Illinois who had worked with at least a score of Teacher Corps interns put it, "They were sloppy and offensive. There were several draft dodgers in the group. I don't think they were really interested in teaching, and they certainly were not disciplined. You see, they were too different, they really weren't our kind of people. I'd have to say, honestly, that they were really, when it comes right down to it, a bunch of *heathens*." No one in the planning stages of the Teacher Corps had anticipated this clash in values and life-styles, though some of them might have been headed off by better program design or pilot-project testing. Incentives might have been developed to make older teachers less resentful and jealous, and to make Teacher Corpsmen more understanding of their beliefs and ways of doing things. Little or nothing of this sort was devised ahead of time, and neglect of such details came back to haunt the Teacher Corps. Local principals complained to Washington, to the participating school of education, and sometimes to their congressman that they wanted more control over selection and appointment of Teacher Corps personnel. Schools of education complained of too much red tape in the application process and of too many delays in funding or guidance from Washington.

But the real taming of the Teacher Corps reform derived from the way in which local schoolmen used the federal program funds to further their own interests. There was nothing exactly devious about this practice.

In the first place, the guidelines of the program called for local control. Local schools of education, the very institutions that were to be the object of Teacher Corps reforms, were given substantial discretion for recruiting Teacher Corps members, designing curriculum, and organizing highly decentralized operations. Despite the burst of presidential level publicity about reform and innovation that preceded the implementation of the Teacher Corps, local school principals and local schools of education believed that the funds were available in order for them to do better at the job they were already doing.

THE WASHINGTON BATTLES
OVER CONTROL AND FUNDING

At the same time that the Corps was sinking into the quagmire of ill-defined objectives and implementation difficulties, with next to no White House attention, presidential involvement with the program continued — confined, however, to publicity and legislative persuasion. Johnson often spontaneously praised the Teacher Corps as a "symbol of new hope for America's poor children." [9] He also made personal appeals to Congress for money to assure that the Teacher Corps got off the drawing boards and into the classrooms. In 1967 the White House obtained barely enough funding to keep the Teacher Corps alive.

At about the same time, local school superintendents demanded the right to select local team leaders and have more of a say in screening prospective team members for their system. This was an obvious attempt to gain control over the program and to ensure that the "new people" were compatible with the existing order. Washington officials balked at first but then consented, as the educational lobbies and conservative members of Congress argued the merits of more local control. Eventually USOE aides reasoned that this concession was necessary for program survival and even rationalized that if the local system felt too threatened and lacked "change-oriented people" to start with, it was highly unlikely that the Teacher Corps could take root anyway.

The Teacher Corps experienced its greatest congressional difficulties in 1967. Easy and quick passage of the 1965 bill did not imply easy appropriations. On the contrary, precisely because many in Congress resented the manner in which it had been rushed by them initially, they were ready to exact retribution. Democratic Representative Edith Green of Oregon, together with several House Republicans, offered various amendments designed to increase local control. One journalist summed up the Teacher Corps' growing congressional problems this way: "The Teacher Corps has few jobs and little money for congressmen to disperse. It questions the value and relevancy of current practices in teacher training. It illuminates the failure of public schools to reach and elevate large numbers of disad-vantaged children. No wonder it's under attack." [10]

The most influential critic of the Teacher Corps was Congresswoman Green, a former public-school teacher and staff member for the Oregon Education Association. She was known as persistent, stubborn, knowledge-able, and decidedly partial to local and state school officials. She felt that the regular students at teachers colleges who were earning their own way or perhaps borrowing under NDEA might be just as dedicated to teaching as Teacher Corpsmen. She insisted that the special attention and subsidies to Teacher Corps members would encourage a form of elitism and divide the teaching ranks.[11]

> I am suggesting that I don't think this [the Teacher Corps] necessarily goes to the heart of the problem. I don't think we have made enough of a study of the slum school to know how we can attract and retain teachers there. Maybe it is going to be by a big salary increment. Maybe it is going to be through means of compensatory education . . . , with very small classes. There are a lot of alternatives that should be explored. I think to say that the Teacher Corps is the answer is perhaps a super-ficial answer.[12]

The White House cautioned that Green should not be allowed to get too upset, that compromise over jurisdictional (local versus federal control) matters could be lived with, although USOE officials should not have to accept substantive compromises that would materially damage the pro-gram. But jurisdictional compromises turned out to involve substance.

Teacher Corps officials took a conciliatory approach to nearly any member of the Congress who had complaints. Organizational survival de-pended on it, or so it seemed to them. Consequently, one former Teacher Corps aide reports, "Our first priority was to put programs in our Senate and House Appropriations Committee members' districts. Second, we tried to put programs in the districts of members of Congress serving on our authorization committees, and last, we tried to have the programs spread around the fifty states." In this way, "we hoped the program would become a salesman for itself and thereby win congressmen [in whose districts pro-grams were operating] over to our side."

Though the Washington office was successful in locating programs in appropriate congressional districts, this priority had the effect of inhibiting a concentration of funds in any one locality or in a limited number of universities. This is a common problem for new federal programs. But a program that has its funds thinly scattered around thirty states when its initial funding is less than $20 million often has difficulty attracting talented local leadership or the commitment of local political elites. The question that arises is how can the federal government initiate pilot proj-ects in order to test new types of programs without being obliged to conduct them simultaneously in every state and community?

Despite the careful selling of Teacher Corps programs and intensive lobbying on their behalf, by late 1967 Edith Green and her allies in Congress had been successful in changing the character of the National Teacher Corps. Some of these changes were manifest in amendments to the Teacher Corps legislation in 1967. Others were brought about by private consultations with HEW officials, committee reports, or merely the volume of congressional attention and criticism aimed at the program. The net effect was that the Teacher Corps was no longer a national program; it became a series of local programs, locally controlled. Local schools and local Teacher Corps teams chose teaching approaches and curriculum emphases at their own discretion. This satisfied most educational lobbies and school people and made it more likely that local principals would select trusted friends within their own school to serve as Teacher Corps team leaders, ensuring that however idealistic or even radical the Teacher Corps interns might be, the program would be closely monitored and controlled by local hierarchies.

By 1968 most HEW officials were frustrated at the amount of time required to defend the Teacher Corps. Said one, "I have worked with at least one hundred pieces of legislation that have been made into law. The most difficult of those hundred has been the Teacher Corps — absolutely without question. . . ."

THE EXECUTIVE AND CONGRESS LOSE INTEREST

As the Johnson administration moved into its lame-duck phase and as the Nixon presidency took hold, the life of the Teacher Corps became very much a congressional matter. Congressional "angels" of the Teacher Corps, like Senators Nelson and Edward Kennedy and Democratic Congressman John Brademas of Indiana, were sought out continuously by Teacher Corps officials who were trying to extend the life of the program, enlarge its funding, and liberate it from the interior of the USOE labyrinth.

Until fiscal 1972 the program's funding gradually increased, rising from $11.3 million in fiscal 1967 to $37.4 million, although it remained well below authorized levels. After 1972, its appropriation was fixed at $37.5 million annually (see table 9.2).

By 1971, when the 1972 budget was drawn up, the Nixon administration had indicated little interest in this Democratic program. Teacher Corps officials had attempted to gain endorsement of the program from the Nixon White House but gained neither access nor attention. Said a former Teacher Corps senior aide, "Not only don't they know about the Teacher Corps, they don't care about us." The director was reassigned in early 1971, and for over a year the Teacher Corps was again allowed to drift.

Yet the program continued. Late in the first Nixon administration it

TABLE 9.2 TEACHER CORPS:
AUTHORIZATIONS AND APPROPRIATIONS
FY 1966–FY 1976 (IN MILLIONS)

Fiscal Year	Authorized	Appropriated
1966	$ 36.1	$ 9.5
1967	64.7	11.3
1968	33.0	13.5
1969	36.1	20.9
1970	80.0	21.7
1971	100.0	30.8
1972	100.0	37.4
1973	37.5	37.5
1974	37.5	37.5
1975	37.5	37.5
1976	37.5	37.5

Source: "Teacher Corps Past or Prologue?" Report by the National Advisory Committee on Education Professions Development (Washington, D.C., July 1975); and U.S. Budget, Fiscal Year 1977.

won a measure of bureaucratic independence and was transferred from its home bureau to the office of the commissioner of education. In 1973–74, it ran 94 projects in 158 school districts and 93 institutions of higher education. And later in the 1970s it became primarily a means to support demonstration projects for retraining educational personnel in poverty-area schools. The Teacher Corps became locked in limbo: its supporters couldn't make it grow, its detractors couldn't kill it.

RESISTANCE TO EVALUATION

During its lengthy fight for survival, the Teacher Corps tried to minimize evaluations of its operations. Aides acknowledged that during its early years the program hierarchy was defensive toward researchers and evaluations. "The director would always dispute their findings and say that on the contrary the program results were really great. He was an optimist and disregarded critical evaluations of any type." Since the program was doing rather poorly by many objective yardsticks, the corps' reluctance to undergo vigorous examination was understandable.

The only sort of evaluation that the program's directors would accept was a rose-tinted one. One such evaluation attempt came in the form of a "Special Report on the Teacher Corps" issued in 1967 from the presidentially appointed National Advisory Council on the Education of Disadvantaged Children. As is frequently the practice of such councils, this analysis was exclusively the work of a few staff in collaboration with a few hired consultants. The report was superficial. Prepared for White House transmission to Congress during debate over future funding for the Teacher Corps, the report glossed over the problems facing the agency and emphasized only the enthusiastic support enjoyed by some local programs. It contained no data, many half-truths, and a few completely inaccurate statements.

In-house capabilities for research and evaluation at the Teacher Corps were always puny. The Teacher Corps was defensive about this but claimed that inadequacy of funds, time pressure, and the practical necessity of generating publicity and accentuating "successes" made it impossible to undertake evaluation. However, evaluation aides in Teacher Corps staff positions were underused, bypassed, and soon disillusioned. Moreover, a presidentially appointed advisory council on the Teacher Corps was similarly disregarded, save as a potential lobbying ally. A prominent state school official who served on this council in the late 1960s summed up its role in this way: "[This] advisory council I serve on is more window dressing than actual service — [it is] used to get higher federal appropriations. Staff does as it pleases after the meetings." In lieu of systematic evaluation, the staff settled for letters from mayors and school superintendents who praised the existing program and called on Congress to expand it. The staff aggressively solicited "success stories" whenever possible and diverted problems as much as it could from attention by White House and Congress.

The corps' reluctance to submit to real evaluation was an understandable strategy, but it had serious consequences. The substitution of puffery for study doubtless misled some members of Congress and the media, by portraying a program in a growing administrative morass as an outstanding success. Representative John Brademas, for instance, proudly referred to the Teacher Corps as "one of the most innovative and successful education programs which Congress has initiated" and claimed that it had been "remarkably successful in meeting the purposes that Congress has assigned it." [13] Even worse, the refusal to do serious in-house research left the corps blind to problems in its objectives and operations, unable to justify itself before congressional skeptics, without an understanding of the import of proposals to alter it, incapable of recasting itself.

THE RESULTS OF THE TEACHER CORPS

Despite the Teacher Corps' early reluctance to submit to evaluations, enough evidence exists to render some sort of judgment on its effectiveness. On the whole, the record of the Teacher Corps must be judged unfavorably. The Teacher Corps has done little to promote its declared objectives and has proven far costlier than anticipated. Thus, according to figures provided by the USOE, in the early 1970s it cost well over $20,000 to train a single Teacher Corps intern over a twenty-month program.

The high cost of educating a Teacher Corpsman might, of course, be worth the investment if most of the recruits stayed in teaching, continued to work in areas with large concentrations of low-income students, and brought to their jobs special abilities and commitment, as the program originally promised that they would. This has not been the case. Attrition has been high. Fifty-one percent dropped out of the first cycle and 27 percent from the second. About 10 percent of the interns have dropped out in more recent cycles. Additional surveys suggest that close to 30 percent more did not plan to stay in teaching even though they completed the program. Thus only about half of them would have entered teaching even without the program. Moreover, of the corps alumni who plan to teach, a third or more do not plan to work in "disadvantaged" schools. Consequently, of the individuals who begin Teacher Corps training, perhaps a mere third or so actually become teachers in poverty areas.

How cost effective, then, is the Teacher Corps? Ten years after its beginning, government officials were unable to answer this question. In a report to the president and the Congress in July 1975, the National Advisory Council on Education Professions Development could only rather weakly observe:

> It would be helpful in assessing the Teacher Corps to know how it compares in terms of cost effectiveness with other teacher education programs. We would like to be able to offer some evidence, but we lack satisfactory data.
>
> There are only crude, incomparable data available on the costs of educating teachers. Nor have we been able to calculate a true cost of educating teachers in the Teacher Corps, either pre-service or in-service. Until better data are available, comparisons are not possible.[14]

Of course there are those who ask whether the $37.5 million now going annually to the Teacher Corps might not be more effectively invested elsewhere, but the Teacher Corps and HEW officials are apparently not about to provide the information and evaluations needed to make such rational calculations. And so it goes.

Another major goal of the Teacher Corps was to bring fresh new talent into the schools, but studies for the Ford Foundation completed in the early 1970s found little evidence that Teacher Corpsmen were statistically different from teachers ordinarily attracted to the education profession. It is clear that in the beginning the Teacher Corps attracted a good many people who would not have otherwise joined the ranks of the teaching profession, but significantly it was these corpsmen who tended to have one of the highest dropout rates from the program. Moreover, according to one estimate, the brightest of America's young adults were not being attracted to the program in its first years: "most interns scored in the lowest quartile of the Graduate Record Examination."

Another objective of the program was to spur reform in teacher training and make schools of education more sensitive to the needs of disadvantaged pupils. Social psychologist Ronald Corwin offers evidence that though new courses were introduced under the sponsorship of the Teacher Corps at numerous schools of education, there was little evidence that either these new courses or the presence of the Teacher Corps on campus had any real impact on improvements within the participating education schools.[15] Frequently, it turns out, the Teacher Corps was viewed as a short-term undertaking, staffed by temporary or junior faculty. When Teacher Corps grants or the university's goodwill toward the Teacher Corps ran out, the program and its temporary faculty were expendable. This problem was of course exacerbated by the national Teacher Corps' own policy of trying to spread the funds to all the states, with emphasis on politically significant districts.

CONCLUSION

By Washington standards, the Teacher Corps was a modest undertaking. But in spite of its modest size, its variety of good intentions, and its earnest objectives, it failed to do much of what was expected of it. Eventually it would become merely one more teacher-training grant program for schools of education and local school systems, a program comfortably controlled by its clientele.

In fairness to the officials who administered the Teacher Corps, it must be pointed out that they worked under difficult conditions. Presidential interest was substantial, but it was evidenced almost entirely in symbolic and public-relations efforts. Congressional support waxed and waned. Educational associations, which never wanted a centralized program that would threaten existing schools of education, worked to minimize the role of the Washington office. The war in Vietnam and escalation in defense budgets came at precisely the same time that Teacher Corps expansions might have taken place. Once a program that seemed likely to grow with national revenues, it became a program that had to compete with less threatening and more cherished subsidy programs. Small and unsure of itself from its creation, the Teacher Corps quickly got pushed to a back burner.

What lessons can we draw from the fate of the Teacher Corps?

1. *The need for prompt action conflicts with the need for thorough analysis and scrutiny of proposals.* When the Teacher Corps was established, conventional wisdom held that the answer to poor education in poor schools was to recruit and train better teachers for these schools. It

seemed like common sense to senators, to presidential assistants, and, in this case, to President Lyndon Johnson. Much of what the federal government attempts to do is based upon such commonsense assumptions; some programs grow, some fade away. The Teacher Corps offers a good example of how commonsense solutions can go awry.

The assumption that small bands of Teacher Corps interns could change the system was in retrospect an assumption egregiously oversold. To have expected these recent college graduates, new to teaching and new to the community, viewed with suspicion by the long-term teachers, without clearly defined responsibilities and with academic course loads at nearby universities consuming much of their time, to change the quality of education in the nation's toughest schools was as unrealistic as it was altruistic. That hopes were inflated became clear as several school systems from Boston to Cairo, Illinois, threw the Teacher Corps out. Not only did the intern-participant dropout rate average nearly 30 percent in the first three or four years in each two-year training cycle but an equally high percentage left the teaching of low-income students a year or two later.

At least some of the problems that the Teacher Corps was to encounter could have been anticipated. However, the political pressures of the moment meant that the Teacher Corps legislation was enacted with little forethought or planning. The dilemma facing politicians is clear: rush reform and risk failure or study reform and endanger passage.

2. *The need for clear objectives conflicts with the need to build political support.* In the case of the Teacher Corps, the drive for passage and funding meant that program officials promised to attain an ever-expanding roster of goals. Paralyzing conflicts among goals became endemic; some were due to the program's poor initial planning, but others arose because the administrators promised too much. In any event, the corps committed itself to so much that it was able to do very little.

3. *Federal reform often will arouse local resistance; local control often will impede federal reform.* The establishment of a federal reform program means that local authorities, for some reason or other, have failed — or revenue in sufficient quantity is not available. In general, however, the same interests that led to error or inaction at the local level are likely to oppose and try to co-opt federal action. The Teacher Corps, for instance, foundered because it was first resisted and then ultimately controlled by the very local teachers colleges and school systems it had been designed to change. Established interest groups are usually more concerned with what they might lose than with what they might gain. As this example shows, in the case of reform programs jurisdictional compromise is fraught with substantive significance. Efforts to bring reform programs under local control are often disguised efforts to gut them.

4. *Congress and the president are often unable (or unwilling) to monitor the implementation of newly enacted programs effectively.* Neither the

president nor his senior domestic policy advisers were aware of the major difficulties besetting the implementation of the Teacher Corps. Top HEW officials were aware of many of them but did not pass the word to a White House increasingly consumed with the war in Vietnam. Congressmen who were advocates of the Teacher Corps in its early days often became emotional in their defense of it. Just as they had been overly optimistic in their early claims for what it might accomplish, so now they became overly charitable in their claims for what it had achieved. Teacher Corps officials controlled most of the information flow to the Congress (and to the White House). And "evaluations," if they can be called that, were made by those who were implementing the program.

5. *Co-opted reforms can become self-perpetuating.* The very interests that struggle to thwart a program may ensure its continuance once they have seized control of it, even though, like the Teacher Corps, the program never fulfills its promise. Ironically, support for the program grows as sponsors, participants, and beneficiaries acknowledge their self-interest. To paraphrase Daniel Webster, the Teacher Corps is a small federal effort, but there are those who love it.

More generally, it is plain that the implementation strategies of the Teacher Corps were not directly related to goal achievement. Improvement of education in poverty areas was approached indirectly through teacher-training programs in which trainees were under no contract to work in depressed-area schools. Providing assistance to school superintendents and principals with few use restrictions for money received parallels the Economic Development Administration's arrangements with World Airways in Oakland, California, described by Pressman and Wildavsky.[16] Similarly, the strategy of rushing a reform through Congress and risking failure of the program, as opposed to studying it in advance and endangering passage, directly parallels Daniel P. Moynihan's general finding in *Maximum Feasible Misunderstanding,* a study of community action in the war on poverty.[17] The findings in this case study also illustrate many of the factors that Bardach points to as complicating the implementation process.[18] Specifically, these factors in the Teacher Corps case include ambiguous executive decisions, major policy changes that violate standard operating procedures of agencies, a large number of officials who act independently on an issue, and too much leeway given to the organization implementing policy.

Finally, we see in the Teacher Corps another phenomenon that several analysts have found in other policy areas, in which grant recipients focus on *program outputs* rather than *policy outcomes.* In this case, what counted was the training of the Teacher Corps interns rather than an assessment of how the education of children in poverty areas was improved.

Making governmental programs work effectively and efficiently is plainly an exacting task. Public officials need encouragement and help in these functions, and they deserve to be praised when they are successful. We need case analyses and comparative studies of both successful and unsuccessful governmental operations to learn how programs can be shaped and guided to achieve intended objectives.

NOTES

1. John F. Kennedy, "State of the Union Address, 1963," *Public Papers of the Presidents of the United States* (U.S. Government Printing Office, 1964), p. 13.

2. U.S. Senate statements and testimony of Senator Edward M. Kennedy, William Vanden Heuvel, and Dr. Neil Sullivan, *Hearings on S. 600, Part III, Subcommittee on Education of the Committee on Labor and Public Welfare,* 89th Cong., 1st sess., 11 June 1965, pp. 1346–51, 1362–68, 1428–37.

3. John Kenneth Galbraith, "Let Us Begin: An Invitation to Action on Poverty," *Harper's,* March 1964, p. 26.

4. Merriman Smith, *A White House Memoir* (Norton, 1972), p. 36.

5. Interview quotes without reference notes come from a series of interviews conducted by the author.

6. Lyndon B. Johnson, speech at University of Michigan, 22 May 1964, *Presidential Papers* (U.S. Government Printing Office, 1965), pp. 705–06. See also Doris Kearns, *Lyndon Johnson and the American Dream* (Harper & Row, 1976).

7. Address to the annual convention of the National Education Association, 2 July 1965, *Public Papers of the Presidents of the United States* (U.S. Government Printing Office, 1966), p. 718.

8. See Jerald G. Bachman, Swazzer Green, and Ilona Wirtanen, *Dropping Out — Problem or Symptom?* (University of Michigan Institute for Social Research, 1971).

9. Lyndon B. Johnson, statements, 20 April 1967, 28 February 1967, and 29 June 1967, *Public Papers of the Presidents of the United States* (U.S. Government Printing Office, 1968), pp. 455, 248, 667–68.

10. John Egerton, "Odds Against the Teacher Corps," *Saturday Review,* 17 Dec. 1966, p. 71.

11. Representative Edith Green, *Hearings on H.R. 6230,* Elementary and Secondary Education Amendments of 1967, Committee on Education and Labor, U.S. House of Representatives, 90th Cong., pp. 215–16.

12. Representative Edith Green, "A Congresswoman Discusses the Politics of Education," *Phi Delta Kappan,* February 1966, p. 232.

13. Representative John Brademas, *Congressional Record* 116, no. 96 (11 June 1970), H. 5477.

14. *Teacher Corps: Past or Prologue?* A report by the National Advisory Council on Education Professions Development, July 1975, p. 19.

15. These generalizations derive from a study of the Teacher Corps funded by the Ford Foundation and directed by Professor Ronald G. Corwin of Ohio State University. Findings cited here are from Corwin's report to Ford, entitled "The Fate of a National Program for Educational Reform" (mimeo, 1971). See also Corwin's book, *Reform and Organizational Survival: The Teacher Corps as an Instrument of Educational Change* (Wiley & Sons, 1974).

16. See Jeffrey L. Pressman and Aaron Wildavsky, *Implementation* (University of California Press, 1973).

17. Daniel P. Moynihan, *Maximum Feasible Misunderstanding* (Free Press, 1969).

18. Eugene Bardach, *The Implementation Game* (M.I.T. Press, 1977).

CHAPTER 10

PRESIDENTIAL ACCOUNTABILITY

People yith vast power at their disposal get cut off from reality, and their power is inevitably misused. One Administration will have its Watergate, another its Vietnam. Clearly, there is a need for Congress, the courts, the media and the general public, each in its own way to work to lessen both the power and the aura of divine right that now surround our President.

> — Jeb S. Magruder, convicted Nixon White House aide,
> *Los Angeles Times*, 22 May 1974, p. II-7.

Anybody who wants the presidency so much that he'll spend two years organizing and campaigning for it is not to be trusted with the office.

> — David Broder's "law." *Time*,
> 26 February 1979, p. 25.

If men were angels, no government would be necessary. If angels were to govern man, neither external nor internal controls in government would be necessary. In framing a government which is to be administered by men over men the great difficulty lies in this, you must first enable the government to control the government and in the next place oblige it to control itself. A dependence on the people is no doubt the primary control on the government. But experience has taught mankind the necessity for auxiliary precautions.

> — James Madison, *The Federalist*, No. 51.

We want to be led, yet we wish to remain free. We want a "take charge" leader in the White House, yet we demand accountable and responsive leadership. Many Americans are now less content to hold presidents to account only every four years when they go to the polls. Our system is built on distrust of powerful leaders and the need for their accountability. This chapter will examine existing and proposed accountability processes.

ACCOUNTABILITY QUESTIONS

Any discussion of presidential leadership and accountability must take into account the ever-present paradoxes of the presidency. Some part of us wants a larger-than-life, two-gun, king-size leader. On the other hand, there is the remarkably enduring antigovernment, antileadership, chronic-complainer syndrome in America. We want strong, gutsy leadership to operate on alternate days with caged, tamed leadership.

One thing seems certain: Presidential powers are not likely to be reduced in the future. James S. Young suggests another enduring reality: "Once seen as a solution to problems, the centralization of power in the White House has come to be seen as a source of problems in the society." [1]

What judgment can be reached about the accountability of the American presidency? How can the people hold presidents answerable between elections? What are the means by which to influence, overrule, or even remove an irresponsible president? Accountability implies not only responsiveness to majority desires and answerability for actions but also taking the people and their views into account. It also implies a performance guided by integrity. Accountability implies as well that important decisions should be explained to the people to allow them the opportunity to appraise how well a president is handling his responsibilities.

Several basic questions arise. To whom is accountability owed? No president, it would seem, can be more than partially accountable to the people, for each will listen to some people and some points of view more than to others. If we have learned anything in recent years, however, it is that the doctrine of presidential infallibility has been rejected. Arbitrary rule by powerful executives has always been rejected here. But what should be done when there are sharp differences between experts or when expert opinion differs sharply from the preponderance of public opinion? How much accountability, and what kind, is desirable? Is it not possible that the quest for ultimate accountability will result in a presidency without the prerogatives and independent discretion necessary for creative leadership? Is what is popular the same as what is right? Will making the presidency more accountable to the majority of the moment make it any more responsible in dealing with problems originating in the preferences, fear, or thoughtlessness of majorities, such as issues of radical injustice, capital punishment, and poverty?

The modern presidency, in fact, may be unaccountable because it is too strong and independent in certain areas and too weak and dependent in others. One of the most troublesome circumstances characterizing the state of the modern presidency is that awesome restraints often exist where restraints are undesirable and only inadequate restraints are available where they are most needed. Presidential weakness often results in an inability to respond. On the other hand, presidential strength is no guarantee that a president will be responsive or answerable. Indeed, significant independent strength may encourage low answerability when it suits a president's short-term personal power goals. A strong presidency may also respond most dutifully to majoritarian desires — some of which may have been created by manipulation, as in the case of the Vietnam War or the law-and-order crusade — but remain largely unanswerable for the actions taken in responding to these desires.

Complicating any discussion of presidential accountability is the fact that public expectations about the strength and powers of the presidency may not correspond to reality. Expectations in excess of actual power surely promote, if not invite, the reality of unaccountability, a fact of life with which presidents are plagued constantly. Demands in excess of the president's capacity to respond often weaken his position; they certainly do not increase his answerability to the people. On the other hand, they can as easily prompt a president to take ill-planned and even irrational action in those areas in which restraints on him are either weak or altogether nonexistent. Surrounded by limitations, especially in the field of domestic activity, a president is tempted, understandably, to move into areas in which accountability always is less.

THE PROBLEM AND THE POSSIBILITIES

In a strict sense, of course, government is always government by the few; the concern is whether government operates in the name of the few, the one, or the many, and whether it is alert and responsive to the views of the many. The ideal conditions for presidential accountability are difficult to spell out, but the public should know what a president's priorities are, how they will be financed, who will gain and who will lose, and what the alternatives are. The public and its representatives in normal circumstances should be given a chance to evaluate presidential priorities and give their views. Substantial controversy exists, however, over the extent to which public opinion should shape or dictate presidential choices. Government by public opinion, however it is devised, can never guarantee justice or wisdom.

It is valid, on the one hand, to complain about the paucity of formal means and the decline in the effectiveness of informal checks for making a president accountable. It is also valid, on the other hand, to appreciate that presidents need flexibility — perhaps today more than ever. No one seriously proposes that a president's decisions should merely reflect majority opinion. The structure of the office in part reflects the desire of its designers to prevent presidents from being threatened or rushed into action by the shifting gusts of public passion. In practice, the definition of acceptable limits for presidential accountability will vary over time. If the standards for presidential accountability tilt too far in the direction either of public opinion or of independence and isolation, a president is less able to provide those subtle accommodating and mediating elements of leadership that are essential for effective democratic government. No task defines the essence of presidential leadership in a pluralistic society better than that of devising a workable and purposeful adjustment of the conflicting views of experts, elite groups, and the people as a whole.

Although certain presidents have tried on occasion to govern without the benefit of considerable public and partisan support, they seldom have succeeded. A president can usually act as he thinks best, but presidents are often heavily influenced by their anticipation not only of the next election but also of tomorrow's headlines and editorials, next week's Gallup poll, next month's congressional hearings, and possible reprisals against their programs by Congress, the Supreme Court, the opposition party, and other institutions. In what other nation can a chief executive be overruled in the courts? A judicial check on a chief executive seldom exists in parliamentary systems if the leader retains his party's backing. In what other countries do the Jack Andersons and legions of underground newspapers and pamphleteers flourish with such tolerance and even encouragement?

Higher literacy rates and growing attention to public events increase the opportunities for the public to comprehend what is going on and to react accordingly. As voter knowledge and attention is improving, so also public-opinion polls are beginning to weigh levels of intensity and information. Today, a presidential candidate who campaigns in most of the fifty states and enters dozens of state primaries is forced to learn the major complaints people have about the performance of their government, which is a vast improvement over the days when presidential candidates conducted national campaigns from their front porches. Although the modern candidate has more opportunities to educate and shape public opinion, it is nearly impossible for him not to learn in turn as he watches the faces of his audiences and gauges the manner in which people respond to what he is saying. Washington reporters may only count the number of times his speech is interrupted by applause, but his staff is more keenly sensitive to what it is that evokes applause or silence.

One of the more confusing aspects of presidential accountability is the way the American people find it convenient to blame presidents for a whole range of problems, regardless of whether the problems have been subject to presidential control. We generally withhold our applause when a president's work is good, but we seldom fail to hiss his blunders. No matter what presidents do, their popularity declines. It hardly seems to matter what they attempt or even who is president. When news is good, a president's popularity goes down or stays about the same; when news is terrible, it merely goes down faster and farther. The decline in approval of the president is in large part a function of the inability and unlikelihood of a president to live up to the buildup he received during the presidential honeymoon. Presidents, of course, have often kindled the buildups by promising more than can be done. Heightened expectations are invariably followed by disappointment. Sometimes the disappointment occasions despair and retribution; people turn on a president almost as if he were the sole cause of everything that is wrong in their lives.

According to some studies, certain segments of the population are more likely to rally around the presidency, both in crises and in general. But it may be that many of these groups are diminishing in size and importance vis-à-vis the rest of the population:

> Our analysis suggests that generalized support for presidents among citizens can be expected to decline over time. The kinds of people who are disposed to give the most support make up an increasingly smaller proportion of the total public while those least supportive are growing. Presidential support is disproportionately located among citizens who are older, of fundamentalist religious persuasion, have fewer years of formal schooling, and may be described as psychologically inflexible. Yet the population is becoming younger, less likely to belong to fundamentalist sects, possessing additional years of formal education, and is more likely to be psychologically flexible. Other things being equal, therefore, these long-term secular changes in the population would lead to a drop in support for presidents.[2]

The authors concede, however, that things are not necessarily equal. Changes do occur, and presidents who can discern the difference between popular and political leadership and who can use the presidency for the noble ends that will best serve the nation can affect how the public will regard them, as well as the office of the president.

Most presidents concede that the man who uses presidential power must understand that by spending it he dissipates it. No president has had as much power in his last year in office as he had in his first. Several presidential resources wane as the years roll by. The presidential honeymoon

FIGURE 10.1
PRESIDENTIAL POPULARITY (ASSESSED AT 3–5 MONTH INTERVALS,
JUNE 1945–JULY 1979)

Question: "Do you approve of the way _____ is handling
his job as president?"

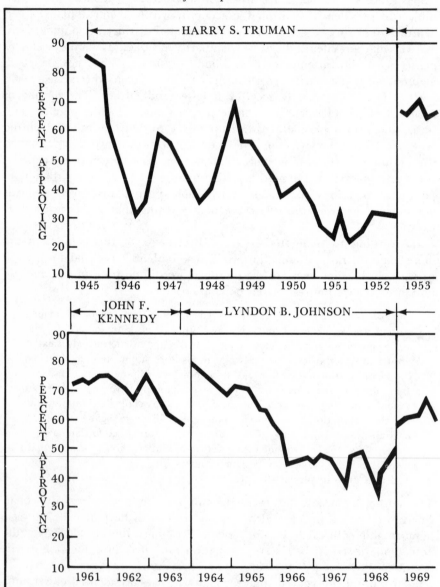

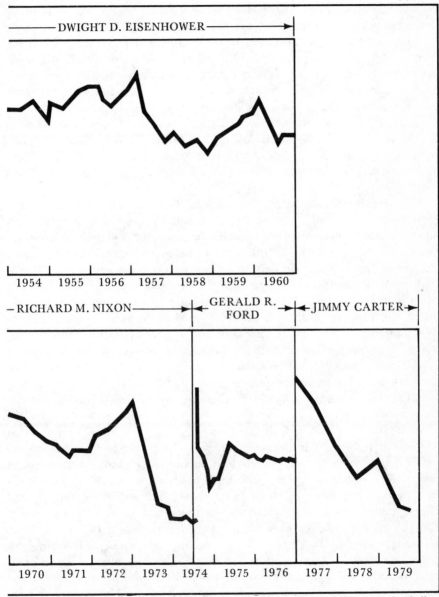

Source: G. Gallup, Gallup Poll Index, 1935–1971 (Random House, 1972); also the Gallup Opinion Index, monthly reports.

comes to an end. Prominent politicians who are rivals for the office begin, after a short grace period, to attack a president's positions, partisan followings crystallize, and the ranks of those who disapprove of the way a president is doing his job begin to swell. Presidential promises, at least many of them, go unachieved. Factions in the president's own party inevitably develop. Press criticism increases. And persons whose pressing claims go unheeded become disaffected.

The frequency and duration of these ebbs and flows of approval between the president and the public are not well understood. Although presidents lose popularity during congressional elections and most presidents' popularity declines considerably in the public-opinion polls over time, Eisenhower was apparently immune to this cyclic factor. Legislative activists like Truman and Johnson have suffered most in the polls, whereas Eisenhower and Nixon, until Watergate, enjoyed more stable support. Is more expected of Democrats? Johnson enjoyed a comfortable margin of American trust for at least two and a half years, then suddenly it was irretrievably gone.

Apparently, legislative activists such as Truman and Johnson suffered great declines in public approval in part because they were outspoken on domestic issues. Perhaps the expectations generated by these administrations were more difficult to fulfill, and the greater heterogeneity of the Democratic party made opposition to any presidential action more likely. Each time a president is forced to act on such controversial domestic issues as racial integration or the separation of church and state, he risks losing the support of intense minorities.[3] How to please both conservative southerners and blacks, Baptists and Catholics, farmers and housewives? The temptation to become the people's source of inspiration for every worthy policy can overcommit the political resources, as well as the institutional prestige, of the presidency.

The public's rhythmic "issue-attention cycle" also tends to restrict the president's leeway in maneuvering to seek solutions to the nation's domestic problems. Economist Anthony Downs persuasively argues that "American public attention rarely remains sharply focused upon any domestic issue for very long — even if it involves a continuing problem of crucial importance to society. . . . Each of these problems suddenly leaps into prominence, remains there for a short time and then, though still largely unresolved, gradually fades from the center of public attention."[4] But the main problem comes when a president is forced to act on a controversial issue; he is likely to create intense and often unforgiving opponents among his former supporters. Even without taking action, a president is likely to come under attack from those who voted for him but find themselves neglected in the distribution of federal patronage or contracts or otherwise disappointed by their inability to influence future presidential policies. Because modern press and television coverage gives so much emphasis to the presidency, they serve to quicken and intensify these reactions. Precisely because a president can gain immediate publicity, he is expected to communicate his views quickly. Precisely because he is supposed to be a shaper of public opinion, he is expected to inspire the country to great causes.

That presidents are firmly hedged in by public opinion is particularly evident and frequently substantiated by presidential avoidance of politically sensitive issues that clearly lack majority support. The question of dispersing low-income housing throughout metropolitan areas is a prime example of such issues. The matter of civil rights, which most presidents have approached with timidity, is another. Recent presidents have shied away from progressive leadership in civil rights until either their hands were forced by intense minority protests or until sizable majorities of the public at last became favorable to the goals of the policy in question. Then, too, the courts had taken the lead and had, in essence, imposed the need for leadership on a very reluctant president. If a president has been ineffectual in winning congressional approval of his domestic program, his failure may indicate no more than that a national consensus does not yet exist for his initiatives and that he has been unable or unwilling to educate and energize the public about the desirability of his proposed changes. Tax reform is one area in which presidents often enjoy substantial general support but are unable to win the specific support needed for controversial change. Former Nixon cabinet member George Romney assessed the impact of public opinion this way:

> Even our most successful political leaders of recent times are limited in what they can do to what is politically possible. Congress, itself, enacts what it believes is politically possible. What determines what is politically possible? The level of understanding by the general public of the crucial issues at stake. The public's awareness or unawareness of the decisively important problems, the alternative political courses of action that are open to the nation, and the sacrifices and necessity for determination of priorities — the general public's awareness of all these things determines what is politically possible.[5]

Another factor mitigating against national leadership in behalf of social reform and redistribution has been the distinctively self-centered mood of contemporary voters, many if not most of whom tire of purposive leaders calling for more sacrifice. Sacrifice translated into the language of the common man means higher taxes and, in return, a government that tells him far too much about what he can and cannot do. Much of the performance of the American presidency is largely a function of its constituency. That constituency is often largely uninterested in the collective pursuit of noble goals that run counter to personal satisfactions. Andrew Hacker offers this gloomy prospect:

Much talk is heard, for example, of the need for purposive leadership. The argument runs that while the American people may be overly self-centered, this condition could be overcome by the emergence of leaders capable of inspiring citizenry to personal sacrifices for public ends. Yet the fact remains that there arrives a time in a nation's history when its people have lost the capacity for being led. Contemporary Americans simply do not want — and will not accept — political leadership that makes more than marginal demands on their emotions or energies. Thus, for all the eloquence about the need for leadership, Americans are temperamentally unsuited for even a partial merger of personality in pursuit of a common cause.[6]

CONSTRAINING BRAKES
ON A PRESIDENT

So highly decentralized and slow in operation is the American governmental system that it seems designed for the protection of the status quo and the compromise of any crusade for redistributive change. Fundamental reforms depend on the status quo's becoming significantly more painful than change or on the occurrence of crises. Short of such dramatic crises as the Great Depression, Pearl Harbor, and the Cuban missiles in 1962, presidents usually have felt the muscular disapproval of interest groups whenever they have embarked on new policy ventures that in any way threatened the existing distribution of power. Veteran White House counselors consider it almost axiomatic that crises must be exploited because of the special but quite temporary support that coalesces for the president at such times. Under more usual circumstances, presidential policies will become greatly adjusted and compromised as they proceed through legislative and, later, a variety of administrative processes.

In attempting to make innovations, the American presidency operates within a system of shared power, one in which the claims of many groups constantly compete. Presidential struggles with other governmental and extragovernmental centers of power stem from the larger societal conflicts over values and the allocation of wealth and opportunity. As a result, the presidency becomes a place in which few radical decisions are made; most of its domestic policies are exploratory, remedial, or experimental modifications of past practices.

Limitations on a president's freedom of action are, to be sure, often desirable. Many of the checks and balances that are still at work today were deliberately designed by the framers of the Constitution. In some measure, presidents should be the captives of their campaign commitments, their parties, and their announced programs. They should be responsive most of the time to the views of the majority of the American people. Presidential behavior should be informed by the Constitution, existing laws, and the generally understood, albeit hazier, values that define democratic procedure. The notion that party programs, spelled out in campaigns, allow the public some control over policy through the election process, is a valuable brake, one that needs, if anything, to be revitalized. Other brakes that limit presidential discretion may be viewed as positive or negative, depending on an individual's political and economic views. The constraining of a president by the bureaucracy and by special interests is implicitly, if not explicitly, a kind of accountability — albeit not the kind we necessarily want as our prime constitutional safeguard against the abuse of power.

Constraints Imposed
by the Bureaucracy

The federal bureaucracy, greatly swollen by the New Deal and the cold-war agencies, as well as by the Great Society, is one of the most visible checks on a president. Indeed presidents are quick to fault the bureaucracy for the many problems that beset the implementation and evaluation of presidential programs. One is reminded of Harry Truman's observation about what it would be like for his successor to be a president rather than a general: "He will sit here and he'll say, 'Do this! Do that!' And nothing will happen. Poor Ike — it won't be a bit like the Army! He'll find it very frustrating." [7]

The problem of how to control the bureaucracy has become a major preoccupation for presidents. Even persons who championed the New Deal now recognize that the executive bureaucracy can be a presidential curse. Arthur Schlesinger, Jr., writes that "as any sensible person should have known, the permanent government has turned out to be, at least against innovating Presidents, a conservatizing rather than liberalizing force." [8] Concern about taming the bureaucracy comes from the right, from the revisionist left, and from moderates. Participants in the Nixon administration constantly embraced the same theme, even to the extent of claiming that their programs were being sabotaged from all directions. One of the key factors in former President Nixon's continuing attempts to centralize more authority either in the White House or in the hands of a few trusted and strong cabinet officials was this very suspicion about the loyalties and parochialism of federal civil servants.

Gaining control over existing bureaucracies and making them work with and for the White House is an enormous burden on the president. He must constantly delegate, he must be most precise about what he is delegating, and he must know whether and for what reasons the agencies to which he is delegating share his general outlook. He must be sensitive to bureaucratic politics, to the incentives that motivate bureaucrats, and to the intricacies of their standard operating procedures. He must have some assurance (and hence an adequate intelligence system) that what he is delegating will be carried out properly.

Recent presidents, doubtless because they were trained as legislators and not as executives, have tended to misunderstand the workings of bureaucracy. They have little appreciation for bureaucrats' considerable concern about organizational essence, organizational morale, and organizational integrity. Presidents mistakenly but invariably look upon the executive branch as a monolith, and they are especially offended when senior bureaucrats differ with them or otherwise refuse to cooperate. Presidents quickly become defensive and critical of the bureaucracy. They fear, sometimes with reason, that their pet programs will get buried in the inert custodial hands of old-line bureaucracies. As a result, as mentioned in the previous chapter, presidents have often sought shortcuts by setting up new agencies for each of their pet projects and relying increasingly on separate advisory and staff units within the executive office. However, the creation of a new agency does not guarantee presidential control. Indeed, some of the most independent, even maverick, federal agencies were originally set up to bypass the so-called old-line departments. Among such agencies are the Atomic Energy Commission, the Office of Economic Opportunity, and the Department of Energy.

Bureau chiefs and career civil servants often do avoid initiative, taking risks, and responsibility, opting instead for routine and security. The bureaucracy most assuredly has its own way of doing things, often more conservative or more liberal than what the president wants. But the fact that bureaucratic interests and presidential interests often differ does not mean that the permanent employees of the federal executive branch constitute an active enemy force. Bureaucratic organizations act, rather, in reasonable, rational ways to enhance their influence, budget, and autonomy. And they generally believe that in doing so they act in the nation's interest.

Thus, the bureaucracy often defines the national interest quite differently from the way it is defined in the White House. But a close examination of these two definitions often reveals that both are valid and representative views of what is desirable about which reasonable people can legitimately differ. The task for a president, then, is to understand the strategies and tactics of federal bureaus and appreciate the underlying motivations. Properly diagnosed, the bureaucratic instinct for competition, survival, and autonomy can be creatively harnessed by the White House both to educate itself and to develop cooperative alliances.

Bureaucratic Vetoes

One major cause of the distance and frequent distrust between the presidency and the rest of the executive branch lies in the nature of the bureaucracy and of bureaucrats.

Consider the official who directs the day-to-day operations of even a broadly defined program; let us call him the bureau chief. He directs the work of large numbers of people, he disposes of large sums of money, he deals every day with weighty, intricate, and delicate problems. He has probably spent most of his adult years in the highly specialized activity over which he now presides. He lives at the center of a special world inhabited by persons and groups in the private sector who stand to gain or lose by what he does, certain members of Congress who have a special interest in his actions, and a specialized press to which he is a figure of central importance. The approbation which is most meaningful to him is likely to be the approbation of the other inhabitants of this special world. The rest of the federal government may seem vague and remote, and the President will loom as a distant and shadowy figure who will, in any event, be succeeded by someone else in a few years. It would be unreasonable to expect this official to see his program in the Presidential perspective.[9]

Seldom is there a passion as keen as that of functionaries for their functions. The bureaucrats whose basic loyalty is to the established way of doing things and whose job survival and promotion are tied directly to program survival and expansion, instinctively, but rationally, resist threats to program control or coordination from the White House.

Consequently, although the bureaucracy was intended to be neutral and nonpolitical, the bureau chief will extend his allegiance to persons or groups who will aid and abet the enlargement of his program or, at the least, its stability. Knowing that presidential and congressional support are only won when the bureau can demonstrate widespread and intense public support, that a president wants to be associated with popular programs, many bureaus and even departments willingly invite capture by special interests in order to gain what they perceive as indispensable clientele and grass-roots support. Where little special-interest support exists, shrewd bureau chiefs do everything possible to create it. Moreover, they spend considerable time forging alliances with well-situated members of Congress and their staffs.

How entrenched these relations can become can be inferred from the fact that, whereas tenure on the White House staff averages less than three years and even less than that among cabinet appointees, the bureau chiefs, senior members of Congress, senior staff in Congress, and veteran Washington lobbyists often endure in their posts for ten or fifteen years or more. Former Secretary of Health, Education and Welfare John W. Gardner told the Senate Government Operations Committee:

> As everyone in this room knows but few people outside of Washington understand, questions of public policy nominally lodged with the Secretary are often decided far beyond the Secretary's reach by a trinity consisting of [1] representatives of an outside body, [2] middle level bureaucrats and [3] selected members of Congress, particularly those concerned with appropriations. In a given field these people may have collaborated for years. They have a durable alliance that cranks out

legislation and appropriations in behalf of their special interest. Participants in such durable alliances do not want the Department Secretaries strengthened. The outside special interests are particularly resistant to such change. It took them years to dig their particular tunnel into the public vault, and they don't want the vault moved.[10]

Practically any new presidential initiative, therefore, faces a strategically placed potential veto group with major allies within the executive branch itself: a social services bureaucracy to resist a negative income tax, an Office of Education to resist measures that would undermine traditional school-of-education training programs, a defense establishment to resist disarmament agreements, and so forth.

The professionalization of many sections of the federal government has created another potentially powerful constraint on presidential action. Professionals in government — for example, senior engineers and physicists in the National Aeronautics and Space Administration or the Defense Department, physicians and biologists at the National Institutes of Health, and economists throughout the government — ordinarily are more committed to the values of their profession than to the political fortunes of presidents. Professionals are more likely to move in and out of government than are other career civil servants. Once outside, the professionals can use their inside knowledge to become effective critics of official decisions as well as lobbyists for interest groups. Those remaining inside can resist the administration by leaking documents or key findings or by threatening collective resignations.

The Nixon administration, for example, was challenged on the usefulness and desirability of the supersonic transport by some of its leading science counselors, who made their professional views public. During the debates over antiballistic missiles, one member of the president's Science Advisory Committee questioned the feasibility of the proposed limited ABM. Similar instances of professionals voicing independent views occurred with respect to the war on crime and various environmental-protection issues. In the Watergate episodes those persons who attempted to curb the various excesses or who stood firm against egregious cover-up activities were senior professionals in the FBI, CIA, and Justice Department, who were supported by the professional code of standards of their bureaus and colleagues.

Constraints Imposed by Special Interests

The American political system is deliberately designed to enhance the chances of special interests to veto policies that affect them. Although the various economic and professional elites may not be as cohesive and omnipotent as the power-elite school suggests, the wealthier interest groups have perpetuated decidedly favorable governmental privileges to advance their business and professional goals. Although at times of crisis there are substantial incentives for subordinating special claims to the nation's well-being, such times are a presidential luxury. Under normal conditions, an elaborate network of influences and obligations may frustrate presidential objectives, especially in the area of domestic policy.

Multiple strategies are available to well-financed interest groups for representing policy ideas that may contravene the president's. They may appeal to Congress or to the White House staff, to friends in the cabinet or in departments and agencies, to advisory commissions, or to the press. Wealthy special-interest groups can hire lawyers to represent them in courts, lobbyists to advance their interests in legislatures, and a variety of other specialists and public-relations consultants to plead their causes to the administrators responsible for implementing federal policy. As the growing White House and executive-office bureaucracies subsume a growing number of interest-group representatives — that is, staffs or offices established to deal with various industrial, regional, professional, minority, or class interests — a mosaic of symbiotic professional and consulting ties emerges between public officials and special-interest and policy elites. Other opportunities to influence the formulation and implementation of policy include: helping to recruit and approve executive-branch advisers; suggesting the framework within which policy changes are made; proposing and framing special legislation; building coalitions of support for, or opposition to, policy changes; and influencing the research and evaluation that take place in particular policy areas. These affiliations and activities substantially affect the manner in which policies are adopted, perpetuated, and administered. Invariably, new ideas seldom compete solely on their merits; and who will have the advantage or disadvantage, who pays and who holds the political clout, is always taken into account as well. To see that this is the case, more than ten thousand lobbyists are currently operating in Washington, D.C.

To believe that as a representative of an outside elite comes closer to the center of national policymaking, the more he will temper the blatantly selfish goals of his interest group is as much an illusion as the schoolbook myth that an ordinary citizen on becoming president is somehow transformed into one of the wisest and most informed of human beings.

Presidents must live with a vast array of venerable subsidy programs that are well protected by Congress and by influential interests. These programs inhibit serious reconsideration of the distribution of economic and political power. Corporate dairy farmers, the oil industry, homebuilders associations, and the maritime industry, for example, carefully protect their cherished governmental shields. The highway, farm, and public-works lobbies also look more powerful from within than from outside the White House. White House aides in every administration learn quickly, if they did not already know, how deep and wide ranging the political opposition to foreign textile imports is, not only from outside the government but also from the Commerce, Labor, and Treasury departments.

Throughout the 1960s, administration efforts for tax reform were frustrated or stillborn. Kennedy administration proposals for the deregulation of transportation made no progress. Johnson and Nixon administration attempts to curtail federal largess in impacted-area educational grants were repeatedly defeated. Congress regularly fails to move on administration initiatives for higher charges for use of federal facilities. One of Johnson's economic advisers summed up the unpromising outcomes of nearly all such attempts as follows:

> Particularly in the early 1960s, far greater gains were to be made by fighting to enlarge the size of the economic pie than by pressing proposals to increase equity and efficiency in sharing the pie. Improved overall performance of the national economy could be legitimately sold as a good for everybody, and thus fitted into the Johnsonian consensus approach. Thus for understandable — though regrettable — reasons [the strength and the bitterness of the opposition], the shields and subsidies continue on the statute books into the seventies.[11]

Often, local special interests who run federal grant programs are the most intense supporters of the status quo; they have high investments in specific policy options and explicitly desired outcomes. Often, too, they benefit as much, if not more, than the intended beneficiaries. As economist Alice Rivlin sees it:

> Most of these programs support the services of particular professional groups — librarians, vocational education teachers, veterinarians, psychiatric social workers, sanitary engineers. Each of these groups believes it is doing something important and useful — and it doubtless is — and fights to preserve and expand the programs it knows will support its activities. The professionals tend — far more than the beneficiaries — to be articulate, conscious of their joint interest and able to impress a Congressman with the importance of what they do.[12]

A president's latitude for achievement can be determined by the degree to which consensus or conflict exists among elite interest groups within a particular arena of public policy. If the policy elite of a given profession or industry agrees on a particular issue, it is nearly impossible for a president to effect an opposing point of view. Exceptions such as medicare, automobile safety devices, and antipollution legislation are not persuasive, because the profession or industry in question seldom lost much and the costs for such programs were in each case passed on in some way to the consumer or taxpayer. If, however, cleavage or confusion occurs over substantive or procedural matters, a president has some independent influence; although even then, the scope and type of his influence will be shaped by the character of the conflict among these elite. Thus, Johnson's efforts to create model cities as demonstrations of how social and physical planning could produce decent and livable cities soon was heavily influenced by determined pressures from home builders, developers, real-estate associations, big-city mayors, and other strategically positioned interests. Likewise, despite widespread public support for rapid progress on the environmental front, Carter's environmental-protection recommendations soon became influenced by the views of the automobile manufacturers as well as by the unions potentially affected by stringent standards and too rapid implementation. Sometimes, a consensus among policy elites may be the product of presidential commitment, but the reverse is more likely to be the case.

Prior commitments to special interests inhibit planning, brake a president's capacity to focus on new problems, and help to exhaust his political credit. Despite high expectations, a president may find himself merely a strategically situated broker for his own party, able only in a limited way to affect existing patterns of grants or subsidies.

Every grant program generates concrete benefits to a particular group, and possessiveness characterizes nearly every group that has participated in the growth of federal-aid programs since the New Deal. According to the doctrine of interest groups, the unorganized are left out of most policy-making equations. In fact, seldom does an interest group emerge that has as its aim the promotion of the public benefit, a program that would benefit everybody. Theodore Lowi lamented the eventual consequences: "Liberalism has become a doctrine whose means are its ends, whose combatants are its clientele, whose standards are not even those of the mob, but worse, are those the bargainers can fashion to fit the bargain." [13] At the same time, the standards of justice and respect for law deteriorate amid informal, frankly feudal negotiations among those stronger interests who can adjust the laws to their own advantage and profit.

In the end all three branches of government and the bureaucracy listen more attentively and usually yield to the arguments and ideas from those segments of society able to represent themselves, able to shape the character of those branches, and able to supply precisely that information and argumentation needed to make the system move. So it is that the many well-heeled interests continue to enjoy a special advantage in any contest with a president who genuinely is a redistributionist. As historian Bert Cochran observed in speaking of the net impact of the New Deal: "When the smoke of controversy cleared, the social and economic contours of the landscape were essentially undisturbed." [14] So, too, after the Great Society various minorities had gained opportunities and access to desired goods and experiences, but the inequitable distribution of wealth in the nation remained fairly constant. Nixon aide Jeb Magruder put it this way: "We didn't spend time on the disadvantaged for the simple reason that there were no votes there. . . . We don't have a democracy of the people. We have a special-interest democracy." [15]

IMPEACHMENT AND REMOVAL —
THE ULTIMATE CHECK

Impeachment is obviously one of the most potent checks against the abuse of executive power, yet over the nation's history it has been one of the least used. For practical purposes, it is a political action, phrased in legal terminology, against an official of the federal government. The Constitution deals with the subject of impeachment and conviction in six places, but the scope of the power is readily outlined in Article II, Section 4.

> The President, Vice President and all civil officers of the United States, shall be removed from Office on Impeachment for, and Conviction of, Treason, Bribery, or other high Crimes and Misdemeanors.

In the impeachment proceeding, the House of Representatives acts as the prosecutor, and the Senate serves as the judge and jury. Any member of the House may initiate impeachment proceedings by introducing a resolution to that effect in the House. The House Judiciary Committee then has to conduct hearings and investigations. The committee then decides either in favor of or against an impeachment verdict and sends its conclusions on to the full House. A 50 percent vote in the House is needed to impeach. Select members of the House, if an impeachment is enacted, would then try the case before the U.S. Senate. In the Senate a two-thirds vote of those members present is needed for conviction and removal.

Only thirteen national officials have been impeached by the House since 1789. Of these, eleven were tried in the Senate; four were convicted, six were acquitted, and one resigned before the Senate took action. In the two remaining cases, the charges were dismissed after the person had been forced to resign national office. Nine of these cases involved federal judges, one involved a senator, one a secretary of war, and one a president, Andrew Johnson, who was overwhelmingly impeached by the House in February 1868 but missed conviction in the Senate by one vote (35–19) in May of that same year.

The impeachment and removal of a president has been a much misunderstood and an obviously cumbersome means of accountability. Its use is fraught with emotion and hazardous side effects, and it necessarily remains a device to be used only as a last resort.

One of President Richard Nixon's involuntary contributions to our understanding of presidential politics is that he provided the occasion for clarifying the character and usage of the impeachment and removal power, for the most significant controversial constitutional question about impeachment had been what were the appropriate grounds for this action. "Treason" and "Bribery" are clear legal terms and cause no problem. It was the phrase "other high Crimes and Misdemeanors" that raised so many hard-to-answer questions. As one group of lawyers put it:

> Is that phrase limited to acts which would be indictable as criminal offenses, or was it intended to reach abuses of office or breaches of trust not constituting criminal acts? If impeachment and removal may properly rest on activities which do not constitute crimes, are there any limits in principle on the type of conduct which can be the basis for impeachment and removal, or should the exercise of these powers be governed solely by the free play of our political system? [16]

Some analysts, especially lawyers defending the potentially impeached, have argued that a person can be impeached and removed from office only on criminal charges or on offenses that would be indictable in a criminal court. The weight of most recent scholarship however, Nixon's defense to the contrary notwithstanding, supports the construction of "high crimes and misdemeanors" as not limited to offenses under ordinary criminal law.[17] The framers intended that the language of impeachment should refer to major injuries or abuses of our constitutional institutions. To confine impeachable conduct to indictable offenses would set a standard so restrictive as not to include conduct that might seriously undermine our governance practices. Some of the worst offenses against our form of government may not consist of violations of criminal law.

One possible view is that an impeachable offense is whatever a majority of the House says it is. The extreme opposite view, or the Nixon defense view, holds that impeachment should be voted only on proof of serious, indictable crimes. In the celebrated Richard Nixon impeachment proceedings, the House Judiciary Committee adopted a middle stance, one that is likely to have a controlling, if not legal, influence upon future impeachment efforts. The Judiciary Committee in 1974 held that violation of a criminal statute is not a prerequisite for impeachment as long as the offense is a serious one. They were well aware that an impeachable offense should not be taken to mean anything around which political expediency might organize a majority in the House and two-thirds in the Senate. In effect, the majority of the House Judiciary believed that a gross breach of trust or serious abuse of power was necessary before passage of an impeachment resolution. Constitutional restraint would have to be very much in order to ensure that a measure of this kind would be adopted only if Congress would also take this step against another president who engaged in comparable conduct in similar circumstances.

One of the lawyers for the House Judiciary Committee, in a particularly probing analysis of the impeachment power, concluded that there are four general ways a president can violate his constitutional duty to see that the laws are faithfully executed — all of which could justify impeachment investigations: (1) If the president attempts, either directly or indirectly, to induce a subordinate to engage in illegal activity, (2) if the president believes that some form of misconduct on the part of a subordinate within the executive branch has occurred and he takes no action to correct it or even to respond to it properly, (3) if the president asks an official or assistant to take ethically questionable steps and does not supervise his or her activity, and (4) if a president does not oversee adequately the actions of his subordinates. It is suggested in this latter case that a president is accountable for any misconduct even if it takes place without his immediate knowledge.[18]

President Nixon resigned before the House impeached him. The House Judiciary Committee, however, had voted to approve impeachment on three counts. It was the view of almost every observer that Nixon would have been impeached and doubtless convicted and removed from office by the Senate shortly thereafter. He chose to resign, in part many feel, because he would have lost the right to his pension and other postpresidency fringe benefits had he been convicted in the Senate. He doubtless decided to resign as well because he had lost the backing of the country and the public support needed to function even at minimal levels in that office.

Many observers have noted that impeachment is a time-consuming and highly traumatic instrument to put into use. This is so. But there is no reason to suppose in most instances that impeachment would be any more traumatic than having a person such as Richard Nixon continue in office for another two years when he has long since lost the ability to govern effectively. The impeachment and removal powers may well be an elaborate and difficult-to-use means to hold presidents to account, but as the Andrew Johnson and Richard Nixon cases attest, each in its own way, it can be used. More important, its availability is an ever-constant reminder to presidents that their power is constrained, that their tenure is not absolutely guaranteed.

PROVIDING FOR FUTURE
SPECIAL PROSECUTORS

Only a handful of the more than one hundred Watergate-related reform bills ever made it through Congress. One of the more controversial ones that did was a provision that would establish, under certain circumstances, a temporary special prosecutor to investigate and prosecute executive-branch conflict-of-interest allegations.

In 1976 the U.S. Senate, under proddings from Senators Sam Ervin and Abraham Ribicoff, overwhelmingly passed a measure creating a permanent special prosecutor who would investigate wrongdoing and conflict of interest by top government officials. The proposed bill would have created a permanent independent office of special prosecutor within the Department of Justice, to be headed for a single three-year term by someone appointed by the president and confirmed by the Senate. The Senate acted because of the belief that top Justice Department officials had an obvious conflict of interest when they investigated whether crimes had been committed either in their own election campaign or by high-ranking officers in the executive branch.

The justification for a permanent public prosecutor was perhaps best outlined by noted Washington attorney Lloyd N. Cutler:

> We have recognized this need for an independent prosecuting official every two or three decades, when instances of official misconduct and conflict of interest have become particularly notorious. Our experience with these special prosecutors has been salutory. Not only have they successfully developed cases that had already surfaced; in the course of their investigations, they have discovered and prosecuted additional crimes that we would never have known about if they had not been appointed. Mr. Cox and Mr. Jaworski, for example, have filed and successfully prosecuted the only significant campaign financing cases that have been brought by the Government of the United States in the last 40 years.
>
> What independent prosecutors uncover once we appoint them suggests that official and campaign misconduct is not rare, but rather that it tends to flourish whenever there is little reason to fear prosecution. Teapot Dome and Watergate may have provided us rare glimpses of predators that regularly roam beneath the surface of the political waters. . . .
>
> We should not be content with a system that requires massive purgatives over a generation. An ongoing institution devoted to the investigation and prosecution of such offenses would increase the likelihood of bringing offenders to justice, and its very existence could deter the commission of offenses that would be committed in its absence. Most important, a continuing public prosecutor might go a long way to restore the public confidence in our institutions that is essential to the operation of a democracy, and that seems to be diminishing with every passing day.[19]

But reaction against the Ervin-Ribicoff Special Prosecutor bill was substantial. Many lawyers and political analysts deemed the idea neither necessary nor desirable. They feared excessive zeal by such a prosecutor could readily lead to petty prosecutions and harassment of executive-branch officials. According to Clark Clifford, one result of this might be "stultification of bureaucratic practices by those who would fear legal attack if they showed any flexibility or departed in any way from past policies. Yet, innovation and decisive action by government officials should be encouraged, not discouraged." [20]

Others feared a permanent special prosecutor would have a staff that would invariably expand with the constant pressure to find things to do. The net result would be a continuing interference with the conduct of the executive branch. Many people doubted whether a person of the stature of an Archibald Cox or a Leon Jaworski would accept appointment to such a permanent position. Cox and Jaworski, the special prosecutors in the Nixon case, both counseled against a permanent prosecutor. Critics feared that someday a Joe McCarthy type might wind up in that office, creating his own police force, faking crimes, and violating the civil liberties of suspects in an effort to smear others and advance himself. Observers worried that a permanent independent prosecutor would be "a free agent, exercising extraordinary power without check. He is, in short, the very kind of official that Watergate should have warned us against." [21] Another general opinion about the Senate's proposal was: "If and when another presidential administration appears to be involved in some gross misconduct, it will be time enough, as the experiences of the Watergate Special Prosecutor's office shows, to respond to the problem specifically and directly." [22]

After two years of further consideration, Congress passed a much watered down version of the Special Prosecutor Act. This 1978 measure calls for the creation of an independent prosecutor only under certain limited circumstances.

Under this new legislation it is up to the attorney general to determine whether or not a case of conflict of interest is valid enough to warrant further investigation and prosecution. This would apply in the cases of about one hundred top executive-office and Justice Department posts and top officers of a presidential election campaign. The statute mandates the appointment by a designated panel of three federal judges of a special prosecutor whenever charges of a violation of federal criminal law arise in connection with these top officials.

There are flaws in the statute. An attorney general, in effect, can decide whether or not to trigger into existence the temporary special prosecutor. If he decides a case is so unsubstantiated as to warrant no further effort, he can prevent investigation and prosecution when others believe it might be justified. As an aide to Senator Ribicoff put it, "While this screening out of frivolous cases had to be done by someone so there would not be a special prosecutor appointed for every crank letter, this is an area of potential abuse if an Attorney General wanted to violate the statute." [23]

Still this post-Watergate measure should have a positive impact on keeping top officials accountable to the criminal law. They now know that their conduct may well have to be judged not by their own political appointees but by an independent prosecutor chosen by the court. This measure also makes clear that even government attorneys in the Department of Justice can have a conflict of interest of an institutional nature. "For too long we have permitted government attorneys to act in situations which clearly presented a conflict — where a private attorney would never be permitted to continue functioning as an attorney." [24]

Although no one can be sure how this reform will work and we can all hope the process will seldom be used, we will just have to wait to see how it works.

THE NO-CONFIDENCE, OR PRESIDENTIAL RECALL, PROPOSAL

One of the more drastic responses to Watergate and the abuse of power by Richard Nixon was the proposed constitutional amendment providing for a vote by Congress of no confidence in a president. The effect would be similar to the recall, now provided for in about sixteen states. Introduced in Congress by Representative Henry Reuss on August 15, 1974, H.J. Resolution 1111 gained little attention and even less support.[25] But it merits some attention in our discussion of presidential accountability, if only because it poses a rather strong alternative to current practices. Indeed, the vote of confidence if introduced has far-reaching consequences, so much so that it might substantially transform the system of government in the United States as we now know it.

How would the no-confidence amendment work? A three-fifths vote of the members of each House present and voting would be necessary. Such a resolution would take priority over any other pending issue before Congress. If adopted, Congress would fix a date, between 90 and 110 days, for a special election for the president and vice president as well as for members of Congress. If it occurs near the regular congressional election date, that date would be used. Note that the incumbent president is eligible to stand for reelection even though he was the target of the no-confidence vote.

A main reason put forward in defense of the no-confidence proposal is that the presidency in modern times has grown too powerful, especially in crisis contexts and in foreign affairs. Presidential power, it is argued, has risen above the level where the system of checks and balances can be effective in countering presidential actions. More bluntly, however, advocates of the no-confidence or similar national recall proposals believe that the four-year fixed term is a liability if and when we have incompetent presidents who lose the confidence of the nation. Incompetence, they point out, is not an impeachable offense.

A main goal of the proposed vote of confidence is to make future presidents more accountable to Congress, as well as more accountable to the American people. A president, it is assumed, would realize that he is accountable for his actions, proposed programs, negotiations, policies, and decisions and would have to face up to criticisms by Congress. The commision of high crimes and misdemeanors would no longer be needed to justify a president's dismissal. Maintaining the confidence of Congress and the general public would be an ongoing necessity. Matters such as Vietnam policy, for example, would have to be discussed in greater detail with congressional leaders to ensure that a president had the support of Congress. The vote of no confidence would be a means of retaliation against a president who too often worked behind the scenes or otherwise manipulated the spirit of checks and balances. Advocates reason that major decisions would have to be made by consultation, instead of by one man. To some extent, then, this constitutional amendment would introduce a certain amount of plural or shared decision making in our national government. The fundamental dangers of decisions by a Lone Ranger president would be thereby reduced.

A primary advantage of the Reuss amendment, of course, is that it does not require proof of illegal conduct. With the impeachment process, high crimes and misdemeanors must be proved. But as James Sundquist writes, "In today's meanings of those words, a president who has simply lost his capacity to lead and govern because of bungling, betrayal by ill-chosen subordinates, or any of the other weaknesses that can lead to misuse of presidential power, cannot for that reason be relieved of power." [26] The Reuss proposal, however, could be used as a clear statement of dissatisfaction with a president's leadership abilities or his policies or lack thereof.

In a nutshell, the chief arguments in favor of the vote of no confidence are these:

Impeachment is an inefficient check. At best it protects against criminal violations of the public trust but not against presidential incompetence.

The president would be more disposed to working with Congress, explaining his policies and educating Congress and the general public about his plans and conduct in office.

This proposal would force more presidential consultation with Congress and the leaders of the major parties and lessen the secrecy surrounding presidential policymaking.

The proposal does not take power away from the president; it only makes him more responsible for how he uses his powers. It might prevent a president from trying to be "above politics" and from isolating himself from criticism.

It would allow Congress to act in the face of negligence, gross incompetence, and disastrous policies, not just explicitly criminal abuses.

The Case Against the
No-Confidence Amendment

Critics viewed the Reuss amendment as an example of "good intentions, bad policy." They pointed out that Congress has plenty of resources with which to check a president if only they would use them. Further, even though presidents have become paramount in the conduct of foreign affairs, Congress has numerous means at its disposal to oversee this exercise of power.

In certain situations it would seem that the vote of no confidence would give Congress the power to continually frustrate a president with whom it disagreed. The alternatives are a government of continuous presidential elections and overall paralysis or a government in which president and Congress are so close as to defeat the basic concept of the separation of powers so fundamental to our system. Perhaps this later condition of power centralized in an overly united president and Congress would, under certain circumstances, be more dangerous to the basic freedom and spirit of the United States than any single "imperial" president.

Moreover, the elections that would be the result of a vote of no confidence might well produce governmental instability and make the development and implementation of long-term programs very uncertain. This would, of course, have a marked effect upon the conduct of our foreign policy.

There is also the argument that a vote of no confidence could actually be used to strengthen the hand of an already strong leader, much as Hitler and de Gaulle used plebiscites to weaken their opposition. If he times it properly, a president who wins a vote of no confidence with a strong show of votes can use it as a false rally of support. One imagines, for example, that Lyndon Johnson could have won a vote of no confidence on his Vietnam policy in 1966. Or Richard Nixon might have won a vote of no confidence during the early stages, say the spring or summer of 1973, of his Watergate crisis. In both cases, these "victories" might have strengthened the hand of those men in defiance of a more responsive, accountable posture.

A vote of no-confidence arrangement might lead presidents to avoid making significant changes in policy that would antagonize Congress. Innovative leadership would be thwarted as presidents might gear most of their actions to public-opinion polls or to the wishes of the majority at the expense of minority rights. The proposal could lead a president to concentrate on short-term or immediately popular initiatives to "create" favorable public approval at the expense of long-term planning.

In short, the cure is worse than the occasional ailment.[27] The vote of no-confidence procedure would not necessarily improve the quality of presidential leadership, nor would it enhance accountability in any significant way. Presidents do not intentionally make poor decisions. What could result might be far worse than the rare arrogant president we have had to endure. This measure might make presidents too dependent on Congress. This measure might make presidents conform too closely with popular opinion. This measure might at some future time give us an endless line of unsuccessful short-term presidents and as a result a paralyzed nation. We risk the unwise weakening of the presidency by such an amendment. Abuses of presidential power do need to be curbed, but this proposal is not the way to do it. We need better leadership, not a weakened presidency.

THE NATIONAL INITIATIVE

One of the controversial political changes Americans have advocated in recent years is the right to initiate or rewrite important national legislation. By a majority of 57 to 21 percent (with 22 percent undecided), in a 1977 Gallup poll, citizens supported a constitutional amendment that would allow voters to initiate national legislation when a group of voters equal to 3 percent of the number who voted in the last presidential election sign a petition requesting such a vote.[28]

Although this change would be new to the national government, it is a familiar practice in about twenty-three states and hundreds of cities. The idea persists that some between-election sanction short of impeachment should be available when a substantial number of Americans believe their president and other national officials are being unresponsive or irresponsible. For those who do not want to go so far as to institute a national recall or a vote of confidence procedure, the idea of impeaching specific national policies (either legislation or executive actions) suggests itself. The impeachment of a policy could, in theory at least, be done by forcing a national policy to be referred to the voters for a vote. Voters have this opportunity in some form or another in more than forty states. The procedure is known as the referendum process. Or the voters could simply, again in theory, initiate a new policy by voting to approve a citizen-initiated measure at the next election.

A proposed national initiative has been the subject of considerable attention on Capitol Hill in the past few years. Hearings were held on the measure in the U.S. Senate in December 1977.[29] About fifty sponsors of the measure introduced variations on this idea in the 96th Congress (1979–1980). The most popular version of the national voter initiative says that the people can write binding national laws with the exception of declaring war, calling up troops, or amending the Constitution. Signatures equal to 3 percent of the ballots cast in the last presidential election and a minimum distribution of 3 percent of registered voters in each of ten states must be gathered in an eighteen-month period. If enough signatures are gathered, the proposition is placed on the next general election ballot. If a majority of those voting vote for it, it becomes law thirty days after the election. It is considered as any other law passed by Congress and signed by the president. A presidential veto is not permitted. However, there is one check on this citizen lawmaking procedure: the measure can be amended if two-thirds of each House vote to amend, although this can be done only after a two-year period. The judiciary, of course, would have the right of judicial review.

What is the rationale for supporting the national initiative? The rising demand for more direct democracy occurs now, as it has in the past, when there is growing discontent with legislative bodies and when there is a decline in the trust of the executive. Such has clearly been the case in recent years. More and more people say our elections are an inadequate accountability mechanism. Elections, proponents of the initiative point out, are a highly imperfect means for popular control of public policy, especially when issues raised during a campaign are not necessarily those that become the important issues later during a president's term. Once elected, a president may alter relations with other nations (as Carter did with Taiwan, for example) or commit the nation to war. A president's fiscal and budgetary policies, which may be quite unrelated to anything he may have pledged in the campaign, can also have extraordinary consequences.

What are the pros and cons of the proposed national voter initiative? Among the more important claims in behalf of this initiative are these:

The citizen initiative would enhance government responsiveness and accountability. It is the ultimate check on nationally elected leaders. If presidents and members of Congress together ignore the will of the people, the people would have this available means to make needed law or to reverse unwanted policies.

It is a desirable safety valve that can be called into use when legislators and presidents become dominated by narrow special-interest groups. Citizen initiative procedures are, the claim is made, freer of special-interest domination than the legislative and policymaking operations in Washington, D.C. As evidence of this, supporters point to Gallup poll data that indicate tough gun-control laws requiring the licensing of all firearms carried outside the home would be enacted by 77 percent of the voters if the measure were in effect now. But the influence of the National Rifle Association in Washington and in individual congressional elections has thus far prevented the adoption of such a measure in Washington by our elected leaders.

Initiative voting would produce an open, educational debate on critical issues that otherwise might be inadequately discussed or discussed only behind closed doors. It is a way, defenders say, of taking personalities out of politics and focusing thoughtful national deliberation on issues instead.

It is a peaceful, nonviolent means of political participation, particularly when people are angry about their governmental leadership or non-leadership. It is also a way of fulfilling a citizen's right to petition the government for redress of grievances.

The national voter initiative might increase voter interest and increase election-day turnout, not a small consideration in a nation of increasingly empty voting booths. Perhaps, too, the very act of giving the citizen more of an active role and more responsibility in governmental processes might help lessen the sense of alienation from government felt by some people.

This kind of referendum voting would also be a vote of confidence in the common sense of the common person. Proponents say the voters are not fools; on the contrary, most voters can see through phoniness and government by public relations — if only they are given a chance. Politics, it is added, must not be left just to the professionals. Much if not all the time, the ordinary citizen is just as capable of making sound decisions as are the experts, politicians, intellectuals, and bureaucrats. Lest we forget, the "best and the brightest" and the "action intellectuals" gave us Vietnam, Watergate, the Korean influence-buying scandal, and much more.

Finally, the national voter initiative is needed because presidents and members of Congress often evade the tough and controversial issues. They fear being in advance of their times. Their concern with staying in office sometimes makes them timid, wedded to the status quo, or overly influenced by narrow constituencies built up around existing government programs. Thus they often delay or duck issues altogether, one result of which is that controversial social issues frequently have to be resolved in the judicial branch. But who elects federal judges?

In short, advocates of the national voter initiative claim that it should help expedite passage of legislation that gets bottled up in Congress or vetoed by presidents. It would be both an action-forcing instrument of the people and a major new means of accountability — of making our national institutions more democratic.

For nearly every claim put forward in behalf of the national initiative there is an equally compelling criticism. The main criticisms are these:

The initiative undermines our representative form of government. The framers of the Constitution purposely constructed a republic because the average person could not be counted on to act for the common good of everyone and preserve individual freedoms, especially minority rights.

The national initiative might further complicate the ballot and confuse the average person who has not kept up with complicated national policy developments.

The national initiative process might be dominated by monied interests who would use the media to sway the average voter with manipulative ad campaigns.

It would often stimulate the rise of hate and fear issues. Hate issues, such as busing, abortion, death penalty, affirmative-action policies, and immigration policies, would raise the emotions of the politically uneducated and nonparticipants and would lead to unsound or unwise or even un-American laws.

National referendum voting would also increase the likelihood of dividing or possibly polarizing the country at a time requiring national unity. Consider the possibilities of a proposition on gas rationing or pornography statutes, not to mention wartime mobilization efforts.

Past uses of the referendum at the state and local levels warn of further difficulties. A lower turnout of voters consistently occurs for referenda than for the election of candidates to national and state offices. Further, the correlation of those who do vote to those in the upper socioeconomic class is nearly always high. Contrary to the expectation of its proponents, therefore, the initiative referenda outcomes have generally strengthened the stalwarts supporting the status quo. Issues of metropolitan reorganization, civil liberties, and civil rights sometimes have suffered setbacks in the marketplace of public referenda. Referenda are used regularly for school-bond issues and property-tax increases to support education, and the results have been frequently conservative and negative.

Referenda also are imperfect at weighing the intensity of people's views. How is it possible to weigh the fact that some people care more intensely about certain issues than others? Once an issue has been posed in a referendum that has binding force, the possibility of any compromise between a lukewarm majority and an intense minority virtually disappears. The notion that a majority is never enough for proper public legitimacy remains basic to democratic theory; minority rights constantly must be taken into account. Processes leaving room for subtle compromise often may be preferable to plebiscitary techniques. Political scientists Raymond Wolfinger and Fred Greenstein argue, for example, that "while politicians inevitably are imperfect in their calculations about intensity, voters are unlikely to make such judgments at all, particularly when their views are channeled through the referenda process." [30] Frequently, no clearly defined set of public attitudes exists at all; the will of the people often is divided, if not confused. For example, in foreign policy, precisely the area in which criticism of an imperial presidency is so great, Gabriel Almond's caution is appropriate:

> Where public policy impinges directly on their interest, as in questions of local improvements, taxation, or social security policy, there are more likely to develop views and opinions resting on some kind of intellectual structure. But on the questions of a more remote nature, such as foreign policy, they tend to react in more undifferentiated ways, with formless and plastic moods which undergo frequent alteration in response to changes in events. The characteristic response to questions of foreign policy is one of indifference. A foreign policy crisis, short of the immediate threat of war, may transform indifference to vague apprehension, to fatalism, to anger; but the reaction is still a mood, a superficial and fluctuating response.[31]

Other deficiencies of the referendum approach lie in its cumbersome, after-the-fact, and often irrelevant character. For the public ire to become sufficiently aroused to mobilize and focus on specific issues takes a long time. John Kennedy and Lyndon Johnson should not have been able to get the country into Vietnam without the knowledge or consent of anybody else, including Congress, but they did. Debates came only years later. In an age of instant decisions — to drop bombs, to send federal troops to a city, or to make crucial calculations about the gold standard — much of what the public might want to object to is already past history, presumably irreversible. Even if a policy is impeached before the fact, this may be insufficient to solve the problem at hand; merely nullifying or curbing the specific acts of the presidency seldom suggests or supplies the alternative policy that might be needed.

Further, there is the classic question of how much a nation wants or can afford to permit public opinion to guide its national leadership. In the yearning for high levels of accountability, a presidency could be devised which would register only the demands of the most boisterous elements in the constituency, perhaps the worst passions and prejudices of a majority. The old political saw "There go my people. I must follow them, for I am their leader" could well become strictly true of the presidency. Walter Lippmann argued that to adhere too closely to listening to the people would constitute a devitalization of governmental power and a malady that could be fatal; that is, when leaders become preoccupied with whether a decision is popular rather than whether it is good, they have, in effect, lost their power to decide, a condition deadly to the survival of a nation as a free society.

In one sense, the issue boils down to this: Does power, properly won, tend to ennoble? Woodrow Wilson thought so: "The best rulers are always those to whom great power is entrusted in such a manner as to make them feel that they will surely be abundantly honored and recompensed for a just and patriotic use of it, and to make them know that nothing can shield them from full retribution for every abuse of it."[32] One may agree with Wilson in most cases, most of the time, but the rare exceptions could prove fatal. Even so, direct government is not the same as self-government. In all probability, to require total accountability to the people would paralyze the presidency and leave it even more impotent than it already is, at least in many areas. Presidential power, properly defined, must consist not merely of the power to persuade; it must consist as well of the power to achieve results. These results, in turn, must be arrived at in ways sufficiently open to permit a public accounting of means as well as ends.

THE SIX-YEAR NONRENEWABLE TERM PROPOSAL

One of the more curious remedies persistently suggested in recent discussions of reforming the presidency is the idea of a single six-year presidential term. This is certainly not a new idea, having been originally proposed in Congress as early as 1826. It has been reintroduced some 150 times since then and has won backing from at least ten presidents, including Presidents Johnson, Nixon, and Carter. The Gallup Opinion organization in 1973 reported that nearly one-third of those polled favored changing to a single six-year term. Presidential candidate John Connally launched his 1980 bid with an endorsement of this reform. This reform could only be achieved by amending our Constitution.

In April 1979 President Carter allowed that the press would ascribe purer motives to his policies if he did not have the option of seeking reelection. And so he endorsed the six-year term as a sensible reform. His attorney general, Griffin B. Bell, called the six-year term an idea whose time has come:

> This change will enable a President to devote 100 percent of his or her attention to the office. No time would be spent in seeking reelection. Under the present system, the President serves three years and then must spend a substantial part of the fourth year in running for reelection. . . .
>
> Moreover, the current four-year term is actually too short to achieve any of the major changes and improvements that a President should accomplish. The funding cycles are so long that it is well into a President's third year before his own program changes take effect. This leaves the bureaucracy in control.

A single six-year term would permit the long-term study, planning, and implementation that our government needs, plus saving that fourth year now lost to campaigning.[33]

Proponents contend that the single six-year term would remove a president from the negative kind of partisan politics. The assumption is that once elected to such a term, with no possibility of reelection, presidents would cast aside partisan calculations and provide leadership for all of the people. He would do what is right even if this meant that his party would lose votes, his friends would suffer financial losses, or his own political future would be damaged. Former Johnson aide Jack Valenti writes that "if the Watergate mess tells us anything it is that the reelection of a President is the most nagging concern in the White House. . . ." Further, he asserts that "Watergate would never have occurred if Presidential aides were not obsessed with reelection. If they had been comfortable in tenure, knowing that in six years they would lose their lease — and in that short time they must write their record as bravely and wisely as possible — is it not possible that their arrogance might have softened and their reach for power might have shortened?" [34]

Advocates of the single six-year term see it as a means of making the presidency more nonpartisan, that is, more objective, "neutral," and "reasonable." They want to take the politics out of the presidency, to de-emphasize the divisive aspects of electoral and partisan politics, to elevate the presidency above selfish or factional ambitions. Some of those who favor this idea see it also as a means of making sure that no president succeeds himself. They prize the concept of citizen-politicians assuming the office of president for a fixed term and then retiring. Some say, too, that a term of six years would strengthen a president's hand in recruiting top managers to the executive departments. Implicit in all these arguments is the hope that the dignity of the office can be enhanced by encouraging presidents to act so as to never favor one party over another, one region over another, or one class over another. Also implicit is the verdict that the roles of politician and statesman are incompatible. Presidents look unstatesmanlike to some people when they appear at party fund-raising dinners or intervene in state and congressional elections.

Arguing that we must liberate the presidency from "unnecessary political burdens," Senator Mike Mansfield said in 1971 that it is intolerable that a president "is compelled to devote his time, energy and talents to what can be termed only as purely political tasks. . . . A president facing reelection faces . . . a host of demands that range from attending the needs of political office holders, office seekers, financial backers and all the rest to riding herd on the day-to-day developments within the pedestrian partisan arena." [35] Others also feel that the country's chief executive should be more businesslike and that reducing his reelection activities would assure more time and energy for substantive planning and systematic program implementation. Some hope, moreover, that the six-year term would enable a president to overcome both his deference to special interests and the timidity that results from having to keep his eye on the forthcoming election.

Several former White House aides have given support to the concept of a six-year term. A former administrative aide to Lyndon Johnson offered this rationale: "I would favor one six-year term for the presidency. I don't think the president should be concerned and involved with politics and the considerations of becoming elected for another term. The president's obligations should be devoted to a whole nation and not to any one section of it." A Nixon foreign-policy aide provided this view: "I am in favor of a six-year term because we frankly don't have enough time to get going as it is. We are working on several things now that are just developing and will have to be dropped this year or next because of the political restraints involved in the 1972 election. . . . There can be some excellent results if we keep pushing. But we are being held back — some of the president's political aides are already sending us memos to that effect." And a former national-security counselor to President Johnson wrote: "The four year presidential term with its tremendous pressures on the incumbent to lay the groundwork for his reelection inhibits . . . long-range non-partisan political thinking. . . . We have seen all too much of White House pressures for dramatic quick fixes on the grounds that 'the president needs something fast before he comes up for reelection.' The single six-year term would seem to provide an atmosphere in which . . . long-term planning and less partisan solutions might have a chance to flourish." [36]

Support for a six-year term without reelection also came from President Johnson, who felt that the most needed reforms take more than four years to formulate, pass, fund, and implement. From the day a new president assumes office, he feels he is racing against an almost impossible time schedule. National budgets are made a year and a half or two years in advance; and, in addition, uncontrollable fiscal and political factors make it difficult for a new president to reorder national priorities significantly. The case for this reform, said Johnson in 1971, is stronger now than ever before: "The growing burdens of the office exact an enormous physical toll on the man himself and place incredible demands on his time. Under these circumstances the old belief that a President can carry out the responsibilities of the office and at the same time undergo the rigors of campaigning is, in my opinion, no longer valid." [37]

In short, the case in favor of the single six-year term is based on several expectations. Namely, that it would:

reduce the role of *politics* in the White House

liberate a president from the worries and indignities of a reelection effort

allow more time to concentrate on policy planning and program implementation

liberate a president from the pressures of special-interest groups and party-line politics, allowing him to exercise greater independence of judgment and nonpartisan leadership

eliminate the advantages of incumbency from presidential elections

allow a president to make decisions free from the temptation of political expediency

enforce the commonsense idea that a period of six years is enough even for the most robust individual

The Case Against the Six-Year Term

Despite some attractive features, the six-year term would cause more problems than it would solve. The required reelection after four years is one of the most democratic aspects of the presidency. It affords an opportunity for assessment. It enhances the likelihood that a president will carefully weigh the effects of whatever he does on his reelection chances. At the core of our system is the belief that our president should have to worry about reelection and be subject to all the same vicissitudes of politics as other elected officials. Moreover, a political party should retain the threat of dumping a president as a check upon the incumbent and the office, especially upon a president who refuses to honor his party's pledges.

When the U.S. Senate in 1913 passed a resolution in favor of the single six-year term, Woodrow Wilson argued against it and his reasoning still seems valid: "The argument is not that it is clearly known now just how long each President should remain in office. Four years is too long a term for a President who is not the true spokesman of the people, who is imposed upon and does not lead. It is too short a term for a President who is doing, or attempting, a great work of reform, and who has not had time to finish it." Wilson also contended that "to change the term to six years would be to increase the likelihood of its being too long without any assurance that it would, in happy cases, be long enough. A fixed constitutional limitation to a single term of office is highly arbitrary and unsatisfactory from any point of view." [38]

The proposed divorce between the presidency and politics presupposes a significantly different kind of political system from that of the United States, which is glued together largely by ambiguity, compromise, and the extensive sharing of powers. In light of the requisites of democracy, the presidency must be a highly political office, and the president an expert practitioner of the art of politics. Quite simply, there is no other way for presidents to negotiate favorable coalitions within the country,

Congress, and the executive branch and to gather the authority needed to translate ideas into accomplishments. A president who remains aloof from politics, campaigns, and partisan alliances does so at the risk of becoming the prisoner of events, special interests, or his own whims.

The very means for bringing a president in touch with reality is the process of political debate and political bargaining, with all of the necessary changes of course, arguments, and listening to other points of view. What makes domestic politics so distasteful to presidents, that it is full of groups to persuade and committees to inform, is precisely its virtue; indeed, it is the major hope for maintaining an open presidency, one neither bound by its own sources of information nor aloof to the point that it will no longer listen.

By calling the president "more presidential" whenever he ignores partisan politics, citizens encourage him to even greater isolation. By turning up their noses at politics in the White House and urging the president to get on with his real business of guiding the nation, they also help to establish the two important conditions for secrecy and duplicity, with which the nation has become so familiar. First, with all the apparatus and technology for secret statesmanship at hand, a president can more easily call upon aides when something needs fixing than persuade the public or Congress to his point of view. Second, because the president will look unpresidential if he participates in normal party politics, his aides must go through grotesque contortions to prove that their boss has never thought about anything except being president of all the people. The tactic of secrecy, so tempting to those who have it within their grasp, amounts to insulating the president from the normal checks and balances of the political system. New bait will be needed to lure presidents out of this comfortable sanctuary and into the morass of open politics, for the present enticements are small.

The premise that politics stops at the water's edge must also be rejected. To bring too little politics and partisanship to bear on foreign-policy matters often means that political parties are not responding to critical issues or are not debating worthwhile alternative policies and deep-seated differences of opinion. Neither of the major American political parties is constituted along neat liberal and conservative lines. A realignment, even a moderate realignment, surely would help to create more effective opposition parties and, hence, the politics of opposition that is so vital on occasion.

One way to prevent future abuses of presidential power, as others have noted, is to make the White House more open; and one way to do that, as has not been suggested so often, is to begin regarding a president as a politician once again. Politics, in the best sense of that term, is the art of making decisions in the context of debate, dialogue, and open two-way conversations, the art of making the difficult and desirable possible.

This kind of politics at the White House should not be diminished. Indeed, as pointed out above, it is highly desirable that presidents be great practitioners of the craft of politics. They, as well as Congress and our parties, would profit from more politics, not less.

Most of the effective presidents have also been highly political. They knew how to stretch the limited resources of the office, and they loved politics and enjoyed the responsibilities of party leadership. The nation has been well served by sensitive politicians disciplined by the general thrust of partisan and public thinking. Many of the least political presidents were also the least successful and seemingly the least suited temperamentally to the rigors of the office. The best have been those who listened to people, who responded to majority as well as to intense minority sentiment, who saw that political parties are often the most important vehicle for communicating voter preferences to those in public office, and who were attentive to the diversity and intensity of public attitudes even as they attempted to educate and to influence the direction of opinion.

President Nixon told the nation during his Watergate crisis that the presidency had to come first and politics second. This, he said, is why he did not involve himself in the 1972 election campaign. So too, Presidents Kennedy and Ford tried on occasion to argue that the problems facing the nation were so technical and administrative in character that they did not lend themselves to the clash of partisan and ideological debate. In essence, they appealed to the belief that highly political decisions must now be placed in the hands of dispassionate bipartisan experts, a notion that is certainly as dangerous as it is blatantly undemocratic.

Everything a president does has political consequences, and every political act by a president has implications for the state of the presidency. The nation must fully recognize that presidents will and must be political, that they ought to be vigorous partisan leaders. Bipartisanship rarely has served the nation well. James MacGregor Burns aptly noted that "almost as many crimes have been committed in the name of mindless bipartisanship as in the name of mindless patriotism." [39] If patriotism in an autocratic system implies blind loyalty to the regime, then patriotism in a democracy must include a responsibility and even obligation to speak out as a citizen whenever one believes that the government is following an unjust or misguided course of action. (Recognizing presidents as partisan political leaders also underscores our lack of an opposition party. Such a party could challenge a president's program and the presidential establishment and would be eager and able to proclaim alternative national priorities.) Decision-making processes in a democracy will be messier and often more confusing than in alternative systems, but if the dreams of Jackson and Van Buren are to be taken seriously, then the real secret and strength of democracy rests in encouraging regular elections and vigorous opposition politics.

If national leaders do become isolated or insulated from the mood of the public, then electing presidents for longer terms would only encourage this tendency.[40] Frequent elections necessarily remain a major means of motivating responsive and responsible behavior. An apolitical president, disinterested in reelection, motivated by personal principle or moralistic abstractions, and aloof from the concerns of our political parties, could become a highly irresponsible president. Elections customarily force an assessment of presidential performance. They are welcomed when promises have been kept and feared when performance has been unsatisfactory. Was it, for example, a mere coincidence, or were President Nixon's troop-withdrawal rates calculated with the election of 1972 in mind? Was the Johnson-Humphrey bombing halt of 1968 aimed toward that year's election? Nixon's economic game-plan reversal in 1971 and Johnson's vain efforts at peace negotiations in 1967 and 1968 were unmistakably related to the positive, constructive, and dynamic character of American elections.

Although change in important national policy is a slow process, a six-year term is not necessarily an appropriate remedy for this. Frequently, policy changes whose pace has frustrated the White House have come slowly because they have been highly controversial and adequate support had not yet been assembled. Mobilizing support is just as much a presidential responsibility as proclaiming the need, and support would be no less crucial with a seven-year or a seventeen-year term. Only a shrewdly political president who is also his party's leader, who is sensitive to political moods, and who is allied with dozens of the political party elite can build those coalitions able to bridge the separation of powers in Washington and to offset the strong forces bent on thwarting progress.

Often, when the White House is frustrated in attempting reform, the proposed changes have not been adequately planned or tested. In the case of the Johnson administration, as has been noted earlier, too many policies were pronounced prematurely — sometimes policy was "made" by press release — and the administration acted as though bill-signing ceremonies were the culmination of the policymaking process. The administration also was frustrated in its attempt to implement sweeping domestic policy changes precisely because too much emphasis was placed on getting the laws on the books, to the neglect of developing the managerial and bureaucratic organizations necessary for imaginative administration of these laws. A White House that becomes overly transfixed with a legislative box score, or that succumbs to the unquenchable thirst for quick political credit, may appear, at least for a while, to be accomplishing great innovations. But translating paper victories into genuine policy accomplishments requires far more than monopolizing the legislative process.

The president who cannot be reelected after four years is unlikely to accomplish anything of value if he is given a free ride for another two. What was true in the past remains true today: effective national leadership requires what the Constitution actually tried to discourage, that a party or faction disperse its members or its influence across the branches of government. Under normal circumstances, a president who ignores this maxim or retreats from these partisan and political responsibilities is unlikely to achieve much in the way of substantive policy innovation. Further, as one former counselor to three presidents put it: "A President who can never again be a candidate is a president whose coattails are permanently in mothballs." [41] A president elected to a single six-year term would be a president inescapably confronted with a bureaucracy as well as senior political appointees even less responsive to him than now. Even when presidents are both popular and eligible for reelection, they depend on senior and mid-career civil servants, a situation summed up in the wry Washington saying that "the bureaucracy eats presidents for lunch." When it is known that a chief executive is to leave by a certain date, bureaucratic entrepreneurs suddenly enjoy wider degrees of discretion and independence. Reeligibility, used or not, is a potentially significant political resource in the hands of a president; and denying that resource, even in the more limited way that the Twenty-second Amendment has done, will diminish the leadership discretion of future presidents who desire to be activist initiators of policy. President Truman spoke to this point, "You do not have to be very smart to know that an officeholder who is not eligible for reelection loses a lot of influence. . . . It makes no sense to treat a President this way — no matter who he is — Republican or Democrat. He is still President of the whole country and all of us are dependent on him; and we ought to give him the tools to do his job." [42]

Political analyst Stephen Hess calls our attention to another practical consideration about the six-year term: If we elect a truly outstanding president under this proposed reform we have him or her in the White House for two years less than under the present practice that would have provided them eight years. If we elect a really bad president we are stuck for two years more than under the present system which provides for getting rid of such types at the end of four years. [43]

The single-term proposal has a comforting ring of good, old-time government and nonpartisanship to it. Yet it represents the last gasp of those who cling to the hope that we can separate national leadership from the crucible of politics and of those who contend that our presidency is too beholden to the workings of a patronage or spoils system. Neither is the case: the former remains an impossibility — it is impossible to take the politics out of public leadership in a democracy — whereas the latter is a problem whose time largely has passed. Equally undesirable is the notion that intense conflict over policy choices, that is, intense political activity, somehow can be removed from the presidency. The conflicts that surround the presidency and require a president to act as a public mediator to mirror those existing and potential conflicts over values that exist within the American society at large. If presidents were not required to resolve political conflicts by making political choices, they would not be fulfilling those responsibilities we rightly associate with democratic leadership.

A PLURAL EXECUTIVE?

The job of the president, some feel, has now become too complex and its reach too extended to be entrusted to one individual's fallible judgment. What can be done to lessen our excessive dependence on the accident of presidential personalities? One solution is to have several presidents. The idea of a plural executive received consideration and some support at the 1787 Constitutional Convention.

The vast responsibilities of an executive who is also chief of state and top party leader are nowhere else expected. Political scientist Herman Finer was sufficiently alarmed by the growth of presidential power that he came out strongly in favor of introducing some kind of plural or collegial element to our national leadership: "The burdens . . . are necessarily so multifarious that to avoid a fatal collapse of efficiency and responsibility the President would have to be a titan and a genius. A collective Presidency might have these qualities, but not a solitary man. A solitary President is a gamble this nation cannot afford." [44] Hence, Finer suggested having one president and eleven vice presidents.

There are numerous variations of the plural executive concept. Some persons have advocated the election of two or three presidents, separating domestic and foreign responsibilities, or separating ceremonial from policy duties, or dividing up the policy formulation and implementation tasks of the presidency. Republican Senator Mark Hatfield suggested that we have an elected vice president, an elected attorney general, and elected heads of the major domestic departments. The Hatfield proposal suggests a plural executive similar to that found in most of the states. [45]

A more modest suggestion, made by former FDR adviser Benjamin Cohen, calls for the creation of a small executive council of not less than five nor more than eight distinguished citizens who would be consulted by a president prior to crucial policy decisions. The Cohen proposal seeks to achieve some of the aims of a plural presidency while leaving our existing singular presidency almost intact. His executive council members would be nominated by a president but subject to Senate confirmation. The council members would be persons of independent political position, widely respected in and out of Congress.

Membership in this executive council would be a full-time job, according to Cohen. The idea is to oblige a president to consult this group of eminent persons *before* he acts on critical national-security matters, although he and he alone would have the ultimate power of decision and the last word.

> The Executive Council should constitute a small super-cabinet with authority to participate in the decision-making process before important or potentially important Presidential plans, programs, and policies are finalized. Its members should have access to reports, memoranda, and other information on any matter within the purview of the Council. They should have authority to request additional information regarding any such matter from responsible sources in the executive establishments, in the Congress or elsewhere. . . .
>
> The members of the Executive Council, individually or collectively, should also have adequate authority within the limits prescribed and guidelines set by the President to act for him in monitoring, approving, and in coordinating the policies and programs of various departments and agencies in order to keep them within and abreast of the Presidential guidelines. But the members of the Executive Council should scrupulously avoid involvement in the minutia of departmental or agency operations. They should operate with very limited staffs of their own and avoid duplicating the staffs of the departments and agencies, although they should have authority to request permission of the heads of departments and agencies to borrow qualified persons for work on particular assignments. . . .[46]

Cohen's proposal emphasizes that the real dangers to presidential leadership come from isolation from peers. Presidents are human beings subject to human frailties. They have their off days, their blind spots, their periods of emotional anxiety, their occasional needs to display a macho aggressiveness. "Quiet consultation by our Presidents before they make their momentous decisions with a small Council of wise and respected persons may protect our Presidents, our nation and our world from much of the hazards of fateful decisions which ultimately must be made by one man." [47]

The Cohen proposal is one of the few plural executive ideas that might be created through legislation rather than through constitutional amendment. It might yield some of the benefits of the plural presidency without inviting most of the liabilities. Although it was one of the few post-Vietnam, post-Watergate reform suggestions to warrant careful consideration, it has received little attention and no support, because most Americans retain the idea that a single executive has to be in charge. Moreover, even the Cohen proposal would further confuse the role of the cabinet and the vice president. Inevitably, too, many in Congress would contend that such an executive council would be a further aggrandizement by the executive of legislative and policymaking powers that rightly belong to Congress — a contention that is not without some merit.

The defects of most plural executive schemes are fairly self-evident:

competition and conflict within the executive, a further swelling of the size of the presidency, and a diffusion and confusion of responsibilities. In times of crisis the members of a truly collective presidency would be expected to show unanimity. But what if they did not come to an agreement? Would the public have confidence in a major policy arrived at by a 3 to 2 or 2 to 1 decision? Surely the bureaucracy might heed such decisions less assiduously. Might not a collectivized presidency court paralysis or indecision, or both, in a nuclear attack or in an international monetary crisis, when swiftness and decisiveness are often most needed?

A plural executive might compound the problems of the already swollen presidential establishment. Conceivably, for example, each president, or each vice president, would want to have his or her own staff, his or her own legislative liaison operation, public-relations staff, and press secretary. Soon, every major interest group would want access to or even representation in each of the various executive staffs. Presidential bureaucratization might become rampant as each of the executives vies for credit, publicity, loyalty, and the appearance of "success."

Plainly, a plural executive would have more difficulty in establishing priorities for the nation. For better or worse, the nation and especially Congress look to the White House for its public-policy agenda. The president must possess the ability to integrate, synthesize, and especially assess the relative merits of one policy with respect to others. How well can this be performed by a collective presidency, where each executive is in charge of just a part or even a fraction of the whole?

A plural executive might encourage excessive internal competition and conflict among the leaders in the executive branch. An intraexecutive veto process might emerge that would weaken executive unity, energy, and dispatch. Our existing system of checks and balances and limited government already seems, according to many people, designed more for paralysis than leadership. The plural executive would just accentuate this characteristic.

Perhaps the most frequent complaint about the plural executive idea is that it would create great difficulties in assigning accountability. Alexander Hamilton argued that the restraints of public opinion on the presidency would lose their efficacy if there were several executives rather than one. Whom should the people blame when things went wrong? Which one or set of executives should be impeached? Far better that there should be a single person for the people to oversee. Hamilton's brief in behalf of a single executive remains compelling:

> . . . the plurality of the Executive tends to deprive the people of the two greatest securities they can have for the faithful exercise of any delegated power, first, the restraints of public opinion, which lose their efficacy as well as on account of the division of the censure attendant

on bad measures among a number, as on account of the uncertainty on whom it ought to fall; and, secondly, the opportunity of discovering with facility and clearness the misconduct of the persons they trust, in order either to their removal from office, or to their actual punishment in cases which admit of it.[48]

Under the existing system, a president already has substantial leeway in creating subordinate positions for sharing his burden. If he so desires, he can appoint a chief of staff or create a de facto assistant president to assume major responsibilities. Many presidents have done precisely this. From a president's point of view, one of the advantages of the current system is that all such assistants or deputy presidents are on a temporary assignment and serve at the pleasure of the president. They can leave once a major assignment is completed. They are expendable, can be shifted to some independent agency or even used as a scapegoat when things go wrong. Under the existing system, a president need not be saddled with permanent deputies with whom he or she may have major disagreements.

In general, suggestions for institutionalizing more help for presidents by fixing into law or grafting onto the Constitution any plan for a plural executive should be treated skeptically. The presidency, as opposed to the president, is already a collective entity, and individual presidents usually have ample discretion to organize their own office as they please. Thus, Franklin Roosevelt during World War II shared substantial presidential authority with such eminent leaders as James Byrnes, Henry Stimson, Cordell Hull, Harold Ickes, Henry Wallace, and Harry Hopkins. In short, the presidency now involves a number of related political leaders, of whom the nominal chief executive is just one, even if almost always the most important one.

PRESIDENTIAL ACCOUNTABILITY AND THE AMERICAN PEOPLE

The basic question here and throughout this book is not whether government by the people is possible or even desirable in the modern world but rather how the political system and the relationship between the leadership and the citizens can be transformed so that they will approach more closely the ideals of democracy. This argument has explicitly rejected the view that things must remain as they are because that is the way underlying forces make them. These pages have often emphasized the need for a strong but also a lean and accountable presidency, a presidency that could achieve the reforms and innovative changes that would broaden the economic and political share of the common person.

The simplistic notion that returning to the drawing boards and coming up with a new charter or a new constitution will provide the needed solutions must be rejected. A new constitutional convention is not needed. Improving and fulfilling national priorities and a better control over the presidency are likely to be accomplished by political rather than constitutional means. No single institutional innovation this writer has ever heard of could guarantee a commitment to truth, compassion, and justice. Formal constitutional provisions to guard against presidential isolation, such as the institutionalization of government-sponsored votes of confidence or a lengthened presidential term, are not the most sensible way to increase accountability.

The fact the American political system and leaders are asked to undertake much of what the rest of society refuses to do is a continual problem in this nation. The promise of the presidency symbolizes the hopes of the people, and certainly there is nothing wrong in calling on our president to summon up exalted national instincts and commitments. But the attempt to reconstitute any single institution in a large, complex society may be rather futile if the fundamental purpose of that institution is to represent and respond to the dominant values of the society. There is little doubt that this society's values are rooted in a strong faith in political and social gradualism, in a deep fear of revolutionary change, and in a steadfast devotion to most of what constitutes the existing order and the existing distribution of wealth and advantages. This is what leads many people to the view that the country by and large gets the kind of leadership it deserves — and that it wants.

Political controls, however, do need to be sharpened and strengthened to ensure a continual public and congressional scrutiny of presidential activity. To describe fully all of the potentially available mechanisms would require another book. But it is clear that openness and candor have been lacking. Presidents and their aides supply disappointingly little information to the press, to Congress, or to the public on matters of impoundment, executive agreements, vetoes, executive orders, and a vast list of other subtle shifts in administrative emphasis. In the seemingly endless attempt to accentuate the positive, White House image-makers too often have distorted news and thereby aggravated difficulties in credibility by claiming too much credit for fortuitous events or for policy initiatives that may or may not achieve sustained or desirable ends, and by projecting the appearance of novelty and boldness usually at the expense of candid discussions of the complexity of problems, the modesty of proposed solutions, and the realities of who must pay and how much.

A free society must mean a society based explicitly on free competition, most particularly competition in ideas and opinions, and by frank discussions of alternative national purposes and goals. Elected leaders and a vigorous press must ceaselessly attack ignorance, apathy, and mindless nationalism — the classic enemies of democracy. The citizen must resist sentimental and rhetorical patriotism that espouses everything as a matter for top priority but in practice eschews the tough political programs that must be begun and implemented. What is needed is a far more thoughtful way of looking at the presidency, leadership, and at citizen responsibilities.

In addition, Congress, the press, and the public must use all existing political controls as a means to inspire as well as to check their presidents. Citizens must insist that their president lend his voice and energies to the weak and the have-not sectors of society. Strengthening the have-not sectors of society and giving a fair hearing to minorities will always remain major presidential responsibilities and an essential part of the legitimacy of the modern presidency. Yet it is well to remember, as most authorities on political change constantly warn, that the way of the reformer, of the catalyst, of creative political change, is always hard: he necessarily fights a two-front war against reactionaries on the one hand and impractical revolutionaries on the other.

In the end, presidents will be kept in line only if the people, according to their own personal views, exercise their rights and their political responsibilities. If the people insist both at and between elections that there be more respect for the doctrine of self-restraint, which all branches, especially the presidency, have been violating in recent years, it will happen. People can "vote" between elections in innumerable ways — by changing parties, by organizing protests, by civil suits and litigation; in short, by "sending them a message." Persistence and intensity will have impact, especially if the political parties can be recast as educational and communications vehicles. The best insurance system to prevent presidential autocracy, on the one hand, and presidential feebleness, on the other, lies in investment in education, dialogue, and rigorous political organizing, in the renewal of our parties, and in the strengthening of citizen-politics at all levels of government.

NOTES

1. James S. Young, "The Troubled Presidency: I" *New York Times,* 6 December 1978, p. A-25.

2. Sam Kernell, Peter Sperlich, and Aaron Wildavsky, "Public Support for Presidents," in Aaron Wildavsky, ed., *Perspectives on the Presidency* (Little, Brown, 1975), p. 178.

3. See John Mueller, *War, Presidents and Public Opinion* (Wiley & Sons, 1973), pp. 196–250.

4. Anthony Downs, "Up and Down with Ecology — The Issue-Attention Cycle," *Public Interest,* September 1972, p. 38.

5. George Romney, "The Citizen Movement" (Paper presented at the Center for the Study of Democratic Institutions, Santa Barbara, Calif., 2 February 1973), p. 3.

6. Andrew Hacker, *The End of the American Era* (Atheneum, 1970), pp. 142–43.

7. Harry Truman, quoted in Richard Neustadt, *Presidential Power* (Mentor, 1960), p. 22.

8. Arthur M. Schlesinger, Jr., *The Crisis of Confidence* (Houghton Mifflin, 1969), p. 291.

9. Kermit Gordon, "Reflections on Spending," in J. D. Montgomery and A. Smithies, eds., *Public Policy* (Harvard University Press, 1966), 15:13.

10. John W. Gardner, testimony before the Senate Government Operations Committee, *Congressional Record*, 92nd Cong., 1st sess., 3 June 1971, S. 8140,

11. Arthur M. Okun, *The Political Economy of Prosperity* (Brookings Institution, 1970), p. 9.

12. Alice M. Rivlin, "Dear Voter: Your Taxes Are Going Up (No Matter Who Wins Tuesday)," *New York Times Magazine*, 5 November 1972, p. 114.

13. Theodore Lowi, *The End of Liberalism* (Norton, 1969), p. 288.

14. Bert Cochran, *Harry Truman and the Crisis Presidency* (Funk & Wagnalls, 1973), p. 8.

15. Studs Terkel, "Jeb Magruder Reflects," *Harper's*, October 1973, p. 72.

16. Committee on Federal Legislation, Bar Association of the City of New York, *The Law of Presidential Impeachment* (Harrow Books, 1974), pp. 5–6.

17. John R. Labovitz, *Presidential Impeachment* (Yale University Press, 1978). See also Charles Black, *Impeachment: A Handbook* (Yale University Press, 1974), Raoul Berger, *Impeachment: The Constitutional Problems* (Harvard University Press, 1973), and Murray C. Havens and Dixie M. McNeil, "Presidents, Impeachment and Political Accountability," *Presidential Studies Quarterly*, Winter 1978, pp. 5–18.

18. Labovitz, *op. cit.*

19. Lloyd N. Cutler, "A Proposal for a Continuing Public Prosecutor," a talk at the University of California, 18 November 1974, reprinted in *Watergate Reorganization and Reform Act of 1975*, Hearings before the Committee on Government Operations, U.S. Senate, July 1975, pp. 208–10.

20. Clark Clifford, letter, in *Watergate Reorganization and Reform Act of 1975*, *op. cit.*, p. 204.

21. David Broder, "Watergate Reform Act: Dangerous and Offensive," *Washington Post* column, reprinted in *Congressional Record*, 29 July 1976, p. E. 4174.

22. Philip A. LaCovara, Statement in *Watergate Reorganization and Reform Act of 1975*, *op. cit.*, p. 264.

23. David R. Schaefer to Thomas E. Cronin, personal letter, 17 January 1979.

24. *Ibid*. On the other hand, some critics are still worried about the possible abuses of even a temporary special prosecutor; see, for example, Steven J. Heyman, "A Bad Idea Whose Time Has Come," *Commonweal* 26 May 1978, pp. 329–31.

25. The constitutional amendment proposed by Representative Henry S. Reuss can be found in *Congressional Record*, II 7158, 21 July 1975. The one place where it received attention and scrutiny was in the *George Washington Law Review*, which contained a symposium on the no-confidence proposal (January 1975): 328–500.

26. James Sundquist, "Needed: A Workable Check on the Presidency," *Brookings Bulletin* 10, no. 4 (1973): 7.

27. Samuel H. Beer puts it well from a comparative perspective: "The lesson of British experience, and indeed of comparative government generally, is that the vote of confidence device might unduly weaken the executive, or unduly strengthen the executive, or, possibly, bring about the nice adjustment that Representative Reuss desires. In short, the consequences of the proposed reform are incalculable. In view of the further fact that the impeachment process did work in the case of President Nixon, these prospects indicate to this author that Congress should leave things as they are." *George Washington Law Review*, January 1975, p. 371.

28. See Hearings, *Voter Initiative Constitutional Amendment*, Subcommittee on the Constitution of the Committee on the Judiciary, U.S. Senate, 95th Cong., 13–14 December

1977, p. 646. See also Ronald J. Allen, "The National Initiative Proposal: A Preliminary Analysis" *Nebraska Law Review*, 1979.

29. *Ibid.*

30. Raymond Wolfinger and Fred Greenstein, "The Repeal of Fair Housing in California: An Analysis of Referendum Voting," *American Political Science Review*, September 1968, p. 769. On the limits of referenda and initiative, see also V. O. Key, Jr., and Winston Crouch, *The Initiative and the Referendum in California* (University of California Press, 1939), and Lindsay Rodgers, *The Pollsters, Public Opinion, Politics and Democratic Leadership* (Knopf, 1949).

31. Gabriel Almond, *The American People and Foreign Policy* (Praeger, 1950), p. 53.

32. Woodrow Wilson, *Congressional Government* (1885; reprint ed., Meridian Books, 1936), p. 187.

33. Attorney General Griffin B. Bell, Address before the faculty and students, University of Kansas, Lawrence, Kans., 25 January 1979, mimeo, p. 5. It might also be mentioned that the founders of the southern Confederacy were also proponents of this idea and indeed provided for a six-year single term for their president. More recently a Washington-based foundation has been organized to limit congressional terms and press for the adoption of a six-year single presidential term. The Foundation for the Study of Presidential and Congressional Terms was established under the National Heritage Foundation in July 1977 as a nonpartisan, nonprofit organization.

34. Jack Valenti, "A Six-Year Presidency?" *Newsweek*, 4 February 1974, p. 11. See also Charles Bartlett, "That Six-Year Term," *Washington Star* 2 May 1979, p. A-19.

35. Mike Mansfield, *Statement in Support of Senate Joint Resolution 77*, before the Subcommittee on Constitutional Amendments of the Senate, Committee on the Judiciary, 28 October 1971; processed. For his extended views and those of several other witnesses, see U.S. Congress, Senate, Committee on the Judiciary, Subcommittee on Constitutional Amendments *Singles Six-Year Term for President*, 92nd Cong., 1st Sess., 1972, p. 32.

36. Chester Cooper, *Perspective*, March 1972, p. 47.

37. Lyndon B. Johnson, *The Vantage Point* (Holt, Rinehart and Winston, 1971), p. 344. Jimmy Carter's similar views are found in *Family Weekly*, 23 Sept. 1979, p. 8.

38. Woodrow Wilson, letter placed in the *Congressional Record*, 64th Cong., 2d sess., 15 August 1916, 53, pt. 13:12620.

39. James MacGregor Burns, "Keeping the President in Line," *New York Times*, 8 April 1973, p. E-15.

40. The possibility also exists that a six-year term, or "a term-and-a-half" as some call it, with reelection precluded, would intensify the presidential selection process. Certainly in such a winner-take-more situation, there is the likelihood that ideological competition would be more aggressive and perhaps more bitter than at present. Conflict would assuredly be heightened. How harmful this would be is difficult to assess, but judging from how corrupt the 1972 reelection campaign became this factor must be considered.

41. Clark Clifford, in hearings before the Subcommittee on Constitutional Amendments of the U.S. Senate, Committee on the Judiciary, October 1971; processed, 92nd Cong., 1st sess.

42. Harry S. Truman, testimony before the Subcommittee on Constitutional Amendments of the U.S. Senate, Committee on the Judiciary, Hearings on S.J. Resolution II: "Presidential Term of Office," 86th Cong., 1st sess., 1959, Part I, p. 7.

43. Stephen Hess, "Espousing a Six-Year Presidency," *Rocky Mountain News*, 11 March 1979, p. 73.

44. Herman Finer, *The Presidency: Crisis and Regeneration* (University of Chicago Press, 1960), p. viii. See also a more recent plea for a more collective presidency: Milton Eisenhower, *The President Is Calling* (Doubleday, 1974).

45. See Mark O. Hatfield, "Resurrecting Political Life in America . . .," *Congressional Record,* 93rd Cong., 1st sess., 12 October 1973, 119, no. 153, S. 19104–07.

46. Benjamin V. Cohen, "Presidential Responsibility and American Democracy" (1974 Royer Lecture, University of California, Berkeley, 23 May 1974; processed), pp. 24–25.

47. *Ibid.*, p. 29. See also George Reedy, *The Twilight of the Presidency* (World, 1970).

48. Alexander Hamilton, *The Federalist,* No. 70 (Modern Library, 1937), pp. 460–67.

CHAPTER 11

PRESIDENTIAL LEADERSHIP

. . . there is a natural aristocracy among men. The grounds of this are virtue and talents. . . . There is also an artificial aristocracy founded on wealth and birth, without either virtue or talents; for with these it would belong to the first class. The natural aristocracy I consider as the most precious gift of nature for the instruction, the trusts, and government of society. . . . May we not even say that that form of government is best which provides the most effectually for a pure selection of these natural aristoi into the offices of government?

Thomas Jefferson to John Adams, 28 October 1813,
The Adams-Jefferson Letters, Lester J. Cappon,
ed. (University of North Carolina Press, 1959), p. 388.

The American political system, though misconceived by some as made up of three coordinate branches of equal powers, has worked best as a presidential system. Only strong Presidents have been able to overcome the tendencies toward inertia inherent in a structure so cunningly composed of checks and balances.

— Arthur M. Schlesinger, Jr., *The Politics of Hope* (Houghton Mifflin, 1962), p. 9.

Most great (not just capable) leaders are the product of major emergencies or disasters. No doubt there are many born leaders, but it is generally only in times of trouble that we let their potentialities blossom into greatness. Great leaders — Roosevelt, Churchill, De Gaulle in our time — appear when a society needs them desperately: only under such conditions are there likely to be both the mandate and the highly motivated followers that great leadership requires. Clearly then, no society should expect to have an endless succession of extraordinary leaders. A healthy society, especially one with our tradition of dispersed power, should be able to function well with good rather than great leaders. Indeed, one of the glories of our society is that "the system" is not excessively dependent on the leader.

— John W. Gardner, *Morale* (Norton, 1978), p. 133.

Presidents in our time are regularly condemned for providing either the wrong kind of leadership or not enough leadership. Yet the presidency was not exactly designed to be the prime source of leadership for the American Republic.[1] Presidents were not expected to be party or legislative leaders. A president was to be a chief administrator and at times the commander in war. The founding politicians vainly hoped the legislature would be the prime leadership branch.

All that has long since changed. Wars, emergencies, national growth, industrialization, and the vast interdependency of our economy with the economies of the rest of the world have had their impact on the presidency. The overall effect has been an almost continual growth in presidential powers and responsibilities. It has meant an enlarged job description for presidents and an ever larger demand that presidents assume the central responsibility for national leadership.

But how much leadership can a president provide? Do we turn too frequently to presidents? Have we in our preoccupation with the larger-than-life heroic leader blocked our recognition of other forms and other locations of leadership that could be more relevant for today's policy problems? I would like to offer a political scientist's thoughts on these questions and to make some suggestions about what might be done to help the situation.

Leadership is an elusive term. We know it when we have it, or see it, but it defies easy definition. Leadership is generally defined as the capacity to make things happen that would otherwise not happen. We think of national leadership as the ability to mobilize human resources in pursuit of desired societal goals. But societal leadership is often an especially untidy process, an untidy process of both national problem solving and national morale building. There is seldom a fixed route, an available recipe book, that guides the way. That's not the way significant policy change comes about. Inventive breakthroughs more often than not occur through a long and disorderly process. Purposive social change often occurs in a way similar to the process involved as an infant learns to walk:

"the society tries, fails, learns, has partial success, bumps its nose, cries, tries again." [2] Experimentation and learning-by-doing rather than preconceived theories have been the animating spirit of American leadership. "Experience," James Madison advised, "is the guide that ought always to be followed whenever it can be found."

Some observers suggest that we seldom, if ever, recruit gifted leaders — men and women with demostrated intellectual and leadership abilities. Instead, they contend, we elect "nice guys" who may talk about change but don't really want it. In other words, we elect those who have a stake in the status quo. If the choice is between the brilliant and the safe, the safe candidate always wins. A stark version of this proposition was put forward a while ago by a retired United States senator: "Anybody who really would change things for the better in this country could never be elected President. . . ." [3] We like our candidates to be sensible, vigorous, and likable, but originality and an independence of mind is not especially sought.

Many of our best presidential leaders were not viewed as such as they entered the White House. Most were "not-rock-the-boat" types. Moreover most of them did not have a sweeping or clear mandate to embark upon bold change. Lincoln, Wilson, Kennedy, all were minority presidents (winning less than 50 percent of those who turned out to vote). Teddy Roosevelt and Lyndon Johnson had no mandate at all, having come to the office because of the death of their predecessor. Franklin Roosevelt ran more as a conservative "balance-the-budget" man than as a bold innovator. And he won at a time when almost anyone who won the Democratic nomination was assured of victory in November.

Most presidents we have come to label as great served in office when there were great challenges to the nation — wars and depressions especially. Confronted with emergencies, they devised programs and worked actively to get them through Congress or they helped devise strategies and worked to get them implemented. In times of trouble, presidents identify themselves with the whole people and the people in turn have usually given these presidents an in-between election mandate without which purposive leadership simply cannot occur. To be sure, there are exceptions, but this has been the general pattern.

The American public often complains that we lack "the truly great" leaders the times demand. We have only "politicians," or so the lament usually goes. They complain that these highly political candidates take money from the rich and votes from the poor on the false promise of protecting each from the other. They contend, too, that presidential candidates approach every question with an open mouth and raise vacillation to the level of moral principle. National politicians, in short, are the public's favorite punching bag.

High-minded people who look down their noses at the politicians should take another look. The art of politics is vital in a democratic society. Politics is the arena in which conflict gets managed, issues get clarified, and problems get resolved. Politics is often defined as the art of the possible. The job of the politician — the creative political leader — is to help us to stretch, to set our sights higher, and to pull together our talent and resources to overcome difficulties and achieve desired breakthroughs.

We will have to enlist and support the best of politicians if we would have competent problem solvers in Washington. We will have to enlist and recruit the best of our young to the craft and profession of politics. We have little choice: we will either have to shoot it out in the streets or reconcile ourselves to the often untidy processes of politics — most notably the haggling, bargaining, compromising, and pulling and hauling that are the everyday essence of political life.

At the same time we have to remind ourselves that presidents must first and foremost be political brokers. That is, they must balance competing interests and seek to please as many people as possible. They are asked to serve majorities. We don't elect prophets, we elect politicians. There is a major difference. Politicians, for obvious reasons, try to tell us what we want to hear. Prophets tell us what is right. "They [the prophets] set impossibly high standards for the rest of us. They make us appreciate the purely political virtues of compromise, easily pleased vanity and mediocre expectation." [4]

The creative politician and the prophet-educator have some characteristics in common. Both have a sense of drive and know that excessive modesty can paralyze. Both know that fatalism can sap the will. Both know that every calling is great when greatly pursued. Both know that stamina, focus, enthusiasm, and timing are the essentials of national revitalization and purposive social change.

John W. Gardner comments on the requisites of leadership: "The future is not shaped by people who don't believe in the future. It will be built by people who see the complexities that lie ahead but are not deterred; people who are conscious of the flaws in humankind but not overwhelmed by the doubts and anxieties of life; people with the vitality to gamble on their future, whatever the odds. . . ." [5] Gardner adds that significant achievements usually have been brought about by people with at least a touch of irrational self-confidence. "Men and women of vitality have always been prepared to bet their futures, even their lives, on ventures of unknown outcome. If they had all looked before they leaped, we would still be crouched in caves sketching animal pictures on the wall." [6] In short, a crucial need for both the politician and the prophet: Acknowledge human fallibility but believe in oneself; acknowledge the complexity of today's problems but still be prepared to act.

Americans hold exaggerated expectations about the political process as a whole. They expect that a great proportion of national or local problems can somehow be alleviated through politics or government and that the right person at the right time in the right office (usually the presidency) can solve society's most complex problems. But the so-called executive virtues of unity, expertise, secrecy, and dispatch do not always characterize the contemporary presidency and most assuredly not the sprawling executive branch. On too many occasions the executive branch is more aptly characterized as splintered, stumbling, leaky, and caught in a web of red tape and cost overruns. Many actions boldly proclaimed by a president in behalf of the public interest have an unreasonably high cost in terms of basic freedoms and civil liberties. Those persons who look to the presidency as a moral anchor or as the nation's hope for progressive, reformist breakthroughs must be mindful also of some of the more dubious presidential commitments of the recent past: the Bay of Pigs, the bombing of North Vietnam, the invasion of a handful of small nations, the spiraling arms race, the perpetuation of an unjust tax structure, Watergate, and the general permissiveness toward the white majority's reluctance to accept black and Spanish-speaking minorities on terms of equality.

Needed is the practical realization that only rarely can a president succeed in bringing about large-scale innovative social changes, and that presidents who would be representatives and activists in behalf of the have-not sectors need extensive support from sizable numbers of those in middle- and upper-income groups. We need to more fully appreciate that "the basic reason why neither Congress nor the President is truly liberal is that liberalism normally represents a minority position in the United States — a fact often obscured by the assumption that the Democratic Party is a liberal party, rather than an exceedingly broad coalition." [7]

The more we learn about the workings of the presidency, the more it appears that a president cannot act as a serious initiator of reforms in more than a few areas at a time. If a president is forced to respond to all the major issues of the day, he doubtless will be forced to respond mainly on the plane of symbolic and superficial politics. Such overloading invites a new kind of weakened presidency in an era in which many problems — such as inflation and recession — require strong longer-range measures. To ensure that presidents do respond — and are to respond — to the most salient problems, to keep presidents accountable, the public should have recourse to vigorous education and political campaigns.

Simultaneously, a renewed respect for, and attention to, other institutions, in and out of government, would strengthen them as alternative sources of reform, policy experimentation, and problem-solving leadership. Congress should be encouraged to play a larger role as a forum for new policy ideas; courts should be encouraged to exercise their powers to curb the Congress and the executive from delegating away to the special interests all of their leadership discretion; states should be recognized as necessary laboratories of reform leadership and enlightened experimentation; foundations and universities should be more accountable as pedagogical and experimental research centers; and public-interest lobbies and legal-aid societies should assume more of the burden of representing the unrepresented. The presidency must not be allowed to become the only, or even the primary, instrument for the realization of government of, by, and for the people.

More often than not, new issues and ideas enter the public arena from outside the political system and impose themselves on political leaders, rather than vice versa. To vest all hope in the wisdom or omniscience of one person is to ignore the vital role of persistent extragovernmental pressures, both elite and grass roots, in bringing about desirable national policies. Too much credit is bestowed on executive leadership or the political entrepreneur and too much glamorization of presidential achievements has occurred, to the neglect of how policy issues and ideas really are generated and develop a life of their own.

Nobody really voted for the New Deal, the Great Society, or the New Federalism. Presidents and Congress respond to crises and issues as they arise, and nearly always they arise between rather than during elections. Activist and effective presidential leadership (or what is often celebrated in textbooks as the promise of the presidency) has been elicited almost exclusively by war, depression, or rare periods of vastly accelerating national revenues. Hence, the frequent presidential lament, that it will take a crisis to bring about change, that unless the people are jolted out of their complacency they will not be aroused and without an aroused public a leader's opportunity to lead is minimal. In the late 1970s a pollster is alleged to have asked interviewees: "Which is the greatest problem facing democracy in the United States today: public ignorance or public apathy?" To which one person replied: "I don't know and I don't care." That's what presidents regularly confront.

The yearning for a nuclear-age philosopher-king can lead only to generalized disappointment or perhaps to the end of democracy as it has been known in America. In a majoritarian democratic republic, policies will change slowly. With few exceptions, the impressive limits and constraints on presidential leadership, especially in the domestic-policy area, can be removed only through the undermining of the processes of coalition-based government and cooperative federalism.

It has been fashionable in recent years to urge our presidents to be national educators. This is, of course, hardly a novel injunction. Ever since George Washington held the post, Americans have eagerly sought a president's guidance. But it seems to me that we now ask our presidents to be visionaries, unusually possessed of a conviction about the direction in which they want to take the nation.

A careful reading of history suggests, however, that this has seldom been the case. The real visionaries and significant educators in the nation have usually operated outside the White House and often outside Washington, D.C.

Adlai Stevenson said that major issues could neither be developed nor effectively presented during presidential campaigns. They must be sharpened and defined and clarified largely through the legislative process between elections. Stevenson did not overstate the matter. If he erred, it was probably in overdrawing the role of the legislature.

Time and again we witness the strategic consciousness-raising and clarification functions of societal leadership coming from persons quite unlike presidents who have a major stake in change and who could seldom be mistaken as presidential candidates.

When one recalls the civil-rights movement, the women's liberation campaign, the anti–Vietnam War effort, consumer and environmental protection, budget cutting protests and kindred crusades, one cannot remember any president who provided the vision, who seized the opportunity to be the educator, or who played a significant role as even a consciousness raiser. As has been mentioned earlier in this book, national politicians fear being right too early, fear being in advance of their times. They want and need to be at the center of things, including the center of political thinking.

If this is so, we shall have to look elsewhere for our national educators. We shall have to look to those interest group leaders, citizen and social movement leaders and those unreasonable and often unelectable types who dream dreams of a more ideal world.

The reality is that all too often on the long road to the White House our sometime-to-be-presidents become the servants of what is, rather than the visionary shapers of what could be. In the long process of working their way up and learning to operate within the system they become rewarded for playing along with the dominant interests and for playing within the traditional rules of the game. "By the time they reach the top, they are very likely to be trained prisoners of the structure. This is not all bad; every vital system reaffirms itself. But no system can stay vital for long unless some of its leaders remain sufficiently independent to help it change and grow." [8]

What have the Martin Luther Kings, the Ralph Naders, the John Gardners, the Rachel Carsons, the I. F. Stones, the Barry Commoners, the Howard Jarvises, and the Bella Abzugs in common? They dared to be different. They sought to understand what it was that was wrong and dared to share that understanding with large numbers of others. Most also were willing to engage in a form of political education and political mobilization that was irritating to the centrist custodians of the status quo. They were willing to rock the boat, chart out higher standards and forgo political careers.

Progress comes about in America not because we elect visionary presidents but because of the way our political system gradually responds to militant mobilizers and political prophets whose views take hold around the country. It is in this sense that presidents can be said to be followers as much as, or more than, they are leaders. When the country's consciousness has been raised by trailblazers, muckrakers, or out-of-office programmatic activists, it is then, and perhaps only then, that a president can provide the acceptance, approval, and spirit of renewal that can accommodate change.[9]

It is in this sense that presidents, in theatrical parlance, provide a kind of Act III leadership. Theirs is no less crucial for coming late in the "performance." But what is essential to understand here is that Act I and Act II leadership are similarly crucial and more often than not these initial phases of leadership must be provided by nonpresidential actors, very often indeed by non-Washingtonians.

It is just too simple to say that great presidential leadership arises when a nation finds itself in great trouble. There are enough Buchanans, Grants, Hoovers, and Fords who have failed this test. James MacGregor Burns writes that "great leadership requires great followership. Leaders mobilize the best in their followers, who in turn demand more from their leaders." [10] Could it not also be the case that great leadership comes about at the top when there has developed middle-level political or social movement leaders who in effect clarify, define, set the agenda, and mobilize the nation in such a way that presidents must join in and, in effect, both follow and lead.

If this is the case, as I think it often is, the competent president must recognize this and be willing to enlist the leadership talents of individuals — both political and nonpolitical — throughout society. The creative president in the words of Bruce Miroff would "reawaken in Americans a sense of their own capacity for political freedom." [11] He would reawaken in people a sense of their own leadership potential, of their own responsibility to partake of society's leadership needs. Thus the competent president sets the tone — a tone that positively encourages Act I and Act II leadership and knows how and when to respond to it.

The realistic presidential leader knows that we define too many of our problems as solvable only by the national government. Many of the problems of both the imperial and the imperiled presidency arise because we have turned too frequently to presidents for the answers to our problems. Those who are concerned with the preservation of individual responsibility and the vitality of nongovernmental institutions must help nurture multiple kinds of leadership at all levels in private as well as public sectors. We shall, of course, need a strengthened and effective presidency. We shall, of course, need brilliant, talented presidents. But we need to deflate the notion that presidents can provide all or even the major amount of our national leadership.

We could achieve this in part by strengthening local, state, and regional government to address problems that should be solved at those levels. We need to strengthen and renew political parties and encourage educators, researchers, enlightened business officials, and other professional leaders to speak out on national issues and to assume some of the responsibility for problem solving, educating and mobilizing the public. We might also more systematically nurture and reward the role of the critic-prophet. We need to expand and replicate leadership development programs for young potential leaders — programs that help our highly specialized young to become generalists and the broken-field runners who can begin to see the interrelationship. The White House Fellows program (at the national level) and programs such as Leadership Corpus Christi (at the city level) are indispensable and illustrative in this connection.

Prudent efforts along these lines will help us overcome our naive preoccupation with the "storybook presidency," with the illusion that only presidents can solve our problems. We must take the initiative to assume responsibility for our problems instead of looking always to the national government to do it all. We must refine our expectations of the president and raise our expectations of ourselves.

I should like to repeat the quote from John Steinbeck with which I began this book:

> We give the President more work than a man can do, more responsibility than a man should take, more pressure than a man can bear. We abuse him often and rarely praise him. We wear him out, use him up, eat him up. And with all this, Americans have a love for the President that goes beyond loyalty or party nationality [sic]; he is ours and we exercise the right to destroy him.[12]

NOTES

1. James MacGregor Burns, *Leadership* (Harper & Row, 1978), p. 385.

2. I am in debt to John W. Gardner for this observation and related observations that have influenced my thoughts in this section. Personal letter to the author, 17 October 1978. Also see his *Morale* (Norton, 1978).

3. James Abourezk, "Life Inside the Congressional Cookie Jar," *Playboy*, March 1979, pp. 105–06.

4. Garry Wills, *Confessions of a Conservative* (Doubleday, 1979), p. 167.

5. Gardner, *Morale, op. cit.*, p. 152.

6. *Ibid.*

7. Gary Orfield, *Congressional Power* (Harcourt, Brace, Jovanavich, 1978), p. 323.

8. John W. Gardner, personal communication, 17 October 1978.

9. James L. Sundquist develops a similar but more Washington-based thesis in his excellent *Politics and Policy: The Eisenhower, Kennedy and Johnson Years* (Brookings Institution, 1968), see chaps. 10–12.

10. James MacGregor Burns, "More Than Merely Power: II" *New York Times,* 17 November 1978, p. A29.

11. Bruce Miroff, *Pragmatic Illusions: The Presidential Politics of John F. Kennedy* (McKay, 1976), p. 293.

12. John Steinbeck, *America and Americans* (Bonanza Books, 1966), p. 46.

APPENDIX

SELECTED
INFORMATION
ON THE
PRESIDENCY

TABLE A.1   PRESIDENTS, THEIR TERMS AND EXPERIENCE

President	Term	Party	VP	Cab-inet	Cong.	Gov.	Gen.
1. George Washington	1789–97	Fed.					x
2. John Adams	1797–1801	Fed.	x				
3. Thomas Jefferson	1801–09	D/R	x	x		x	
4. James Madison	1809–17	D/R		x	x		
5. James Monroe	1817–25	D/R		x	x	x	
6. John Quincy Adams	1825–29	D/R		x	x		
7. Andrew Jackson	1829–37	Dem.			x	x a	x
8. Martin Van Buren	1837–41	Dem.	x	x	x	x	
9. William Harrison	1841	Whig			x	x a	x
10. John Tyler	1841–45	Whig	x		x	x	
11. James Polk	1845–49	Dem.			x	x	
12. Zachary Taylor	1849–50	Whig					x
13. Millard Fillmore	1850–53	Whig	x		x		
14. Franklin Pierce	1853–57	Dem.			x		x
15. James Buchanan	1857–61	Dem.		x	x		
16. Abraham Lincoln	1861–65	Rep.			x		
17. Andrew Johnson	1865–69	Union	x		x	x	
18. U. S. Grant	1869–77	Rep.		x			x
19. Rutherford Hayes	1877–81	Rep.			x	x	x
20. James Garfield	1881	Rep.			x		x
21. Chester Arthur	1881–85	Rep.	x				x
22. Grover Cleveland	1885–89	Dem.				x	
23. Benjamin Harrison	1889–93	Rep.			x		x
24. Grover Cleveland	1893–97	Dem.				x	
25. William McKinley	1897–1901	Rep.			x	x	
26. Theodore Roosevelt	1901–09	Rep.	x			x	
27. William Taft	1909–13	Rep.		x		x a	
28. Woodrow Wilson	1913–21	Dem.				x	
29. Warren Harding	1921–23	Rep.			x		
30. Calvin Coolidge	1923–29	Rep.	x			x	
31. Herbert Hoover	1929–33	Rep.		x			
32. Franklin Roosevelt	1933–45	Dem.				x	
33. Harry Truman	1945–53	Dem.	x		x		
34. Dwight Eisenhower	1953–61	Rep.					x
35. John Kennedy	1961–63	Dem.			x		
36. Lyndon Johnson	1963–69	Dem.	x		x		
37. Richard Nixon	1969–74	Rep.	x		x		
38. Gerald Ford	1974–77	Rep.	x		x		
39. Jimmy Carter	1977–81	Dem.				x	
Totals (to 1981)			13	9	23	17 b	11

a Denotes territorial governorship.

b Total is less than the number of items listed because Cleveland appears twice but served as governor only once.

TABLE A.2   PRESIDENTIAL ELECTION RESULTS

Year	Candidates	Party	Popular Vote	Electoral Vote
1789	**George Washington**			69
	John Adams			34
	Others			35
1792	**George Washington**			132
	John Adams			77
	George Clinton			50
	Others			5
1796	**John Adams**	Federalist		71
	Thomas Jefferson	Democratic-Republican		68
	Thomas Pinckney	Federalist		59
	Aaron Burr	Democratic-Republican		30
	Others			48
1800	**Thomas Jefferson**	Democratic-Republican		73
	Aaron Burr	Democratic-Republican		73
	John Adams	Federalist		65
	Charles C. Pinckney	Federalist		64
1804	**Thomas Jefferson**	Democratic-Republican		162
	Charles C. Pinckney	Federalist		14
1808	**James Madison**	Democratic-Republican		122
	Charles C. Pinckney	Federalist		47
	George Clinton	Independent-Republican		6
1812	**James Madison**	Democratic-Republican		128
	DeWitt Clinton	Federalist		89
1816	**James Monroe**	Democratic-Republican		183
	Rufus King	Federalist		34
1820	**James Monroe**	Democratic-Republican		231
	John Quincy Adams	Independent-Republican		1
1824	**John Quincy Adams**	Democratic-Republican	108,740 (30.5%)	84
	Andrew Jackson	Democratic-Republican	153,544 (43.1%)	99
	Henry Clay	Democratic-Republican	47,136 (13.2%)	37
	William H. Crawford	Democratic-Republican	46,618 (13.1%)	41
1828	**Andrew Jackson**	Democratic	647,231 (56.0%)	178
	John Quincy Adams	National Republican	509,097 (44.0%)	83
1832	**Andrew Jackson**	Democratic	687,502 (55.0%)	219
	Henry Clay	National Republican	530,189 (42.4%)	49
	William Wirt	Anti-Masonic ⎱		7
	John Floyd	National Republican ⎰	33,108 (2.6%)	11
1836	**Martin Van Buren**	Democratic	761,549 (50.9%)	170
	William H. Harrison	Whig	549,567 (36.7%)	73
	Hugh L. White	Whig	145,396 (9.7%)	26
	Daniel Webster	Whig	41,287 (2.7%)	14
1840	**William H. Harrison**	Whig	1,275,017 (53.1%)	234
	Martin Van Buren	Democratic	1,128,702 (46.9%)	60
1844	**James K. Polk**	Democratic	1,337,243 (49.6%)	170
	Henry Clay	Whig	1,299,068 (48.1%)	105
	James G. Birney	Liberty	62,300 (2.3%)	

TABLE A.2   *(Continued)*

Year	Candidates	Party	Popular Vote	Electoral Vote
1848	**Zachary Taylor**	Whig	1,360,101 (47.4%)	163
	Lewis Cass	Democratic	1,220,544 (42.5%)	127
	Martin Van Buren	Free Soil	291,263 (10.1%)	
1852	**Franklin Pierce**	Democratic	1,601,474 (50.9%)	254
	Winfield Scott	Whig	1,386,578 (44.1%)	42
1856	**James Buchanan**	Democratic	1,838,169 (45.4%)	174
	John C. Frémont	Republican	1,335,264 (33.0%)	114
	Millard Fillmore	American	874,534 (21.6%)	8
1860	**Abraham Lincoln**	Republican	1,865,593 (39.8%)	180
	Stephen A. Douglas	Democratic	1,382,713 (29.5%)	12
	John C. Breckinridge	Democratic	848,356 (18.1%)	72
	John Bell	Constitutional Union	592,906 (12.6%)	39
1864	**Abraham Lincoln**	Republican	2,206,938 (55.0%)	212
	George B. McClellan	Democratic	1,803,787 (45.0%)	21
1868	**Ulysses S. Grant**	Republican	3,013,421 (52.7%)	214
	Horatio Seymour	Democratic	2,706,829 (47.3%)	80
1872	**Ulysses S. Grant**	Republican	3,596,745 (55.6%)	286
	Horace Greeley	Democratic	2,843,446 (43.9%)	66
1876	**Rutherford B. Hayes**	Republican	4,036,572 (48.0%)	185
	Samuel J. Tilden	Democratic	4,284,020 (51.0%)	184
1880	**James A. Garfield**	Republican	4,449,053 (48.3%)	214
	Winfield S. Hancock	Democratic	4,442,035 (48.2%)	155
	James B. Weaver	Greenback-Labor	308,578 (3.4%)	
1884	**Grover Cleveland**	Democratic	4,874,986 (48.5%)	219
	James G. Blaine	Republican	4,851,981 (48.2%)	182
	Benjamin F. Butler	Greenback-Labor	175,370 (1.8%)	
1888	**Benjamin Harrison**	Republican	5,444,337 (47.8%)	233
	Grover Cleveland	Democratic	5,540,050 (48.6%)	168
1892	**Grover Cleveland**	Democratic	5,554,414 (46.0%)	277
	Benjamin Harrison	Republican	5,190,802 (43.0%)	145
	James B. Weaver	People's	1,027,329 (8.5%)	22
1896	**William McKinley**	Republican	7,035,638 (50.8%)	271
	William J. Bryan	Democratic; Populist	6,467,946 (46.7%)	176
1900	**William McKinley**	Republican	7,219,530 (51.7%)	292
	William J. Bryan	Democratic; Populist	6,356,734 (45.5%)	155
1904	**Theodore Roosevelt**	Republican	7,628,834 (56.4%)	336
	Alton B. Parker	Democratic	5,084,401 (37.6%)	140
	Eugene V. Debs	Socialist	402,460 (3.0%)	
1908	**William H. Taft**	Republican	7,679,006 (51.6%)	321
	William J. Bryan	Democratic	6,409,106 (43.1%)	162
	Eugene V. Debs	Socialist	420,820 (2.8%)	
1912	**Woodrow Wilson**	Democratic	6,286,820 (41.8%)	435
	Theodore Roosevelt	Progressive	4,126,020 (27.4%)	88
	William H. Taft	Republican	3,483,922 (23.2%)	8
	Eugene V. Debs	Socialist	897,011 (6.0%)	
1916	**Woodrow Wilson**	Democratic	9,129,606 (49.3%)	277
	Charles E. Hughes	Republican	8,538,221 (46.1%)	254

TABLE A.2 *(Continued)*

Year	Candidates	Party	Popular Vote	Electoral Vote
1920	**Warren G. Harding**	Republican	16,152,200 (61.0%)	404
	James M. Cox	Democratic	9,147,353 (34.6%)	127
	Eugene V. Debs	Socialist	919,799 (3.5%)	
1924	**Calvin Coolidge**	Republican	15,725,016 (54.1%)	382
	John W. Davis	Democratic	8,385,586 (28.8%)	136
	Robert M. La Follette	Progressive	4,822,856 (16.6%)	13
1928	**Herbert C. Hoover**	Republican	21,392,190 (58.2%)	444
	Alfred E. Smith	Democratic	15,016,443 (40.8%)	87
1932	**Franklin D. Roosevelt**	Democratic	22,809,638 (57.3%)	472
	Herbert C. Hoover	Republican	15,758,901 (39.6%)	59
	Norman Thomas	Socialist	881,951 (2.2%)	
1936	**Franklin D. Roosevelt**	Democratic	27,751,612 (60.7%)	523
	Alfred M. Landon	Republican	16,681,913 (36.4%)	8
	William Lemke	Union	891,858 (1.9%)	
1940	**Franklin D. Roosevelt**	Democratic	27,243,466 (54.7%)	449
	Wendell L. Willkie	Republican	22,304,755 (44.8%)	82
1944	**Franklin D. Roosevelt**	Democratic	25,602,505 (52.8%)	432
	Thomas E. Dewey	Republican	22,006,278 (44.5%)	99
1948	**Harry S. Truman**	Democratic	24,105,812 (49.5%)	303
	Thomas E. Dewey	Republican	21,970,065 (45.1%)	189
	J. Strom Thurmond	States' Rights	1,169,063 (2.4%)	39
	Henry A. Wallace	Progressive	1,157,172 (2.4%)	
1952	**Dwight D. Eisenhower**	Republican	33,936,234 (55.2%)	442
	Adlai E. Stevenson	Democratic	27,314,992 (44.5%)	89
1956	**Dwight D. Eisenhower**	Republican	35,590,472 (57.4%)	457
	Adlai E. Stevenson	Democratic	26,022,752 (42.0%)	73
1960	**John F. Kennedy**	Democratic	34,227,096 (49.9%)	303
	Richard M. Nixon	Republican	34,108,546 (49.6%)	219
1964	**Lyndon B. Johnson**	Democratic	43,126,233 (61.1%)	486
	Barry M. Goldwater	Republican	27,174,989 (38.5%)	52
1968	**Richard M. Nixon**	Republican	31,783,783 (43.4%)	301
	Hubert H. Humphrey	Democratic	31,271,839 (42.7%)	191
	George C. Wallace	American Independent	9,899,557 (13.5%)	46
1972	**Richard M. Nixon**	Republican	46,631,189 (61.3%)	521
	George McGovern	Democratic	28,422,015 (37.3%)	17
1976	**Jimmy Carter**	Democratic	40,828,587 (50.1%)	297
	Gerald R. Ford	Republican	39,147,613 (48.0%)	240

Source: From Arthur Schlesinger, Sr., "The U.S. Presidents," *Life* (November 1, 1948), p. 65; Arthur Schlesinger, Sr., "Our Presidents: A Rating by 75 Historians," *New York Times Magazine* (July 29, 1962), pp. 12ff; Gary Maranell and Richard Dodder, "Political Orientation and Evaluation of Presidential Prestige: A Study of American Historians," *Social Science Quarterly*, vol. 51, no. 2 (September 1970), p. 418, copyright © 1970 by The University of Texas Press; *The Gallup Opinion Index* (February 1976), pp. 14, 15; U.S. Historical Society survey (1977). Compiled in Robert E. DiClerico, *The American President* (Englewood Cliffs: Prentice-Hall, Inc.), © 1979, p. 332. Reprinted by permission of Prentice-Hall, Inc., Englewood Cliffs, New Jersey and the above sources.

TABLE A.3   EXECUTIVE OFFICE
OF THE PRESIDENT UNITS SINCE 1939 [a]

The White House Office, 1939–
Council on Personnel Administration, 1939–1940
Office of Government Reports, 1939–1942
Liaison Office for Personnel Management, 1939–1943
National Resources Planning Board, 1939–1943
Bureau of the Budget, 1939–1970
Office of Emergency Management, 1940–1954
Committee for Congested Production Areas, 1943–1944
War Refugee Board, 1944–1945
Council of Economic Advisers, 1946–
National Security Council, 1947–
National Security Resources Board, 1947–1953
Telecommunications Adviser to the President, 1951–1953
Office of Director of Mutual Security, 1951–1954
Office of Defense Mobilization, 1952–1959
Permanent Advisory Committee on Government Organization, 1953–1961
Operations Coordinating Board, 1953–1961
The President's Board of Consultants on Foreign Intelligence Activities, 1956–1961
Office of Civil and Defense Mobilization, 1958–1962
National Aeronautics and Space Council, 1958–1973
The President's Foreign Intelligence Advisory Board, 1961–1977
Office of Emergency Planning, 1962–1969
Office of Science and Technology, 1962–1973
Office of Special Representative for Trade Negotiations, 1963–
Office of Economic Opportunity, 1964–1975
Office of Emergency Preparedness, 1965–1973
National Council on Marine Resources and Engineering Development, 1966–1971
Council on Environmental Quality, 1969–
Council for Urban Affairs, 1969–1970
Office of Intergovernmental Relations, 1969–1973
Domestic Council, 1970–1978
Office of Telecommunications Policy, 1970–1977
Council on International Economic Policy, 1971–1977
Office of Consumer Affairs, 1971–1973
Special Action Office for Drug Abuse Prevention, 1971–1975
Federal Property Council, 1973–1977
Council on Economic Policy, 1973–1974
Energy Policy Office, 1973–1974
Federal Energy Office, 1973–1974
Council on Wage and Price Stability, 1974–
Energy Resource Council, 1974–1977
Office of Science and Technology Policy, 1976–
Office of Administration, 1977–
Domestic Policy Staff, 1978–

[a] This listing does not include the dozens of short-term advisory commissions, study councils, and cabinet level coordinating committees that often exist to help advise and guide a president and his staff.

The Central Intelligence Agency since 1947 is formally listed as part of the Executive Office of the President, although in practice it operates as an independent agency.

TABLE A.4   PRESIDENTIAL LEADERSHIP RANKINGS

Schlesinger Poll 1948	Schlesinger Poll 1962	Maranell-Dodder Poll 1970	Gallup Poll 1975	U.S. Historical Society Poll 1977
Great	*Great*	*Overall Prestige*	*What three U.S. presidents do you regard as the greatest?* %	*Ten greatest presidents* — Votes
(1) Lincoln	(1) Lincoln	(1) Lincoln	Kennedy 52	Lincoln 85
(2) Washington	(2) Washington	(2) Washington	Lincoln 49	Washington 84
(3) F. Roosevelt	(3) F. Roosevelt	(3) F. Roosevelt	F. Roosevelt 45	F. Roosevelt 81
(4) Wilson	(4) Wilson	(4) Jefferson	Truman 37	Jefferson 79
(5) Jefferson	(5) Jefferson	(5) T. Roosevelt	Washington 25	T. Roosevelt 79
(6) Jackson	*Near Great*	(6) Wilson	Eisenhower 24	Wilson 74
Near Great	(6) Jackson	(7) Truman	T. Roosevelt 9	Jackson 74
(7) T. Roosevelt	(7) T. Roosevelt	(8) Jackson	L. Johnson 9	Truman 64
(8) Cleveland	(8) Polk	(9) Kennedy	Jefferson 8	Polk 38
(9) J. Adams	(8) Truman	(10) J. Adams	Wilson 5	J. Adams 35
(10) Polk	(9) J. Adams	(11) Polk	Nixon 9	L. Johnson 24
Average	(10) Cleveland	(12) Cleveland	All others 9	Cleveland 21
(11) J. Q. Adams	*Average*	(13) Madison	Don't know 3	Kennedy 19
(12) Monroe	(11) Madison	(14) Monroe		Madison 16
(13) Hayes	(12) J. Q. Adams	(15) J. Q. Adams		J. Q. Adams 14
(14) Madison	(13) Hayes	(16) L. Johnson		Eisenhower 14
(15) Van Buren	(14) McKinley	(17) Taft		Monroe 7
(16) Taft	(15) Taft	(18) Hoover		Hoover 6
(17) Arthur	(16) Van Buren	(19) Eisenhower		McKinley 4
(18) McKinley	(17) Monroe	(20) A. Johnson		Van Buren 2
(19) A. Johnson	(18) Hoover	(21) Van Buren		Arthur 2
(20) Hoover	(19) Harrison	(22) McKinley		Tyler 1
(21) Harrison	(20) Arthur	(23) Arthur		Buchanan 1
	(20) Eisenhower	(24) Hayes		Grant 1
	(21) A. Johnson	(25) Tyler		
		(26) Harrison		

TABLE A.4 (Continued)

Schlesinger Poll 1948	Schlesinger Poll 1962	Maranell-Dodder Poll 1970	Gallup Poll 1975	U.S. Historical Society Poll 1977	
Below Average	Below Average	(27) Taylor		Hayes	1
(22) Tyler	(22) Taylor	(28) Coolidge		Taft	1
(23) Coolidge	(23) Tyler	(29) Fillmore		Coolidge	1
(24) Fillmore	(24) Fillmore	(30) Buchanan		Nixon	1
(25) Taylor	(25) Coolidge	(31) Pierce		W. Harrison	0
(26) Buchanan	(26) Pierce	(32) Grant		Taylor	0
(27) Pierce	(27) Buchanan	(33) Harding		Fillmore	0
		(Harrison and Garfield not included due to brevity of tenure)		Pierce	0
Failure	Failure			A. Johnson	0
(28) Grant	(28) Grant			Garfield	0
(29) Harding	(29) Harding			B. Harrison	0
				Harding	0
				Ford	0

Source: Table from Robert E. DiClerico, *The American President*, 1979, p. 332; © 1979 by Prentice-Hall, Inc. Reprinted by permission of Prentice-Hall, Inc., Englewood Cliffs, N.J. Data from Arthur Schlesinger, Sr., "The U.S. Presidents," *Life*, 1 November 1948, p. 65; Arthur Schlesinger, Sr., "Our Presidents: A Rating by 75 Historians," *New York Times Magazine*, 29 July 1962, pp. 12ff.; Gary Maranell and Richard Dodder, "Political Orientation and Evaluation of Presidential Prestige: A Study of American Historians," *Social Science Quarterly* 51 (September 1970): 418; *The Gallup Opinion Index*, February 1976, pp. 14, 15. U.S. Historical Society provided the results of its survey.

TABLE A.5   RELEVANT SECTIONS OF THE CONSTITUTION OF THE UNITED STATES

ARTICLE I — The Legislative Article

SECTION. 1. All legislative Powers herein granted shall be vested in a Congress of the United States, which shall consist of a Senate and House of Representatives.

SECTION. 2. The House of Representatives shall be composed of Members chosen every second Year by the People of the several States, and the Electors in each State shall have the Qualifications requisite for Electors of the most numerous Branch of the State Legislature. . . .

SECTION. 3. The Senate of the United States shall be composed of two Senators from each State, [chosen by the Legislature thereof,] for six Years; and each Senator shall have one Vote. . . .

The Vice President of the United States shall be President of the Senate, but shall have no Vote, unless they be equally divided.

The Senate shall chuse their other Officers, and also a President pro tempore, in the Absence of the Vice President, or when he shall exercise the Office of President of the United States.

The Senate shall have the sole Power to try all Impeachments. When sitting for that Purpose, they shall be on Oath or Affirmation. When the President of the United States is tried, the Chief Justice shall preside: And no Person shall be convicted without the Concurrence of two thirds of the Members present.

Judgment in Cases of Impeachment shall not extend further than to removal from Office, and disqualification to hold and enjoy any Office of honor, Trust or Profit under the United States: but the Party convicted shall nevertheless be liable and subject to Indictment, Trial, Judgment and Punishment, according to Law. . . .

SECTION. 7. All Bills for raising revenue shall originate in the House of Representatives; but the Senate may propose or concur with Amendments as on other Bills.

Every Bill which shall have passed the House of Representatives and the Senate, shall, before it become a Law, be presented to the President of the United States; If he approve he shall sign it, but if not he shall return it, with his Objections to that House in which it shall have originated, who shall enter the Objections at large on their Journal, and proceed to reconsider it. If after such Reconsideration two thirds of that House shall agree to pass the Bill, it shall be sent, together with the Objections, to the other House, by which it shall likewise be reconsidered, and if approved by two thirds of that House, it shall become a Law. But in all such Cases the Votes of both Houses shall be determined by yeas and Nays, and the Names of the Persons voting for and against the Bill shall be entered on the Journal of each House respectively. If any Bill shall not be returned by the President within ten Days (Sundays excepted) after it shall have been presented to him, the Same shall be a Law, in like Manner as if he had signed it, unless the Congress by their Adjournment prevent its Return, in which Case it shall not be a Law.

Every Order, Resolution, or Vote to which the Concurrence of the Senate and House of Representatives may be necessary (except on a question of Adjournment) shall be presented to the President of the United States; and before the Same shall take Effect, shall be approved by him, or being disapproved by him, shall be repassed by two thirds of the Senate and House of Representatives, according to the Rules and Limitations prescribed in the Case of a Bill.

SECTION. 8. The Congress shall have Power To Lay and collect Taxes, Duties, Imposts and Excises, to pay the Debts and provide for the common Defence and general Welfare of the United States; but all Duties, Imposts and Excises shall be uniform throughout the United States;

TABLE A.5 *(Continued)*

To borrow Money on the credit of the United States;

To regulate Commerce with foreign Nations, and among the several States, and with the Indian Tribes;

To establish a uniform Rule of Naturalization, and uniform Laws on the subject of Bankruptcies throughout the United States;

To coin Money, regulate the Value thereof, and of foreign Coin, and fix the Standard of Weights and Measures;

To provide for the Punishment of counterfeiting the Securities and current Coin of the United States;

To establish Post Offices and post Roads;

To promote the Progress of Science and useful Arts, by securing for limited Times to Authors and Inventors the exclusive Right to their respective Writings and Discoveries;

To constitute Tribunals inferior to the supreme Court;

To define and punish Piracies and Felonies committed on the high Seas, and Offences against the Law of Nations;

To declare War, grant Letters of Marque and Reprisal, and make Rules concerning Captures on Land and Water;

To raise and support Armies, but no Appropriation of Money to that Use shall be for a longer Term than two Years;

To provide and maintain a Navy;

To make Rules for the Government and Regulation of the land and naval Forces;

To provide for calling forth the Militia to execute the Laws of the Union, suppress Insurrections and repel Invasions;

To provide for organizing, arming, and disciplining, the Militia, and for governing such Part of them as may be employed in the Service of the United States, reserving to the States respectively, the Appointment of the Officers, and the Authority of training the Militia according to the discipline prescribed by Congress;

To exercise exclusive Legislation in all Cases whatsoever, over such District (not exceeding ten Miles Square) as may, by Cession of particular States, and the Acceptance of Congress, become the Seat of the Government of the United States, and to exercise like Authority over all Places purchased by the Consent of the Legislature of the State in which the Same shall be, for the Erection of Forts, Magazines, Arsenals, dock-Yards, and other needful Buildings: — And

To make all Laws which shall be necessary and proper for carrying into Execution the foregoing Powers, and all other Powers vested by this Constitution in the Government of the United States, or in any Department or Officer thereof. . . .

ARTICLE II — The Executive Article

SECTION. 1. The executive Power shall be vested in a President of the United States of America. He shall hold his Office during the Term of four Years, and, together with the Vice President, chosen for the same Term, be elected, as follows

Each State shall appoint, in such Manner as the Legislature thereof may direct, a Number of Electors, equal to the whole Number of Senators and Representatives to which the State may be entitled in the Congress: but no Senator or Representative, or Person holding an Office of Trust or Profit under the United States, shall be appointed an Elector.

[The Electors shall meet in their respective States, and vote by Ballot for two Persons, of whom one at least shall not be an Inhabitant of the same State with themselves. And they shall make a List of all the Persons voted for, and of the Number of Votes for each; which List they shall sign and certify, and transmit sealed to the Seat of

TABLE A.5 (*Continued*)

the Government of the United States, directed to the President of the Senate. The President of the Senate shall, in the Presence of the Senate and House of Representatives, open all the Certificates, and the Votes shall then be counted. The Person having the greatest Number of Votes shall be President, if such Number be a Majority of the whole Number of Electors appointed; and if there be more than one who have such Majority, and have an equal Number of Votes, then the House of Representatives shall immediately chuse by Ballot one of them for President; and if no Person have a Majority, then from the five highest on the List the said House shall in like Manner chuse the President. But in chusing the President, the Votes shall be taken by States, the Representation from each State having one Vote; A quorum for this purpose shall consist of a Member or Members from two thirds of the States, and a Majority of all the States shall be necessary to a Choice. In every Case, after the Choice of the President, the Person having the greatest Number of Votes of the Electors shall be the Vice President. But if there should remain two or more who have equal Votes, the Senate chuse from them by Ballot the Vice President.] a

The Congress may determine the Time of chusing the Electors, and the Day on which they shall give their Votes; which Day shall be the same throughout the United States.

No Person except a natural born Citizen, or a Citizen of the United States, at the time of the Adoption of this Constitution, shall be eligible to the Office of President; neither shall any Person be eligible to that Office who shall not have attained to the Age of thirty five Years, and been fourteen Years a Resident within the United States.

[In Case of the Removal of the President from Office, or of his Death, Resignation, or Inability to discharge the Powers and Duties of the said Office, the Same shall devolve on the Vice President, and the Congress may by Law provide for the Case of Removal, Death, Resignation or Inability, both of the President and Vice President, declaring what Officer shall then act as President, and such Officer shall act accordingly, until the Disability be removed, or a President shall be elected.] b

The President shall, at stated Times, receive for his Services, a Compensation, which shall neither be encreased nor diminished during the Period for which he shall have been elected, and he shall not receive within that Period any other Emolument from the United States, or any of them.

Before he enter on the Execution of his Office, he shall take the following Oath or Affirmation: — "I do solemnly swear (or affirm) that I will faithfully execute the Office of President of the United States, and will to the best of my Ability, preserve, protect and defend the Constitution of the United States."

SECTION. 2. The President shall be Commander in Chief of the Army and Navy of the United States, and of the Militia of the several States, when called into the actual Service of the United States; he may require the Opinion, in writing, of the principal Officer in each of the executive Departments, upon any Subject relating to the Duties of their respective Offices, and he shall have Power to grant Reprieves and Pardons for Offences against the United States, except in Cases of Impeachment.

He shall have Power, by and with the Advice and Consent of the Senate, to make Treaties, provided two thirds of the Senators present concur; and he shall nominate, and by and with the Advice and Consent of the Senate, shall appoint Ambassadors, other public Ministers and Consuls, Judges of the supreme Court, and all other Officers of the United States, whose Appointments are not herein otherwise provided for, and which

a Superseded by the Twelfth Amendment.

b Superseded by the Twenty-fifth Amendment.

TABLE A.5 *(Continued)*

shall be established by Law: but the Congress may by Law vest the Appointment of such inferior Offices, as they think proper, in the President alone, in the Courts of Law, or in the Heads of Departments.

The President shall have Power to fill up all Vacancies that may happen during the Recess of the Senate, by granting Commissions which shall expire at the End of their next Session.

SECTION. 3. He shall from time to time give to the Congress Information of the State of the Union, and recommend to their Consideration such Measures as he shall judge necessary and expedient; he may, on extraordinary Occasions, convene both Houses, or either of them, and in Case of Disagreement between them, with Respect to the Time of Adjournment, he may adjourn them to such Time as he shall think proper; he shall receive Ambassadors and other public Ministers; he shall take Care that the Laws be faithfully executed, and shall Commission all the Officers of the United States.

SECTION. 4. The President, Vice President and all civil Officers of the United States, shall be removed from Office on Impeachment for, and Conviction of, Treason, Bribery, or other high Crimes and Misdemeanors.

RELEVANT AMENDMENTS TO THE CONSTITUTION

AMENDMENT XII (1804) — Election of the President
The Electors shall meet in their respective states, and vote by ballot for President and Vice President, one of whom, at least, shall not be an inhabitant of the same state with themselves; they shall name in their ballots the person voted for as President, and in distinct ballots the person voted for as Vice President, and they shall make distinct lists of all persons voted for as President, and of all persons voted for as Vice President, and of the number of votes for each, which lists they shall sign and certify, and transmit sealed to the seat of the government of the United States, directed to the President of the Senate; — The President of the Senate shall, in the presence of the Senate and House of Representatives, open all the certificates and the votes shall then be counted; — The person having the greatest number of votes for President, shall be the President, if such number be a majority of the whole number of Electors appointed; and if no person have such majority, then from the persons having the highest numbers not exceeding three on the list of those voted for as President, the House of Representatives shall choose immediately, by ballot, the President. But in choosing the President, the votes shall be taken by states, the representation from each state having one vote; a quorum for this purpose shall consist of a member or members from two-thirds of the states, and a majority of all the states shall be necessary to a choice. And if the House of Representatives shall not choose a President whenever the right of choice shall devolve upon them, before the fourth day of March next following,a then the Vice President shall act as President, as in the case of the death or other constitutional disability of the President. — The person having the greatest number of votes as Vice President, shall be the Vice President, if such number be a majority of the whole number of Electors appointed, and if no person have a majority, then from the two highest numbers on the list, the Senate shall choose the Vice President; a quorum for the purpose shall consist of two-thirds of the whole number of Senators, and a majority of the whole number shall be necessary to a choice. But no person constitutionally ineligible to the office of President shall be eligible to that of Vice President of the United States. . . .

a Modified by the Twentieth Amendment.

TABLE A.5   (*Continued*)

AMENDMENT XX (1933) — The Lame-Duck Amendment

SECTION 1. The terms of the President and Vice President shall end at noon on the 20th day of January, and the terms of Senators and Representatives at noon on the 3d day of January, of the years in which such terms would have ended if this article had not been ratified; and the terms of their successors shall then begin.

SECTION 2. The Congress shall assemble at least once in every year, and such meeting shall begin at noon on the 3d day of January, unless they shall by law appoint a different day.

SECTION 3. If, at the time fixed for the beginning of the term of the President, the President elect shall have died, the Vice President elect shall become President. If a President shall not have been chosen before the time fixed for the beginning of his term, or if the President elect shall have failed to qualify, then the Vice President elect shall act as President until a President shall have qualified; and the Congress may by law provide for the case wherein neither a President elect nor a Vice President elect shall have qualified, declaring who shall then act as President, or the manner in which one who is to act shall be selected, and such person shall act accordingly until a President or Vice President shall have qualified.

SECTION 4. The Congress may by law provide for the case of the death of any of the persons from whom the House of Representatives may choose a President whenever the right of choice shall have devolved upon them, and for the case of the death of any of the persons from whom the Senate may choose a Vice President whenever the right of choice shall have devolved upon them.

SECTION 5. Sections 1 and 2 shall take effect on the 15th day of October following the ratification of this article.

SECTION 6. This article shall be inoperative unless it shall have been ratified as an amendment to the Constitution by the legislatures of three-fourths of the several States within seven years from the date of its submission.

AMENDMENT XXII (1951) — Number of Presidential Terms

SECTION 1. No person shall be elected to the office of the President more than twice, and no person who has held the office of President, or acted as President, for more than two years of a term to which some other person was elected President shall be elected to the office of the President more than once. But this Article shall not apply to any person holding the office of President when this Article was proposed by the Congress, and shall not prevent any person who may be holding the office of President, or acting as President, during the term within which this article becomes operative from holding the office of President or acting as President during the remainder of such term.

SECTION 2. This Article shall be inoperative unless it shall have been ratified as an amendment to the Constitution by the legislatures of three-fourths of the several States within seven years from the date of its submission to the States by the Congress.

AMENDMENT XXV (1967) — Presidential Disability, Vice-Presidency Vacancy

SECTION 1. In case of the removal of the President from office or of his death or resignation, the Vice President shall become President.[1]

SECTION 2. Whenever there is a vacancy in the office of the Vice President, the President shall nominate a Vice President who shall take the office upon confirmation by a majority vote of both houses of Congress.[2]

SECTION 3. Whenever the President transmits to the President pro tempore of the Senate and the Speaker of the House of Representatives his written declaration that he is unable to discharge the powers and duties of his office, and until he transmits to them

TABLE A.5 (*Continued*)

a written declaration to the contrary, such powers and duties shall be discharged by the Vice President as Acting President.[3]

SECTION 4. Whenever the Vice President and a majority of either the principal officers of the executive departments or of such other body as Congress may by law provide, transmit to the President pro tempore of the Senate and the Speaker of the House of Representatives their written declaration that the President is unable to discharge the powers and duties of his office, the Vice President shall immedaitely assume the powers and duties of the office as Acting President.

Thereafter, when the President transmits to the President pro tempore of the Senate and the Speaker of the House of Representatives his written declaration that no inability exists, he shall resume the powers and duties of his office unless the Vice President and a majority of either the principal officers of the executive department or of such other body as Congress may by law provide, transmit within four days to the President pro tempore of the Senate and the Speaker of the House of Representatives their written declaration that the President is unable to discharge the powers and duties of his office. Thereupon Congress shall decide the issue, assembling within forty-eight hours for that purpose if not in session. If the Congress within twenty-one days after receipt of the latter written declaration, or, if Congress is not in session, within twenty-one days after Congress is required to assemble, determines by two-thirds vote of both Houses that the President is unable to discharge the powers and duties of his office, the Vice President shall continue to discharge the same as Acting President; otherwise, the President shall resume the powers and duties of his office.

[1] Superseded by the Twelfth Amendment.
[2] Superseded by the Twenty-fifth Amendment.
[3] Modified by the Twentieth Amendment.

SELECTED BIBLIOGRAPHY

This bibliography, not intended to be comprehensive, includes important political analyses of the office of the president and the people who have held it. Many of the studies cited here treat major controversies surrounding this embattled institution. More generally, this listing permits me the chance to single out books that were helpful in writing about the state of the presidency.

1. THE PRESIDENCY IN GENERAL

Abraham, Henry. *Justices and Presidents.* New York: Oxford University Press, 1974.

Anderson, Patrick. *The Presidents' Men.* Garden City, N.Y.: Doubleday, 1968.

Bailey, Thomas A. *Presidential Greatness.* New York: Appleton-Century-Crofts, 1966.

Barber, James David. *The Presidential Character,* 2nd ed. Englewood Cliffs, N.J.: Prentice-Hall, 1977.

Berger, Raoul. *Impeachment: The Constitutional Problems.* Cambridge: Harvard University Press, 1973.

——. *Executive Privilege: A Constitutional Myth.* Cambridge: Harvard University Press, 1974.

Binkley, Wilfred E. *The Man in the White House.* Baltimore: Johns Hopkins University Press, 1958.

Brant, Irving. *Impeachment.* New York: Knopf, 1972.

Broder, David S. *The Party's Over.* New York: Harper & Row, 1971.

Brownlow, Louis. *The President and the Presidency.* Chicago: University of Chicago Press, 1949.

Buchanan, Bruce. *The Presidential Experience.* Englewood Cliffs, N.J.: Prentice-Hall, 1978.

Bundy, McGeorge. *The Strength of Government.* Cambridge: Harvard University Press, 1968.

Burns, James MacGregor. *Leadership.* New York: Harper & Row, 1978.

——. *Presidential Government.* Boston: Houghton Mifflin, 1966.

Chamberlain, Lawrence H. *The President, Congress and Legislation.* New York: Columbia University Press, 1946.

Cornwell, Elmer E. *Presidential Leadership of Public Opinion.* Bloomington: University of Indiana Press, 1962.

Corwin, Edward S. *The President: Office and Powers.* New York: New York University Press, 1940.

Cotter, C. P., and J. M. Smith. *Powers of the President During National Crises.* Washington: Public Affairs Press, 1961.

Cunliffe, Marcus. *American Presidents and The Presidency.* N.Y.: American Heritage, 1968.

DiClerico, Robert E. *The American President.* Englewood Cliffs, N.J.: Prentice-Hall, 1979.

Dunn, Delmer D. *Financing Presidential Campaigns.* Washington: Brookings Institution, 1972.

Edwards, George. *Presidential Influence and Congress.* San Francisco: W. H. Freeman, 1980.

Fenno, Richard F. *The President's Cabinet.* New York: Vintage, 1959.

Finer, Herman. *The Presidency: Crisis and Regeneration.* Chicago: University of Chicago Press, 1960.

Fisher, Louis. *President and Congress.* New York: Free Press, 1972.

——. *The Constitution Between Friends.* New York: St. Martin's Press, 1978.

Goldsmith, William M. *The Growth of Presidential Power: A Documented History.* New York: Chelsea House, 1974.

Grabner, Doris. *Public Opinion, the President and Foreign Policy.* New York: Holt, Rinehart and Winston, 1968.

Greenstein, Fred, and others. *Evolution of the Modern Presidency: A Bibliographical Survey*. Washington: American Enterprise Institute, 1977.

George, Alexander. *Presidential Decision-Making in Foreign Policy*. Boulder, Colo.: Westview Press, 1979.

Griffith, Ernest S. *The American Presidency: The Dilemmas of Shared Power and Divided Government*. New York: New York University Press, 1976.

Grossman, Michael B. and Martha J. Kumar, *Portraying The President: White House Press Operations and the News Media*. Baltimore, Md.: Johns Hopkins Press, 1980.

Hardin, Charles. *Presidential Power and Accountability*. Chicago: University of Chicago Press, 1974.

Hargrove, Erwin C. *Presidential Leadership*. New York: Macmillan, 1966.

————. *The Power of the Modern Presidency*. New York: Knopf, 1974.

Herring, Pendleton. *Presidential Leadership*. New York: Farrar and Rinehart, 1940.

Hess, Stephen. *Organizing the Presidency*. Washington: Brookings Institution, 1976.

Hobbs, Edward. *Behind the President: A Study of Executive Office Agencies*. Washington: Public Affairs Press, 1954.

Hofstadter, Richard. *The American Political Tradition*. New York: Vintage, 1948.

Holtzman, Abraham. *Legislative Liaison: Executive Leadership in Congress*. Chicago: Rand McNally, 1970.

Hoxie, R. Gordon. *Command Decision and The Presidency*. New York: Crowell and Reader's Digest Press, 1977.

Hughes, Emmet John. *The Living Presidency*. New York: Coward, McCann & Geoghegan, 1973.

Hyman, Sidney. *The American President*. New York: Harper and Bros., 1954.

James, Dorothy B. *The Contemporary Presidency*. New York: Pegasus, 1969.

Kallenbach, Joseph E. *The American Chief Executive*. New York: Harper & Row, 1966.

Koenig, Louis. *The Chief Executive*. Rev. ed. New York: Harcourt, Brace and World, 1968.

Labovitz, John R. *Presidential Impeachment*. New Haven, Conn.: Yale University Press, 1978.

Lammers, William W. *Presidential Politics: Patterns and Prospects*. New York: Harper & Row, 1976.

Laski, Harold. *The American Presidency*. New York: Grosset & Dunlap, 1940.

Loss, Richard, ed. *Presidential Power and the Constitution: Essays by Edward S. Corwin*. Ithaca, N.Y.: Cornell University Press, 1976.

McConnell, Grant. *The Modern Presidency*. New York: St. Martin's Press, 1967.

McGinniss, Joe. *The Selling of the President 1968*. New York: Trident Press, 1969.

Milton, George F. *The Use of Presidential Power*. Boston: Little, Brown, 1944.

Minow, Newton M., and others. *Presidential Television*. New York: Basic Books, 1973.

Mueller, John E. *War, Presidents and Public Opinion*. New York: Wiley & Sons, 1973.

Mullen, William F. *Presidential Power and Politics*. New York: St. Martin's Press, 1976.

Nathan, Richard P. *The Plot That Failed: Nixon and the Administrative Presidency*. New York: Wiley & Sons, 1976.

Neustadt, Richard. *Presidential Power*. New York: Wiley & Sons, 1960.

Novak, Michael. *Choosing Our King*. New York: Macmillan, 1974.

Patterson, C. P. *Presidential Government in the United States*. Chapel Hill: University of North Carolina Press, 1947.

Pious, Richard M. *The American Presidency*. New York: Basic Books, 1979.

Pollard, James F. *The Presidents and the Press*. Washington: Public Affairs Press, 1964.

Polsby, Nelson W. *Congress and the Presidency*. Englewood Cliffs, N.J.: Prentice-Hall, 1971.

Reedy, George E. *The Twilight of the Presidency*. New York: World, 1970.

Rose, Richard. *Managing Presidential Objectives*. New York: Free Press, 1976.

Rossiter, Clinton. *Constitutional Dictatorship*. New York: Harcourt, Brace, 1948.

————. *The American Presidency*. Rev. ed. New York: Harcourt, Brace and World, 1960.

————, with Richard P. Longaker. *The Supreme Court and the Commander in Chief*. Expanded ed. Ithaca, N.Y.: Cornell University Press, 1976.

Schlesinger, Arthur M., Jr. *The Imperial Presidency*. Boston: Houghton Mifflin, 1973.

————, and Alfred deGrazia. *Congress and the Presidency: Their Role in Modern Times*. Washington: American Enterprise Institute for Public Policy, 1967.

Schubert, Glendon. *The Presidency in the Courts*. Minneapolis: University of Minnesota Press, 1957.

Scigliano, Robert. *The Supreme Court and the Presidency*. New York: Free Press, 1971.

Shull, Steven A. *Presidential Policy Making*. King Court Communications, 1979.

Sorensen, Theodore C. *Decision-Making in the White House*. New York: Columbia University Press, 1963.

————. *Watchman in the Night: Presidential Accountability and Watergate*. Cambridge, Mass.: M.I.T. Press, 1975.

Sickels, Robert, *The Presidency: An Introduction*. Englewood Cliffs, N.J.: Prentice Hall, 1980.

Strum, Philippa. *Presidential Power and American Democracy*. 2nd ed. Pacific Palisades, Calif.: Goodyear, 1979.

Sundquist, James L. *Politics and Policy: The Eisenhower, Kennedy, and Johnson Years*. Washington: Brookings Institution, 1968.

Tourtellot, Arthur B. *The Presidents on the Presidency*. Garden City, New York: Doubleday, 1964.

Tugwell, Rexford G. *The Enlargement of the Presidency*. Garden City, N.Y.: Doubleday, 1960.

Vinyard, Dale. *The Presidency*. New York: Scribner's, 1971.

Wayne, Stephen J. *The Legislative Presidency*. New York: Harper & Row, 1978.

White, Theodore H. *The Making of the President 1960; 1964; 1968; 1972*. New York: Atheneum, 1961; 1965; 1969; 1973.

Wilson, Woodrow. *Congressional Government*. 1885. Reprint edition, New York: Meridian Books, 1956.

Wolanin, Thomas. *Presidential Advisory Commissions* Madison, Wisc.: University of Wisconsin Press, 1975.

Young, James S. *The Washington Community 1800–1820*. New York: Columbia University Press, 1966.

2. THE PRESIDENTIAL SELECTION PROCESS

Alexander, Herbert E. *Financing Politics*. Washington: Congressional Quarterly, 1976.

Asher, Herbert. *Presidential Elections and American Politics*. Homewood, Ill.: Dorsey, 1976.

Barber, James David, ed. *Race for the Presidency: The Media and the Nominating Process*. Englewood Cliffs, N.J.: Prentice-Hall, 1978.

Bishop, George F., et. al. *The Presidential Debates: Media, Electoral and Policy Perspectives*. New York: Harper & Row, 1978.

Brams, Stephen J. *The Presidential Election Game*. New Haven: Yale University Press, 1978.

Burnham, Walter Dean. *Critical Elections and the Mainsprings of American Politics*. New York: Norton, 1970.

Campbell, Angus, and others. *The American Voter*. New York: Wiley & Sons, 1960.

Campbell, Bruce A. *The American Electorate*. New York: Holt, Rinehart and Winston, 1979.

Ceaser, James W. *Presidential Selection: Theory and Development.* Princeton: Princeton University Press, 1979.

Crouse, Timothy. *The Boys on the Bus.* New York: Random House, 1973.

Davis, James W. *Presidential Primaries: Road to the White House.* New York: Crowell, 1967.

Hadley, Arthur. *The Empty Polling Booth.* Englewood Cliffs, N.J.: Prentice-Hall, 1978.

Hess, Stephen. *The Presidential Campaign.* rev. ed. Washington: Brookings Institution, 1978.

Keech, William, and Donald Matthews. *The Party's Choice.* Washington: Brookings Institution, 1976.

Kessel, John. *Presidential Campaign Strategies and Citizen Response.* Homewood, Ill.: The Dorsey Press, 1980.

Lengle, James I., and Byron E. Shafer, eds. *Presidential Politics: Readings on Nominations and Elections.* New York: St. Martin's Press, 1980.

Longley, Lawrence D., and Alan G. Braun. *The Politics of Electoral College Reform.* New Haven: Yale University Press, 1972.

Nie, Norman, Sidney Verba, and John Petrocik. *The Changing American Voter.* Cambridge, Harvard University Press, 1976.

Page, Benjamin I. *Choices and Echoes in Presidential Elections.* Chicago: University of Chicago Press, 1978.

Parris, Judith H. *The Convention Problem.* Washington: Brookings Institution, 1972.

Peirce, Neal R. *The People's President: The Electoral College in American History and the Direct-Vote Alternative.* New York: Simon & Schuster, 1968.

Polsby, Nelson, and Aaron Wildavsky. *Presidential Election.* 4th ed. New York: Scribner's, 1975.

Pomper, Gerald M. *Elections in America.* New York: Dodd, Mead, 1970.

———. *The Election of 1976: Reports and Interpretations.* New York: McKay, 1977.

Ranney, Austin, ed. *The Past and Future of Presidential Debates.* Washington, D.C.: American Enterprise Institute, 1979.

Sayre, Wallace S., and Judith H. Parris. *Voting for President.* Washington: Brookings Institution, 1970.

Scammon, Richard M., and Ben J. Wattenberg. *The Real Majority.* New York: Coward-McCann, 1970.

Schlesinger, Arthur M. Jr. and Fred Israel, eds. *History of American Presidential Elections 1789–1968.* 4 vols. N.Y.: Chelsea House, 1971.

Thompson, Hunter. *Fear and Loathing: On the Campaign Trail '72.* San Francisco: Straight Arrow Books, 1973.

Tugwell, Rexford G. *How They Became President.* New York: Simon & Schuster, 1965.

Watson, Richard. *The Presidential Contest.* New York: John Wiley, 1979.

Wayne, Stephen J. *The Road to the White House.* New York: St. Martin's Press, 1980.

Winner Take All. Report of the Twentieth Century Fund Task Force on Reform of the Presidential Election Process. New York: Holmes and Meier, 1978.

Witcover, Jules. *Marathon: The Pursuit of the Presidency, 1972–1976.* New York: Viking, 1977.

With The Nation Watching. Report of the Twentieth Century Fund Task Force on Televised Presidential Debates. Lexington, Mass.: Lexington Books, 1979.

3. USEFUL ANTHOLOGIES ON THE PRESIDENCY

Bach, Stanley, and George T. Sulzner, eds. *Perspective on the Presidency.* Lexington, Mass.: D. C. Heath, 1974.

Barber, James David, ed. *Choosing the President.* Englewood Cliffs, N.J.: Prentice-Hall, 1974.

Burnham, Walter Dean, and Martha Weinberg, eds. *American Politics and Public Policy.* Cambridge, Mass.: M.I.T. Press, 1978.

Clark, Keith, and Lawrence Legere, eds. *The President and the Management of National Security.* New York: Praeger, 1969.

Cornwell, Elmer E., ed. *The American Presidency: Vital Center.* Chicago: Scott, Foresman, 1966.

Cronin, Thomas E., and Sanford D. Greenberg, eds. *The Presidential Advisory System.* New York: Harper & Row, 1969.

————, and Rexford G. Tugwell, eds. *The Presidency Reappraised.* 2nd ed. New York: Praeger, 1977.

Dunn, Charles, ed. *The Future of the American Presidency.* Morristown, N.J.: General Learning Press, 1975.

Haight, David E., and Larry D. Johnson, eds. *The President: Roles and Powers.* Chicago: Rand McNally, 1965.

Halpern, Paul, ed. *Why Watergate?* Pacific Palisades, Calif.: Palisades Press, 1975.

Hirschfield, Robert S., ed. *The Power of the Presidency.* New York: Atherton, 1968.

Hoxie, R. Gordon, ed. *The White House: Organization and Operation.* New York: Center for the Study of the Presidency, 1971.

————, ed. *The Presidency of the 1970s.* New York: Center for the Study of the Presidency, 1973.

Jackson, Henry M., ed. *The National Security Council.* New York: Praeger, 1965.

Johnson, Donald B., and Jack L. Walker, eds. *The Dynamics of the American Presidency.* New York: Wiley & Sons, 1964.

Mansfield, Harvey C., Sr., ed. *Congress Against the President.* New York: Harper & Row, 1975.

Moe, Ronald C., ed. *Congress and the President.* Pacific Palisades, Calif.: Goodyear, 1971.

Polsby, Nelson W., ed. *The Modern Presidency.* New York: Random House, 1973.

Pomper, Gerald, ed. *Party Renewal: Theory and Practice.* New York: Praeger-Holt, 1980.

Roberts, Charles, ed. *Has the President Too Much Power?* New York: Harper's, 1974.

Saffell, David C., ed. *Watergate: Its Effects on the American Political System.* Cambridge, Mass.: Winthrop, 1974.

Shull, Steven A. and Lance T. LeLoup, eds. *The Presidency: Studies in Public Policy.* King's Court Communications, 1979.

Sindler, Allan P., ed. *America in the Seventies: Problems, Policies and Politics.* Boston: Little, Brown, 1977.

Thomas, Norman C., and Hans W. Baade, eds. *The Institutionalized Presidency.* Dobbs Ferry, New York: Oceana, 1972.

————, ed. *The Presidency in Contemporary Context.* New York: Dodd, Mead, 1975.

Wildavsky, Aaron, ed. *The Presidency.* Boston: Little, Brown, 1969.

4. SPECIFIC PRESIDENTS AND THEIR ADMINISTRATIONS

Acheson, Dean. *Present at the Creation.* New York: Norton, 1969.

Adams, Sherman. *First-Hand Report.* New York: Harper and Bros., 1961.

Albertson, Dean, ed. *Eisenhower as President.* New York: Hill & Wang, 1963.

Bernstein, Barton J., ed. *Politics and Policies of the Truman Administration.* Chicago: Quadrangle, 1970.

Burns, James M. *The Lion and the Fox.* New York: Harcourt, Brace, 1956.

————. *Roosevelt: Soldier of Freedom.* New York: Harcourt, Brace, 1971.

Califano, Joseph A. Jr. *A Presidential Nation.* N.Y.: Norton, 1975.

Cochran, Bert. *Harry Truman and the Crisis Presidency*. New York: Funk & Wagnalls, 1973.

Dean, John W. *Blind Ambition*. New York: Simon & Schuster, 1976.

Donald, Aida DiPace, ed. *John F. Kennedy and the New Frontier*. New York: Hill & Wang, 1966.

Donovan, Robert J. *Eisenhower, The Inside Story*. New York: Harper and Bros., 1956.

Eisenhower, Dwight D. *Mandate for Change*. Garden City, N.Y.: Doubleday, 1963.

Evans, Rowland, and Robert Novak. *Lyndon B. Johnson: The Exercise of Power*. New York: New American Library, 1966.

——. *Nixon in the White House*. New York: Random House, 1971.

Fairlie, Henry. *The Kennedy Promise*. Garden City, N.Y.: Doubleday, 1973.

Flexner, James Thomas. *Washington: The Indispensable Man*. Boston: Little, Brown, 1974.

Ford, Gerald R. *A Time to Heal*. New York: Harper & Row/Reader's Digest Press, 1979.

George, Alexander L., and Juliette L. George. *Woodrow Wilson and Colonel House*. New York: Dover, 1956.

Goldman, Eric F. *The Tragedy of Lyndon Johnson*. New York: Knopf, 1969.

Gosnell, Harold. *Harry Truman: A Political Biography*. Westport, Conn.: Greenwood Press, 1980.

Haldeman, H. R., with Joseph DiMona. *The Ends of Power*. New York: New York Times Books, 1978.

Hughes, Emmet John. *The Ordeal of Power*. New York: Dell, 1962.

Johnson, Lyndon B. *The Vantage Point*. New York: Holt, Rinehart and Winston, 1971.

Johnstone, Robert M. Jr. *Jefferson and the Presidency*. Ithaca, N.Y.: Cornell University Press, 1978.

Kearns, Doris. *Lyndon Johnson and the American Dream*. New York: Harper & Row, 1976.

Latham, Earl, ed. *J. F. Kennedy and Presidential Power*. Lexington, Mass.: D. C. Heath, 1972.

Lyon, Peter. *Eisenhower: Portrait of the Hero*. Boston: Little, Brown, 1974.

McPherson, Harry C. *A Political Education*. Boston: Atlantic-Little, Brown, 1972.

Magruder, Jeb Stewart. *An American Life*. New York: Atheneum, 1974.

Miller, Merle. *Plain Speaking: An Oral Biography of Harry S. Truman*. New York: Medallion, 1974.

Miller, William Lee. *Yankee From Georgia: The Emergence of Jimmy Carter*. New York: Times Books, 1978.

Miroff, Bruce. *Pragmatic Illusions: The Presidential Politics of John F. Kennedy*. New York: McKay, 1976.

Nessen, Ron. *It Sure Looks Different from the Inside*. New York: Playboy Press, 1978.

Nixon, Richard M. *RN: The Memoirs of Richard Nixon*. New York: Grosset & Dunlap, 1978.

O'Brien, Lawrence. *No Final Victories: From John F. Kennedy to Watergate*. Garden City, N.Y.: Doubleday, 1974.

Osborne, John. *The Nixon Watch*. (A series.) New York: Liveright, 1970–75.

Phillips, Cabell. *The Truman Presidency*. New York: Macmillan, 1966.

Rather, Dan, and Gary Paul Gates. *The Palace Guard*. New York: Harper & Row, 1974.

Schlesinger, Arthur M., Jr. *A Thousand Days: John F. Kennedy in the White House*. Boston: Houghton Mifflin, 1965.

——. *The Age of Roosevelt*. 3 vols. Boston: Houghton Mifflin, 1957, 1958, 1960.

Sherwood, Robert E. *Roosevelt and Hopkins*. New York: Harper and Bros., 1948.

Sidey, Hugh. *A Very Personal Presidency: Lyndon Johnson in the White House*. New York: Atheneum, 1968.

Sirica, John J. *To Set the Record Straight: The Break-In, The Tapes, The Conspirators, The Pardon*. New York: Norton, 1979.

Sorensen, Theodore. *Kennedy.* New York: Harper & Row, 1965.

Truman, Harry S. *Memoirs.* 2 vols. Garden City, N.Y.: Doubleday, 1955, 1956.

Tugwell, Rexford G. *In Search of Roosevelt.* Cambridge: Harvard University Press, 1972.

———. *The Democratic Roosevelt.* Garden City, N.Y.: Doubleday, 1957.

Wills, Garry. *Nixon Agonistes.* Boston: Houghton Mifflin, 1970.

Woodward, Bob, and Carl Bernstein. *All the President's Men.* New York: Simon & Schuster, 1974.

———. *The Final Days.* New York: Simon & Schuster, 1976.

Young, James S. *The Washington Community: 1800–1825.* N.Y.: Columbia University Press, 1966.

5. BUREAUCRATIC POLITICS AND PROGRAM IMPLEMENTATION

Allison, Graham T. *Essence of Decision: Explaining the Cuban Missile Crisis.* Boston: Little, Brown, 1971.

Berman, Larry. *The Office of Management and Budget and the Presidency, 1921–1979.* Princeton, N.J.: Princeton University Press, 1979.

Brauer, Carl M. *John F. Kennedy and the Second Reconstruction.* New York: Columbia University Press, 1978.

Davis, James W., Jr. *The National Executive Branch.* New York: Free Press, 1970.

Derthick, Martha. *New Towns In-Town.* Washington: Urban Institute, 1972.

Destler, I. M. *Presidents, Bureaucrats and Foreign Policy.* Princeton, N.J.: Princeton University Press, 1972.

Donovan, John C. *The Policy-Makers.* Indianapolis: Pegasus, 1970.

Downs, Anthony. *Inside Bureaucracy.* Boston: Little, Brown, 1967.

Enthovan, Alain C., and Wayne Smith. *How Much Is Enough? Shaping the Defense Program, 1961–1969.* New York: Harper & Row, 1971.

Finn, Chester. *Education and The Presidency.* Lexington, Mass.: Lexington Books, 1977.

Freeman, J. Leiper. *The Political Process.* Rev. ed. New York: Random House, 1965.

George, Alexander, and others. *The Limits of Coercive Diplomacy.* Boston: Little, Brown, 1971.

Hadwiger, Don F. and Ross B. Talbot, *Pressures and Protests: The Kennedy Farm Program and the Wheat Referendum of 1963.* San Francisco: Chandler Publishing Company, 1965.

Halberstam, David. *The Best and the Brightest.* New York: Random House, 1972.

Halperin, Morton H. *Bureaucratic Politics and Foreign Policy.* Washington: Brookings Institution, 1974.

Heath, James F. *John F. Kennedy and the Business Community.* Chicago: University of Chicago Press, 1969.

Hickel, Walter J. *Who Owns America?* Englewood Cliffs, N.J.: Prentice-Hall, 1971.

Hilsman, Roger. *To Move a Nation.* Garden City, N.Y.: Doubleday, 1967.

Hoopes, Townsend. *The Limits of Intervention.* New York: McKay, 1969.

Janis, Irving L. *Victims of Groupthink.* Boston: Houghton Mifflin, 1972.

Katz, James E. *Presidential Politics and Science Policy.* New York: Harper & Row, 1978.

Kaufman, Herbert. *The Limits of Organizational Change.* University, Ala.: University of Alabama Press, 1971.

Kennedy, Robert F. *Thirteen Days: A Memoir of the Cuban Missile Crisis.* New York: Norton, 1969.

Kessel, John. *The Domestic Presidency.* Scituate, Mass.: Duxbury Press, 1975.

Kistiakowsky, George B. *A Scientist at the White House.* Cambridge, Mass.: Harvard University Press, 1976.

Lowi, Theodore J. *The End of Liberalism.* New York: Norton, 1969.

McConnell, Grant. *Steel and the Presidency*. New York: Norton, 1963.

MacMahon, Arthur W. *Administering Federalism in a Democracy*. New York: Oxford University Press, 1972.

Marcus, Maeva. *Truman and the Steel Seizure Case: The Limits of Presidential Power*. New York: Columbia University Press, 1979.

Morgan, Ruth P. *The President and Civil Rights*. New York: St. Martin's Press, 1970.

Moynihan, Daniel P. *Maximum Feasible Misunderstanding*. New York: Free Press, 1969.

——. *The Politics of a Guaranteed Income*. New York: Random House, 1973.

Neustadt, Richard E. *Alliance Politics*. New York: Columbia University Press, 1970.

Orfield, Gary. *The Reconstruction of Southern Education*. New York: Wiley & Sons, 1969.

Pfiffner, James P. *The President, the Budget and Congress: Impoundment and the 1974 Budget Act*. Boulder, Colo.: Westview Press, 1979.

Pressman, Jeffrey, and Aaron Wildavsky. *Implementation*. Berkeley: University of California Press, 1973.

Reagan, Michael. *The New Federalism*. New York: Oxford University Press, 1972.

Rivlin, Alice M. *Systematic Thinking for Social Action*. Washington: Brookings Institution, 1971.

Rourke, Francis E. *Bureaucracy, Politics and Public Policy*. Boston: Little, Brown, 1969.

Safire, William. *Before the Fall: An Inside View of the Pre-Watergate White House*. New York: Belmont Towers Books, 1975.

Seidman, Harold. *Politics, Position and Power*. New York: Oxford University Press, 1970.

Sichel, Werner, ed. *Economic Advice and Executive Policy: Recommendations from Past Members of the Council of Economic Advisers*. New York: Harper & Row, 1978.

Steiner, Gilbert Y. *The State of Welfare*. Washington: Brookings Institution, 1971.

Stockwell, John. *In Search of Enemies: A CIA Story*. New York: Norton, 1978.

Sundquist, James L. *Making Federalism Work*. Washington: Brookings Institution, 1969.

Thomas, Norman C. *Politics in National Education*. New York: David McKay, 1975.

Tobin, James. *The New Economics One Decade Older*. Princeton, N.J.: Princeton University Press, 1974.

Wann, A. J. *The President as Chief Administrator*. Washington: Public Affairs Press, 1968.

Wildavsky, Aaron. *The Politics of the Budgetary Process*. Boston: Little, Brown, 1964.

Wise, David. *The Politics of Lying*. New York: Random House, 1973.

Wolman, Harold. *Politics of Federal Housing*. New York: Dodd, Mead, 1971.

ACKNOWLEDGMENTS

This study has benefited from the assistance and criticism of numerous friends and professional colleagues. Foremost in this category are the hundreds of White House aides, cabinet officers, and other Washington political elite who allowed me to interview them over the past ten years. This book could not have been written without their frank answers to my countless questions. I wish to thank the following persons for sharing ideas with me or reading portions of this study at one stage or another: Harold Barger, Dom Bonafede, James MacGregor Burns, Craig Charney, Benjamin Cohen, Tania Cronin, Delmer Dunn, John Gardner, Stephen Hess, Donald Johnson, Landis Jones, Herbert Kaufman, William Keech, John Kessel, William Livingston, Bruce Miroff, William Morrow, Bruce Oppenheimer, Gary Orfield, Alan Otten, Judith Parris, Jeffrey Pressman, Laurence Radway, Peter Rofes, Richard Scammon, Arthur Schlesinger, Lester Seligman, Hedrick Smith, James Soles, James Sundquist, Norman Thomas, Rexford Tugwell, Jack Wann, and John Whelan. Please know that this is but a partial list of those who have given me suggestions, encouragement, and advice (although it has not always been taken). Greg Franklin, Cynthia Chapin, and Amy Bartlett at Little, Brown ably assisted me during the editing and publishing stages of the book, and I am much in their debt.

INDEX